WORKS ISSUED BY

THE HAKLUYT SOCIETY

———————

THE JOURNAL AND LETTERS OF
CAPTAIN CHARLES BISHOP
ON THE NORTH-WEST COAST OF
AMERICA, IN THE PACIFIC AND
IN NEW SOUTH WALES

1794–1799

SECOND SERIES
No. CXXXI

ISSUED FOR 1966

The annual subscription to the Society is £2. 2s. sterling ($6 U.S. currency) payable
on 1 January. There is no entrance fee.

Members are entitled to all volumes issued by the Society (other than those of the
Extra Series) during the period of their membership. As a rule, two volumes are produced each year.

Applications for membership may be addressed to any of the Honorary Secretaries.
No proposer is necessary.

124/ The King having meditated a plan to cut off the Missionaries, for the sake of their property, soon as we should sail, and had already committed hostilities on part of them who went to endeavour to recover our boat and People. they all met in Council and the Majority resolved, if we would take them on board, to leave the Island and go with us to Port Jackson, agreeing to draw Bill on the Directors of the Missionary Society, for the Expenses which would arise for their Passage. and it having been our intention, previous to leaving the Society Islands to lay in such a Stock of Provisions, as would prevent the necessity of our purchasing much at Port Jackson, where of course we expected it would be dear. we agreed to take them on Condition they would pay the difference of Price between buying them here and at Port Jackson and work their passage down in the vessel. and on 29th March we received on board 11 Men 4 Women 4 Children with all their cloths and Effects, and on 31st we got under way and sailed our Anchor being hooked to a rock we unfortunately parted the Cable and lost it, and put to sea, Harrassed and oppressed in mind with a leaky Ship & with only one Anchor — on the 8th April a Ruptive of a blood vessel in my Stomach which continued, with intermissions of a few hours, four days, had very nigh put a period to my sufferings and life together. however it happily stopped on the 12th and in the course of a few weeks I became pretty well. — on the 14th May we arrived Safe at Port Jackson. the vessel making about 2 feet water ⅔ hours.

The next day being 15th May I signified to Richd Atkins Esqr. deputy Judge Advocate for the Colony, that we would Protest as to the necessity of our coming to Port Jackson, and on the 18th the following Protest, and general Statement of the occurrence was made by myself Officers & part of the Crew.

Protest Barque Nautilus.

By this Public instrument of Protest, be it known unto all Men who shall see these presents, that on 18th day of May, in year of our Lord one thousand seven hundred and ninety Eight. Before me, Richd Atkins Esquire His Majesty's acting Judge Advocate of the Territory of new South Wales and

The Journal and Letters of Captain Charles Bishop on the North-West Coast of America, in the Pacific and in New South Wales 1794-1799

Edited by

MICHAEL ROE

CAMBRIDGE

Published for the Hakluyt Society

AT THE UNIVERSITY PRESS

1967

Published by the Syndics of the Cambridge University Press
Bentley House, 200 Euston Road, London, N.W. 1
American Branch: 32 East 57th Street, New York, N.Y. 10022

Library of Congress Catalogue Card Number: 66–27453

Printed in Great Britain
at the University Printing House, Cambridge
(Brooke Crutchley, University Printer)

PREFACE

My acknowledgements range as widely as did Bishop's voyages. Footnotes specify particular obligations, but some demand more emphatic notice. My first debt is to the Trustees of the two institutions which possess Bishop's documents, namely the Mitchell Library, Sydney, and the Provincial Archives of British Columbia. Their permission to publish was quick and cordial; moreover Mrs Marjorie Hancock and G. D. Richardson, of the Mitchell Library, and W. E. Ireland, of the Provincial Archives, answered many wearisome questions. Scarcely less crucial in this book's appearance has been the co-operation of Miss E. M. J. Campbell, honorary secretary of the Hakluyt Society; her efforts largely dissolved problems consequent upon my living farther from Bishop's homeland than even he penetrated. Mrs Kathleen King, of the University of London, drew the maps. The University of Tasmania has provided a congenial atmosphere, clerical and financial assistance, and an efficient Library service. Many fellow-workers have answered my importunings. I would mention K. M. Bowden, H. E. Maude, J. C. Beaglehole, J. S. Cumpston, and especially J. W. Earnshaw. Earnshaw, having learned that there were two sections of Bishop's manuscript, brought them together (by having a microfilm copy of the British Columbia section lodged in the Mitchell Library), and investigated Bishop's career. He has made his knowledge available with splendid good-will.

This work is scarcely mine to dedicate. But Bishop's ghost must approve when I offer the book to K. M. Dallas—native of Tasmania, with the history of which Bishop had a unique connexion; lover of the sea, and erudite in its lore; paramount among historians who have seen Australia's foundation in terms of the world-wide movement which Bishop represented; a true friend.

Hobart   M. R.
1962–66

v

CONTENTS

vii

LIST OF ILLUSTRATIONS

A page of Bishop's Memoranda on ship *Nautilus*,
Amboyna to Port Jackson, 1796–99. Mitchell
Library, MS. C 192, fol. 124   *frontispiece*

Map I(*a*) South-east Australia: the approximate
route of the *Nautilus* on her first trip
to the sealing grounds, October 1798
                                        facing p. xli

Map I(*b*) The southern coast of Cape Barren
Island: the location of Bishop's seal-
fishing 1798–99 (*Source:* Flinders,
Atlas, 1814).

Map II   Chart of the Gilbert Islands, based on
information from Bishop, Simpson and
Bass, published by Alexander Dalrymple,
1802   xliv

Map III   Chart of the Marshall Islands, based on
information from Bishop, Simpson and
Bass, published by Alexander Dalrymple,
1802   xlv

Map IV   Bishop's voyages on the coast of North-
west America   51

Map V   Bishop's voyages in the eastern seas
                            Pull-out at end of volume

The frontispiece is reproduced by courtesy of the Trustees of the
Public Library of New South Wales, Map I(*b*) by courtesy of the
Trustees of the British Museum, Maps II and III by permission
of the Library of Congress. Maps I(*a*), IV and V were drawn by
Mrs Kathleen King.

ABBREVIATIONS AND USAGES

O.E.D.   *The Oxford English Dictionary.*

R.B.A.A.S.   *Report of the British Association for the Advancement of Science.*

Sandwich Islands is used to describe the group otherwise known as the Hawaiian Islands, Hawaii being reserved for the particular island of that name.

INTRODUCTION

I. THE TEXT

In October 1794 the *Ruby*, Charles Bishop master, sailed from Bristol, bound for the otter-fur trade of North-west America; before returning to England six years later Bishop had ranged over the Pacific from Cape Horn to Kamchatka, from Alaska to Tasmania. Records of that voyage constitute the text here published. Bishop kept log-books as a matter of course, and these have disappeared; but there survives a manuscript to which Bishop gave the title-page:

> Commercial Journal—
> Copy's of Letters, and acc^{ts} of Ship Rubys
> voyage to N.W^t coast of America
> and China, 1794.5.6
> By Chas Bishop, commander.

The book in which Bishop wrote was of hand-made paper, folio size, in six-sheet quires. The 'Commercial Journal', describing the voyage to, proceedings at, and departure from the North-west coast, extended to page 127. After five blank leaves there began, with new pagination, the 'Copy's of Letters' and other memoranda, which occupied a further 162 pages.

At some time the book was split at page 62 of the memoranda. This division corresponds to the point at which Bishop sold the *Ruby* (at Amboyna, in the Moluccas, November 1796) and purchased another vessel, the *Nautilus*; at this point, too, Bishop's interest shifted from the northern to the southern hemisphere. The second section has, in place of a title, this inscription:

> Nautilus at Sea Latt 12°: 20′ N Longitude
> 130 degrees E^t of Greenwich
> Thursday 2^d Feby 1797

This Book, is particularly Intended, by me, for Mr William Bishop, Attorney at Basingstoke in Hamshire and it is my ernest

desire, and request, if any accident should overtake me, that it
may be forwarded to him by the first safe conveyance—

Given from under my hand
and Seal, the date above written

Chaˢ Bishop[1]

To the Person who shall
succeed me in Command or
situation, or who shall take
cognisance of my Effects.

Like the 'Commercial Journal' title, this inscription is on a
slip now pasted to a folio, but from appearances may earlier
have been stuck to a cover or an end-paper.

The two sections of the book are now in different institutions: that concerning the *Ruby* is in the Provincial Archives
of British Columbia, Victoria, B.C.; that concerning the
Nautilus is in the Mitchell Library, Sydney, New South
Wales. Each library acquired its holding in 1912–13; this,
together with the obvious logic for Bishop's purpose of maintaining the record intact, suggests that the split might not
have occurred until well after the document's composition.
Yet the evidence is stronger for supposing that Bishop himself split the book, in February 1797. His writing the inscription to William Bishop points to this, as does the note (in an
alien hand) on the sheepskin binding of the *Ruby* manuscript:
'Charles Bishop/M[hiatus] 2 April 1797/Anno 1797'. The
best hypotheses would seem to be that the 'M' stood for
Macao, that the note was the work of the contemporary
binder, and that he returned the bound volume in April 1797.
Bishop evidently had the manuscript beside him as late as
10 June 1797, for his letter of that date refers by numeration
to earlier pages. That letter also refers to Captain W. R.
Broughton having undertaken to carry a journal to Britain.
Broughton left China on 26 June 1797, although not directly
for Britain—which raises the further, but unsolved, puzzle
why he was chosen as courier. Almost certainly it was this
manuscript which Broughton transmitted. On scrutiny, the
reasons for supposing that Bishop might have kept the docu-

---

[1] There follows a rough seal, subscribed 'W. Allen'.

ment intact do not prove invincible. Probably he could dispense with this record because he had yet other copies of his papers: a proposition which has independent support in the time-gaps and dis-sequence with which items appear in the extant book. If both sections made their way to William Bishop, their simultaneous acquisition by the libraries presents no problem. The documents' interim history is blank.

Bishop kept the journal with care, and the memoranda adequately. He cancelled some pages in the journal, and tore out others. His writing was always legible, and the ink has weathered well. His spelling was up to the eighteenth-century average. Like such contemporaries as James Cook he stumbled over consecutive vowels, aspirates, and 'wh' sounds. The one orthographic oddity was occasional transposition of letters to produce such words as 'fater' and 'noly'. Bishop's punctuation was likewise characteristic of the times, having (by modern standards) too many commas and dashes and too few stops; if his sentence closed at the end of a line he used no point at all. Bishop revised his own work, and someone has corrected the journal further. Capitalization was eccentric not only in choice of words, but in formation of letters: for many, Bishop used an upper and lower case form, but often wrote the former small and the latter big.

The editor has handled stylistic problems in the usual way, diverging from the original only where necessary to ensure sense. Place-names have remained precisely as Bishop wrote them. The size rather than the form of letters has determined capitalization. No indication is given where modification of punctuation has occurred, nor where Bishop's repetition of a word has been eliminated. Bishop's own emendations have been incorporated as a matter of course and those of his earlier editor ignored: having to work from photostats may have led the present editor into error in distinguishing the two sets of corrections.

At some points more direct intervention has taken place. The manuscript sometimes requires an added word or phrase to make sense, and these the editor has supplied. Some letters repeat information which the earlier text has given; brief summaries replace these passages. Letters have been shorn of salutations and farewells, and information as to their address, date, and destination given at their head. Abbreviations not in axiomatic use (a subjective but genuine distinction) have been filled out. All words and letters supplied for one or other of these purposes appear in italics; where Bishop underlined, the printed text is in small capitals. Conformity has been imposed on the presentation of Latitude and Longitude in margins; on the form adopted within each statistical table; and on the placing (either up or down) of terminal letters in those abbreviations which remain.

The annotations are modest, seeking to clarify rather than to amplify. They are the work of a general historian, not of an economist, cartographer, anthropologist, botanist, or zoologist. At some points the editor has failed to satisfy himself, and readers will no doubt find other grievances. The notes do not explain words defined in *The Shorter Oxford English Dictionary* (third revised edition, 1950).

At the top of the journal sheets Bishop wrote (with variations) at the appropriate stages: 'From Bristol towards the North West coast of America'; 'On the North West coast of America' (often with the particular region following); 'From N.W. America towards Sandwich Islands'; and 'At Sandwich Islands 1796'. The journal is now divided into chapters accordingly, the latter two sections being conflated. Bishop gave running date-heads in his margins and this practice has been followed.

Bishop attempted occasional illustrations. They comprise a Sun Fish, an Easter Island couple, rocks off Cape Blanco, an American Indian in his canoe, 'A Beauty of the N.W^t coast of America', another shapely female, a small sailing vessel, and a sea-maiden clasping an anchor. Only the last, a miniature, has any power. The page on which it appears is reproduced, while Bishop's other artistic efforts go ignored. At the beginning of the manuscript journal is a map, showing with some care the *Ruby* voyage, and the outline of many others. Who drew these outlines and what they represent are unanswered queries. They do not stand for Bishop's movements during his own later voyages, thus confirming the probability that he did not then have the *Ruby* manuscript in his possession. Because it confuses rather than clarifies, this map also is not reproduced. Instead Bishop's routes are shown in maps prepared by the editor.

Several historians have known Bishop's manuscript.[1] F. W. Howay used the *Ruby* section extensively in his various studies of the otter-fur trade. In the 1920s T. C. Elliott published two articles which extracted substantial passages from this document: one (1927) reproduced all entries from Bishop's sojourns at the Columbia River; the other (1928) transcribed the introductory paragraph of the journal, some paragraphs from the instructions to Bishop, and the entries from 7 to 22 May 1795; H. R. Wagner and H. W. Bradley were two other historians of the North-west to refer (very sparingly) to the *Ruby* manuscript. The archives of Hawaii have long held a typescript of this material,[2] from which R. S. Kuykendall and H. B. Restarick drew. In Australia K. M. Bowden has used the whole manuscript, and H. E. Maude the *Nautilus* section.

II. CAPTAIN CHARLES BISHOP AND HIS VOYAGES

Bishop's voyage of 1794–1800 and his later life epitomized what V. T. Harlow has termed 'the swing to the East'— Britain's concern in the later eighteenth century to find wealth and power among the littorals and islands of the eastern seas.[3] Especially did Bishop's experience typify European contact with the Pacific, that story of endless interaction between trader, missionary, administrator, and primitive person. Thus the text gives a paradigm of Pacific history source-material. Furthermore, it relates a minor epic of adventure, courage, and turbulent fortune.

[1] See the Bibliography under names mentioned.
[2] Information from Miss A. Conrad, archivist.
[3] *The Founding of the Second British Empire 1763–1793* (London, 1952 and 1964), I, 62–102, and II, especially chapters 5–8 (chapter 7 giving the best background account of 'the China Trade and the Canadian Pacific Coast').

Bishop was born to a middle-class Hampshire family, probably in the late 1760s.[1] The text indicates a fair education; the spelling is sometimes odd, but Bishop has a decent vocabulary and manages an occasional literary allusion. He joined the Navy around 1780, and reached midshipman's rank. But no patron appeared who might grant Bishop the commission which he believed himself to have merited, and so after about ten years he transferred to private employ. Such exchange was common, part of the intimacy between adventurers and government which pervaded 'the swing to the East'.

Bishop's employer was Sydenham (or Sidenham) Teast of Bristol. Men of that name had played a sizeable part in Bristol commerce throughout the century, as ship-builders and merchants.[2] The most lucrative trade of the time and place was the transport of slaves from Africa to America and the Indies. The Teasts pursued other interests. These included whaling in the South Atlantic, and in 1790 the South Sea Company granted licences for two Teast ships probably bent on that business.[3] At first, Bishop did not venture so far. The opening lines of the text indicate that late in 1792 he went, as second-in-command of the *Ruby*, to north-west Africa. Operating from Portendick, near Marsa,[4] the crew gathered ivory and other produce. In 1789 Sydenham Teast (either father or son) had spoken about this trade before the Committee of the Privy Council on Trade and Plantations, as it studied the Slave traffic. Since he had embarked on the business a few years earlier, five of his vessels had returned from Africa; ivory, gum copal, and various woods were the major items. Not that they won much profit, only five per cent 'beyond

[1] He was described in 1804 as 'about 35' (W. S. Hill-Reid, *John Grant's Journey* (London, 1957), 58). All quotations and facts from Hill-Reid, who does not treat his subject with the stringent criticism Grant requires, have been checked against the J. Grant papers (National Library of Australia, Canberra); and, where possible, other sources.

[2] Information from J. W. Earnshaw; C. M. MacInnes in C. N. Parkinson (ed.), *The Trade Winds* (London, 1948), 67.

[3] Committee of Treasury of South Sea Company, 16 September 1790 (British Museum); W. E. Minchinton (ed.), *The Trade of Bristol in the Eighteenth Century* (Bristol, 1957), 53.

[4] Shown in Bishop's MS. map. Marsa is at 18° 20′ N., 16° 00′ W.

legal Interest'. Other traders might have done better because high mortality among their sailors reduced wage costs, but Teast ships carried surgeons and had lost only ten men from disease (but even this was ten per cent). Teast appears to have been an intelligent witness, and expressed interest in further development of African commerce.[1]

The Teasts were quick to venture into the otter-fur trade. The pursuit of furs had always been a prime economic force in North America, and the otter of the North-west waters (*Enhydra lutis*) had attracted Japanese hunters before 1600. Four to five feet in length, weighing up to eighty pounds, the animal is amphibious, its brown-black fur warm and rich.[2] Following the Japanese, Russians and Spaniards entered the hunt from their dominions to north and south. By the late eighteenth century Russia was becoming steadily more interested in the area,[3] while Spain still explored the coast and regarded it as an adjunct of her American empire. But early in 1778 James Cook arrived off the coast, beginning the heroic era in otter-fur history and the incursion of British and New England mariners into this cock-pit of competitive imperialisms. Even Austria and France were to show some interest.

Cook and his men appreciated the quality of the otter-furs, gathering some at Nootka (which he first called King George's) Sound and Prince William Sound. The Indians were co-operative; the climate bearable for a fair part of the year. Altogether, the great navigator ruminated, 'the discovery of this part of the continent of North America, where so valuable an article of commerce may be met with, cannot be a matter of indifference'.[4] Cook did not live to see the confirmation which this forecast received when his expedition reached Canton. The pelts returned as much as 120 dollars each; many seamen wanted to sail back to the North-west

---

[1] C. E. Fayle in Parkinson (1948), 77; Minchinton (1957), xv; House of Commons Sessional Papers, 1789, paper 646*a*, part one.
[2] See T. A. Rickard, 'The Sea-otter in History', *British Columbia Historical Quarterly*, **11**, 15–31.
[3] See H. McCracken, *Hunters of the Stormy Sea* (London, 1957).
[4] *A Voyage to the Pacific Ocean...for Making Discoveries in the Northern Hemisphere...* (London, 1785), **11**, 296.

coast and become rich on its furs. James King, chronicler of the voyage after Cook's death, agreed as to 'the advantages that might be derived from a voyage to that part of the American coast, undertaken with commercial views'. He suggested that the East India Company might sponsor an expedition, which would complete the surveying of both the Asian and American coasts of the North Pacific, and pay for itself by fur-trading. The vessels should take wrought iron and a forge to shape it to the Indians' needs, knives, coarse cloth, and trinkets.[1]

The diffusion of knowledge concerning the furs took time, and not until April 1785 did the Briton James Hanna set off from Canton as the first English-speaking adventurer to follow where Cook had pointed. Over the next thirty years an average of about eight ships pursued the business each season, although from around 1800 Yankees increasingly outnumbered Hanna's compatriots. In 1810 the genius of the United States of America's fur industry, J. J. Astor, extended his interest to this region and founded the Pacific Fur Company, which established its 'Astoria' base at the mouth of the Columbia River. Astor soon withdrew from this venture, but meanwhile he had inspired the British-Canadian North-West Company also to build a station on the Columbia (1811). This became a focus for the trade, and continued as such after the North-west Company merged with the Hudson's Bay Company in 1821.[2] But by then the otters had dwindled far. The relative paucity of animals meant that the trade was never more than a by-way of fur-trade history. Yet it had intrinsic interest, and the very shallowness and uncertainty of its largesse made it typical of all Pacific trade. Riches for some, usually the pioneers; frustration for the rest—that chorus was to resound again and again, for Bishop and for many others.

Hanna's expedition was successful,[3] and the first product of a few years' intense British activity, concerning which this

[1] *A Voyage to the Pacific Ocean...* II, 434 ff.
[2] P. C. Phillips and J. W. Smurr, *The Fur Trade* (Norman, 1961), II, 36–66, 270–388.
[3] M. E. Wilbur, *The East India Company...* (Stamford, 1945), 337 ff.

account notices only the passages significant for Bishop's voyage. During 1785, London interests formed the King George's Sound Company to pursue the business; its backers included Sir Joseph Banks who, especially as President of the Royal Society (1778–1820), encouraged many aspects of 'the swing to the East'. The Company planned to settle a factory at Nootka, and to use it as a springboard for trade throughout the North Pacific, especially with Japan. Thus the expansionists aimed not merely to follow Cook's track, but to go where his final voyage might have led had he survived. British interest in Japan and Korea appeared often throughout these years, *inter alia* in Teast's programme for Bishop. The Government and the East India Company approved the King George's plan. The venture set off in late summer 1785, commanded by Nathaniel Portlock and George Dixon, both veterans of the Cook voyage. They had fair success, although never approaching fulfilment of the original scheme.[1]

Among others on the coast in 1786 was a two-ship expedition financed by the East India Company at Madras, at the persuasion of J. C. Strange. This venture too had abortive plans of making a settlement; Strange kept a journal, but its publication waited until 1928. The voyage had mediocre fortune, and so interest from Madras died away.

More important was the concurrent activity of the Bengal Fur Society. Its finance came from men of respectability in that district, but its inspiration from J. H. Cox. This vigorous agent for India-based merchants spent most of the 1780s in Canton, defying the East India Company's ban on private British entrepreneurs there.[2] He backed Hanna's venture, and then persuaded his Indian associates to launch the Bengal company. It commissioned John Meares, erstwhile lieutenant in the Navy, to lead yet another expedition of 1786. Meares enjoyed good trade, but lost his accompanying sloop and saw

---

[1] V. T. Harlow and F. Madden (eds.), *British Colonial Developments 1774–1834. Select Documents* (Oxford, 1953), 21–30.
[2] M. Greenberg, *British Trade and the Opening of China 1800–42* (Cambridge, 1951), 23 ff.; H. B. Morse, *The Chronicles of the East India Company Trading to China 1635–1834* (Oxford, 1926), II, 142. Harlow questions Cox's backing of the first voyage (II, 435 n.); Greenberg might be inaccurate.

twenty-three of his men die during a fearful winter in Prince William Sound. With spring, he sailed back to Canton, sold his furs, and prepared for a second voyage under the same aegis. By May 1788 he was back on the coast in the *Felice*, with his consort the *Iphigenia*, William Douglas. The two carried Portuguese colours, thus evading the need to obtain licences from the East India and South Sea Companies, which had monopolies over British trade in the area. At Nootka Meares acquired title to land from the chief Maquinna, established a factory upon it, and built the sloop *Northwest America*. His contacts with Portlock and Dixon were hostile, signifying the fierce competitiveness of the trade. The *Iphigenia* and the *Northwest America* traded northward.

While they wintered on the coast, Meares returned to Canton late in 1788 and sold his furs with great profit. Also in port was R. C. Etches, driving force behind the King George's Sound Company. The two evidently decided that monopoly would give best and most enduring returns, and so pooled their resources. Another associate was Daniel Beal(e), who took over Cox's business on the latter's expulsion by the East India Company in 1788, himself avoiding that fate by becoming Prussian consul. For their joint venture they retained the *Princess Royal*, a King George's Sound Company vessel, and commissioned also the more imposing *Argonaut*. In command of her and the expedition they placed James Colnett, another interesting figure. He had served as a midshipman on Cook's northern voyage and remained in the navy until August 1786, then retiring on half-pay.

Colnett sailed in April 1789, first for the Japanese coast and then for Nootka, intending to expand the settlement there. In April too the *Iphigenia* and the *Northwest America* arrived at Nootka from the north, finding two Americans there. The *Northwest America* soon departed on a trading cruise. The next arrivals, early in May, were two Spanish warships. Spain, or at least the Viceroy of Mexico, had determined to assert hegenomy. E. J. Martinez, in command of the warships, declared Nootka Spanish territory, and seized first the *Iphigenia* and then the *Northwest America*, the *Princess Royal*, and the *Argonaut* as they entered in June and July. The seizures were brief and largely painless, but the Nootka Sound incident had begun.

Concurrent events in Britain heightened its explosive potential. In 1789 both Portlock and Dixon published narratives which stressed the wealth offered by the trade. Alexander Dalrymple, most vigorous of all publicists for expansion in the eastern seas, issued his *Plan for Promoting the Fur-trade*. Thus opinion was averse to acceptance of a note presented to the British Government on 11 February 1790, asking that it restrain its subjects from quasi-colonization on Spanish territory. After some equivocation, William Pitt used his heaviest diplomatic armament to force Spain's withdrawal from this position. In October the two powers signed a Convention which declared that Britons should be free from restraint 'either in navigating or in carrying on their fisheries in the Pacific Ocean or in the South Seas, or in landing on the coasts of these places not already occupied, for the purpose of carrying on their commerce with the natives of the country or of making establishments there'.[1] The whole coast north of California ranked as 'not already occupied'. Spain was to restore the territory and goods confiscated at Nootka. In asserting itself over this incident the British Government showed its determination to facilitate 'the swing to the East', especially but not only as it concerned the North-west coast.

As such a demonstration, the episode was but part of a very large programme, which Harlow has sought to delineate in the mass. The sponsorship of Cook's voyages was one dramatic product of the Government's concern with eastern trade and, in close connexion, with revived hopes for the discovery of a North-west passage.[2] Henry Dundas, second only to Pitt in the Government, was to become the father-in-law of J. C. Strange, and encouraged the latter's venture.[3] The King

[1] Quoted, L. Mills, 'The Real Significance of the Nootka Sound Incident', *Canadian Historical Review*, 6, 119.
[2] G. Williams, *The British Search for the Northwest Passage in the Eighteenth Century* (London, 1962), illuminates this aspect.
[3] J. M. Norris, 'The Policy of the British Cabinet in the Nootka Crisis', *English Historical Review*, 70, 565–6.

George's Sound Company acted under ministerial approval. In the late 1780s Government planned to send another expedition to the Pacific, aiming especially for the North-west coast. Henry Roberts was to lead it, with George Vancouver as his second-in-command. News of Martinez's actions at Nootka led to this scheme acquiring a more aggressive character: the expedition was to establish a Nootkan settlement, intended to assist the fur trade, in defiance of Spain.[1] The Convention made such drama superfluous, and Vancouver's actual voyage belongs later in the narrative.

Tied with this sensitivity for the North-west coast was the Government's espousal of the whaling industry. Cook had noted the existence of whales and seals thereabouts, and the loss of the American colonies did more to provoke interest. Were Britain to remain dominant over the seas then she must attend to this business, important both for its own sake and as a nursery for mariners. The northern fisheries (around Greenland and Newfoundland) no longer met all needs, so British attention focused on the fields reached by sailing south—the South Atlantic immediately, but in prospect the whole Pacific. Lord Hawkesbury (formerly Charles Jenkinson, afterwards Lord Liverpool) was especially solicitous of the industry as President since 1786 of the Committee on Trade and Plantations.[2] Government approved Portlock's efforts to establish a fishing base on Staten Island (Isla de Los Estados) in the South Atlantic. The Government deliberately used the Nootka incident as an occasion for opening the Pacific to British whalers.

One notable indication of the Government's sympathy for the North-west entrepreneurs was the respect it granted Meares during the diplomatic crisis of 1790. Arriving in England in early April he urged the toughest possible line against Spain. His accounts of the seizures at Nootka exaggerated Martinez's severity; the factory at Nootka assumed

---

[1] G. Greenwood, *Early American–Australian Relations* (Melbourne, 1944), 57–8; Harlow, II, 439–40.
[2] Harlow and Madden, 367–80; Harlow, II, 293–328.

proportions beyond reality; and his own flying of Portuguese colours in 1788 received less notice than its pertinence demanded. Meares told the Committee on Trade and Plantations of his hopes for the trade, the opening of Japan prominent among them.[1] His protestations won acceptance at face value.

Above all Meares published his *Voyages*, which was Bishop's text-book and remains the classic of the trade. Its subscribers included Cox, Hawkesbury, and Evan Nepean, under-secretary at the Home Office and a key figure among those pushing 'the swing'. The book's refrain was the felicitous amalgam of Providence, British power, and Pacific commerce. The prospects of trade with Japan; the necessity of annexing the Sandwich Islands as a base for shipping; the value of a colony in south Korea which would serve to 'annihilate' Russian activity in those seas—these were among the lessons Meares taught.[2] Siberia, north China, and the Philippines also came within his vision of boundless trade. He mentioned the riches which whalers might find in the Pacific, and urged that an embassy be sent to China as a first move in persuading the authorities there to relax controls over trade. All this was in the introduction, while the body of the work gave an interesting and encouraging account of Meares's and Douglas's experiences on the coast.

Early in 1791 the British Government moved to finalize the Nootka Convention by sending out Vancouver to accept the due restitution on the spot. The expedition, intended also to survey unknown coasts, comprised Vancouver's *Discovery* and the armed tender *Chatham*, W. R. Broughton. Sailing by way of the Cape of Good Hope and the south Australian coast, Vancouver reached Nootka in August 1792. He found there his Spanish counterpart, J. F. Quadra. The two became personal friends, but interpreted the Convention differently. Vancouver wanted cession to Britain of the whole port, without implication that he was admitting Spanish rights elsewhere; Quadra would restore only the territory

[1] Harlow and Madden, 33–5.
[2] *Voyages Made in the Years 1788 and 1789...* (London, 1790), lxxxiii–xcv.

occupied by Meares's fort (itself a matter of controversy), at least unless Vancouver would adopt a more conciliatory attitude apropos possession of the southward coast. The impasse dragged along, but Vancouver used his time profitably in survey work and wintered at the Sandwich Islands. He returned Broughton to England to put the diplomatic problem before the metropolitan powers. In January 1794 they agreed, in terms more like Quadra's than Vancouver's, that Meares's ground was alone to be restored formally; for the rest Britain was satisfied with a mutual guarantee that neither power should seek exclusive rights of settlement. Vancouver left Nootka in October 1794 before news of the settlement reached him; he spent his last unhappy years preparing his narrative for publication. The restitution at Nootka took place in March 1795, between commissioners of the two nations. In anti-climax, both then withdrew.

Broughton meanwhile had taken command of the *Providence* (October 1793), in which he was to return to Nootka and also to survey north Asian waters, including the coasts of Japan and Korea. The early 1790s saw a surge of British interest thither, as Dundas advised Lord Macartney to spy out trade possibilities as an ancillary to the famous, fruitless, embassy to China, and the Government asked the East India Company to report on the same subject, which it did in discouraging terms.[1] Awaiting Broughton with the Indians at Nootka were letters left by the commissioners telling him that the controversy was over; Bishop, arriving in the interim, guessed wrongly that they proposed formal British settlement there.[2] Broughton collected the letters and continued with his surveys. He lost the *Providence* off Formosa in May 1797, but carried on in his tender, soon reaching Canton, there to become Bishop's post-boy.

★ ★ ★

[1] G. Macartney, *An Embassy to China* (ed. J. L. Cranmer-Byng) (London, 1962), 16, 380; W. G. Beasley, *Great Britain and the Opening of Japan 1834–1858* (London, 1951), 4.
[2] W. R. Broughton, *A Voyage of Discovery to the North Pacific Ocean* (London, 1804), 50; see below, p. 95.

While these events proceeded at the national level, men like Teast made them meaningful in terms of commerce. On 8 January 1791 Teast interrogated the Board of Trade about the Nootka Convention 'so that he may know how to carry on the Trade and Fishery in the Southern Seas and pacifick Ocean with benefit to himself, but without infringing any part of the said Convention'; in June he despatched to North America the *Jenny*, 78 tons, James Baker, which sailed in June 1791.[1] On his way to the coast Baker called at Easter Island, Tahiti, Christmas (Line) Island, and the Sandwich Islands, from which last he carried two native girls. Moving over to the coast in mid-1792 Baker discovered what he called Sidenham Harbour, at the mouth of the Umpqua. Then the *Jenny* traded to the north, reaching Nootka on 7 October. Vancouver was just about to leave for the Sandwich Islands and at Baker's request agreed to return the girls. The naval man felt that his compatriot had erred in taking the Islanders from home, but discounted the suspicion of the Spaniards that Baker had intended to exchange them for furs; he believed this report invented by Americans seeking 'the prejudice and dishonour of the British subjects trading on the coast'.[2] Anyway, Baker would seem to have been employing a somewhat ruthless variant of the use of Islanders' labour by many traders, Bishop among them. The Americans further charged Baker with piracy and firing upon the Indians of Clayoquot Sound.[3] After leaving Nootka, Baker moved south. Broughton met him at the mouth of the Columbia and called the spot (Meares's Deception Bay) Baker Bay, which name still applies. The two vessels sailed out together on 10 November into storms which damaged the *Jenny* severely.

She carried her furs not to Canton but to England. They must have sold well enough to maintain Teast's interest in the trade. He determined to return the ship to the coast in

[1] Harlow, II, 320 n.; minutes of Court of Directors of South Sea Company, 15 September 1791; generally, F. W. Howay and T. C. Elliott, 'Voyages of the "Jenny" to Oregon, 1792–94', *Oregon Historical Quarterly*, **30**, 197–206.
[2] *A Voyage of Discovery to the North Pacific Ocean...* (London, 1798), II, 226.
[3] B. Anderson, *Surveyor of the Sea* (Seattle, 1960), 111–12.

1793–4, although the command now went to J. W. Adamson. The new master had great experience, having been Douglas's second-in-command on the *Iphigenia* and again on the coast in 1791–2. The reports of Baker and Adamson doubtless shaped the instructions, knowledge, and ideas with which Bishop set forth. Under Adamson, the *Jenny* traded very successfully. She made Nootka late in September 1794. Vancouver, just about to depart, remarked how 'very small' she was; yet on board were 2000 skins. Adamson told Vancouver of his plan to sail for Canton, thence to return to England under charter from the East India Company.[1]

In a way characteristic of the trade, these preparations misfired. Adamson, obviously a very competent man, played out his part: the *Jenny* was at Canton on 25 December and ready to leave six weeks later. But she lacked a homeward cargo, probably because the East India Company had reneged its undertaking to provide one. Confounding this confusion, the Hoppo (Chinese chief port-officer) prohibited the *Jenny* from sailing, as an empty ship yielded no customs revenue. The Company still did not help, so she got away only by paying duties on a cargo of silk put down in her name, but not in her holds.[2]

By then the *Ruby* was far on her voyage. The text indicates that Teast's decision to send her in late 1794 was rather tardy. On 10 September the directors of the East India Company agreed that the *Ruby* 'be licensed to proceed from the North West coast of America to the Japanese Islands and China'; eight days later the South Sea Company added its permission for the voyage.[3] The petition to the South Sea Company came not direct from Teast, but from the house of St Barbe, an important whaling firm. So negotiations proceeded with the two companies, whose privileges and behaviour provoked vast controversy in the eighteenth and

[1] Vancouver, III, 314–15.
[2] Morse, II, 259–60. Note that Morse says the *Jenny* carried but 1600 skins.
[3] Minutes of Court of Directors of East India Company (Commonwealth Relations Office, London) and Minutes of Court of Directors of South Sea Company for dates cited.

early nineteenth centuries. The South Sea Company by now maintained only the form of its monopoly over all southern excursions, but the East India Company still had forty important years ahead. Many ardent advocates of 'the swing to the East' criticized the Company for allegedly hindering expansion, but it fought back. The Act 33 George III, cap. 52, had established a new compromise. Its chief purpose was to require the Company to make 3,000 tons of shipping annually available to private merchants in the Indian trade. Proponents of the fur-trade had campaigned for recognition from the Company, and Section 78 met this demand:

> And, for the further encouragement of trade to the north-west coast of *America* and the islands adjacent, under the limitations contained in the convention made by his Majesty with the King of *Spain*, of twenty-eighth day of October one thousand seven hundred and ninety, it may be expedient that ships fitted out for those parts should in certain cases be permitted by licence from the said company to proceed from the said coast and islands direct to the isles of *Japan* and the coasts of *Korea* and *Canton*, there to dispose of their cargoes obtained on the said north-west coast of *America*, and to return from thence direct to the same north-west coast or islands adjacent, and there dispose of their returns in trade, the owners and commanders of such ships entering into such covenants with, and giving such security to the said company, and submitting to be bound by such rules and regulations as shall appear to the best adapted for preserving to the said company the exercise and benefits of their commercial privileges, and conduce to the preservation of good order and regularity of the ships companies, and their observance of the law prescribed by the native states...

The text indicates how heavily the Company's demands weighed on both Teast and Bishop: no wonder men of their class came to look upon monopoly privileges as abominable heresies, defying the new revelation of *laissez faire*.

The *Ruby* was an American-built ship of 101 tons, extensively reconstructed in 1785 and 1787.[1] As a ship-builder Teast must have chosen her with care, and evidently attended

---

[1] Information from Lloyd's Register of Shipping for 1795, conveyed by J. W. Earnshaw. The Register gives the weight as one hundred tons, but Bishop adds the extra (see below, p. 3).

to some defects after she returned from Africa. The selection of trade-goods was comprehensive and sensible; the instructions presented to Bishop clear, forceful, and optimistic. All appeared ready for a happy voyage.

Its early stages were orthodox. Calls at São Tiago and Rio de Janeiro were routine for southward voyages. The Falklands had fewer visitors, but a generation earlier had been the subject of dispute between Britain and Spain, in a way anticipatory of the Nootka incident. In 1764 the Government despatched John Byron to explore the south seas, the voyage linking with Francis Drake's of the past and Cook's of the future.[1] Byron had little success, but he did fulfil the instruction to locate and survey the Falklands. Early in 1765 he established a settlement at Port Egmont, on the western island, as a token of claiming possession. A year earlier the Frenchman L. A. de Bougainville had established Port Louis at Berkeley Sound in the east. Spain looked askance at this action of her ally, believing that it might assist English penetration of Hispanic America. France therefore ceded Port Louis to Spain in 1767. Both before and after that event friction existed between the two colonies, and the metropolitan powers took up these quarrels. In 1770 Spain seized Port Egmont, and war with Britain hovered. France discouraged such militancy, however, and Port Egmont was restored. In 1774 Britain evacuated the colony while maintaining right of possession; the Spaniards remained at Port Louis.

Easter Island, Bishop's next resort, had a strategic position comparable to the Falklands, but lacked a decent harbour and never figured in world affairs. Bishop accepted a common error in supposing that the British privateer Edward Davis had landed there in 1687.[2] Actually not until 1722 did Jacob Roggeveen discover the island, which then waited forty-eight years for its next European visitors: Spaniards, whose report prompted the Viceroy of Peru to have serious but unrealized thoughts of annexation.[3] Cook (1774), J. F. de la Perouse

---

[1] Harlow, I, 22 ff.
[2] See *The Journals of Captain James Cook*... (ed. J. C. Beaglehole) (Cambridge, 1961), II, 326 n., 348 n.
[3] Harlow, I, 51–3.

(1786), the *Jenny*, and presumably some other traders also called there before the *Ruby*.

Bishop's journal to the coast shows him in a pleasing aspect. His narration was competent, and included some striking phrases. He was an interested observer at the various ports, noticing not only armament and produce but also social and human characteristics. He speculated on waterspouts, and attempted some zoological description. Typical eighteenth-century attitudes appeared too in his indulgent scorn of Catholic ceremony at Rio, albeit his own public prayer-reading on Sundays aboard ship. Generous good-will so far pervaded Bishop's account of the Easter Islanders that he wrongly exculpated them of cannibalism. At the Island he enjoyed the pleasures of Pacific women, and was happy that his men shared the boon. Concern for the crew showed also in a surgeon's presence aboard the *Ruby* (a practice not enforced by law),[1] and in the serving of treacle as an anti-scorbutic. Overall Bishop's text tells a little more about the rank-and-file than do most comparable records. His seamanship to this point was competent, if not inspired, and drew on careful reading of pertinent narratives. Throbbing throughout the journal was Bishop's passion to succeed, and so win honour for himself and profit for Teast. This rather morbid fervour was a notable peculiarity of Bishop's character, yet similar attitudes must have upheld other men who withstood the torment and troubles of 'the swing to the East'.

Further identifying Bishop with his age was the coincidence between his world-view and that of the poet James Thomson (1700–48). Their attitudes to all things were similar, and the ruling passions of both were love of Britain and love of Nature. Moreover, the reader of today will judge both as naïve and smug on the former theme, affecting and interesting on the latter. Bishop quoted Thomson's 'Summer' in the journal, and another, yet unidentified, extract is from the same school. Bishop himself might have been the emulator: a description of him as 'a poet in his way' appears below, and his prose sometimes suggests a versifier lurking behind the

---

[1] J. A. Nixon in Parkinson (1948), 136–7.

lines. No doubt Bishop knew Thomson's 'Rule, Britannia' and perhaps a passage from 'Liberty' which hailed precisely such Britons as himself:

> Even, yet untouched by daring keel, be theirs
> The vast Pacific—that on other worlds,
> Their future conquests, rolls resounding tides.

The poet joined navigators, statesmen, and merchants in pointing eastward.

The *Ruby* reached 'New Albion', as Bishop followed Drake in terming the mid-continental coast, in April, and anchored in the Columbia on 22 May. Already she lagged behind Teast's schedule, but not irreparably. Ambivalence remained the key-note throughout 1795, as Bishop traded up the coast to about 55° N. and back again to the Columbia. Disappointment alternated with success, anxiety with pleasure. Especially equivocal was Bishop's attitude to the Indians, on whom he depended not only for furs and food but also for human contact. He could truly respect and like them, yet as the season passed he became increasingly prone to fear and suspicion. This tension helped the journal acquire one of its most notable qualities: illumination of the intercourse between the two races. But Bishop also revealed how the actual situation on the coast forced cordiality and even co-operation with other European traders, contrary to the isolation ordered by Teast. The text gives an exact picture of what goods sold on the coast, and of the process of trade. Above all, it sounds the refrain of 'mortification': all the bright moments could not compensate for the long, cold, grim months of business.

Bishop's chronicle has some faults. He was neither anthropologist, nor zoologist, nor botanist. More culpably, he did not always make his precise route clear. His account is less significant than Meares's and those connected with the American vessel, *Columbia*.[1] The unpublished account of Joseph Ingraham's trade in 1792 has similar quality and better illustrations. Otherwise, Bishop gives as good an

[1] F. W. Howay (ed.), *Voyages of the 'Columbia' to the Northwest Coast 1787–90 and 1790–93* (Boston, 1941).

account of the trade as does anyone, either historian or participant.[1]

Bishop spent the early winter months, October to January, at the Columbia, and then determined to seek refreshment at the Sandwich Islands. Boredom and misery rather than sheer need probably forced this decision, and Bishop's capitulation to them suggests that he lacked the toughness, inhuman if not superhuman, which the trade required. Perhaps, however, his flaw lay in seamanship. In the very crossing of the bar at the river's mouth the *Ruby* suffered damage which doomed the enterprise. She had to struggle to reach her destination.

In using the Sandwich Islands as a base, Bishop followed the common route of fur-traders, both British and American. Their contact had profoundly influenced Hawaiian politics, facilitating chief Kamehameha's establishment of dominion throughout the group. Bishop witnessed an important stage in this process, and grasped its significance; his detail, however, was faulty.[2] The text's relation of the experiences ashore of the ship's surgeon has more peculiar and authentic value. For Bishop himself these weeks were important because he then met his future associate, Roger Simpson, then aboard the American (*Lady*) *Washington*. Simpson gave Bishop much help, but insufficient to stem all the latter's 'mortification'. Provisions were scarce; the *Ruby* became more dilapidated; as Bishop had feared, the crew fell victim to the delights of tropic love, and rebelled at the prospect of returning to the coast in their leaky vessel. Bishop just failed to meet here with Broughton, whom he assumed would lend the protection of the British Navy while the *Ruby* was careened.

Thus circumstances forced Bishop to sail for Canton, whence he might refit for a further trip to the coast the following

[1] For a review of the literature, see F. W. Howay, 'Indian Attacks upon Maritime Traders of the North-West Coast, 1785–1805', *Canadian Historical Review*, **6**, 287–305; and 'A List of Trading Vessels in the Maritime Fur Trade', *Royal Society of Canada, Proceedings and Transactions. Third Series*, **24**, ii, 111–34; **25**, ii, 117–49; **26**, ii, 43–86; **27**, ii, 119–47; **28**, ii, 11–49.

[2] R. S. Kuykendall, *The Hawaiian Kingdom* (Honolulu, 1947), 22 ff., especially 47 n.

season. In China, however, 'mortification' became more intense and varied than ever. The market for furs was low; the cost of provisions high. Bishop, rightly, saw himself as too much the simple man of the sea to manage the intricacies of commerce. On Simpson's advice he engaged as agent one John Howel. An erstwhile clergyman of the Church of England, Howel migrated to New England some time before 1790 and became associated with the fur trade. He himself went to the coast in 1792 and then to Canton where he became part-owner (the exact situation is vague and shady) of the *Washington*. In her Howel sailed to the Sandwich Islands, spending some months there in 1793–4 before returning to China.[1]

Simpson's reference notwithstanding, Howel proved a confidence man. In appointing him Bishop made the classic mistake of an innocent abroad. The text shows the high cost of his error—not so much, ultimately, in cash, but in Bishop's nervous energy and self-confidence. His affairs further suffered all the notorious impositions, delays, and resistance imposed by the Chinese Government.[2] The East India Company's local executive, the 'select committee of supercargoes', gave their distressed compatriot but passive aid. The exception was James Drummond, a sympathetic and distinguished man: his home at Macao had housed Lord Macartney recently, and in the past Luiz de Camoens as he wrote 'The Lusiad'.[3] Drummond's interest in Bishop was deep and ready. Whether it was entirely free of commercial interest remains obscure; Drummond protested that the Company allowed him no private investments, but perhaps he did have some arrangement with the Chinese merchant Conse(e)qua whom he subsequently encouraged to back Bishop.

In mid-1796 Bishop considered ending the long torture of business negotiation, cutting the expedition's losses, and him-

[1] H. B. Restarick, 'The first clergyman resident in Hawaii', *Hawaiian Historical Society, 32nd Annual Report*, 54–61.
[2] See, for example, K. S. Latourette, 'The history of early relations between the United States and China', *Transactions of the Connecticut Academy of Arts and Sciences*, 22, 20–6.
[3] Macartney (ed. Cranmer-Byng), 219, 383.

self re-joining the Navy at the invitation of Peter Rainier, Commodore and effective commander of the East Indies fleet. A few months earlier Rainier had struck major *coups* against the Dutch by capturing Amboyna, capital of the Moluccas (February), and Banda (March).[1] Bishop tentatively sold the *Ruby* and her cargo to one Robert Pavin, who however was beset with financial problems of his own. In hopes of profitably selling the cargo, the two mariners took the *Ruby* down to Amboyna. So trade followed the flag; and it proved good trade. At Amboyna, therefore, Bishop finally sold the *Ruby* to Pavin and bought the *Nautilus*, the qualities of which moved him to almost poetic enthusiasm. In a sense the move was rash, even hysterical, and Bishop himself was soon to regret it. Yet it showed too a remarkable durability of optimism and adventure.

Bishop met further troubles on returning to China (February 1797), but struggled on with his arrangements for a return to the coast. He planned as well to détour to Más Afuera for seal skins and oil. Although the idea fell through it had interest in illustrating the process of exploitation of fresh fields. Philip Carteret of H.M.S. *Swallow* had sheltered at Más Afuera in May 1767 and noticed the abundant seals; in 1773 John Hawkesworth published Carteret's account for Bishop and the world to read:[2] yet only in these very months burst the brief, intense, profitable, destruction of those animals.[3]

Bishop at last sailed from Canton in June 1797, with Simpson his deputy, only to meet a series of devastating storms. These drove him first to Formosa, where the natives proved savage and nearly killed second-officer John Harbottle. Next Bishop sheltered at Petropavlovsk, Kamchatka; the Russians' hospitality melted away the acrimony with which Bishop had regarded their compatriots as rival traders on the coast. The *Nautilus* then sailed south into further tempests,

[1] C. N. Parkinson, *War in the Eastern Seas 1793–1815* (London, 1954), 94.
[2] J. Hawkesworth, *An Account of the Voyage Undertaken by the Order of His Present Majesty for Making Discoveries in the Southern Hemisphere*... (London, 1773), I, 555–6.
[3] Phillips and Smurr, II, 63.

which did not even allow a return to Kamchatka. Instead Bishop made again for the Sandwich Islands, planning to refit there and, the coast being now out of the question for 1797, to sail direct for Más Afuera. The islands lacked material to restore the *Nautilus* completely, and the next bad weather forced her to Matavai Bay, Tahiti, early March 1798.

Bishop now contacted representatives of the cross, which with flag and trade-good has ever composed the guiding trinity of European expansion. Exactly one year earlier the London Missionary Society had established on Tahiti the first British missionary station in the Pacific. From the outset the natives had seen the missionaries as likely providers not of divine truth, but of European technique and material, especially firearms. When these anticipations proved false, tension arose. Bishop, the first European to arrive since the mission's foundation, was ready to trade firearms. To prevent him from doing so, the missionaries supplied his needs from their own resources. Bishop accepted the arrangement, but the natives became still angrier. The *Nautilus* departed on 10 March, leaving behind an ugly situation and five Hawaiian deserters.

With the *Nautilus* gone, animosities at Tahiti became more explicit. The natives' anger, reported one missionary, left them 'in one continual Broil'; the deserters spent all their time fomenting this.[1] The situation could have ended with massacre of the missionaries; it could have righted itself. The opportunity for a different resolution appeared when the *Nautilus*, having met yet another storm, sailed back into harbour on 24 March.

Immediately, the natives became still more hostile. When the missionaries sought to help Bishop by sending a delegation to the natives to urge the deserters' return, their emissaries suffered rough handling. On 28 March two further deserters (evidently the Europeans Reidson and McDonald)

---

[1] London Missionary Society papers; South Seas Journals; journal of R. Hassall, dated from Parramatta (New South Wales), 1 September 1799 (papers held by the Society, London). This and the following missionary references overlap, altogether providing a good account of the situation at Tahiti and the trip to Port Jackson.

came to the mission house and alleged that the natives were preparing a mass attack; so ugly was their temper that they had turned vicious when the seamen advised moderation. The missionaries debated with 'great altercation and great searchings of heart'.[1] Some estimated Bishop's return as 'a very Singular providence', and believed that they must take the escape which the *Nautilus* offered;[2] others 'would give all to the Natives rather than leave the Island to go in such a Leaky Ship'.[3] The majority were for departure, but wanted only to move to another island, whereas Bishop would take them only to his own new-chosen target of Port Jackson, New South Wales. Eleven of the eighteen missionaries determined to accompany him. The eleven had six dependants, so it was probably to make room as well as to maintain discipline that Bishop refused to receive back McDonald and Reidson. All was ready to sail on 30 March. But that day was a Friday, and the sailors' superstition forced a day's postponement of the departure of the vessel, with all her Christian cargo.

The *Nautilus*, damaged and crowded, had a rough journey. An anchor broke loose as they left Matavai Bay. Bishop burst a blood-vessel, and the missionary (S. H. Clode) who tended him agreed that it threatened death. The accident forced abandonment of plans to refresh at the Tonga (Friendly) Islands. Bad weather cancelled a projected call at Norfolk Island, and also the taking of observations for a few days. In consequence navigation went astray and the vessel nearly wrecked on the rocky outcrop of Ball's Pyramid one day, and on Lord Howe Island the next. On 14 May she reached Sydney, the settlement on the magnificent harbour-estuary of Port Jackson.

Bishop presented his bill to the missionaries.[4] Clode be-

[1] London Missionary Society papers; South Seas Letters; J. Harris to the Society, 29 March 1798.

[2] London Missionary Society papers; Hassall, *loc. cit.*; and South Seas Letters; J. Jefferson to missionaries on Tongatapu, 5 February 1799.

[3] London Missionary Society papers; Australian Letters; S. H. Clode to Society, 26 September 1798 (first copy).

[4] London Missionary Society papers; South Seas Letters; J. Eyre and J. Hardcastle to missionaries in New South Wales, 3 September 1799 (draft).

wailed its size, remarking that the Tahiti station had supplied all provisions for everyone aboard, and that the 'passengers' in fact had kept watch and joined the constant pumping. The Directors of the London Missionary Society in turn took a critical view of the whole episode when at length they heard of it, initially through Teast.[1] But by then the bill had long been paid.

Bishop's resort to New South Wales has an interesting place in the early history of British Australia. The pioneering settlements at Sydney and Norfolk Island had existed only since 1788. The declared motive for planting these colonies was to provide a gaol, with the proviso that the land's natural products, especially naval stores, might be a useful side-line. By 1798 the population was about 5,500 at Sydney and 900 at Norfolk Island; throughout the decade over 6,000 persons had landed as convicts.[2] The major tradition among Australian historians has been to accept the 'dumping of convicts' as the true reason for settlement, and to concentrate their attention on the society which convicts, ex-convicts, and their gaolers developed. Some students however would see the colonies as significant primarily for their place in British commercial imperialism, that is, in 'the swing to the East'.

Before 1788 several publicists had urged the potential value of trade based on Australia. John Campbell, geographer and editor of travel literature, had argued in 1744 that the known parts of New Guinea, Australia, Tasmania, and the Solomon Islands, were all parts of *terra australis incognita* and offered the brightest promise for Britain's future wealth.[3] J. M. Matra, a midshipman on Cook's first great voyage, proposed in 1783 that a settlement in Australia could open trade with the North-west coast of America (in furs), the Moluccas, Japan, Korea, South America and New Zealand. In 1785 Sir George Young, naval officer and expansionist, argued in similar vein; Secretary of State Lord Sydney endorsed Young's idea and after delay it went before a committee of merchants, upon which, in the ambiguous phrase of a letter

[1] London Missionary Society papers, *idem.*
[2] E. M. O'Brien, *The Foundation of Australia (1768–1800)* (Sydney, 1950), 253, 286.   [3] Harlow, I, 34.

of Young's eight years later, 'it was immediately adopted in the manner you so well know'. In the mid-eighties Alexander Dalrymple had warned the Directors of the East India Company that the establishment of a colony in Australia or Norfolk Island might threaten the Company's monopoly by establishing a rival and independent focus for trade. Presumably many other contemporaries thought of potential Australian colonization in similar terms, although sometimes their emphasis was on the produce of the settlements rather than their service as entrepôts. Such was the case with a plan of Young's for the establishment of a proprietary colony at Norfolk Island (1788), and that of an anonymous contemporary who looked to Norfolk, New Zealand, and New Caledonia as the most promising lands.[1]

After foundation the settlements served a function something like that which these discussions had postulated. Early in 1790 the British Government planned that the intended colony at Nootka might receive men and stores from New South Wales; and this relation survived the change of official tactics, in that Vancouver did draw some stores from Sydney.[2] Before Bishop himself thought of sailing to Port Jackson, he met other ships which had touched there before going to the North-west coast. James Drummond, shrewd man of business, was alive to the lucrative market for general cargo at Sydney in 1796–8; Bishop would have done well to accept his advice and exploit this opening.

The colonies' great service to British commercial expansion was to assist the South Sea whalers. Probably the whaling interest was among those which approved Young's plan. In January 1789 Samuel Enderby, a leader of this interest, told the Secretary of the Committee on Trade and Plantation that were the whalers allowed full access into the Pacific (in

[1] On this subject see J. M. Ward, *British Policy in the South Pacific (1786–1893)* (Sydney, 1948), 1–13; K. M. Dallas, 'The first settlement in Australia, considered in relation to sea-power in world politics', *Tasmanian Historical Research Association Papers and Proceedings*, 2, 4–12; and M. Roe, 'Australia's place in "The swing to the East", 1788–1810', *Historical Studies, Australia and New Zealand*, 8, 202–13. The texts of the known plans are in F. M. Bladen (ed.), *Historical Records of New South Wales* (Sydney, 1892), I, ii, 1–14, 141–2; and *ibid*. II, 359–67.
[2] Greenwood, 59–62.

modification of the chartered monopolies) 'the settlements of New Holland would be often visited as there are many whales in those seas'.[1] At Enderby's request, five vessels which took convicts to Port Jackson in 1791 were whalers, which after unloading their cargo investigated the neighbouring seas. The commanding officers at both Sydney (Arthur Phillip) and Norfolk Island (P. G. King) encouraged their work; King, who was to take charge in Sydney 1800–6, had financial and personal ties with the Enderbys. The whaler-captains reported finding many whales and seals, but inclement weather hindered their capture. Not until 1796 did outbreak of war with Spain force British whalers to leave South American waters and push farther west for their prey. The East India Company modified its restrictions on whalers' movements, and whaling based on Australian ports began a fifty-year boom.

Meanwhile the colonies otherwise served the exploitation of the eastern seas. They provided a springboard whence a few adventurers defied Spain's monopoly of commerce with her American colonies. In 1806 eminent Britons even considered using Sydney as a base for armed attack on Panama and Peru.[2] The Pacific offered more congenial and continuing enterprise. 'Trade in all the main island groups of the Pacific, with the exception of Hawaii, began as a consequence of the settlement of New South Wales; and until the middle of the nineteenth century nearly all its major developments occurred as aspects of Australian expansion.'[3] In this story Bishop played a characteristic and significant part.

For years after 1788 the British Government paid little attention to the colonies' own resources, but in 1802 it took one step which further linked Australia with 'the swing to the East'. Two Navy ships went to Sydney to gather samples of timber and other produce, and at their command was James Colnett! Since his release from Spanish confinement

[1] Quoted, W. J. Dakin, *Whalemen Adventurers* (Sydney, 1938), xviii.
[2] B. Atkins, 'Australia's place in the "Swing to the East", 1788–1810: Addendum', *Historical Studies, Australia and New Zealand*, 8, 317–18.
[3] Naval Intelligence Division, *Geographical Handbook Series, Pacific Islands* (London, 1945), I, 268–9.

at Nootka, Colnett had pursued a career which made him perhaps the outstanding single representative of 'the swing'. After fair trading on the coast, he carried his furs to Canton only to find a glutted market. On Daniel Beale's advice he determined to seek more profitable sale for them in Japan and Korea. His efforts constituted the most positive British attempt to open trade thither until well into the nineteenth century, but had little success.[1] He returned to England and in 1793-4 commanded an expedition, financed by whaling interests, but endorsed by the Government. Colnett described this episode in the text and title of the book he published from London in 1798: *A Voyage to the South Atlantic and round Cape Horn into the Pacific Ocean, for the Purpose of Extending the Spermaceti Whale Fisheries, and Other Objects of Commerce, by Ascertaining the Ports, Bays, Harbours, and Anchoring Births in Certain Islands and Coasts in those Seas, at which the Ships of the British Merchants Might Be Refitted.* In his introduction Colnett upheld brighter hopes for trade with Japan and Korea than his own experience justified. Finished with this venture, Colnett rejoined the Navy.

So some people before 1788 discussed Australia's potential value in commerce, and others after 1788 sought to realize that value. Was the 'dumping of convicts' therefore not the true motive for settlement, but a shield against the jealous hostility of the East India Company? The idea is somewhat melodramatic and probably beyond proof. The strongest documentary evidence in its support is a letter from P. G. King to Evan Nepean of 4 March 1795, which listed the qualities of Norfolk Island and remarked 'how far they may appear to render this Island of Value to Government, or a resource to the Colony in New South Wales, must depend upon the Object Government had in View when the Colony in New South Wales was formed, which I shall not presume to form an Opinion of'.[2] The weight even this can bear is limited, but probably it is enough to confirm that the

---

[1] Beasley, 2-3; *The Journal of Captain James Colnett aboard the Argonaut from April 26, 1789, to Nov. 3, 1791* (ed. F. W. Howay) (Toronto, 1940), 230 ff.
[2] Colonial Office papers 201/18 (Public Record Office).

historians of early Australia should attend more to these commercial aspects than they generally have done.[1]

For Bishop no ambiguity existed. His text gives the merest hint of the penal character of New South Wales; to him the colony was significant exclusively as a base for trade. Sydney provided an officer of British law before whom he could 'protest' the reasons for his departure from the plan designed at Canton. Local artisans repaired the *Nautilus* and merchants supplied stores—all being very expensive, but efficient. The colony offered too a labour force, and as many ex-convicts yearned to return to England they would accept little or no wages if carried towards that goal. Bishop even found in Sydney scope for public service—as member of a court which investigated a mutiny on a convict transport.[2] Throughout he met the ready co-operation of colonial authorities, especially Governor (1795–1800) John Hunter and Naval Officer William Kent.

Above all, Bishop learned in Sydney of new fields for adventure: the seal fisheries of Bass Strait. Their existence had been known for some time, to the British whalers of 1791 for example. George Bass, the young naval surgeon who since 1795 had won distinction as an explorer of south-east Australia, noticed in the summer of 1797–8 that many seals abounded in the islands off the south-east mainland and that someone (probably escaped convicts) had been destroying them. More positive information resulted from the Bengal vessel *Sydney Cove* being wrecked between Preservation and Rum Islands in the Furneaux group in January 1797.[3] Her longboat set off for Port Jackson with seventeen men, while the rest remained, salvaging what they could. The longboat wrecked in turn, but three survivors carried their tale to Sydney. Hunter despatched a series of expeditions to bring back all the men and stores. The final excursion, February–March 1798, was that of the sloop *Francis* under

---

[1] A last-moment footnote must hail a crucial exception: G. Blainey, *The Tyranny of Distance* (Melbourne, 1966).

[2] *Historical Records of New South Wales*, III, 453 ff.

[3] See appropriate chart in M. Flinders, *Observations on the Coasts of Van Diemen's Land, on Bass's Strait and its Islands, and on Part of the Coasts of New South Wales* (ed. G. Mackaness) (Sydney, 1946).

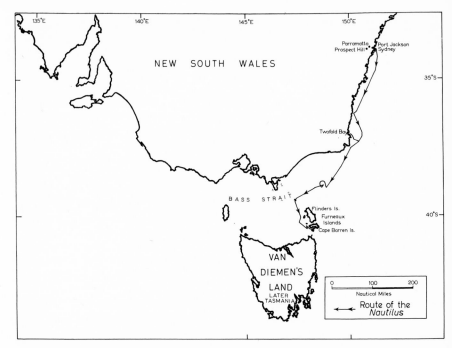

Map I(a)   South-east Australia: the approximate route of the *Nautilus* on her first trip to the sealing grounds, October 1798 (*Source: Historical Records of New South Wales*, III, map facing p. 769).

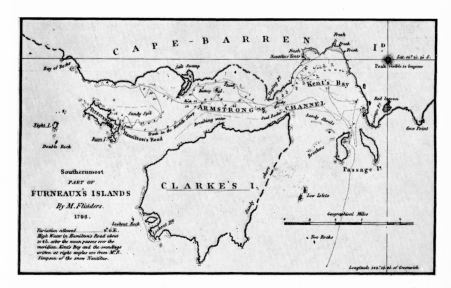

Map I(b)   The southern coast of Cape Barren Island: the location of Bishop's seal-fishing 1798–9 (*Source:* Flinders, *Atlas*, 1814).

the command of Lieutenant Matthew Flinders, also currently winning renown for his explorations.

All engaged in this saga must have seen many seals around the Furneaux Islands, but Flinders later wrote that it was his own report which 'induced Messrs. Bishop and Simpson...to prepare their vessel for a sealing speculation to that quarter'.[1] This was the first planned venture into an industry which was to retain importance for a generation. Bishop was now to enjoy skimming the cream of Pacific wealth; many who followed were to experience the same frustration as he had known on the North-west coast.

The *Nautilus* left for the south on 7 October 1798. She accompanied the sloop *Norfolk*, in which Bass and Flinders were to circumnavigate Tasmania. As the two vessels sailed down the Australian coast Simpson assisted Flinders in surveying Twofold Bay.[2] Arrived at the Furneauxs Flinders 'proposed to go ahead of the *Nautilus* with the sloop, into Armstrong's Channel, and ascertain the nearest situation of the sealing points for her to lay in'.[3] Perhaps this marked the apogee of official assistance for Bishop's adventures: having as his pilot the man second only to Cook in British exploration of Australian coasts. The vessels proceeded from the west along the southern coast of Cape Barren Island, skirting many rocks and shoals. On 22 October the *Nautilus* anchored at what Simpson (and posterity) called Kent Bay; Flinders would have nominated another spot, but recognized that the actual choice was wiser.

Bishop and Simpson pitched camp on a stream, about a mile north of their anchorage. As at the Columbia, Bishop planted a garden, which yielded 'tolerable vegetables' and probably fathered the seas of parsley now rolling over the area.[4] So began deliberate European settlement on territory which was to become the colony of Van Diemen's Land, later the State of Tasmania. Maritime industry was to be vital in the early history of that community: with the evaporation of

[1] *A Voyage to Terra Australis...* (London, 1814), I, cxxxviii.
[2] *Ibid.* I, cxxix. See Maps I(*a*) and I(*b*) for this voyage.
[3] *Historical Records of New South Wales*, III, 774.
[4] Flinders (1814), I, cxlvii.

Pacific commerce its hey-day passed, apparently never to return. Thus Tasmania remains close to the sea, in fact and in sympathy. It is appropriate both that Charles Bishop should have played such a part in Tasmania's history and that this account of his life should come from its shores.

The adventurers spared some time for enquiry. Simpson surveyed Kent Bay, Flinders afterwards publishing his observations. Bishop sailed the passage between Flinders and Cape Barren Islands. 'From him we learn', reported Flinders, 'that there are many rocks and isles in it, whose exact situation and form are not ascertained; but it appears, that there is a safe passage through the strait, and some well-sheltered anchoring places in it.'[1] The *Norfolk* called back at the camp on 24 November, so that Bishop might carry its news to Hunter. Flinders was pleased to note that the adventure proceeded well, albeit hampered by the seals being distant at the eastern extremity of the island.[2]

At Christmas, Bishop ferried to Sydney the produce gathered so far, his arrival attracting some notice. David Collins, splendid annalist of New South Wales's early history, remarked this and other movements of the *Nautilus*.[3] Bishop's business interested other entrepreneurs, especially a group headed by T. F. Palmer, an erstwhile Fellow of Queens' College, Cambridge, who had suffered transportation in 1794 for his democratic politics. Palmer's 'company' arranged that Bishop should leave a party on Cape Barren over the winter. To others Bishop probably concealed his success,[4] in the hope of preserving the field for Palmer's men.

Bishop returned to the fisheries before anchoring at Sydney again late in February 1799. His next recorded act was to head a subscription in favour of Rowland Hassall, one of the Tahitian missionaries and a victim of robbery.[5] On 5 March the American whaler *Rebecca*, William Campbell, came into

---

[1] Flinders (ed. Mackaness) (1946), 44.
[2] Flinders (1814), I, clx.
[3] *An Account of the English Colony in New South Wales* (London, 1802), II, 110–11, 131, 142 ff., 288.
[4] See letter of J. Thomson, 8 September 1799, *Historical Records of New South Wales*, III, 717.
[5] London Missionary Society papers, Hassall's journal.

port with a cargo of general merchandise. The current market in Sydney was weak, so Campbell decided that his wares might sell better at Norfolk Island.[1] He engaged Bishop and the *Nautilus* to carry the cargo thither, which duly took place. Bishop might have added a private investment, for the commandant at Norfolk recorded the purchase from him of 'Sugar, Canvass, etc.' worth £816. 19s.; alternatively he could have been acting as Campbell's agent.[2] The *Nautilus* returned to Port Jackson on 24 April.

Before departing for Canton on 29 May, Bishop planned further commercial enterprise in Australian waters.[3] Success in the fisheries had invigorated his optimism, dissolving the bitter experience of 1795–8. The new scheme was for Bishop to join with George Bass and to bring out a well-chosen cargo, the sale of which would be the centrepiece of a brilliant enterprise; further profits would be found wherever the southern oceans might offer them. In becoming Bass's partner Bishop filled an office sought by Flinders with an ardour which to modern senses appears more characteristic of an aspiring lover than of a colleague.[4] Bishop came to develop a similar affection for Bass, a man of cruel and potent charm.

Several figures among the respectability of New South Wales helped finance the Bass–Bishop plan. Joining Naval Officer Kent in displaying this particular facet of the tie between government and adventure were Thomas Jamison, a colonial surgeon, and James Williamson, the Deputy Commissary. Kent and Williamson also backed Bishop in his current application for letters of marque, under which he could seek plunder and 'prizes' from the shipping of the King's enemies.[5] Just a few weeks before, Port Jackson had served a further role in oceanic expansion by receiving a 'prize' captured off the Peru coast by two whalers, but Bishop was the first to seek and gain letters of marque from the local authorities.

[1] Collins, II, 201.
[2] Colonial Office papers, 201/15, 155.
[3] K. M. Bowden, *George Bass 1771–1803* (Melbourne, 1952), 91 ff.
[4] K. M. Bowden, 'George Bass, 1771–1803, surgeon and sailor', *Bulletin of the Post-Graduate Committee in Medicine University of Sydney*, 17, 54–5.   [5] See below, pp. 314–15.

The voyage to Canton, for which Bass joined the comple-
ment, achieved distinction not in battle but in discovery.
Passing through the Gilberts 1–5 July the *Nautilus* explored
the Tabiteuea, Nonouti, and Abemama atolls. Conscious of
their achievement, the adventurers scattered names in self-
commemoration: Bishop's Islands, Drummond's Island,
Sidenham Teast's Islands, Harbottle Island, Roger Simpson's
Islands. These designations were transitory, but in charting
and naming Nautilus Shoal, off Tabiteuea, the leaders did
mark posterity. At Tabiteuea the *Nautilus* anchored and
communicated pleasurably with the natives. Moving on to
the Marshalls in mid-July, the expedition charted Maloelap,
Erikub, and Jemo; ignorant of the work of Thomas Gilbert
and John Marshall, Bass and Bishop again gave their names
to various atolls. Their observations in the Gilberts and
Marshalls provided Dalrymple with the material for two
charts published in 1802; the readings are accurate, deficient
only in longitudes being a degree or so east.[1] The *Nautilus*
then made for the Marianas Islands, where, Bishop told the
Canton supercargoes, she made her sole halt of the voyage.
The *Ruby–Nautilus* voyage ended at Macao on 18 August
1799.

The *Ruby* accounts, finalized at Macao in February 1797,
showed Teast to have grossed just under 9,000 Spanish
Dollars (£2,250) from the North-west venture. Against this
his costs were the vessel itself (£300–350 on Bishop's grudg-
ing estimate), the trade cargo (£1,450), insurance, and presumably interest forsaken on the East India Company bond.
This was a poor return; coming after the difficulties suffered
by the *Jenny* it explains why Teast, like his fellow Britons
at large, left the trade to the Americans. The *Nautilus* venture
showed a net loss of some 10,500 Dollars. Teast bore about
5,500 Dollars of this, Conseequa about 4,500, Bishop himself
about 450.

[1] H. E. Maude, 'Post-Spanish discoveries in the Central Pacific',
Journal of the Polynesian Society, **70**, 82–3; Bowden (1952), 89; A. Sharp,
The Discovery of the Pacific Islands (Oxford, 1960), 152–5, 183–4; further
information from Maude (Australian National University, Canberra). See
Maps II and III.

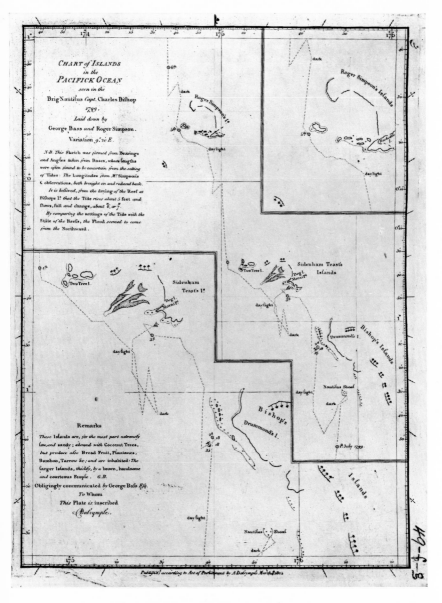

Map II Chart of the Gilbert Islands, based on information from Bishop, Simpson and Bass, published by Alexander Dalrymple, 1802. 'Bishop's Island' is Tabiteuea; 'Dog Island', Nonouti; 'Harbottle Island', Abemama.

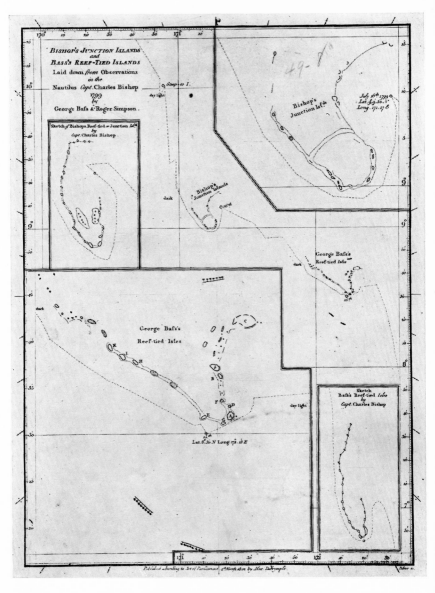

Map III   Chart of the Marshall Islands, based on information from Bishop, Simpson and Bass, published by Alexander Dalrymple, 1802. 'George Bass's Reef-tied Isles' is Maloelap; the stopping-place of 16 July, Erikub; 'Steep-to I', Jemo.

Bishop's financial records told a little more of the seamen who served such expeditions as his. Mutiny, desertion, and death all briefly appeared. Pacific Islanders, Chinese, and Europeans of various nationalities mingled together on the pay-roll. Bishop's companions ranged from ex-convicts to men of sizeable distinction. Before his death at Sydney in May 1804 Simpson engaged in several more voyages aboard the *Nautilus*, continuing both to trade and to explore.[1] Simpson clearly impressed Flinders and might well have been a more effective seaman and organizer than Bishop. John Harbottle and George McClay found their way back to the Sandwich Islands, where they joined Kamehameha's ring of European aides;[2] Harbottle's was indeed a happy progress from that grim day at Formosa. S. R. Chase (Chace), one of those whom Bishop left on Cape Barren for the winter of 1799, maintained a long connexion with Tasmania. He married Letitia, natural daughter of that David Collins who wrote about the *Nautilus* in his *Account of...New South Wales* and who afterwards (1803–10) was first Lieutenant-Governor of Britain's colony in southern Tasmania. From 1819 Chase was a ship's master in the service of this colony, until he disappeared at sea in about 1827.[3] Probably others of the *Nautilus* crew had comparable, if unrecorded, experiences.

★ ★ ★

The text ends with the settlement of business at Canton, but Bishop's life continued. He probably returned to England during the summer of 1800 and first discharged his obligations to Teast and the East India Company.[4] Then would have followed family visits, and meetings with the Miss Sparkshot whom he soon betrothed.[5] But the 'swing to the East' held

[1] *Sydney Gazette, and New South Wales Advertiser* (29 May 1803, 20 May 1804).
[2] R. S. Kuykendall and A. G. Day, *Hawaii: a History* (New York, 1948), 37; H. H. Gowen, *The Napoleon of the Pacific* (New York, 1919), 279, 282.
[3] Biographical file, Tasmanian State Archives.
[4] A search has not revealed any pertinent documents.
[5] Hill-Reid, 61; J. Grant papers, *passim*. Just possibly, the romance was a later hallucination of Bishop's mind.

Bishop too fiercely to allow much dalliance; his major task was to assist Bass in preparing for the speculative voyage to New South Wales. William Bishop, Charles's brother at Basingstoke, put £444 into the venture. Total funds amounted to £10,890.[1] This purchased the *Venus*, a fine seventy-six foot vessel, the cargo for Sydney, and other goods (including some otter furs!) for Canton. The latter was to be the market for whatever else the adventurers might find in the East Indies, New Guinea, and places yet unknown. In October Bass married Elizabeth Waterhouse, to enjoy three months of marriage before embarking on the enterprise he was to show little desire to end and from which he never returned. Elizabeth Bass's letters to her husband bled with love, despair, and dignity; his were few, brief, smart, and silly. Their incidental references to Bishop show retrospectively that he was close within the Bass family circle in the latter months of 1800, something of a butt for Bass's teasing, and himself paying mock court to Mrs Bass senior.

The *Venus* sailed from Portsmouth on 9 January 1801. She evidently carried letters of marque, for her first adventure was nearly to capture a prize, off the Canary Islands. Her route then led to Salvador, to São Sebastião Island, and to Cape Town, reached on 3 June 1801. Here Bass and Bishop were warned off trade with New Guinea and learned also that the Sydney market was dull. Arriving thither on 29 August they found this report all too true: goods were plentiful and, under the year-old rule of P. G. King, credit was not. The two abandoned their more romantic plans, even considering the task, surely most dreary for Bishop, of looking for seals off the North-west coast.

Governor King offered a brighter prospect. True to his own instinct for commercial enterprise, he had determined to relieve the colony's want of fresh meat by bringing pork from Tahiti.[2] In London in 1799 he had talked with leaders of the London Missionary Society, and on settling in New

---

[1] Bowden (1952), 91 ff.
[2] Roe, *Historical Studies. Australia and New Zealand*, 8, 207–8; H. E. Maude, 'The Tahitian pork trade: 1800–1830', *Journal de la Société des Océanistes*, 15, 58 ff.

South Wales had gathered pertinent information from know-
ledgeable persons, including Rowland Hassall. King sent
greetings both to the depleted mission and to the chieftain Tu
(Otoo, Pomare) within whose realm it survived. These preparations culminated in May 1801 when the government vessel *Porpoise* sailed off to gather pork. It had such success that
at the year's end King not only sent the government's *Norfolk*
in its wake but also contracted with Bass and Bishop for the
same task. 'This adventure is a certain gain', Bass wrote his
wife, 'and has no speculation in it.' He intimated that subsequently the *Venus* would attempt trade with South America:
even if war with Spain continued, 'a few vigorous and wary
exertions will make all go well'.[1] The craft was prepared for
combat, and her cargo deposited — part in store, part for sale.

The journey began on 21 November, and the first call was
6–21 December at Facile Harbour, Dusky Sound, New
Zealand. Here the business was 'cutting down pines and
rummaging the old Endeavour'—a vessel run aground there
in 1795 and still offering worth-while salvage, especially iron
for trade with Pacific Islanders. This done, the *Venus* poked
around harbours in southern New Zealand, Bass naming
them Inlets of Venus but leaving no exact identification. The
next target was the Austral Islands. There Bass discovered
Marotiri (Bass Rocks), and also claimed (but without foundation) that honour apropos Raivavae. This latter the adventurers called Lord Bolton's Island after 'a friend of Bishop's',
Thomas Orde-Powlett, first Lord Bolton (1746–1807), erstwhile Secretary of State and currently Lord Lieutenant of
Hampshire with a seat near Basingstoke. They spoke to the
natives there, but learned nothing of potential profit. Then
the *Venus* turned north; it saw Mehetia on 24 January, and
made the sixty miles westward to Matavai Bay that same day.

Bass sailed again on 5 February for the Sandwich Islands
and perhaps elsewhere in search of pork and other cargo,
leaving Bishop in charge at Tahiti throughout what proved
an exciting period. Trade went well, Bishop outstripping

[1] Bowden (1961), 49 ff. Details of the following voyage are also from
this source.

William House, master of the *Norfolk*. He did so by bartering firearms, which King had forbidden to House and indeed sought to limit to Bass and Bishop. The missionaries apparently favoured the *Venus* people, and Tu did so to the extent of installing Bishop in one of his own houses.[1] Good reason determined the chieftain's support. Since the visit of Cook's second expedition Tu had won consistent British support in Tahiti's civil wars. 'Events now took on a rhythm: so long as a ship was in Matavai Bay Tu would be found on board importuning the captain for muskets or direct military aid against his constantly rebellious "subjects", or ashore supervising the market; when the Bay was empty his enraged rival chiefs, envious of the favours shown him, were apt to put him in his place by divesting him of his coveted acquisitions.'[2] The rhythm was now to reach a crescendo.

The latter months of 1801 had seen Tu's fortunes at low ebb. The missionaries, dependent on him as they were, felt disquiet, and as Tu's defeats continued into 1802 all the British on the island came to share this. Bishop took the initiative with perhaps neurotic enthusiasm. On 23 June, recorded House, he 'reviewed the King's men and made them go through the loading and firing motions English fashion', a few days later he urged the assembled British that they actively lead an attack on Tu's enemies. House had been instructed by King against taking 'any decided part in the affairs of the country', and the missionaries also jibbed at Bishop's proposed aggression. Tu then sought aid from Bishop and from Roger Simpson, now also in port with the *Nautilus*. On Bishop's urging, the British again went into conclave. A mission history records that:

the subject of actively engaging in the present commotions was resumed, Capt. B now informed the Society, that he did not wish them to take part in the business against their inclination; he only requested to know, if it would not be for the Society's interest, that there should be peace; and whether it would not be for the

[1] W. House, Transactions on Board of the Armed Colonial Brig *Norfolk* at Otaheita 1801 and 1802 (Mitchell Library, Sydney); Bass to P. G. King, 31 January 1802, G. W. Rusden papers (Trinity College, University of Melbourne).
[2] Maude (1959), 74.

interest of the Society, that he should go and act against the rebels. The sense of the Society was taken upon the subject, when only one negative was found, who objected thro' a scruple of conscience. Some arguments were now used by Capt. B with Capt. H to induce him to permit his men to be employed in the service. Capt. H agreed, if the Society would indemnify him to Governor King for a breach of orders. This the Society acceded to. Capt. B drew up a certificate for the purpose, and the assenting members signed it.[1]

Bishop led Tu's army into battle on 3 and 4 July. The result was not the annihilating victory for which Bishop yearned, but did guarantee the safety of Tu and the mission for the time being. The *Venus* returned on 1 August, with so favourable an account of the Sandwich Islands that one of the missionaries forthwith suggested to London that a mission might prosper there.[2] Bass joined in discussions concerning the political situation, but no further action resulted. Before the *Venus* sailed on the 19th the missionaries presented a letter of thanks to Bishop—'to whom, under God', one of them had written, 'we are indebted for our preservation'.[3] Bishop was too ill personally to receive these congratulations. In mind, body, and spirit he had moved far from the jesting, indulgent friend of the Easter Islanders.

Bass had planned, after picking up Bishop at Tahiti, to 'jog together down through the Societys, Friendlys, Navigators, Feejees, and Hebrides until we have completed our cargo and found out the best islands for a second trip'.[4] The actual itinerary probably embraced only the first three groups. It ended at Port Jackson on 14 November.

The voyage was a commercial success. It returned fifty-seven tons of pork and 30,034 pounds of salt. The New South Wales government bought most, while private buyers included Nicolas Baudin, commander of the French scientific expedition then investigating Australian waters. The gross

[1] J. Davies, *The History of the Tahitian Mission 1799–1830* (ed. C. W. Newbury) (Cambridge, 1961), 53 ff.
[2] London Missionary Society papers, South Seas Letters; letter of J. Youl, 30 September 1802.
[3] *Ibid.*, letter of J. Jefferson, 8 July 1802.
[4] Bowden (1961), 50–1; Bowden (1952), 112–13. The Navigator Islands are now known as the Samoan Islands; other correct forms for groups named by Bass are Fiji Islands and New Hebrides.

return was about £3,000, and perhaps two-thirds of that was profit. Meanwhile the London cargo had begun to sell, the government taking thence a further £1,000 worth of meat.[1]

Bass considered several prospects—a venture to Batavia, establishing (with King's support) a monopoly over the edible fish in New Zealand waters and supplying New South Wales therewith, returning to Tahiti to salvage the *Norfolk* which had run aground.[2] In the event he left Port Jackson in February 1803, planning first to re-visit Dusky Sound, then to attempt smuggling goods into South America, then to gather more pork at Tahiti. He disappeared early on his route, in circumstances which remain obscure. Bishop survived, having been forsaken by his more resilient comrade in January:

Bishop has been totally useless to me and the concern for many months past, indeed ever since I left him at Otaheite in February, and went to the Sandwich Islands. He is still no better, and that being the case I shall leave him to recover whilst I make the next voyage. It is more than probable he will be in the grave before my return.

Bass recognized that Bishop's health improved a little in the next few weeks, but appears nevertheless to have determined to dissolve the partnership when back in Sydney. Meanwhile Bishop was to try to sell the remaining *Venus* cargo.

The next eighteen months were the most tranquil in Bishop's recorded life. By May 1803 he had enough health and confidence to pay a hundred guineas for two farms, covering altogether a hundred acres, at Prospect Hill, a pleasant farming district twenty miles west of Sydney. In August Governor King granted a further hundred acres to this estate.[3] It took the name 'Bass and Bishop's Prospect', so evidently Bishop considered his farming as an extension of the partnership. Flinders remarked at this time that 'poor Bishop seems to be wholly dispirited' and also implied criti-

[1] J. F. Watson (ed.), *Historical Records of Australia* (Sydney, 1915), I, III, 603.
[2] Bowden (1952), 117 ff.
[3] *Sydney Gazette, and New South Wales Advertiser* (29 May 1803); information from Department of Lands, Sydney.

cism of the farm and its stock, but at least the situation had
improved since the beginning of the year.[1] In late September
Bishop advertised his intention of soon residing on the farm,
warning trespassers that he would curtail their activities 'as
far as he legally can'.[2] The move proceeded in due course.

Meanwhile Bishop had built up his local friendships.
Jamison, Kent, and Williamson still lived in New South
Wales; despite business frictions they probably remained
close to Bishop. The Governor himself was reportedly 'intimate'.[3] As well as associating with the official respectability
Bishop mingled with the colonial *salon* of gentlemen convicts,
among whom sympathy for radical ideas generated criticism
of authority. This tie followed naturally from Bishop's earlier
connexion with T. F. Palmer, himself now dead as the result
of shipwreck on his homeward journey. Maurice Margarot,
one prominent member of the *salon*, like Palmer had been
transported for sedition, while another, Henry Brown Hayes,
aroused King's fears by propagating freemasonry.

From the gentlemen convicts came John Grant, Bishop's
closest associate at this period and the source of most information concerning it. Grant, a highly eccentric man, was transported for shooting the guardian of a girl for whom he had a
vain infatuation. He came to New South Wales with letters
of introduction from ex-Governor Hunter and with liber-
tarian beliefs; thus a double channel mingled his life with
Bishop's. The upshot was that in mid-1804 he went to live
on Bass and Bishop's Prospect, nominally as a servant
'assigned' by government but really as a companion.

Grant's queerness often produced hyperbole, but his happy
picture of Bishop's life at this time was probably accurate.
'He has 3 Men and 1 woman servant, books and every comfort a farm can afford; with a musquet and a horse ready
should I wish to hunt.' Such opulence resulted less from
solid wealth than from Bishop's extravagance, which at this
very time had caused a quarrel with Jamison, who sought to

[1] Letter of 8 August 1803, G. Bass papers (K. M. Bowden, Melbourne).
[2] *Sydney Gazette, and New South Wales Advertiser* (25 September
1803).
[3] Hill-Reid, 58.

supervise Bishop's expenditure of the partnership funds.[1]
Still, Grant was impressed by this apparent material pros-
perity, with which, moreover, went gifts of character:
'Bishop is a man of noble mind tho' fond of women, an
excellent navigator and a poet in his way on sea subjects';
'he possesses a mind very rare for it is open and artless as my
own'. Worried by Bass's long absence, Bishop hoped still to
return with his partner to England and Miss Sparkshot;
meanwhile he made the colony his 'adopted country' and
gave Grant his affectionate sympathy.[2]

Bishop might well have become one of the gentry-farmers
of New South Wales. This path was to attract several mer-
chant-sailors, including Bishop's old associate William Campbell, whose career in the early 1800s precisely followed the
Bass–Bishop pattern, as it ranged over pork-gathering at
Tahiti, sealing at Más Afuera, smuggling and prize-catching
off South America. But Bishop faced no such destiny, for
he was going mad. Whenever the process first became overt
(the quarrel with Jamison? the war-mongering at Tahiti? the
purchase of the *Nautilus* at Amboyna?), by November 1804
it had advanced so far as to cause Bishop to write this letter
to another comrade of happier days, Rowland Hassall, now
a retailer with whom he had considerable business:

Mr Hassal,

As I wish only to recieve Bread from your hands, I hope you
will not think me too particular, in requesting you will not send
my servant, to recieve it from the Baker, but to send your son, or
some one you have confidance in, to get it, as for yourself, I have
private reasons for this request, which I do not chose to avow,
without necessity. Inclosed also is part of some particles of white
matter I picked out of the last pound of Tea—I had from you,
have the goodness, I call on you as *a Christian* and a man who
hath received no ill (at my Hands) to take care nothing un-
wholsome is mixed, in such articles of food &c I may recieve from
you, for having been unaccountably poorly these two or three
days past I begin to assume again the vigilence and caution which

[1] Bishop to Richard Atkins, 21 July 1804, Supreme Court of New
South Wales papers (Archives Office of N.S.W., Sydney), Bundle 29,
item 1165.
[2] Hill-Reid, 58–9; letter of 12 July 1804, J. Grant papers.

under the blessing of God! preserved my life so often before—
and am determined in no instance, to omit, taking the legal courses
of Law, against any one, whom I may feel confident of convicting
of any base attempts, to distroy me, His Majestys Third Son—
Tho' afflicted, and most unhappy in that Title, I most willingly
subscribe myself to your Faithful Friend! and Obedient Servant

Cha⁵ Bishop

Prospect—Wednesday 21 Novʳ 1804[1]

Magnifying the pathos of this letter was its echo of one happy
moment on the North-west coast, when Bishop told the
wondering Indians of the prodigious size of his own and the
Royal families. Perhaps that incident provoked the hallucination. Bishop's condition became so bad about this time that
King had him put under the charge of John Savage, a government surgeon. Savage's station was at Parramatta, situated
between Sydney and Prospect Hill, and Bishop probably
lived at either the hospital or gaol there.

Grant took over the farm and felt much concern at the
situation. Writing home on 1 January 1805 he described
Bishop's condition. Its principal cause was grief for Bass.
Further anguish had accrued from financial difficulties,
brought on by extravagance (evidently Jamison had acted
with good reason in mid-1804). One of Bishop's hallucinations
was that he believed himself Governor of the colony; another
was that he had discovered gold. Grant doubted that this
latter idea *was* senseless; Governor King said the sand was
pyrites but, reasoned Grant, Bishop had seen true gold in
Africa and perhaps government preferred to conceal a discovery. Actually King did send a test sample of the sand to
Sir Joseph Banks, and so Grant had begun a long series of
false allegations that Australian authorities feared and
frustrated the exploitation of mineral wealth.[2] Indeed Grant,
while admitting that King treated Bishop kindly enough,

[1] Letterbook, R. Hassall papers (Mitchell Library, Sydney). Hassall's
record of sales often mentions Bishop.
[2] Letter of December 1804, *Historical Records of New South Wales*, v,
528–9; and see G. Blainey, 'Gold and governors', *Historical Studies.
Australia and New Zealand*, 9, 337–50.

believed his friend's confinement to be yet one further example of government tyranny. Grant made this opinion and his other criticisms of authority so plain and public that in mid-1805 he was re-transported to Norfolk Island.

Yet King apparently was sensitive to Grant's aspersions concerning Bishop. On 14 October 1805 an official precept summoned 'Twelve good and lawful Men (being Free-holders)' to consider Bishop's sanity. There is no record of any civil jury having met earlier in the penal, authoritarian colony of New South Wales. The twelve found that Bishop was indeed a lunatic. Appointed as his trustees were John Macarthur, foremost name in the establishment of the Australian wool industry, and Samuel Marsden, a man of business and of God, who did much to extend Christianity into the South Seas. They quickly called for Bishop's out-standing debts 'that they may be then liquidated as far as we hold unsold assets'.[1]

The finances of Bishop and 'the concern' are obscure. Jamison was in charge, and his sub-agent reported in Sep-tember 1805 that the business involved over £4,000.[2] Jamison was the logical person to have become Bishop's trustee and, after some obstacle disappeared, became so in May 1806. He at once organized the sale of Bishop's property.[3] Yet even before King ceased to be Governor in August 1806 Bishop owed government over £100, which was never paid, and in October Jamison called for further claims against his estate.[4] If these details add up at all, it is to emphasize Bishop's extravagance of 1803–4 and to suggest that 'the concern' took little or no responsibility for his private debts.

In March 1807 plans to return Bishop to England misfired at the last moment.[5] At about this time he may even have

---

[1] *Sydney Gazette, and New South Wales Advertiser* (24 November 1805).
[2] M. Hayes to King (28 September 1805), P. G. King papers, vol. 8 (Mitchell Library, Sydney).
[3] *Sydney Gazette, and New South Wales Advertiser*, 18 May 1805 and 8 June 1806.
[4] Colonial Office papers, 201/128, 137; *Sydney Gazette, and New South Wales Advertiser* (26 October 1806).
[5] *Sydney Gazette, and New South Wales Advertiser* (22 March 1807). Just possibly there were two Charles Bishops in Sydney, and this report referred to the other.

returned to his farm, or at least have hoped to do so.[1] Lodgings were sought for him in August, without known result.[2] A Charles Bishop was among those 'principal inhabitants' of the colony who addressed congratulations to the current Governor, William Bligh, on New Year's Day 1808;[3] some three weeks later a junta led by John Macarthur usurped the Government. During Bligh's term Bishop's debts to government increased by another £20, and soon the Commissioners of the Navy began chasing £84. 12s. which Bishop had owed since his 1798 sojourn in Sydney. Lieutenant-Governor William Paterson, then administering the colony, replied to their letter on 26 March 1809: 'I regret to inform you that this unfortunate man is now Insane,—A Pauper Confined in the Goal without I learn any funds to support him but the Prison Allowance.'[4]

John Grant had now resumed his life in New South Wales and his interest in Bishop's welfare.[5] Two days before Paterson wrote to the Navy Commissioners, Grant wrote to Paterson, urging that he end Bishop's misery by arranging his return to England. A quick decision was necessary, as Jamison (still the lunatic's trustee) himself proposed soon to go thither. Jamison believed that Bishop stayed in a cell more from humiliation than from madness; a sea-voyage might yet cure him. Paterson was sympathetic, and wheels began to turn. When Grant visited Bishop early in April the lunatic was in his usual miserable state, ill-clad and exposing his genitals. Yet a few days later Bishop left confinement. He walked towards Government House, prepared to take up residence. Instead he had to make do with lodgings in 'the Rocks', Sydney's colourful waterfront district; government gave his landlady, Mrs Pugh, an allowance from the gaol fund

[1] See Hill-Reid, 198. I have been unable to locate the documents on which Hill-Reid constructs this passage.
[2] *Sydney Gazette, and New South Wales Advertiser* (23 August 1807).
[3] Sir J. Banks papers, Captain Bligh and New South Wales, 299 (Mitchell Library, Sydney).
[4] *Historical Records of Australia*, I, vii, 35; Letterbook, W. Paterson's papers (Mitchell Library, Sydney).
[5] Documented in the J. Grant papers, but in a notebook written in abbreviations and in pencil, together making reconstruction very difficult.

and a man to attend him. William Bishop contacted the colonial authorities about this time, and Charles's condition seemingly improved a little. Probably in consequence, Paterson now determined that Bishop should return to England. Accompanied by his personal papers, he left Port Jackson aboard the *Mary Ann* on 15 October 1809.[1] There the record of his life ends.

As it stands, that record narrates tragedy. Bishop left England in 1794 an intelligent, competent, and likeable man. Against him thereafter beat many stresses of navigation, of business, of personal relations, and of politics. All these overwhelmed the simple seaman. The lover of Easter Island became the warhawk of Tahiti. By mid-1804 Bishop still appeared 'artless' to Grant, but hovered on lunacy. His last years in Australia passed in darkness and poverty. 'The swing to the East' had thrown Bishop back and forth, and broken him.

[1] J. Finucane to W. Bishop (13 October 1809), Letterbook, W. Paterson's papers.

I

FROM BRISTOL TOWARDS THE
NORTH-WEST COAST OF AMERICA

Earley in the month of June, the Ship Ruby burthen one 1794
hundred & one tons arrived at Bristol from the coast of
Africa with a valuable cargo of Ivory, Red wood, and Malle-
quette Pepper,[1] some Bees wax & Ebony which she had been
collecting about eighteen months, mostly under my command,
the Former Master, John Learne, a worthy character, having
died soon after her arrival on the coast, when the charge
consequently fell to me, and I have the pleasure to think I
gave my merchant every satisfaction. The ship being discharged of her lading was put under repair, and intended for
a voyage simuler to the last, but dureing my absence from
Bristol on a visit to my Friends Mr. Teast had resolved to
fitt her for a voyage to the North West coast of America to
procure Furs and other valuable skins for the China Markett,
he having fitted one ship (the Jenny) the preceeding season.
From him I recieved a letter aquainting me with his intention
and offering me the command, to which I readily acceeded,
NOT WITH OUT considering the arduous undertaking—

Early in the month, the Ship being equipped with every neces- September
sary for three years voyage, arm'd with eight three Pound
carrige Guns, and six half pound swivels, together with a sufficient quantity of small arms, and in every respect well appointed, carrying seventeen men including the officers and four
Boys, took in her cargo for the purchase of the Furs and other
Skins from the Native Indians of America & on the twenty ninth October-
left Bristol and proceeded down to Kingroad when having
taken in our Powder and every other stores we got under weigh
on the sixteenth at noon and made all sail down the Bristol
Channel, with the wind at about South by East, and on passing
Possett Point, Mr. Teast the Owner was observed on shore
and was accordinly saluted with seven Guns, and he took his
farewell of us amidst the Echoing shouts of my happy crew[2]

---

[1] The timber was probably mahogany, possibly ironwood; the pepper
came from Malagueta, the district later known as the Grain Coast.

[2] King Road lies immediately to the west of the junction of the River
Avon, down which the *Ruby* sailed from Bristol, and the River Severn;
Possett Point is Portishead Point, another few hundred yards west.

17th: Friday morning the wind blowing Fresh at South, we continued our course down Channel and at three oclock discharged the Pilot, being then to the East*ward* of Lundy Isle[1] about four miles. At 4 oclock the wind veer'd round to the Westward and blew a strong Gale, that I thought it most prudent to bear up and Anchor in Lundy Road, which we did

20th: at 6 in the Evening and remained here to Monday noon, when the wind Coming fair our anchor was weighed and all sail set, and at 5 in the afternoon we lost sight of Old England—By the Pilot I wrote Letter N° 1 in the Index, and on our leaving Lundy road, wrote letter N° 2,[2] and left it on board the Active, Revenue Cutter, to be forwarded by the first opportunity.

Being now at sea, with a fair wind, and all sail set, the People where mustered to Quarters, and all our Guns loaded with round shott, cannister[3] or Grape, and the whole of the crew seemed active, and willing to defend the ship, as long as I might choose to command them—a very keen lookout was keept by every person in the respective Watches

22^d: In the morning we passed a Schooner standing to the East-
48° 49′ N   *ward*. The Wind continuing in North East Quarter.
10° 20′ W

23^d.   In the forenoon we saw a large schooner standing to the East*ward* which did not alter her course—

Sunday 26th: Saw a Brig standing to the NW. which appeared to avoid us.
38°18′ N   Performed divine service, to which I had the pleasure to see
16° 40′ W   the whole of my crew very attentive.

Tuesday 28th: In the morning at 9 oclock we saw the Isle of Porto Sanco[4] W½S distance 14 leagues, being only eight days and half from Lundy I consider it a very good passage. In the afternoon

---

[1] Lundy Island is in the mouth of the Bristol Channel at 51° 12′ N., 4° 40′ W.
[2] See below, p. 151.
[3] This usage (properly 'canister') to describe small bullets derives from their container, and anticipates the *O.E.D.* ascription by seven years.
[4] Porto Santo Island is the northernmost of the Madeira Islands, the town of that name being at 33° 04′ N., 16° 20′ W.

being then about 6 miles E.N.E. of the Island we saw a large
Frigate to leeward appearing to be in chace of us, standing to
the East*ward*. We haul'd our wind and standing to the N.W.
With the night coming on Soon lost sight of her, and when
dark Bore away and according to my Idea, crossed her track
about 5 miles from her, however at daylight we saw nothing
of her, and continued our course to pass to the West*ward* of
Isles Palma and Ferro.[1]

In the morning at daylight we saw Isle Palma SWbS[2] 15   Thursday 30th
leagues but did not get clear of these Islands 'till saturday
AM owing to Calms

This day we passed the Tropic of Cancer, when Neptune,   November
as usual, came on board and performed the ceremonies to   Tuesday 4th:
initiate our young sailors, who never had passed this line
before, to the clime of the Torrid Zone.[3] The Doctor seem'd
to ingross his attention most, who was well ducked

Here it may not be improper to state the restrictions we are
laid under by the East India company, for the Breach of any
of them Mr. Teast and myself are under heavy penelties—
they are as Following—
1st: The preamble of the Indenture sets forth that the East
India company have by various acts of Parliment the Ex-
cluscive right to trade in the Indian Oacean and Pacific from
Cape Horn West, to the Cape of Good Hope—
2dly. They give us licence for three years under the following
restrictions commencing from the seventeenth September

---

[1] (La) Palma Island and Ferro (Hierro) Island are both in the Canary
Island group at between 28° 28′ N., 17° 49′ W. and 28° 50′ N., 17° 46′ W.
and 27° 45′ N., 18° 00′ W. respectively.
[2] I.e. south-west by south. Such abbreviations are not spelled out. The
points of the compass clockwise from north are north by east, north-
north-east, north-east by north, north-east, north-east by east, east-north-
east, east by north, east, and so on. These are further split by the addition
of fractional bearings, the fraction referring to the direction which follows
it.
[3] This variant of the crossing-the-line ceremony does not, in fact, seem
to have been as common as Bishop implied, especially when the ship
planned ultimately to cross the Equator. See *Mariner's Mirror*, 48 (London,
1962), 73, 231, 314.

1794—That the buisness of our voyage Shall in no way interfere to the prejudice of their trade

That on the ships Arrival at Canton or any other place within the Empire of China we are to obey all orders and instructions we may receive from the East india companys supercargos or agents with respect to our behaviour to the Natives

That we must give a faithful Manifest of our Cargo before we attempt to dispose of it to the Supercargo, any stores Provisions &c not contained in the Manifest to be lieable to Seizure

We are not to obstruct their searching the ship when they please

None of the crew are to be left behind without permission of the Supercargo

We are not permitted to sell anything but the produce of the North West coast of America

All Gold & Silver we recieve from the Natives is to be paid into the Companys treasury taking their Bills at the usual rate of Exchange

We must not go to the South*ward* and West*ward* of Canton nor to the West*ward* of New Holland

We are not to ship any goods or merchandize with out the Express licence of the Supercargo

We are answerable, for any ill behaviour towards the Natives, to the Supercargo, and must submit to his deciscion

We must return direct to Great Brittain, at the Expiration of the licence—

We must within 14 days after our return to England deliver to the East India Company the original Log Book and Journals of the voyage which are not to *be* made Public without our permission, except to Government—

For the true and faithful performance of these we give bonds of twenty five Thousand Pounds

We have also a Free licence from the South sea company for eighteen months, to fish or trade in the south seas

Saturday 8th: Nothing in particular happened to the 8th: except that we where becalmed 2 days between the latitudes of 22 and 20 degrees. In the morning at daylight we saw the Isle of Sal, one of the Northmost of the Cape de Verd Islands, which we left to the Eastward and at noon came in Sight of the Isle of Bonnivista.[1] The North side of this Island is bound by reefs of dangerous Rocks, on which several valuable ships have been lost, and is sopposed to have a Million of spicie lying among them. The Hartwell, Brittish East Indiaman, was the last vessel of consequence. The wreckers from America come here, and with proper machines, taking the advantage of a smooth season, get in amongst the breakers, and the water being very clear, by means of Glasses discover where any thing of value lies and having proper divers, are known to have taken up much of the property lost. We passed this Island also to the West*war*d at the distance of about 4 miles offshore, keeping a Good look out for a small Reef of Rocks lying about SWbW 4 Leagues from the Road of Bonnivista called the Isles of Letten[2]—at 8 in the evening knowing ourselves to be to the South*war*d of them, the Ship was hove too to wait for daylight, at which time we saw the Isle of May and steering away to the East*war*d of it as soon as we came abreast the South Point, saw the Isle of St Jago,[3] the largest of the Cape deverds bearing about South West seven Leagues, and at three oclock we anchored in Port Praya Bay with the small Bower anchor in Seven fathems water, fine Brown Sand, and found riding here the Schooner, Nancy, of Boston, who had been making some attempts at the Wreck of the Hartwell, but without much success, owing to the season being too far advanced, the months of June, July & August being the smoothest times—

Soon as the ship was secured at her Anchor, the Boats where hoisted out, and the Gigg carried me on Shore, where

16° 24′ N

Sunday 9th.

anchors at St Jago

[1] The Isle of Sal and Böa Vista Island are respectively the northernmost and easternmost of the Cape Verde Islands. The Islands have belonged to Portugal since the fifteenth century.

[2] Presumably the shoal Joa Leitao (João Valente) which lies about twenty-one miles west-south-west of Böa Vista.

[3] Bishop referred to Maio and São Tiago (São Thiago, Santiago) Islands. Praia is the port of the latter, on the south coast, at 14° 55′ N., 23° 31′ W.

I waited on the Governor General of the Islands, desiring his permission to Water my ship, to which he readily agree'd. The Governor is a Tall Elderly man, a Native of Europe and, I believe, the only one on the Island. He recieved me with Politness, and was presented with a Cheese and a hamper of Potatoes, with which he appeared to be much pleased. After taking a slight view of the Town and its inhabitants, and of the watering Place, I returned to my[1] Ship for the night.

Monday 10th Early in the morning the Long Boat was dispatched for the Water and made in the day four trips which filled up most of our Punchens, but it soon appeared that it was but Indifferent for the People began to complain of the BELLY AKE. As I concluded we should have enough Bristol water to last us to Rio de Janeiro *this* determined me not to take any more off, and having procured about a thousand of fine oranges at one Shilling p*e*r Hundred we got every thing ready to Sail, leaving a letter, N° 3,[2] on board the American schooner who was going derict to Boston, and a Copy of it, on shore with the Governor, to be forwarded the first opportunity—

Tuesday 11th:
sails from
St Jago

at 9 oclock hoisted in all the boats, and got under weigh, making all Sail to the South*war*d and at noon where five Leagues from the Island, the whole of the Crew in good health.

As these Islands are so generally known, and of which there are good discriptions in the Books of Geography, I shall forbear saying any thing of them here, otherwise than the natives are mostly yellow or Black, live in low mean houses, and in most every respect inferiour to the Native Negros of Africa. Their Islands have a Barren roude appearence and some of them often visited by Famine, owing to the intense heat of the sun, and the little rain that falls, they seldom having any, but dureing the three months of the Tornado

[1] At this and some other like places Bishop has written 'the' above 'my'. This was so plainly an afterthought that 'my' appears the better reading.
[2] See below, p. 151.

8

Season, and while we laid here, a Small vessel arrived from St. Nicholas[1] with an account of twenty Families having perished for want. Provisions at this time, would sell very well at all the Islands, Indeed the Natives are known to be so very indolent, that if they have but a sufficiency of food for the day, they religiously follow one Scripture maxim, of Taking no thought for tomorrow,[2] but will dance half the night, and sleeping the other half, rise with the Sun and like their asses and Goats, in which Islands there are plenty of the former, pick a scanty subsistence for the day—the young men are all Soldiers in their turn for a Month. The Fort has twelve Guns with shattered carriges, once or twice firing would dismount the whole of them. The Generals guard consisted of three Privates a Sargeant and a Corporal, with four rusty musketts, one wanting a Bayonet another a cock to the lock, and only two Cartridge Boxes amongst them, this will be sufficient to convey an Idea of their military strength—I saw but two women who where originally White, these where old, but dressed very elegantly. The most part of them are Mellatoes and many of them well featured. Their dress in general was a striped Cotton cloth round the middle reaching down to the ankles with a nother of a different Pattern, thrown loosly over their Sholders. I saw also some hansome Black Women—

The wind continues favourable in the North East quarter, but the air is become very sultry, the Crew all in good health. The sea has been much rippled since we left St Jago's, hence I conclude the Current is setting to the Westward.

Thursday13th: 10° 24′ N 22° 6′ W

Here, while the ship, in good order, glides gaily on her course and with little variation of circumstance, the liberal instructions I have recieved from my Spirited Employer, are worthy of my strictest attention, they are as follows—

★ ★ ★

[1] São Nicolau Island is one of the Windward Cape Verdes, its chief town being at 16° 37′ N., 24° 18′ W.
[2] 'Take therefore no thought for the morrow: for the morrow shall take thought for the things of itself' (Matthew, vi. 34).

Teast to Bishop,[1] *at Bristol, 24 September 1794:*

I have appointed you to the command of my ship the Ruby, on an intended voyage to the North West coast of America, Japan and China—you are to proceed direct from Bristol to the North West coast of America, touching at such places only, as will be indispensibly necessary to procure Water and Fresh Provisions. As the success of the voyage and all your future proceedings, depend on your early arrival on the N.W. Coast (say by 31ˢᵗ: March 95) I should therefore advise you not to think of touching at the Sandwich Islands, unless you are fairly round Cape Horn by the first of January, but endeavour to make Easter Island, which lies in Latt 26°: 57′ S, and get what refreshments you can there. You must endeavour to make the N.W. Coast in Latitude 35° North or thereabout—and trade the coast up to Port Sidenham, which lies in Latt: 43°: 50′ North, Longitude 124°: 18′ West, you must make your trade outside the Bar. From Port Sidenham you will proceed examining the Coast to deception Bay, which lies in 46°: 20′ North Latitude. I advise your going over the Bar into this bay on the flood tide, as the River Choonock and two other considerable Rivers empties them selves into this bay. There are very fine Sea Otter, River Otter, Fox, Martin, Racoon, Lynx cat, Beavers, Wolves and Bear Skins to be procured there. From deception bay you will proceed to the Northward, touching in at, and carefully examining every streight, sound and river, that appears navagable with Safty to Nootka Sound. You will observe the coast to the North-ward of Nootka, up to Haine's Cove, has not yet been ex-plored. I recommend you to pay particular attention to this part of the coast as also to every port in the Charlotte Islands. From Haines Cove you will proceed to Port Meares, Sea Otter Sound, Norfolk Sound, Bearings Bay, Admiralty Bay, Prince William Sound, and the Islands adjoining—It is probable there are many Harbours and places of trade be-

[1] Places mentioned in this letter will be annotated as Bishop ap-proached them. He never approached Prince William Sound, nor Yakutat Bay, which was Cook's Be(h)ring's Bay and Dixon's Admiralty Sound.

tween the ports I have mentioned, it will be to your Interest and Honour to Examine the coast with Care from one end to the other, and the utmost activity in moving from one port to another in your route to the Northward will be required. The moment your trade is done you must remove, making the Natives sensible nearly the time you purpose to return, and give them every encouragement to keep their Furs for you.

You must keep your Orders, your Route and instructions a profound secret, and if you are not in want of assistance have no entercourse whatever, (Especially while you are making trade) with any other ship, and you MUST NOT PART with any of your articles of trade in Barter with other Ships, NOT EVEN FOR Furs.

I expect you will arrive at Prince Williams Sound, by the 30th: June 1795—and as soon as you have collected all the Furs and Skins there and the adjacent Islands you will return to the South*ward* touching in at every place of trade between Prince Williams Sound and deception Bay and Should you on your arrival on the Coast have procured any quantity of Furs or Skins to the South*ward* of deception Bay, I recommend you to return to those places before you leave the coast. When you pass the Commandant of His Majesties Ships on that station,[1] in your return to the South*ward* Write me three letters stating the Furs &c you have on board, Which letters carefully seal up, and desire the Commandant, to forward two of the Letters by diff*erent* conveyences, keeping the third himself until his arrival in England, to Establish my inshurence in case of Loss.

I am now drawing towards the period necessary for quiting the N.W. Coast of America, and Whether it will be most advisable to proceed to Japan and China or to Canton direct. As this will depend so much on circumstances, I must in a great measure leave it to your Judgment, and determination, not doubting but you will make choice of whichever shall appear to be most for my interest, keeping in view the

---

[1] Teast evidently referred to Nootka Sound.

II

necessity of returning early to the N.W. Coast of America
the ensuing season—The following instructions are for your
government in leaving the N.W. Coast—

Should you have procured 1500 prime sea otter skins,
above the size of Cubs (for Cubs are of little or no value) by
the 31st: August, and you hear a favourable acc*ou*nt of the
trade at the Japanese Islands, you must proceed from the
North West Coast to Japan and from thence to China (Canton)
but should you hear an unfavourable account of the Trade
at Japan, or, should have not procured a sufficient quantity
of skins to authorise you to quit the Coast of America so early
as the first of September 1795, or, on the other hand should
you have plenty of good trade, and a prospect of its con-
tinuance and little opposition, and you find you have the
commanding articles, and that you would leave great quantities of Prime Furs unpurchased, I should advise you not to
leave the coast untill the 15th: October, and then proceed
direct to Canton—I am now going to give you directions how
you are to proceed on your arrival at Canton—

You must immediately on your arrival there, deliver unto
the Honourable the East India companys Supercargo, a True
Manifest of all Gold and Silver (provided you should have
procured any at the Japanese Islands) Furs, Skins and Merchandize then on board the Ruby, and also an account of the
remaining outward bound cargo then on board, stating that
you mean to return to the N.W. Coast of America with the
Said European goods, and request that the Ship may be
Searched—you must be very cautious in the disposal of the
Furs and skins &c at Canton, and as soon as the sale is
compleat, you will deliver into the Hon*our*able East India
Co*mpany* Treasury the whole of the Bullion, you have
recieved for which amount their Supercargos will draw at
the then rate of Exchange Bills on the Hon*our*able East India
Company at 365 days sight in my favour—If Possible get
four setts of these Bills drawn, and forward three of them by
seperate conveyances to me, keeping the fourth set with your-

self. I hope you will have compleated your buisness at Canton by the 15ᵗʰ: January 1796 and that you will arrive on the N.W. Coast of America in about Latitude 35° N by 31ˢᵗ: March following—

You will then proceed in your second purchase of Furs Skins &c trading along the coast as herein before directed, taking advantage of what experience you gained in the first voyage and you must endeavour to dispose of the whole of your European goods on the N.W. Coast to the NATIVES, for their Furs & Skins, but after the 31ˢᵗ: August 1796 you are at liberty to barter any of the remains to any Ship for prime Furs, but you will please to take notice, that you are not to quit the coast of America unless you have disposed of the whole of your goods, before the 10ᵗʰ: September 1796— From the N.W. Coast you must proceed for the Japanese Islands and such ports in the Kingdom of Correa as you may have learned will prove advantageous to the voyage, and lastly to Canton, where you will deliver the Bullion that may be procured for the Furs and Skins sold—In the manner directed in the former part of these orders.—Finish your Buisness with all possible dispatch at Canton and if the Honourable East India Companys Supercargo, will not Charter the vessel as a Packett, or on freight for London, you must proceed direct from Canton to Bristol—

You must keep a regular Account of your trade and every other transaction, and be sure to pay every attention to the limits and regulations, prescribed by the Honourable East India Companys Licence, as any infringement on them or any Injury done by you to the Natives of Japan or China, will be attended by severe consequences and will subject both you and me to immense penalties

There is not any Private adventure allowed any officer or Seaman on board the Ship Ruby—Should any person carry a private adventure he is to forfiet his Whole Wages and Commissions

13

You will please to observe the Expence of this outfitt is more than double the amount it would be in Peace in Wages Provisions & Insurence, and that it will require the strictest attention and active perseverence to make it answer—one thousand prime sea otter skins will barely pay the Expence of the outfitt—Should you not procure the quantity of Prime sea otter skins you expect, you must endeavour to purchase every other sort of Skins that are of a good quality and a few thousand Fur Seals would be worthy of your attention taking care to dry them well

The Prime Sea Otter Skins must be packed in Cases, not Casks, and by no means put a damp or damaged Skin among them, and in fine weather they Should be Examined. Furs if sound and dry, Keep best close packed

I have to recommend to your attention the procuring as many Brazil or south sea Pebbles,[1] (such as you saw at Mr Brodrips) as possible, and a few Casks of shells, also the pearl oyster shell with which the Sandwich Islands abound, and a quantity of Leather War dresses, which you may purchase Cheap to the South*ward*. These and pearl Oyster shell are good articles as you proceed to the Northward

I am informed that Gold do not bear a proportionate value with Silver in China, that an ounce of Gold which here is worth from £3. 15 to £3. 17 is not worth more than 3£ per oz there and that silver (ie) Spanish dollars which are worth here from 4/4 to 4/6 each is worth 5/- in China. I mention this for your government provided you should touch at the Japanese Islands, in Canton you must inform yourself well respecitng the value of each

When you pack the Furs especially the prime sea otter skins, remember to put Ceader shavings amongst them. It will keep them from being eaten by the moth

---

[1] *O.E.D.* notes that Brazil pebbles are lenses ground from a pure, colourless rock-crystal found in that country, but probably Teast did not refer to this. South Sea pebbles might have been a species of spondylus.

Make all possible enquiry for my ship the Jenny J. W. Adamson, Master, and in every letter you write state the time and Place, when and where she arrived on the N.W. Coast of America, and the time she left it, and endeavour to learn whether she was bound to Japan, or to China direct

Capt*ain* Charles Bishop is to have Six pounds p*er* Month Wages and a commission of Six pounds p*er* Cent on the neat sales of the first Cargo of Furs skins &c in Japan and China, but provided the sales of the first Cargo of Furs skins &c should amount to upwards of fifteen thousands pounds neat, he is to have Eight Pounds p*er* Cent commission, on the neat sales of the Second cargo

Mr Joseph Williams (Chief Mate) is to have five Pounds p*er* Month Wages, and a Commission of one Pound p*er* Cent on the neat Sales of the Cargos, and in Case of your death which God forbid! is to succeed you in the command of my Ship the Ruby

Mr. Thomas Hunt (second Mate) is to have four Pounds fifteen shillings p*er* Month, Wages, and a commission of seven shillings and six pence p*er* Cent on the neat sales of the Cargos.

★ ★ ★

I do hereby acknowledge to have recieved an Exact Copy of the foregoing Orders, and I do engage to fullfill the Same and strictly to abide by and comply with the regulations and Limits prescribed by the Hon*oura*ble East India Companys Licence

Sign'd

Bristol 13th: October 1794   CB——

★ ★ ★

FARTHER ORDERS—*13 October 1794:*
The Duty paid by the ship at Canton, being so very heavy, it will not answer for you to proceed there with less than 700 Prime Sea Otter skins, and should you not be so fortunate as

to procure that Quantity, in time to leave the N.W. Coast of America so as to insure your return early the next Season, you must remain on the Southermost part of the coast and trade dureing the Winter. On the other hand should you find plenty of Prime sea otter skins on the Coast, and that by remaining there the first part of the Winter months you could dispose of the whole of your Cargo, BY ALL MEANS continnue your trade, getting to the South*ward* as the Winter draws on. By disposing of the whole of your cargo the first season you will save paying a second duty at Canton—In this Case unless you have good accounts of the trade at Japan, you must give up the Idea of going there

DO NOT SUFFER A REAL PRIME SEA OTTER SKIN TO GO FROM THE SHIPS SIDE—all under Prime, (ie) Brown, Worn, Stag'd[1] or damaged, and inferiour Skins must be bought cheap to make up for the Extraordinary price you pay for the very Prime

Wicinannish, at Port Cox is a very powerful Chief—Dash[2] Him well—give him as a Present the Trunk Marked with my name, a Best Fowling piece, a Silver Mounted Hanger, shott Belt and powder Flask, and a Gold laced Hatt.

* * *

Recieved a Copy of the above orders, Witness my Hand— Signed C.B.—

* * *

Upon Mr. T— taking his farewell of us, he called his Clerk into the Cabbin and desiring him to take notice, that his last declaration was to desire me in every instance to act soley as his representative, well knowing that it was impossible for him to provide by orders or instructions for circumstances that are likely to ensue in a voyage of this discription, and indeed his orders he did not mean, so much for my government, as in case of Accident or Death to me, that they might be directions for the continnuence of the voyage to the person

---

[1] Properly 'stag' or 'stagg', describing raw, unseasoned furs (*O.E.D.*).
[2] This appears the reading, and is acceptable in the sense of 'cut a dash with'.

16

who Should succeed me, from whom he expected an Explicit complyence. But should Death or Accident happen to him, 'you are Witness' (Said he) 'of this my declaration and also, that it is my desire in that case, that, my Executors or who-ever else it may concern, do not censure Mr. B— for any Conduct he might be induced to persue contrary to his instructions, for the good of the voyage—well knowing he will not neglect doing every thing in his power for my interest'

I'll not decieve him—

Since Thursday 13th: we have made but a slow progress to the South*war*d owing to light Baffling winds, which in the course of a few hours has blown from every Quarter, attended with heavy rains thunder and lightning and at times the weather has been very close and sultry. The people however continnues in good health all except the cook, whose illness mostly proceeds from a Bruise in the Side occasioned by a Spar falling on him from the Booms, he is by no means dangerously ill—on Monday we had a number of water Spouts near us, one of which came so close, that we became apprensive that it would pour its deluge of water on our decks. The Guns where primed fore and aft, and two of them fired which had the desired effect, for it ceased in that Quarter and began in a nother more remote from us—These spouts or Cataracts of water, I concieve to be caused, by the great heat of the Sun raryfying the air to that degree, that the encombant clouds become incapable of containing the quantity of water, they had imbibed by evaporation—the Air at this time was very hot, and the heavy cloud from whence these issued, seem'd to drag its weight with reluctance, and very low in the atmosphere[1]

Wednesday 19th:
5° 10′ N
22° 28° W

This day we got a steady Breeze from the S. East with fine Weather and in the afternoon saw a large ship a head of us. The Guns where loaded and the ship clear'd for action, at

Friday 21st:
2° 00′ N
23° 14′ W
Variation
11° 13′ W

---

[1] Bishop's explanation was essentially correct; the cloud forms a funnel which fills with rain. The coinage 'encombant' nicely blends 'incumbent' and 'encompassing'.

Sun set we came abreast of her at the distance of 3 miles to leeward. She appeared to be a Spanish Man of War, but sailed so very ill that she did not offer to chace us, and in the morning was out of Sight astern—

Sunday 23rd:
00° 38′ S
25° 44′ W

This Morning we spoke an American ship called the Olive Branch in Company with another of the same Country bound on the Southern Wale Fishery—in this instance the Ship has given me great satisfaction with respect to her Sailing. These ships where both coppered and carrying the same quantity of sail as our Selves. It was seven oclock when we Spoke them and at noon only one of them was barely in sight astern and to leeward with all—the difference of Sailing must be at least 5 to 3—This day being Sunday, Read prayers to the people who are all in good health except the Cook, and he is much better.

Sunday 30th:
14° 29′ S
33° 47′ W
Variation
00° 47′ W

Nothing very particular has happened this last week. We have had a Strong Breeze from the S East and have made 966 miles on our Course good. The variation of the compass gradually decreasing and now there is little or none—Thursday 27th: a Man of war Bird flying over our ship took hold of the Vane at the main Top Gallant mast head with his beak and Braking the Spindle attempted to fly away with it, but soon drop'd his Prize over board. He continued flying about the Ship sometime, and the seamen, who are generally very Superstitious—was very anxious to shoot him. I fired five times but at a great height, cut his tail feathers off, and some of his Wing, nevertheless he made his Escape—The Cook is quite recovered and all the people in good health attended Divine service this Morning

Sunday 7th
December
1794

At midnight we sounded and had Ground at 50 fathoms coarse Rocky bottom, hence I concluded we where not more than 15 Leagues from Cape Frio which is known to lye 20 Leagues EbN from the Harbour of Rio de Janeiro[1]— The wind Blowing fresh from the Eastward we Steer'd away

[1] Cape Frio is 75 miles from Rio, at 23° 00′ S., 42° 00′ W.

WbS under an easy Sail expecting to see the Cape in the
morning—At daylight we spoke a Portuguese Fishing boat
but neither understanding each others language, we could
not gain any information with respect to the Situation of the
land, and the weather being so thick and rainy we could not
see more than two miles from the ship, with a very heavy
Swell running in on the coast. We where going to heave the
ship too to wait for fairer Weather, when it suddenly clear'd
up and we Saw the Islands lying to the North*ward* of Cape
Frio WbS½S 7 or 8 miles, and passing these at noon, came
abreast of the Cape, and Observed the Lattitude to be
22°: 50′ S. At 5 oclock in the fater noon, having run about
half the distance between Cape Frio and Rio de Janeiro, it
blowing a Fresh Gale with thick dirty weather, we hove the
ship too and plyed under and Easy sail, intending to go into
the Harbour in the Morning.

At daylight saw the Entrance of the Harbour NWbN 7 or Monday 8th:
8 miles the winds light, and Hazy W*eather*. At Noon passed Rio de Janeiro
the Fort of Santa Cruez[1] and saluted it with 5 Guns they
returning an equal number. The Harbour Master came on
board and took charge of the ship and at 7 oclock we anchored
to the North*ward* of the Small Fortified Island lying abreast
the Town, in 6 fathems Fine Soft ground moor'd with half a
Cable each way

As soon as the ship was secured at her Anchors I repaired
on shore in the Harbour masters Boat to the Palace and paid
my respects to the vice Roi,[2] asking permission to water and
refresh my people. To this he readily complyed, and gave me
permission to remain in the Harbour one week after the
proper officers had searched and Examined the Ship and our
Papers to see that we where not on any illicit Trade—this is
always customary—as the Portaguese do not allow any im-
portations, but in their own Vessells—the Vice Roi having
asked the news in Europe at the time we left it, and recieving
as perfect an account as my limited knowledge could give,

---

¹ Santa Cruz.   ² Conde de Rezende, Dom. Jozé de Castro.

dismissed me to go on board and not to visit the shore 'till farther orders but gave us permission to Send a boat to markett under the charge of a Corporals guard—

On my return to the Ship I found the guard Boat had taken her station near the Ship well man'd and arm'd to prevent any Smuggling, nor did they ever leave it night or day 'till relieved by a nother.

Tuesday 9th: This afternoon a number of Civil and Naval officers came on board, and After Examining the Pass, Register Journals &c took down in writing those questions and Answers which I gave with respect to where we came from, where bound, cause of coming here &c &c sending the chief and second mates on shore to be Examined their, after which I was desired to retire, and they called the People in seperately to to see if their should be any difference, when being well satisfied as to the truth of my assertations they directed that myself and officers Should come on shore in the Morning and Sign the protest &c. These formalities I understand are procribed by the Queen[1] to be administered to every Foreign vessel, that should come here—after the buisness was over they where regaled with cheese and Taunton Ale of which they are very fond, and left the ship quite Satisfied—

Wednesday 10th: This Morning myself and officers repaired on shore as before directed and having signed the necessary papers, recieved permission to water and to Ship any Wine, Rum or Stores for the Ship upon which Buisness the Boats were immediately Employed—this day a Spanish Ship from River Plate bound to the Havannahs[2] put in here in distress having Sprung a leak—

Sunday 14th: The Ship being compleatly watered, and having got every necessary on board that this Pleasant clime afords, with an additional Stock of Wine ($\frac{1}{2}$ Pipe Port, 9£)—1200 Billits fire wood &c—she was clear'd for Sea intending to Sail in the

[1] Maria I.   [2] The Spanish West Indies.

Morning—Monday being a favourite day of sailing with me. On this day last voyage when we went to the Coast of Africa, we Sailed on a monday arrived on monday, left the coast monday and arrived in England Monday. The present voyage commenced on Monday and arrived here on monday and now we sail again Monday—the People this afternoon had all liberty to go onshore and returned in the evening in good order

This morning at daylight the Harbour master came off and Monday 15th: we got underweigh with the land breeze and proceeded out of the Harbour, having left two setts of letters N° 4[1] to be forwarded by the first conveyance to Europe. At 9 oclock we where clear of the Harbour and having settled with the Harbour Master for Anchorage 5/6 per Deim and Pilotage in and out, an unnecessary imposition! 7£, he left us, and hoisting in the boats made Sail towards Cape Horn, all, in good health and Spirits

As a discription of this Place the Capital of the Brazils and residence of the Vice Roi, may be expected here, I have only to regret my imperfect knoledge, and abilities in discribing one of the finest Harbours and Places of Refreshment and repair for shipping in the World. The following will only be a faint scetch of it—

Rio de Janeiro on the coast of Brazil is situated just within Rio de Janeiro the tropic of Capricorn, in the Latitude of 22°50′S and longitude 42°44′ West of Greenwich[2]—near the Entrence of the Harbour there are several Small Islands, ships going in or coming out go through between either of them, as the winds may occasion them, there not being any danger in any of the Channels. After passing these Islands about 3 miles you come abreast of the Sugarloaf a Remarkable high Mount, of a conical figure. This is distinctly seen a long way off at Sea, and is a good mark to know the Entrance of the Harbour by,

[1] See below, pp. 152–3.
[2] Actually 22° 54′ S., 43° 10′ W.

the Sea washes its Base on the North Side and I am told a
vessel would not touch the ground close to it—the mouth of
the Harbour here is about one mile broad, a clear open
channel. On the right hand Shore stands the Castle and Forts
of Santa Cruez, a very strong fortification of upwards of
100 large cannons, and over it on a high mountain is a nother
very strong fort which most effectually commands the shipping going in or coming out. It would be next to an impossi-
bility for a Ship to go in by force, and you could not hurt
them by any cannonade afloat—at this fort Strangers going
in must send a Boat to recieve an officer of the Guard who
accompanys that ship up to the City and attends the Captain
to the Palace when his charge ceases—passing between these
two Points, the Sugar loaf and the fort, you sail right up to
the Harbour and pass two small round Islands,[1] which are
also covered with Guns besides Fortifications on both Shores
all the way up to the City. I am told they have near 800
Cannons mounted and capable of attack or defence. Being
come abreast of the City we Anchored outside of a Small
Fortified Island[2] on which stands a nunnery—between this
and the town their Small vessells are loaded and unloaded,
and farther up the Harbour their large vessells are moor'd.
There where at this time about 100 Sail of Shipping, amongst
them a fine Frigate of 48 Guns and a Smaller man of war
lying as Guardships. This is the most spacious and com-
modious harbour in the Brazils, and one of the first rate in
the World. The appeerence of the surrounding land is truly
Picturestic, high lofty mountains whose tops kiss the Clouds,
interspersed with deep, cultivated, valleys, with beautiful
villas seated in the Avenues of the orange Groves, form a
view, which to the Sailor whose eye has long explored the
Horrison round, and met no object to chear his Sight, nothing
but Sea and Clouds, fills his mind with grateful pleasure,
each object joys his heart, and his Sight imbibes a portion
of the surrounding beauties to chear his Memory when
remote at Sea

[1] Probably Laje and Villegaignon.
[2] Probably dos Cobras.

There is a number of small Islands scattered o'er the bosom of the Harbour, cover'd with vegetation, 'The seats of Blameless Pan'.[1] They are in general not inhabitated, except those who from their situation are elegible for fortification.

The City called St Sabastian[2] is a populas well built Place and is sopposed to be 3 miles in circumference, the streets all meet at right angles, some of them are broad, and all of them Paved. The houses are mostly 3 Stories high, and contain several Families, there are few Private houses, They, are mostly shops and warehouses and I generally found the People of the same professions, living all in the same street, thus I counted twenty seven silver smiths shops in one street, and saw no other of that profession in any other—they Reckon the White inhabitants to be one forth of the whole, 15000, the Coloured People one forth, and from twenty to thirty thousand Blacks mostly slaves, natives of Africa—

There is about 6000 troops, seemingly in good order and dicipline, certainly very well clothed. They all wear Side Arms and Chastise the blacks with great severity if they find them quarreling or making any disturbance—dureing the night there is Patrols of Horse and foot in almost every Street of the City, and a Forignor is always accompanyed by one or two of them, even in the day, who can not go any where without them, and they never forsake their Charge till at sun set he Sees you off in your Boat under the care of a nother arm'd Soldier who constantly attends in each boat beloning to the Ship

The pallace is situated in the centre of what they call the great Square. Itt is well built, about 60 feet high, having noly two Stories. In the upper one the Vice Roi resides, where are various appartments for his Court and officers of State—beneath these is the General Guard room, and various offices for transacting the Public buisness, as the Bench of Justice,

---

[1] Quoted from James Thomson, 'Summer' (properly 'seat').
[2] The city's full name is São Sebastião do Rio de Janeiro.

Mint for coining, refining the Gold, silver, stones &c. The Pallace faces the Harbour, and near the Steps for Landing is the great Fountain for Supplying the Ships with water—this is conveyed here by means of a lofty acquduct across a deep Vally from a distant mountain, to the City and there are four large Fountains in different Parts, to supply the natives—the water is in general good, but dureing the rainy Season it is not clear and has a leafy taste—

There is six or seven large Churches. I saw three of them, and they where very richly ornamented, with Gold and Silver and Some very good Paintings where hung up in them. The images of the Virgin our Saviour and his appostles, where as large as life and appeared to be well Executed, but the image of the Virgin to which the Soldiers always Bowed, was dress'd out, in all the tawdry nonsense of a Stage Actress, in room of that Simplicity of dress suitable to the humility of that Person.

I saw while I was here a Buirel, and a Procession sacred to one of their saints—the Buriel was, a Child who had died of the Small Pox, a desease that raged here at this time, and made great havock for they do not innoculate. It was dressed out in Silk, and all the Finery to be imagined, and the ravages the desease had made in its innocent face, was plastered over with a white paste. It was exposed in a Baskett ornamented with flowers dureing the day in the Chuch, and at six oclock it was buired in the following manner. There were four Gentlemen each with a wax taper in their hands standing by the four Corners of the Bier. Soon after a Priest entered and gabbled over in a hasty manner some prayers in latten, which as Soon as finished a vault was opened under the communion table, and it was carried on the bier down. I went amongst the rest to see this dispositary of the dead—it was very large, and there was on a heap a great many human bones, and Some corpses by them that seem'd lately dead—they where all dress'd in the finery they had been buired in and where covered with a little loose sand—this child was

Put beside them, the cloaths opened and a few Shovels of sand thrown over the Body. The flowers where taken up and presented with some degree of ceremony to its Friends, some where given to me, but it appeared that not one of its relations where there. Upon enquiry I find the Corpse is suffered to remain here only till its soul should arrive in heaven, for which voyage they allow about a Month. It is then taken up and buired in the common burying place—the Bones I saw where loose Bones taken out of it, and dispositied here, that those whom they belonged to might know at the general reserection where to find their straggling Members—at least this is their belief it seems—

In the procession there was nothing remarkable more than in the usual ceremonies in the Roman Cathilic countries on the Same occasion, except that they had six small Children dressed out in rich cloaths, each of which had Wings the feathers of which was edged with gold, they where led seperattly by a Priest round the high Priest—the People where all on their Knees in the streets through which they passed, and bowed to the High Priest who carried a Cross—

They have a theatre here, and on Sunday the day before we Sailed thare was to have been a performance—and I obtained permission from the officer of the Guard to remain on shore 'till 12 oclock at night, to see it, but he afterwards came and told me that some of the principal actors being unwell, it was set aside, but at the same time continnued his permission for my staying on Shore under the charge of the Guard who had orders to accompany me where ever I choose to go—by this means I had an opportunity of seeing their Women, for in the day there is not a WHITE woman to be Seen, but in the Evenings to ten oclock they are to be met with every where dressed very richly. After this hour the Modest discription of them retire and leave their city to those of easy virtue of which there are abundance—They seem in general hansome, but here you must allow a Sailor is a bad judge, at least 'till he has been Some time on Shore, they seem'd so

25

to me, but perhaps when compared to the Brittish Fair, they would turn out like the Public house at which I got a horse to carry me to Bristol, when I landed the last voyage. I thought it then a Capital Inn, having been confined for near two years to a small Ship with a Cabbin just room to turn in and a few days before we sailed was at it again, when it appeared in its true light, a mean Country Alehouse—

There is a very good markett here under cover where is to be had Fish Beef and abundance of Poultry, vegetables, Fruit &c all very cheap. Lb Beef $1\frac{1}{2}^d$—a large duck or Fowl 1^s—I saw no mutton—and Goats are very dear, as well as hogs—the Fruits are in great Plenty and in great variety, Pine Apples, Oranges, Cocco nuts, Grapes, Mango's, Mellons, Prickly Pears, Consou Apples,[1] limes, Guaver's, Pomgranites, and number of Berries and other fruit I do not know how to name. They are all Excellent in their kind—'Witness thou best Anana, Thou the Pride of vegetable life:'[2] &c &c.

The Mines, from which the Gold is brought, is at a great distance from here, I am told 500 miles. There is abundance of Gold in those Mountains near the City, but they are not Suffered to be opened. The Severe Penelty of Slaving in the Public Mines, or being sent a Slave to their Settlements in Africa, is inflicted on those, who Attempt to mine, or take Gold from any part, but under Commission of Government. While we where here thare was 5 hundred weight escorted here under a Strong Guard of Horse, there has been none transmitted to Europe these 20 months since the commencement of the war.[3] Their Treasury here must be at this time very rich, besides a great number of precious Stones and Silver— there is, I am told, one diamond weighing an ounce and half brought in lately. They are very jealous of Forignors, and do not care to give much information with respect to their riches, to them—Sugar, Rum, Cotton and Coffee is produced in this

---

[1] Probably the receptacle of the fruit of the cashew tree.
[2] Correctly quoted from James Thomson, 'Summer'.
[3] France declared war on Spain 7 March 1793.

Country the Same as our West Indies, and in the more Southern parts, Weat, but it is of a very inferiour quality— Those People I had any dealings with, seem'd perfectly civil and Polite, the Present Vice Roi has been here about three years—he is an elderly man of a mild and pleasing Aspect and manner—he is treated with all the respect due to his high office and seems much beloved by the inhabitants—having given as full a discription of this Place &c as my Short stay and imperfect information could collect, I shall now persue my voyage towards Cape Horn and the North west coast of America.

We began to here experience variable winds and a Colder Climate and this day it blew very hard for 5 hours from the Southward and a Great number of Birds where flying about the Ship

Sunday 21st:
32° 32′ S
45° 53′ W

Dark squally weather with the winds South westerly. This being Christmas day, Read the Service to the Ships company, who are all in good health, and the circumstance of the day was a good Fresh dinner and a bowl of Grog o'er which true Harmony and Content presided, and each wishing Success to the Ship drank the happiness and health of his Messmates with Pleasure.

Thursday 25th
36° 47′ S
48° 22′ W
South Cape of
River Plate
WbN, Dist*ant*
90 Leagues

The year, with us, is ushered in with a heavy gale of wind from the South west with a Clear cold Air and a high Mountainous sea running. It blows so hard that we are obliged to lay too under a Close Reef Main Topsail and Fore staysail, the ship is very easy under this sail, and ships but little water. We have found the Currents setting strong to the South*ward* two days preceeding this Gale and have great numbers of Birds flying about the ship and yesterday saw a Wale— Monday last, it was a Calm serene day and we caught a Fish the Sailors call a Sun Fish, it weighed about 200 lbs. I never saw one before and am not certain it is named right.[1] When

Thursday 1st
January *1795*
43° 29′ S
50° 59′ W

---

[1] Bishop described the *Mola mola*, which retains the popular title, 'sun fish'.

cut up it appeared the Fleshy parts where covered with a thick grissly coat, hard and white about 2 inches thick. We tried to procure oil from it but the fire reduced it to a Strong fishy gelly—as to the flesh, which was perfectly white, it was a most delicious repast, eating exactly like the Claws of a Crab or lobster, and it Served for a fresh dinner for all hands. Of several that where swimming about the Ship, this was the smallest we Saw, its skin is the same kind as the small Cases of Instriments are cover'd with, thick and rough—its Exteriour Appearence is in this form[1]—

It was about 4 feet long and 20 inches broad and in the thickest part, about the sholder Fin was a foot in diameter.

Monday 5th:
48° 27' S
57° 11' W
Variation
22° East

Since Friday we have Had Moderate breezes and the winds favourable. Our near approach to Falklands Isles is signified by vast quantities of long sea weed and a variety of sea Fowl, as Albatrosses, Sea Mews, Penguins, Sea hens, Gulls and Sea Crows. We have seen also a good many wales. At noon this day Falklands Isles bore nearly S. West distance 65 Leagues—but the wind is now S. West blowing a Fresh Gale, the air very keen, like the N. East winds in Europe. The People all in good health attended prayers yesterday— we find in general a swell from the Southward that at times impeades our progress much—

Wednesday 7th
50° 46' S
59° 46' W

Last night It blew very hard for a few hours from the NW: and apprehending our selves to be no great distance from Falklands Isles, the Ship was hove too to wait for daylight, when with light winds and hazy weather we made all Sail, and at 10 oclock we saw the Jason Isles[2] which lay of the NW Extreme of Falklands Isles, bearing S East 3 Leagues— the wind being far Westerly with thick hazy weather, I determined to proceed round the East End of them altho' I grant it was out of my course, but there is many dangerous low Islands and rocks on the West Side, and not having a good Chart I am induced to think it was Prudent so to do—

---

[1] There follows a rough sketch.   [2] 51° 05' S., 61° 00' W.

Since Wednesday we have been sailing along the North and Friday 9th:
51° 28′ S
58° 26′ W East sides of these Islands with the wind westerly at times blowing Fresh, at times moderate: the land appears broken, and Extremly Barren: not a tree or a Bush to be Seen, as we Sailed past the nearest Points. We observed a few Seals: but not many together—this day at noon being come abreast of Port Lewis, Berkley Sound,[1] the wind came out SSW and blew a Gale, this was directly in our teeth. The ship Since leaving Rio de Janeiro had made a Good deal of water in her upper works, when it blew Fresh and the wind being now foul, I thought it a good time dureing its continnuence to Anchor in Berkley Sound and Caulk the Sides round *and* at same time, fill up our water, and refresh the People: accordingly we beat up the Sound about 16 miles, and anchored in a Sandy Bay, called Freshwater Bay in 7 fathems at 8 oclock in the Evening: dist*ant* from the nearest shore about a mile.

The wind now being shifted to WNW with fair weather: Thursday 15th: The water compleat, The ship Caulk'd: and a fine stock of Fresh Beef, two Bullocks, with abundance of wild ducks and Geese. We prepared to sail, and Friday Morning at daylight got under weigh and proceeded down the Sound, and at 8 oclock took our departure from the South end of the Sound, intending to pass to the Westward of Beauchenes Guions Isle[2] about a degree, but after passing the South East End of Falklands Isles, we experienced a Current which in 8 hours set us thirty miles to the Eastward of our Course, this was proven by our seeing Beauchenes Isle at daylight about 3 Leagues under our Lee Bow: and not being able to weather it we bore up and passed to East*ward*—

At Port Lewis, which is about 9 miles farther up the Sound Falklands
Islands than where we lay: the Spaniards have a Fort and a Church with about a dozen detatch'd houses for the Offices and Crew

[1] Berkeley Sound is at 51° 35′ S., 57° 56′ W., and Port Louis is at its north-west corner.
[2] Beauchene Island is at 52° 55′ S., 59° 15′ W.

of the Guardship the Captain of which is Governor of the Settlement, to this place their convicts from River Plate is brought: to breed and kill the Cattle. The linguist, who is an Irishman told me they where in all about 300 men, for they have NO WOMEN, and that the Gardship is relieved every year. He also told me the principal reason of their Settling here was to prevent any other nation doing so, and by that means have a Port of resort for Shipping which in a war would affect their Trade on the other Side of Cape Horn, The coasts of Peru and Mexico. The French where formerly settled here, but gave it up to the Spaniards. They left them their Cattle &c. These are Suffered to range at large and is computed to the number of twenty Thousand head, they export about 2000 hides every year to the River Plate. The Indians catch these wild Bullocks on horseback, it is really a noble Sight to See with what ease they take them: The Indian being provided with about three Fathems of Strong leather made rope: with a sliding noose on one end: the other made fast to his thigh and saddle: mounts his horse and makes towards the Bull: as soon as he See's him coming after—the Bull Sets off Full speed, but in a course of half a mile is come up with by the horse: the Indian: seeing himself within reach of the Horns, gathers the rope up in his hand: and throwing it at full swing round his head: Putts the noose over his horns and turns his horse round: They never miss their throw: another Indian comes with a Rope and watching the rearing of the Bull: catches him by the leg and throws him down: they then Geld him or kill him as they may have been ordered. The whole is done in about 10 minutes. The Governor and officers treated us very kindly and the day before we Sailed made me a Present of two young Bullocks. They Supplyed us with beef all the time we where here and what vegetables they could afford: for they have but very little: the air is too cold: for even now at midsummer: while the wind is Southerly it is as cold as February in England. There is Plenty of Fresh water all over the Islands: and abundance of wild Fowl of every discription. The Snipes are as large as Cocks, severl kind of Ducks and Geese and there is some wild Hogs on

Some of the Islands, but the land every where exibits nothing but barren heath or Rocks, not a tree, not a Bush, on any of them: some Articles would sell well here to the Spaniards: they bringing a good deal of money from River Plate: on Purpose to trade with any ships that might put in to refresh— and by the Linguist I am Furnished with a list of things in demand—

With respect to natural curiosities: I collected but few, the Principal is the Sea Limpitt which grows on the Rocks. The fish in the Shell is the same as is found on the Rocks of our Sea Coasts: but the shell is of a most beautiful tortoise shell Enamel. They gowr[1] in great abundance here, and I pickd about 600 of them not knowing they might be of value, but this I am Shure they will be very pretty Presents to those ladies who keep Tea caddies[2]

At 8 oclock this Morning we passed Beauchenes Guions Isle: 17th: Saturday it is a Rocky Barren Land of a reasonable height: about 3 miles long and one Broad. Their appeared to be a landing place on the NE side. We saw great abundance of Seals and Penguins on it: but not a tree or a Bush

This Morning we Saw States Island, called most commonly Monday 19th: Staten Land:[3] it *is* a high Woody Broaken Island, but as we where a good way off I cannot give here any farther discription. The N East End bore of us at noon NW½N 10 Leagues: and we observed in the Latitude of 54° 52′ S the wind being Westerly. We are pushing with all Speed to the Southward intending not to attempt to Stand to the Westward till we are at least two degrees to the Southward of Cape Horn: it lies in 55°: 58′ S.[4]

Yesterday and to day it has blown a heavy Gale of wind with Wednesday severe Squalls of Rain, Hail and Sleet, the air very cold— 21st: 56° 31′ S

[1] The oddest of Bishop's inversions.
[2] For a letter written from the Falklands, see below, p. 153.
[3] The eastern tip of Staten Island is at 54° 42′ S., 63° 43′ W.
[4] Actually at 55° 59′ S., 67° 16′ W.

62° 34′ W
Variation
27° East

and a most tremendeous Sea going: one of which struck the ship: unshipped the weel and the cabin door being open: half Fill'd the Cabin and almost floated me out of my Bed where I had just laid down to recruit, having been up for near 48 hours—the Ship however is light and makes but little water: and is an Excelent sea Boat—But full small for these tempestious seas

Friday 23ʳᵈ:
57° 31′ S
63° 57′ W

This is a fine serene day, it joys our hearts after the late severe weather: and the Ship is hung up with wet cloths: to dry. The air is warm clear and pleasent, the Sea smooth, and with gentle breezes from the Southward we are steering away under all sail to the Westward: the Sky to the Southward is remarkably Bright. Hence I conclude we are not more than a degree from the Icce. Cape Horn bore at noon NW½N 53 Leagues—

Wednesday
28ᵗʰ
57° 46′ S
71° 49′ W
Variation
27° East

Thank God we are pretty clear of this Stormy Cape, and Shall steer away as fast as these adverse winds will permit, to warmer climes and temperate Gales. The wind since leaving the latitude of 50°: has always been Westerly: N.W. or S.W. but always Westing in it, but when I look at Ansons tract: I cannot but think we have had a very favourable passage as yet. This day is pretty favourable and we are making a west course good but Alas! here it is fine one hour, the next a Gale of wind and Cold Rain or Hail or Snow. This day at noon the Cape Bore NE½E Distance 72 Leagues. The People are all in good health, and give me as yet no uneasiness by bad behaviour, This I trust will continnue

February 1795
Wednesday
4ᵗʰ:
55° 08′ S
81° 15′ W
Variation
25° East

The whole of this last week, we have had variable weather, calms & Storms alternately, but the winds always westerly, with the South west we Stand to the N.W. and again when it veers to the North west we tack to SW, so that we have made but little Northing tho' a good deal of westing. We pray heartily for Southerly winds to get to the Northward for these adverse winds are bleak, and Cold, and wet. Yesterday it blew a very heavy Gale from Westward and a tremendeous high Sea running, to day it is more Moderate and the Sea

Smoother. The Ship is very easy in a Gale under her Foresail and Stay courses,[1] and ships but little water. On the whole she Proves a lively sea Boat, indeed was she not so, we Should have Suffered Severely in these tempesteous seas. Cape Horn bore at noon East half South distance 150 Leagues, and the South Entrence of the Streights of Magallan East by North ½ North 90 Leagues distance

Since last Thursday, we have had a continual succession of hard Gales and Severe squalls of wind from the South west. It has blown so hard at times, that we could not carry sail, and the sea running so high, that we have scarcely had any thing Dry on us after being on deck Ten minutes. However we have this consolation, that we are getting fast into a more temperate clime: one of the most unpleasant circumstances attending bad weather in so small a Ship is that we cannot Cook, 'But a Sailor is Tar for all weathers'—[2]

Wednesday 11th: 48° 13′ S 83° 45′ W Variation 17° East

Since yesterday noon the almost constant Gale of wind: has abated and we are now Gliding along with a smooth sea and Steady moderate Breezes: from the WSW: the air is warm and the atmosphere clear. This is no more than might be expected after so good a Run to the North*ward* and at this Season of the year: the August of the Southern Hemphosphere. The Albatrosses which has been our constant attendants since coming into the Latitude of 40° S the other side the Cape: has left us, we have not seen one this last day: These Birds seem to enjoy the Stormy Latitudes: and nature has been very provident to them by endowing them with an amazing length of wing: measuring from six to eight feet across: with these by the Slightest motion of the Body they skim along over the mountain billows with great ease, and never hardly have occasion to flutter, like other Sea Fowl: they are to be met with in these high Latitudes from a hundred to a hundred and fifty leagues off the Land: and are seen riding on the Seas with careless ease in the Stormyest Blasts of the

Sunday 15th: 40° 40′ S 85° 30′ W Variation 13° East

---

[1] The stays are the lowest sails on a mast; 'courses' is a synonym for sail.
[2] A corruption of Charles Dibdin's song, 'The Tar for all Weathers' (A. W. Shipps, University of Colorado).

South: in their feathers they look nearly as big as an English Goose: but when striped of their Jackett are not larger than a Duck. The Sailors eat them: but they are very disagreeable to a nicer palate, being full of rancid Fishy oil.

Easter Island bore at noon, North West by West dist*ance* 488 Leagues, it lies in 27°: 4' S Latt: and 109°: 46' West Longitude[1]—

Sunday 22d:
31° 48' S
98° 34' W
Vari*ation*
8° E*ast*

This last week: we have had remarkable steady breezes: with fair weather: and a smooth sea: and have made great progress towards Easter Island: where I mean to put in and try to procure Some Sweet Potatoes, Fowls &c. This last 24 hours we have made 180 miles distance and the Island bears now at noon: N 64° W*est* or NWbW ¾ W distance 216 Leagues: the ships Company continnue in good health: Attended Prayers this Morning: a Circumstance never neglected when the weather will admit—I am sorry to find our wood grows Short and we shall be under the necessity of Cooking once in two days as there is none to be procured at Easter Island. This gives me real concern, as the People has had tea sweetened with Treacle Since we have been out, for Breakfast: in the room of salt meat and which I believe has not contributed a little in preserving them from the appearence of the Scurvy: especially as they where almost continually wet beating round Cape Horn. I shall therefore endeavour to make one of the Isles of Los Majos which lies nearly in the Latitude of 23° North and I am told are covered with wood, and lies in our Direct course towards North west coast of America:[2] we continnue to see a Variety of sea Fowl, tho' the nearest known Land is Easter Isle—

[1] Actually at 27° 05' S., 109° 20' W.
[2] As Bishop was to find, the isles of Los Majos did not exist (see below, p. 45). Their Spanish 'discoverer' had misplaced either the Sandwich or the Revilla Gigedo Islands, which latter lie between 18° 20'–19° 20' N., 110° 45'–114° 50' W. R. A. Skelton (British Museum) suggests that Bishop may have been using the 'Chart, containing the Coasts of California, New Albion...and Islands dispersed over the Pacific Ocean to the North of the Line', by John Green (London, 1753 and many later editions). For detailed discussion of the Islands' location see Anderson, 128–35.

Untill yesterday we have been gliding along for this last Fortnight under all Sail with moderate Breezes and fine Serene weather and a smooth Sea: winds, mostly in the N East and Expected to see Easter Island to day but to our Surprize as well as Mortification the wind veer'd round to NW and has blown Excessive hard with Severe Squalls of wind & rain nor is there at present any appearence of a Change: I am quite at a loss to account for this weather here in so low a Latitude as I find by all the Journals of former navigators: that they always found Easterly winds within the Lattitude of 30th: degree, SE, East, or NE. There is abundance of Sea Fowl hovering round us: small Gulls: Boatswains: Man of war Birds and Pentles.[1] Easter Island bore at noon West ½ South: distance 70 Leagues

Saturday 28th:
26° 45′ S
105° 56′ W
Variation
4° Easterly

Since yesterday we have had fair weather: and Approach Easter Island fast. It bears this day at noon West distance 83 miles by Account: we have not seen so many Birds to day as we did on Sunday. However we hope to see the Island tomorrow morning: the People are all in good health

March 1795
Monday 2d:
27° 03′ S
108° 18′ W
Variation
4° Easterly

Having run by the Log 59 miles West, since yesterday noon, at daylight we saw the Land: Easter Island bearing west 12 or 14 Leagues distance: my Longitude agreeing Exactly with the Longitude of that Excellent navigator Captain Cook, who lays the Island down in 109° degrees 46′ minutes. It has but a Barren appearence: no wood: but is of pretty good height above the level of the Sea: and there are Some Spotts of vegetation on it. We are approaching it fast with a fair wind and all Sail Set and Expect to anchor on the N. West side in the Afternoon: in my next Ill give a farther discription of it—

Tuesday 3d:

Sailing along the North side of the Island two small cannoes came off each carrying two men: they approach'd the ship with much caution, but as they percieved by our Presents of Iron Hoop, that we where Friends: one out of each cannoe

Easter Island

[1] Petrels.

Jumpt overboard and Swam to the ship and was taken in. They gave their Presents to the Cannoes as soon as we made them understand we where going to Anchor in Cooks Bay on the North west side,[1] and dismissed them to go on Shore themselves staying to accompany us round. These Cannoes are of very mean construction: but display what their Genius is capable of if they had any trees of sufficient bigness to make them. These! consist of a great many small Pieces of wood like rough Staves Sewed together, with a high beak and Stern Post, and to Prevent them from oversetting (for they are scarcely wide enough to set down in) they have two long spars secured to the Gunwalls which run out both on one side, and then have another about the Same length of the Cannoe fastened to the Ends of the out riggers which floats along the Surface of the water: this being of light wood the bouyency of it prevents the Cannoe from upsetting that way, and the weight of it, when out of the water, the other, but certainly impedes their Progress much

As we passed along the land we observed a good many natives sitting out on the side of the hills which are covered with Plantations of Sweet Potatoes, Sugar Cane, Yams and other roots and near any of the villeges they have one or two monuments standing on the Sea Shore facing them: these Seem to be intended to represent Human Figures: but done with a very coarse Idea, they stand some of them twenty feet high: and appear to be constructed of Stone: they are certainly Erected either as Monuments of some of their Worthies, or on Some Religious Idea.[2]

Passing round the NW end of the Island about a mile we came to the Bay where Cook anchored, and at the distance of a Mile and a Quarter from the Shore tried to get ground with & upwards of 90 fathems of line but could not effect it. The wind being off the land we beat in Shore under easy Sail, sounding frequently, and at 1 mile from the shore got 70 fathems water:

---

[1] Hanga-roa Bay: see Beaglehole in Cook, II, 339 n.
[2] Knowledge as to the monuments' function remains at about this point.

the next cast 40, 30, 25, and at $\frac{3}{4}$ mile from the Shore Anchored in 23 fathems: coarse sand & shells: the Prevailing winds here is S E*ast*, East and N E*ast*, which blows off the Land: but the other day: we had a Gale of wind from the NW. when this roadstead must have been very dangerous from the vicinity of the land and the wind and sea being right in

The ship being Secured at her Anchor and the Sails furled: Wednesday 4th with every thing in readiness to get under weigh should the wind come in from the Sea, the watch set, the others retired to rest, when at two oclock in the morning about a dozen beautiful young Women came swimming off naked as Nature introduces her children into the World. They came in with the greatest Saing froid, not in the least afraid: the Sight of so much beauty for it was a fine moon light night, did not fail to awaken in the minds of our Weather beaten crew, Sentiments kindred to love[1]—some of them content with the Presents they had recieved, a Knife, a Piece of Iron Hoop, or a looking Glass, Jumpt overboard and Swam on Shore with the news: daylight no sooner appeared than off they came— men, Women, boys, and Girls, the Ship was surrounded with beauties. These would come on board, stay a little time, RECIEVE A PRESENT, and away overboard to refresh themselves, for when they Staid long the motion of the ship would make them sick—the men brought off a good many red yams, and Bannanoes which was mostly bought for short Pieces of Iron Hoop, but brought but few Sweet Potatoes, and no Fowls, though offered the ENORMOUS SUM of two twopenny Knives for each—

In the evening having procured but little VEGETABLE refreshments, and it being now the full of the Moon, fearing a Change of weather, we got underweigh and Stood off to Sea intending to come in in the Morning and try the Effect of another days trade—when having got off about five miles, two young men who had Expressed a desire to accompany us to 'BRITTANNIEE' on Seeing the Ship withdraw from their Native Land, came aft and in a most Expressive and Petious

---

[1] Bishop or his earlier editor here scored out some twenty words.

manner requested me to tack the Ship and land them amongst their Friends again: this I did, the weather looking fair, and Anchored about 8 oclock in the Smae Place we had before.

Thursday 5th: In the Morning as before they came off, the Men brought to day a good many fine Sweet Potatoes and we Procured nearly half a Ton of them but only three Fowls: I believe these had a Sort of relegious Interdiction, called Tabou'ee as we even at last offerd a Hatchett for one which was not a Sufficient inducement, and they where bought here in Plenty in 1793 for a foot of Iron Hoop—In the morning we hoisted out the wale Boat and I went close in Shore: but could not (if inclined to, land) effect it, the Surf beat so hard upon the Rocks and there is no beach. In the evening we got underweigh and made all sail for the North west coast of America—

Situated on the Bosom of the great South sea or Pacific occean 500 Leagues from any known Land, is a small Spott of Earth about twenty five or Thirty miles in circumference. It seems oregionally to have been discovered by one Davis and Called after his Name Davis' Land, but at that time Navigation was very imperfect and he had placed it far out of its real Situation.[1] It was reserved for the Illustrious Cook to adjust this buisness, who touch'd here in March 1772 and renamed it Easter Island. It seems he landed with a Party of arm'd men and traversed o'er the Island, but the natives, fearful he would Seize Some of their Women, from their not seeing any on board the Ship, and so many of the other sex together, hid them away, and as I am informed for I have not read that voyage, he did not see one Female[2]—it is interspersed with hills and vallies, the highest from 6 to 8 hundred feet above the level of the Sea. The Natives seem numerous and we compute them from 1500 to 2000—,[3] their houses resemble so many large Beehives the front discribing the third of a Circle and from their being so near the serface I

---

[1] See above, p. xxviii.
[2] This was an exaggeration: see Cook (ed. Beaglehole), II, 350.
[3] Cook estimated 6–700; Bishop was more accurate, but probably still under the mark. See Beaglehole in Cook, II, 350–1 n.

conclude they must be hollowed out some depth in the Earth similer to what I have Seen on the coast of Africa, the Entrence is right in the centre of the Front and seems to Project like a Porch two or three Feet beyond it. They are composed of reeds such as the Coopers use of which they have abundance—it would have given me great pleasure to have been able to land amongst them with safty, the sides of the hills and vallies are covered with vegetation, and we observed two very clear Runs of water pouring over the Rocks—

The men of Easter Isle are of a middling stature and rather slender and do not appear very strong. They possess in general an open countanance with Black eyes, hair short, and most of them wore their Beards, but this latter I believe is from necessity, as they seemed much Pleased to be shaved by our people. Both men and Women are curiously tattooed about the face thighs and Arms in various figures, of Flying Griffins, Fish, human Faces, Stripes &c—I observed on Shore all the People where cloathed from the Sholders to the Ankles with a kind of white matting composed of the Rind of the Plantane or Palm trees and only those who swam off where naked, men, women, and Children. The women, indeed had a string tied round the waist and Some loose Rushes brought round between their legs—when the Ship Jenny of Bristol touch'd here in 1793 they where so given to theiving that they would Snatch the hatt off their heads, a knife out of their hands and away over board with it. At that time they did not know the use of Fire arms. That ship has touch'd here twice since,[1] or some others whose crews may not have been so humane: for on one of them taking up a knife which was lying on deck and jumped overboard, I had observed him and got a Pistol, without intention of firinge it near him, he immediately held the Knife up in his hand and swam back with it, at the same time an old man (I believe his Father) held my hand making Signs not to fire, throwing himself down on deck and imitating a Person dying. Hence

---

[1] The *Jenny* had touched twice not since 1793, but since 1791 or early 1792, i.e. first on her homeward run from that voyage and again outward bound in 1793–4. Bishop's '1793' probably should read '1792'.

I fear some ship has taught these children of nature a severe lesson, indeed they did not openly Attempt to Steal any thing, and if they had I could not in my heart have considered it a Crime in them, cut off as they are from the world. Every thing they see in us, is a Rare novelty, and one cannot wonder at their desire to retain some mark as a memorial of having been visited by so strange a People as they must consider us to be. The only things we lost was a Cooks Axe and Saw which through the carelessness of the Cook had been left in their way and they got off with them without being observed by any one

These Young women who came on board, had in general either a Father, Husband or Brother attending them, who for the Sake of the Presents of Handkerchiefs or cloaths the Sailors would give them urged them (some times appearently against their own inclinations) to accompany them below— I have seen a variety of Females on the coast of Africa and amongst the Moors,[1] but never so generally well Formed. Their Limbs 'harmonious swell'd by natures FINEST hand'[2] exibited a Figure equal to the finest paintings of Italy, with a chearful open countenance, long Black hair, sparkling Black Eyes and teeth, that rivals Idea—the Sun has shed his influence o'er their Skins which in the women, who are considerably fairer then the men, is of a Bright orange or indeed fairer—resembling a dark coloured Straw. Some of them where painted a little with a Reddish ocre, over the Forhead. Both men and women seem'd very fond of a little Boy I have under my Care, (Son of my Late Captain—John Learne) who is a fine round face chubby Boy, about 10 years of age.[3] They sollicited me often to let him go on Shore, in vain. At one time they where about stealing him, two men being ready to recieve him in the water and two of the Girls had got him in their arms going to let him down the Side, when the boys

[1] Moors penetrated as far south and west as the coast whither Bishop sailed for Teast.

[2] Quoted from James Thomson, 'Summer' (Bishop's emphasis).

[3] The modern mind gawks at Bishop carrying this passenger whose name, and only his name, appears but briefly throughout the whole story (see below, pp. 189 and 193).

cries call'd our attention and prevented them. Not, if they had got him in the water, they could have made off with him, for our boat would have soon have overtaken them. Upon this defeat one of the Women took him in her arms and gave him her Breast, casting a look of so benign and Gentle a discription that I am well perswaded they would have taken care of him, and that it was not, for the unkind supposition of their being cannibals suggested by some of the Crew, that they wished to have him onshore. In confermation of this Idea I observed they had not a weapon, or a Scar or a spot or Blemish on their Skins: and if they where cannibals they would certainly have wars, which I believe is not the case.[1] I Fancy their food consists of Roots, they have some Fowls and there is Fish round the Islands, they have very fine fishing netts made of Grass, thir fish hook is of Bone

Of their language, our short stay prohibited us from aquiring much knoledge. Pe'hee, signifies Friend—new'ee, Big—nid'ee, little—mow'ee, to ly down, sleep—mo'aee, Fowls—Etta'oea Knife—Ear'ee chief &c

The natives when they swim off, tie up a Bundle of Coopers Rushes in the same form I have seen them in England, which they place under them with the peaked end out of the water. This bears them up so that they have only the toil of making way through the water, which they Seem to do with great ease. These Bundles I believe are only intended to support them along side the Ship, where they Stay sometimes four hours for I observed they often threw them away when going for the Shore.

Adieu! ye happy Race! may the Gentleness of our Polished nations still possess your Breasts, untainted with our Crimes, we go from you to the Close dark savage of America.

---

[1] The Islanders engaged in both war and cannibalism, the latter sometimes the result of 'a simple liking for human flesh that could impel a man to kill for no other reason than his desire for fresh meat' (A. Metraux, *Easter Island* (tr. M. Bullock, London, 1957), p.103). In this light even the wet-nursing of chubby young Learne can appear sinister.

In the following leaf I have attempted to represent these People as they came on board. My Colours are Bad as may be seen in the Figure of the Man.[1] I forbear daubing with them the Woman. The original lives in my mind superiour to any ability I have to represent it. She was the daughter of an Old man, who either from his age or situation seem'd to claim a particular respect from the rest, and was in consequence attended to by me, and I found it highly Gratifying to him, as well as service to us, to appoint him as Trade Man, Giving him Several presents, trifling to us but of infinate value to him.[2] Among the rest I gave him a large Brass Dogs coller which he put about his neck, much delighted. His interest taught him to instruct his daughter to be attentive to me—she danced, sang and made use of every art her confined abilety was capable of to please, nor was it in vain. I gave her a White Shirt, and while putting it on her she stole the Knif out of my Pockett, this I could not prevent tho' I percieved it, but as it was of value to me, I sent one of the People with a trade Knife to give it her in the room, when she pulled it out, and with a laugh gave it up. She staid on board till we where under weigh. I laughing askd her to accompany us to Brittannee, she pointed to her Father and they Both jumped overboard and made for the Shore, without staying for the Presents I had intended for them—if I am not mistaken her name is Te'ree having heard her Father make use of the word several times when speaking to her—

Sunday 8th:
22° 30′ S
111° 29′ W
Variation
4° East

Last night at 8 oclock the ship Gliding along under all Sail with Pleas*ant* winds and weather, the People as usual, had a Bottle of Rum to drink ' SATURDAY NIGHT AT SEA ' when we where alarmed with a Quarrel amongst them, and on myself and officers repairing forward, found Rich*ar*d Evans the armorer, had been fighting with John Black, a seaman, and dureing the contest: Evans struck Black so severe a Blow

[1] The sketches show head and torso of the two figures. They are very weak.

[2] On the effective use of a middle-man depends much of the success of trade with primitive (and not only primitive) peoples everywhere. Bishop was very conscious of this.

with an hammer on the face, as to cut the Cheek quite through, Just below the left eye, in a dreadful manner, besides giving him other slight wounds. This being contrary to Humanity, as well as good Order, Evans was seized up to the Main Rigging, and by my directions, recieved a dozen smart lashes on his back, with a Catt & nine tails, and put in Irons. In the morning Evans expressing is sorrow for what he had done, and declaring before all hands, his intention of Paying John Black one months pay 4£ as a compensation for the wounds he had given him: I was induced to let him out of Confinement to his Duty again: after which all hands as usual attended Prayers in good order—They are both very good men, & these circumstances will happen in the best regulated Famelies

We continue Gliding along under all sail with fair serene weather and a smooth sea, and expect to cross the Equator with the sun: 20th: The late Example of Punnishment, has been productive of very good effect. Their assiduity, and attention to their duty, as been persued with as much ardour as good hummor. Black is in fair way, and already does duty in the day, and all hands appeared in clean good order at Prayers to day. We have continnued to see Birds ever since leaving Easter Island: tho' very remote from any known Land.

Sunday 15th:
10° 5′ S
115° 45′ W
Variation
5° East

This day at 4 oclock in Afternoon we passed the Equator, in the Long*itude* 120th degree West. For these last 2 days we have experienced strong Southerly Currents, Saturday it run nearly S*outhwar*d 1½ miles p*er* Hour, and to day S W*ester*ly 2 miles. I intend trying it tomorrow, if the weather continnues moderate.

Sunday 22d:
00° 14′ S
119° 28′ W
Variation
3° East

We have tried the current this morning and find it now set West by North 2 miles p*er* hour. As I can by no means Account for the Variation and Rapidity of this immense body of water I shall say nothing more on the Subject.[1] Of course

Monday 23d:
00° 29′ N
120° 38′ W
Variation
3° 30′ East

[1] The Humboldt current sweeps up the coast of Peru from south to north before moving west at the Equator, but Bishop had met a prevailing current which sets southward from the Gulf of Panama and which is strongest December–February.

our Reckonings are corrected accordingly, for as yet we make but indifferent Lunar Observations, not having a good time piece or watch in the Ship, for among other damage recieved by the sea striking the Ship off Cape Horn: my watch (which was very correct in keeping Time) was hanging over the head of my bed, and getting wett, it has ceased to go ever Since. We have Seen Several turtle, but have not been able to take one, tho' the boat has been constantly lower'd down ever since we have come near the Equator for that purpose— Yesterday there was a good many birds about us, and to day there are a greater Number. As we are Sailing out of any known tract of former Navigators of course a good look out is keept for Land. This last week all hands have been employed in making a boarding netting to go quite round the Ship seven or eight feet deep. The bottom Rope is to be fastened round the rails and the upper one is haul'd out to the Lower yard Arms, so that it is impossible for any Person to come on board by Force without cutting it: and in the act of doing this, a Bayonet stops that as well as every other operation of their Life. These precautions are highly necessary, some of the Strong tribes having been too Successful in their Attempts—

Sunday 29ᵗʰ
5° 29′ N
124° 07′ W
Variation
4° East

This last week we have made but little Progress owing to light Baffling winds, incident to those latitudes situated between the South East and North East trade winds, with some heavy showers of rain, but less Thunder and lightning than I ever knew so near a vertrical Sun. We have been visited by great numbers of Extrodinary large Sharks, many of them has been taken, and now they serve a Fresh meal for all hands. It is the last resource for Fresh Provisions. We have seen some Turtle, but to our mortification have not been able to take one of them—This Morning we first got a Steady N. East wind and are driving away to the Northward under a Croud of Sail, with fair serene weather. The People all in good health Attended Prayers this morning. There continnue to be great many Birds hov'ring about the Ship, altho' as yet we have seen no other indication of the vicinity of Land.

44

Since Sunday last we have had Strong steady Breezes from the North East, with which we rapidly proceed to the North*ward* and Expect, if the Isles of Los Majos are laid down on the Chart right (for they bear no name in any of our navigation Books) we shall See towards tomorrow evening the Isle of Messa whose situation on the chart is marked in the Lattitude of 18°:48′ N and Longitude 134° 45′ W. We have Seen a vast number of sea Fowl, till within this 2 days and now we seldom see one. This day being Easter Sunday, we keept the feast with our last Fresh Stock, a Duck, indeed we have scarcely had a Fresh dinner since coming round Cape Horn but on Sundays. The Sandwich Isles are to leward of us, but too far out of our way to go for Stock (440 Leagues) however we expect to be on the Coast of America by 30th Instant. My crew are all well Except one, whose illness proceeds from an ill cured venereal complaint. This has been revived by feeding so long on salt diet, I fancy, for the Scurvy seems to bear a great proportion in his disorder. However under his present medicines and food he SHALL soon be well—

April 1795
Sunday 5th:
17° 07′ N
132° 21′ W
Variation
6° 30′ East

We are past the Isles of Los Majos, without seeing one of them: Indeed I am well convinced they do not Exist in the Longitude as laid down in the chart: the Spaniards has spread numerous Islands and Shoals over their charts of the Pacific occean which cannot be found by the navigators from England. I do not pretend to Say these Islands have no Existence: but they are certainly erroneously marked on the charts: and it has never been my Fate to hear, from any one who has visited them, their real Situation & Produce.— However I expect to See the coast of America by 30th: Indeed! it is become necessary we should, for our wood is nearly quite Exausted, and we have not more than 5 weeks water remaining. The Crew are all well—we have been visited by 3 or 4 large sea Fowl, two of which I shott. They are of a dark Grey colour, and have extrodinary long wings, one of them measured 7½ feet from tip to tip. They resemble the Albatrosses in the South Pacific, in form and Bill, but are certainly much larger. When skinned and left hanging up a

Sunday 12th
27° 07′ N
136° 10′ W
Variation
10° 40′ East

day or two, We made our dinner of them: but they eat very strong and fish'y: nevertheless being fresh, we considered them a rarity—we begin to experience a change of climate, but three weeks ago, we where panting beneath a Scorching vertrical sun, now with the Present N.E. winds a warm Jackett is comfortable

Sunday 19th:
33° 37′ N
137° 24′ W
Variation
11° 30′ East

This last week nothing worthy of notice has occurr'd and we have made but little Progress on our way towards America, owing to light baffling winds or strong adverse ones. At Present the wind is North westerly a steady Breeze with which we are Standing to the N. East and still expect to see the Land by the 30th: tomorrow noon will compleat Six months since leaving Lundy Isle. It is a long time to be sailing but I cannot help thinking it a remakable good passage and considering our present Situation, when I look at the tracks of other Ships, the least I find is by an American who was eight months: but Some of them have been ten or twelve. The Crew are all in good health, and Prayers where read to day to a very Orderly, clean and Attentive Ships Company.— Both offices and men give me great Satisfaction—as I have said before. I trust it will continnue—

Sunday 26th:
36° 00′ N
132° 23′ W
Variation
13° East

It is just now moderated after one of the most severe Gales of wind I ever experienced: Friday noon it was quite Calm but half an hour after the Meridian a Fresh Gale Sprung up from the S West with continnued increasing to Six oclock, with which we where driving along at an amazing rate to the N East. We where just taking in the Steeringsails when the wind suddenly veer'd to the W.N.W. and as fast as we could take in Sail, brought us in half an hour under Reeft Courses: and at 8 oclock had increased to that degree that the ship could not bear any canvass but the Goose wing of a Reeft Foresail. At 12 oclock the Sea was tremendous beyond discription, and only to be exceeded by what followed on Saturday morning. The wind having veer'd to NNW, blew with increased violence: the sea following this wind crossing the one that had been raised by the W.N.W. wind occasioned for 3 or 4 hours a most dreadful conflict of this raging element. 'Tis well for us the Ship is the most livly Sea Boat I ever knew or (Except by the interposition of Divine Providence) I think She would hardly have existed now. Tho' severely tossed about we shiped but little water, nor did she strain a nail or a Rope in her. The only Damage we sustained (and which shurely is of consequence) is having had most of the Copper sheathing washed off her Bottom, and one man Recieved a severe contusion on his head by being pitched off his feet by the violence of the Ships motion against the Lee Rail. We are in hopes his skull is not fractured, but he is at present very ill. This Storm has driven us much out of our course *so* that unless we have very favourable winds we shall not see the Land so soon as I expected—In the Late gale I had the misfortune to have my India Pilot[1] (an excellent Book of Charts which cost me ten Guineas) wetted with salt water, by a Sea Bursting in the Cabbin Windows. However it will Serve me for the Present voyage, the Success of which I hope will render this Loss trifling—

The 30th. is passed, and we do not See the Land. This is owing to strong adverse winds from the North*ward* and it is now Blowing Strong from the N. W*est*. We can carry but little Sail to it. We see now and then a Solitary Bird and a few days ago where visited by several young Seals. We have also Seen Some Wales. I expect to see the Land tomorrow or next day if this wind continnues, for we are making a great deal of Easting. I have the Pleasure of saying, the People are are all well. The man hurt by the late storm begins to do Duty again this day. As we are full late on the Coast to make a voyage this Season, I am Endeavouring to reach Deception Bay which lies in the Latitude of 46° 16′ N to Procure Wood, Water and Ballast and not loose any time to get to the North*ward* by trying to trade to the South*ward* of that Place as there are few otter Skins to be procured, and for one day

Sunday 3d May
40° 54′ N
124° 42′ W
Variation
16° East

---

[1] Beaglehole remarks that Mount and Page were very popular purveyors of hydrographical material and that Book III of their *The English Pilot* described Oriental Navigation (Beaglehole in Cook, I, 443 n.).

that we might be able to keep in shore we must beat at Sea Six, if I might be left to Judge from the weather we have experienced since Passing to the Northward of the 30th Degree—and there are no KNOWN Ports where we could put in with safty, till we do reach Deception Bay and the Ship is become very Crank, having lightened her a great deal by the Expenditure of wood Provisions &c.

II

ON THE NORTH-WEST COAST
OF AMERICA

the coast of North-west America.

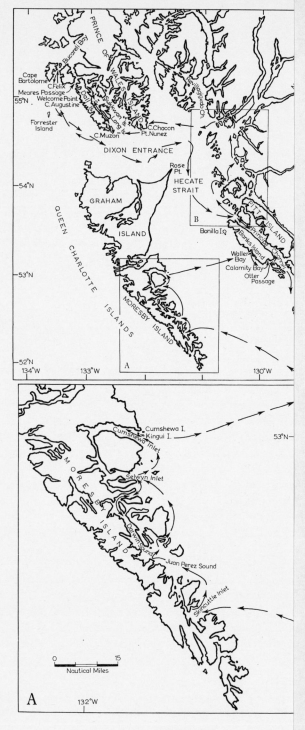

Map IV. Bishop's voyages on

May 1795

This morning at 8 oclock the Man at the Mast head (Lewis Miles) saw the Land, the long look'd for coast of America Extending from NEBN to East, distance about 15 Leagues— it had been blowing since Tuesday noon a Strong Gale from the North*ward* and continnues to blow that we carry but little sail (courses). At 9 the Land was seen Plainly from the Deck. We sounded with 130 fathems but did not get Ground at the Distance of 12 Leagues from the Land. We stood in shore 'till 7 oclock in the Evening when being then about 7 or 8 miles off we could see plainly there was no appearence of an harbour. A Straight coast Extending from S E*ast* to N ½ E*ast* and each extreme terminating in the Horizon to a Point. The land high and hilly and covered with Wood to the sumits of the highest mountains with several spots of Snow on the tops. The wind blowing Excessive hard from the North. We wore the Ship and stood of WNW under courses all night, and Friday morning the land was seen at daylight nearly in the same position it was first discovered. We sounded when we wore the Ship with 100 fathems but did not get ground. The wind still blows from the North: which by us, after this long passage of 29 weeks from Bristol, is severely feelt, especially as the Port where we can refresh and Procure wood, is now 233 miles right in the winds eye. But Fortitude and Patience is the 'Order of the Day', we have had two men ill this few days, but they are recovering. If we hold our Ground Good while this adverse Gale blows it will be as much as we can expect and have only to pray for a favourable change

We continued standing to the West*ward* till Friday evening, when the Gale moderated, and we again Stood in for the Land and at 3 oclock this afternoon was within half a mile of the shore, the Weather fine, breeze steady, and Sea Smooth. We had a fair view of the Coast at least 4 Leagues North and 6 Leagues South of us but find no inlet from the Sea. The Northmost land forms a remarkable Cape being a high Fore-land and which from its Latitude must be the Cape Blanco of the Spaniards.[1] The Land, we observed while so near the shore, has considerable vegetation on it, and Groups of Lofty Pines spread over the sides of the Hills, which are intersected with beautiful vallies, but saw not the least trace of an Human being inhabiting this Solitary shore. The wind still coming from the North we where necessitated again to Stand to Sea

Sunday 10th:
42° 28′ N
124° 15′ W
Variation
19° East

Dureing the Night, the winds where light and variable, and at Daylight the Land was seen at the Distance of six Leagues, nearly in the same Point of view we saw it Yesterday, and at noon after a Calm of 3 hours the wind again sprung up from the North. We stood close in shore 'till seven oclock in the Evening to see if we could discover any harbour or Port of Safty, if only for a few hours, to stop the Ship while we procured a Boatload of wood, but found none, and with the winds light with an appearence of Calm we again stood off to Sea. At this time Cape Blanco Bore North: 6 or 7 miles— S. Westerly of this Cape lye many Rocks and the farthest one appears to be 7 miles from the Shore.[2] Three of these are very remarkable, being much alike in form, and the middle one having a high archway perforated through it, the Cape itself is Steep to the Pitch of it, and together with the Rocks answer well the description of the Cape Lookout of Mears' but we cannot reconcile it to the Latitudes for this lies in 42°: 47′ N and his Cape Lookout is marked in Latt 45°: 30′N.[3]

Monday 11th:
42° 33′ N
125° 4′ W
Variation
19° East

We continnued standing to the Westward with this Adverse North wind 'till six oclock this evening when the wind veering to N.W. we tacked and Stood again in for the Land, carrying a Press of Sail all night, and at daylight (Tuesday morning) the Land was seen in E.N.E. at the distance of 16 or 17

---

[1] The Spaniards' Cape Blanco might well have been Point St George (41° 48′ N., 124° 15′ W.), but Bishop obviously meant the modern Cape Blanco (42° 50′ N., 124° 34′ W.). This and subsequent locational notes draw heavily from H. R. Wagner, *The Cartography of the Northwest Coast of America to the Year 1800* (Berkeley, 1937) and the appropriate *Pilots*.

[2] Blanco Reef.

[3] Bishop then sketches 'a view of Cape Blanco and the Rocks, which we call the thirteen stones'. Meares's Cape Lookout is now Cape Meares, 45° 29′ N., 123° 59′ W.

Leagues—the weather since Friday has been very Pleasant, Moderate Breezes and Smooth Sea, that had the wind been blowing in any other direction we must have made a good progress along the Coast and we are put to the last shifts for firewood—however the Crew are all well, and in good Spirits, tho' all of them look with a degree of anxiety at the Furtile Land of New Albion when we stretch in shore, and cannot help shewing their desire to change the long oceanic Scene—

We stood in Shore, as usual without finding any Harbour[1] and at 7 oclock in the evening stood off for the Night

Tuesday 12th: 43° 06′ N

The greatest part of this day has been calm, so that what ground we gained in the Breeze was lost when it failed owing to a Southwesterly Current and at noon this day we are nearly in the Same situation we where last night, when we tacked— it being calm in the morning the wale Boat was lowerd down and I went to try and shoot some wild fowl, but, altho' many fine Geese and Ducks where Seen, they where too shie to come within shott—a Breeze springing up induced me to return before we had reached the Shore. In our way we fell in with a large Sea otter asleep which on the approach of the Boat instantly disappeared. We have seen several playing in the water: in the Evening the wind died away and it remained Calm all night. In the morning a Breeze again Sprang up off the Land which is now at the Distance of 10 Leagues—

Wednesday 13th: 43° 06′ N

This Morning, after a night of Light winds with intervals of Calm & Rain: we found ourselves off Port Sidenham[2] a Small River which has a Bar at its entrence, and had not a Breeze Sprung up From the South West, We should have attempted getting in here but this Change after so long a

Thursday 14th 43° 31′ N
Friday 15th 43° 40′ N

---

[1] For possible anchorages, see below, p. 110 n.
[2] Almost certainly at the mouth of the Umpqua River, the Light of which is at 43° 40′ N., 124° 12′ W. For discussion see Wagner, 515–16, and T. C. Elliott, 'Journal of Captain Charles Bishop of the "Ruby" in 1795', *Oregon Historical Quarterly*, **29**, 343 n. Both agree that Bishop was now probably at the Umpqua but indicate that he falsely identified the port as Murderers' Harbour, which in fact was probably the present Tillamook Bay, 42 miles south of the Columbia River.

Northerly wind, was too favourable to loose any time in-
dependant of the danger of making free with the Land with
the wind right on and a Fresh Gale. We therefore made all
Sail to the North*ward*—Port Sidenham was first visited by
Captan Grey[1] in the American Sloop Washington in 1788
who got aground and in this situation was attacked by the
Natives who kill'd one of his Crew. He gave it the Name of
Murderers Harbour, But Captain James Baker of Mr. Teasts
Ship the Jenny in his voyage 1791 fell in with this Place and
went in Safe where he continued trading with the Natives
10 or 12 days, but procured few otter skins. The Natives are
discribed as being numerous and of a Savage disposition.
They are very Expert with their Bows & arrows, and made
signs to the Jennys Crew that if they got them onshore, they
would eat them. It is to be observed that a ship cannot come
out but with a leading wind between N E*ast* & S E*ast*—therefore it would be imprudent for a ship in the first part of her
voyage to run the risk of being wind bound, in a Place of no
great trade.—Captain Baker not knowing that it had ever been
visited by any other vessel called it Port Sidenham, in honour
of Mr Sidenham Teast his Spirited commercial owner.

Saturday 16th:
44° 49′ N

We continnued all night under a Press of sail to Stand to the
North*ward* with the wind at West blowing a Fresh Gale.
Passing the Cape Perpetua[2] of Captain Cook, and at 9 oclock
this Morning we where abreast of some Remarkable high
Land, to the East*ward* of which there appear'd an opening:[3]
but it blowing hard from the West*ward* we could not attempt
making free with the Land the Ship being very Crank and a
Considerable Sea Running on the Shore together with Hazy
weather. At noon we where distant from the Land about
5 Leagues when the Latitude was as p*er* Margin. We find
those Places noticed by Captain Cook, answer well the Situation and discription, given in the Account of his voyage.—
At 4 oclock in the Afternoon the wind veerd to the North*ward*

[1] Captain Robert Gray (Grey) for whom see Howay (1941), *passim*.
[2] 44° 19′ N.
[3] Possibly Alsea Bay, a difficult anchorage, about 8·5 miles north of
Cape Perpetua.

when the weather moderated and we stood of till daylight Sunday morning when the ship was tackd and we again stood in, in hopes to find a Port.

At noon this day though the weather was generally Hazy it clear'd away and we Saw the Land Plainly. There appeared to be a Bay or inlet bearing NNE between this and a nother bearing ENE. The Land was high as was also the Land forming the Extremes North and South. At 2 oclock we bore away to explore the Bay in ENE*ast* and at 6 had got within three miles of the shore when to our Mortification we dicerned that the two high lands where joined by a low Sandy Beach. The Land on the North side formed and look'd much like that part of Mount Edgcumbe called Redden Point. The Bay we called False Bay its Latitude will be 45° 10′ N.[1] For the Night we again stood off to sea—Prayers were read to the Crew to day who are all in good health.

Sunday 17th: 45° 06′ N

This morning, after experiencing light Baffling Winds with Foggy weather for these two days past, it clear'd away about 10 oclock and we found ourselves within a few miles of Quicksand Bay,[2] so called by Captain Mears in 1788, who has given it a fair discription in the Book published of his voyages. Nevertheless I believe an Entrence might be effected by small vessells into the Harbour by the South Shore, but it being late in the Evening before we could get in with the appeerence of rough weather from the Sea, precluded us from Exploring the Channel with a Boat: we saw a Smoke where Indians had been but could not percieve any of them, altho' Guns where fired and the Colours displayed to induce Some of them to come off to the Ship we being at one time within ½ mile of the Shore

Wednesday 20th 45° 42′N

---

[1] 'Perhaps the beach between Capes Lookout and Kiwanda' (i.e. about 45° 15–20′ N.), Elliott, *Oregon Historical Quarterly*, **29**, 345 n. Mount Edgcumbe is on the peninsula on the southern side of Plymouth Hoe (England), opposite Plymouth itself; Redding Point is the south-east cape of the peninsula.

[2] Tillamook Bay. There is now an entrance, and if this *was* Gray's 'Murderers' Harbour' it must have been usable then.

Friday 22ᵈ: At daylight Cape Disapointment[1] was seen bearing ENE 7 Leagues and the wind blowing from the South*ward* a Fresh Gale we bore away for Deception Bay[2] and at 7 oclock came on the Bar where we carried a press of sail to get in the Ebb tide setting out at the rate of 5 or six miles an hour. Our soundings where from 12 10 9 8 6 4 3 and over the Bar 2¾ Fathems, a Proatideous rolling sea following the ship. At 8 oclock we gott safe in to the Bay and Anchored within the Bluff at the Dist*ance* of ¼ mile from the Shore

Deception Bay   We continnued here till Friday 5ᵗʰ June, dureing which time we purchased upwards of one hundred good sea otter skins and a variety of others. The ship was ballasted, the hold restowed and compleated with wood and water for three months. Shurely no one can tax us with being Idle when it is considered that all this was done in thirteen days, and more especially as from the few in Number of our crew we where often for nearly the whole day obliged to desist from the work and attend Soley to Guard the Ship having often more than 200 Indians alongside and on the deck and all their Cannoes Plentifully arm'd with Bows & arrows, spears and some Musketts.

As in all probability I shall be better aquainted with these people[3] before we leave the coast of America, I shall forbear, here, to dwell much on the description of them—they where very quiet and peacable but no doubt where ready to Snatch at any advantage that want of caution in us might offer.

On the Evening of the day we arrived, at Sunset a Gun was fired by desire of some of the Natives to inform their brethren up the River of the Arrival of the ship. This had the desired effect, for at daylight the cannoes where seen flocking off

[1] Cape Disappointment Light is at 46° 17′ N., 124° 03′ W.
[2] Baker Bay, on the northern side of the mouth of the Columbia River, eastward of Cape Disappointment. See above, p. xxv. Note that Teast and Bishop, probably following Baker, called the Columbia 'Chinnook' or 'Choonock'.
[3] The Chinook. See below, pp. 113–29.

from every Quarter and brought with them many good skins. We expected of course from the Information we hitherto Saturday 23ᵈ had of these People that with the choice goods that compose our cargo, we should have been Able to Procure them in way of Barter readily and with ease, but our disapointment might be better concieved then Expressed, when after bartering and shewing them a great variety of articles for the whole day, we did not purchase a Single Fur. Tea Kettles, sheet Copper, a variety of fine Cloths and in Short the most valuable Articles of our Cargo where shewn without producing the desired Effect, and in the Evening the whole of them took to their Cannoes and paddled to the Shore, leaving us not more disapointed than surprized. We however learn'd from them that a Captain Moore or Moven had been here and from a variety of circumstances we believe he had wintered in Deception Bay.[1] They also informed us that Captain Adamson had been here in Mr Teasts Ship the Jenny. We could not learn how long since he had left it but the natives seem'd to say he made good trade here

This Morning the natives came off in greater numbers than Sunday 24ᵗʰ yesterday. They had now seen most of the Articles of our Cargo, and began to set their own Price on the Skins: which as may be sopposed from their behaviour yesterday, was not moderate. We where Plegued the whole day to break trade on their own terms, but knowing our Stay here would be at least ten days, we suffered them once more to depart with their skins

This day we broke trade with the Natives and tho' not bought Monday. so cheap as they have been at this place, was more reasonable that we had Expected to have procured them, and having once began we continnued to procure many good Furs daily

---

[1] Moore of the *Phoenix* was in fact probably the first seaman to winter in the Columbia. See F. W. Howay, 'Early followers of Captain Grey', *Washington Historical Quarterly*, **18**, 12. For overall details of shipping on the coast, the basic reference is Howay (1930–4). He indicates that there were twelve traders on the coast in 1794, seven in 1795, and seven in 1796—but even his learning has not established certainty in such estimates.

till Thursday 4ᵗʰ June when the natives very frankly told us they had no more. We purchased dureing this time 111 Skins of the Sea Otter, besides a variety of Fox, Martin, Lynx Catt, Beaver and other Skins—and the ship being compleated with

Friday
5ᵗʰ June:

wood and water we sailed out of the harbour Friday morning with a light breeze from the East*war*d and by 8 oclock where clear over the Bar on which we had only 2¾ fathems with breakers all round us, but we did not come out or Sail in, in the best water owing to the lightness of the Breeze, the Strong Ebb tide setting us over too far the South Shore. While we where in the Harbour, We cleared a small Island and Planted:[1] Peas, Beans, Potatoes and several Peach stones and Sow'd Reddishes, Mustard, Cresses, and Sallery seeds that we are in hopes on our return from the North*war*d we Shall have vegetables for our table: the Natives brought us a Large moose dear and 3 fallow dears which served the whole Crew 9 days. We caught also with the Seine abundance of fish

Sunday 7ᵗʰ
47° 36′ N

Persuing our course to the North*war*d with light variable winds and serene weather, some times near at others distant 2 or 3 Leagues from the Land, this day at noon, we where abreast of Mount Olympus,[2] so called by Captain Mears in 1788. It is an Exceeding high Piece of Land and was covered with Snow halfway down from its sumit. The hills round its base are covered with wood and the brightness of the Snow formed a Striking contrast to the dark woody lands. At 4 oclock We came near the villiges of Queenhithe and Queenuett memorable for their killing and Eating the Crew of a Boat beloning to the Imperial Eagle 1787.[3]

---

[1] The first known garden in the territory which now forms the States of Oregon and Washington. There were two small islands (since eroded) just inside the cape (T. C. Elliott, 'The Journal of the Ship Ruby', *Oregon Historical Quarterly*, **28**, 263 n.).

[2] Now known as the Olympian Range, some fifty miles inland.

[3] Bishop drew his information from Meares, 124–5. Elliott disparaged the story (*ibid.* **28**, 270 n.); he is probably right in doing so, for cannibalism, even as a bond of secret societies, was never a Chinook practice (information from V. E. Garfield, University of Washington). Queen u ett was evidently some minutes north of the modern Quinault, which is on the coast just north of the entrance of the Quinault River, at about 47° 22′ N.; Queen Hythe was on Destruction Island, or on the coast opposite, at about 47° 40′ N.

A Cannoe came off from Queen u ett in which where Six men. They had indeed a much more savage look and Gesture than our Friends in Deception Bay. They had several skins of the sea otter, which we tried to Purchase by shewing them a variety of Articles when suddenly they pushed off and Paddled swiftly to the shore—we are at a loss to account for this Sudden departure as we where cautious not to let but few of our People appear— These people Spoke nearly the same language as those of Deception Bay

We had a Fresh breeze from the South East all night and in the morning it increased to a Gale with thick Rainy weather, and an heavy swell setting in on the Shore. It was our intention to have visited the South Shore of the Straights of John defuca[1] which we where off but this bad weather precluded us from attempting to make free with the Land. At Monday 8th noon the ship was hove too it blowing a Fresh Gale. *I was then* intending to proceed when the weather would permit to Port Effingham and Port Cox,[2] having been driven to the North*w*ard of the Straights of Defuca. But on mature deliberation, it was resolved to Push with this Southe*r*ly Gale to the Charlotte Islands.[3] Our reasons for giving up the Idea of going to Port Effingham &c where we knew a Captain Moore had gone from Deception bay 30 or 40 days before us, and he no doubt took these Ports in his rout. We had seen enough of his goods in deception bay amongst the Natives to be ashured of the goodness and variety of his Cargo as not to leave a doubt of his getting all their Furs, and to loose time, a Fair wind and at this advanced state of the season to get into Ports which have already been visited, where reasons too obvious for our not adopting this Plan of Proceeding. It is to be observed we have been a month on the Coast 25 days of which the winds have been adverse to go to the N West— we therefore Push'd with this Strong Southerly Gale all Tuesday 9th

[1] Juan de Fuca Strait. Map IV illustrates the route hence northward.
[2] Barkley Sound and Clayoquot Sound.
[3] Queen Charlotte Islands.

night Passing Nootka Sound and at noon we saw Woody Point[1] which forms the North Cape of the Sound bearing EbN 4 Leagues

We continnued our rout all night and the next day with *Moderate* breezes, somtimes thick somtimes clear weather, and at noon we Saw the Lancies Isles[2] which are seven in Number and lie nearly in an East and west line with Cape Scott, the farthest one is about 11 Leagues from the Main and lies in the Latt of 51°: 49′ N—the breeze which had increased gradually till midnight blew an excessive hard Gale we could not shew any sail to it and this continnued about 30 hours. The Ship owing to an ugly cross lofty Sea was very Wett and uncomfortable and for the first time began to open the Seams in her upper deck and in several Places

Thursday 11th: In the Evening of this day the Gale abated and we made sail towards Queen Charlotte Islands which we computed to be about 20 Leagues distant—and on Friday morning we saw the Land: it being thick weather we run into the first openin which offered and after beating up the Sound[3] about 4 miles anchored in a Snug and Secure haven formed by Several Small Islands in 15 fathems water, at the distance from the Land of about 200 yards: a Cannoe came up from a village situated on the South Point of the Sound near which we wished to have anchored but could not find any place of securety for the Ship. We purchased several good Skins from them and they promised to return next day for more Clemens as they called our Goods, and bring plenty of Nickies

Sonday 14th: Yesterday we had many cannoes on board and Procured considerable numbers of Furs. These people[4] differ much from

[1] Cape Cook, which at 50° 05′ N., 127° 55′ W. is prominent, but well north of the northern cape of Nootka Sound. Bishop probably saw Maquinna Point, which does fit his description.
[2] Scott Islands, one of the five (by the usual count, but there are several islets) of which is Lanz Island. The westernmost, Triangle Island, is at 50° 52′ N., 129° 05′ W. Cape Scott is at 50° 47′ N., 128° 26′ W.
[3] Bishop was probably in or about Skincuttle Inlet, Moresby Island.
[4] The Haida.

those in deception Bay. They are a stout athletic Race, and
this tribe appears to be Gentle and Easy in their minds and
Actions. But if we where pleased with these Qualifications,
we could not help being disgusted at the Sight of their Women,
who to the constant dirt and Grese, and filth that covers their
Skins, have rendred their faces truly horrible by having the
under lip perforated in which is fixed a Peice of wood of an
oval form about 2½ inches in length, with a Grove round the
Edge to admit the lip to Clasp it close.[1] The upper side of
this Etrodinary decoration is a Concave, and in the middle
are fixed Several Pieces of the Pearl Oyster Shells, and when
they talk or Eatt it comes like a Saucer up to the Point of the
Nose. They are of different Sizes according to the age of the
Person. In the young women it sticks right out, but in the
older Ladies whose lip has been so long on the stretch as to
require a Piece of wood of 9 inches in circumference (I bought
one or two of them of this size) the weight of which cannot
be suspented Horizontally but by Great Exertion of the lip,
and therefore hangs nastily down below the chin and Exposes
their shattered teeth and withered white red Gums. The Men
have nothing of this kind, and I saw several young women
without it, but tho' the men are not thus disfigured they are
Equally disgusting, for these have quantities of flax-coarse
long hair twisted up with Greese and ocre with their own and
forms 8 or 10 large tails hanging down their Backs. Both men
and women kill the Six leg'd Gentry[2] (with which they
Abound) and Eat them. It is extrodinary that altho' many
are among the furs we Purchase from them yet they will not
trouble us—The natives are usually clad in a kind of matt
made of the Bark of the Birch edged with Strips of the Sea
Otter Fur. They have some of them a kind of baskett Hatt
which Ties under the chin. The women wear a Short Petticoat made of leather, and in general display a good deal of
unaffected modesty and delicacy, of either, the men are
totally void—We believe they are not Cannibals. We saw

[1] I.e. a labret, the nature and use of which Bishop described accurately;
see F. Boas '...On the North-Western Tribes of America', *R.B.A.A.S.*
(1889), 808.
[2] I.e. vermin.

several of their burrying places, in Woods near the Shore. These where composed of four Boards about a foot high from the Ground at the feet of the dead and two feet at the head and formed an oblong Square. The bodies where covered with Skins and it appeared that two of three where burried in one House (If I may so call it). Between each was placed a small Box that where Empty, and a large mussel shell was hung over each head. The whole was cover'd with the Rind of the Birch tree and Stones laid on it.[1]

We Procured many large Pearl Oyster Shells and Plenty of fish but did not see the Skin of any land annimal but three or four small Black and Grey foxes. These Sounds abound with Sea otters, and we counted 12 at one time with their heads above water, but they are so hunted by the Natives that they disapear at the least noise—

Sunday morning we got under weigh and where proceeding out of the Sound when 3 strange Cannoes came in from the Southward and brought many Good furs. We therefore anchored again and in the afternoon carried on considerable

Monday 15th trade with them and on Monday Morning we Sailed having bought all their Skins and Proceeded about 6 leagues farther to the northward when we where off a large Sound[2] met by Several large Cannoes who promised us Plenty of Nickies if we would go into their Sound. This we did and anchored in a Snug Sandy bay at sunsett.

Tuesday 16th. No sooner did the day break than many cannoes came along-site full of Men Women and Children and by 6 oclock we had not less than 250 or 300 Indians about the ship. It became necessary to keep a Good lookout and the People where Placed to their Arms and the boarding netting got up, all the Cannoes being Arm'd. They where Extremely Clamerous and Impudent. We however after a great deal of noise pur-chased between 50 and 60 good Skins. The natives seem'd no

---

[1] This was the most usual, but not the sole form of burial among the Haida; see D. Jenness, *The Indians of Canada* (Ottawa, 1958), 335.
[2] Possibly Juan Perez Sound.

ways intimidated by our arms and would but for the boarding netting have all came out of their Cannoes, but we only Suffered the Chiefs in. Seeing so many Women about the Ship one would Suppose nothing hostile was Intended, but it is to be remembered that the Eannas are Kings, and Govern the men throughout these Islands, with a degree of dispotic Athority.[1] What ever they Say the men must do. Nor dare the men Sell a Single fur without first shewing the Goods to Eanna and an American Ship was attacked in one of these Islands,[2] where there was more women in the frey than men, and many of the Natives of both Sexes where killed before they desisted. At Sunset the Natives upon being desired left the ship and took up their abode on the shore abreast of us for the night, and next morning we Purchased the few remaining skins and saild to the North*ward* to look for more trade—

Wednesday 17th 52° 34′ N

We continnued under an Easy sail all night with light Baffling winds when at daylight a Strong Breeze sprung up from N W*est*. We where about 3 Leagues to leeward of a Large Sound into which we attempted to get but after beating 4 hours and not gaining any ground owing to a Strong lee Current we ran in through a Chain of small Islands up an opening three miles and Anchored off a Sandy beach in 15 fatho*m*s where is a Run of Fresh water.[3] The wind contin*uing* to blow adverse we took this opportunity of Painting the sides and blacking the bends which where very Bare, and filling up our Fresh water and Saturday Morning we made sail down the Sound with the wind at

Thursday 18th.

Saturday 20th: 52° 43′ N

[1] The Haida were matrilineal (i.e. traced descent through the mother), but this was not equivalent to matriarchy. Bishop perhaps exaggerated the degree of female authority, although he was not alone in commenting upon it (see Howay (1941), 235).

[2] Most likely Bishop referred either to the attempt on the *Washington* (June, 1791) or to that on the *Hope* (August, 1791); see Howay, *Canadian Historical Review*, 6, 289–92 and *passim*, and below. For the Haida's attitude to the trader see G. M. Dawson, 'Report on the Queen Charlotte Islands', Geological Survey of Canada, *Reports of Explorations and Surveys 1878–9* (Montreal 1880), 160–1.

[3] Bishop might have attempted to enter Selwyn Inlet and then have gone into the northern entrance of Darwin Sound.

S.W. We saw no natives beloning to the Sound, but where visited by some Cannoes from the Northward who brought a few Furs

Having Proceeded to the Northward about 9 or 10 miles and passed several small openings we came to an Island Called by the Natives Lenna Huen on which their Chief Comswa and his tribe have their Habitations during the Summer for Catching and Drying Fish for the Winters Store, and Passing it about two miles Anchored in a Fine Sandy Bay N West of it in 11 fathoms.[1] This Bay is Surrounded by small Woody Islands and Rocky Islets and open only to an E S East wind. The Natives have several Spotts of Land clear'd in which there appear'd to be somthing sow'd and on the Point there are some Hugh Images intended to represent Human Figures. There are several Monuments Erected with Some degree of Order and I understand this is the Place where they Bury their Dead[2]

The ship was no sooner Anchored than we where visited by Cannoes from all Quarters Who brought many good Furs: but the Price as Usual was so high we did not purchase one, and the Natives took them away with seeming unconcern, altho' threatened that we Should Sail before the Morning.—

We had observed that all the Skins we procured since coming among these Islands where newly killed, and by no means equal in general to the winter Furs, but here we learned that a Ship had preceeded us and had gone on to the Northward Sunday 21st: but a little time since. Impressed with this Idea, we Purchased all their Skins Early the next morning and sail'd for the Opposite Shore intending to trade the coast up to the

[1] Bishop presumably had come to Cumshewa Inlet. Lenna Huen was probably Cumshewa Island, possibly Kingui Island. Bishop was not explicit whether he went into the Inlet or farther up the coast; more likely the former, especially as the northern coast has shallow in-shore waters. The harbour remains difficult to identify. The spelling Cumshewa is taken from the geographical features now named after him; whenever present geography gives this lead to past orthography, it is followed.

[2] The images were totem poles. It is most unlikely that Bishop saw any cultivation.

North*w*ard. And here I cannot help observing how Cautious
a Trader should be how he begins trade on his Arrival first
among these Islands, for if he gives any thing Extrodinary
at First, or if there is any thing new and uncommon in his
Cargo, He must consider that the different Tribes communi-
cate with each other, and he must Purchase every Skin at the
Same Price and with the Same Articles, or meet with considerable delay and trouble noise &c[1]

In the after noon we Saw Banks's Island bearing NE 9 or
10 Leagues and dureing the short dark there was in the Sky,
we hove too and then made Sail in for the Land at Daylight.
At 6 oclock a Smoke was Observed ahead for which we stood   Monday 22[d]
and Passed several Rocks and Rocky Islets—when a Cannoe
came off with 5 men in her singing a Song in which there was
a good deal of melody, and Paddled alongside. They made
Signs that there was a good Harbour inside the Small Islands
which we were within a mile of and we Steer'd in for them.
The Entrence is about 500 yards whide and when within
them we anchored in 14 fath*om*s shelly Bottom dist*ant* from
Each Shore 200 yards in a Snug and Secure Haven.[2] We
under stood from the Natives that they had 30 or 40 Skins:
however they only Produced alongside two, that had been
lately taken and was not Cured which we told them, we
would Purchase as soon as the Eannas had Prepared them
for Drying. The Indians now left us and Paddled to the Shore
a little way above us—

In the afternoon the wale Boat was well manned and Arm'd
and I went up the Habour to Explore it and see if there was
any more Indians. Having proceeded about half a mile up we
came to the Wigwam of the Natives who had been on board
which stood within a Point behind which was a snug Bason
for their Cannoes. On our approach the Natives Expressed

[1] Bishop seemingly wrote in retrospect, and in regret of his early
practice.
[2] On the western coast of Banks Island, towards the south. From
Bishop's latitude (see below, p. 67) and description, Waller Bay was
probably the anchorage. He was now among the Tsimshian people.

much fear of us, and with some reason for they had been detected Pilfering several articles while on board. However it was not our intention to offer the least harm to them, but our motives for Landing, was, as well from curiosity, as a desire to see the Quantity of Furs they had. Having Expressed our intention, the Indians very Frankly met us half way, and conducted us up, but not 'till he had considerable conservation with the Women, through the bushes. The first place we came to was the butchery, where lay about 40 dead Seals, newly killed. Ten or 12 more, was on the Fire, Singing the Hair off the Skins. A Woman and a man where Striping the blubber and Skin together, off an other Quantity. Another woman was cutting up and Quartering the Flesh. Many Poles spread from tree to tree about 6 feet over the Fire where Covered with Strips of Blubber, and on bushes all round was hung the Flesh. Blood Gutts and filth formed the comfortable foot Path to the Habitation which lay about 10 yards from the butchery. This was no other than some Poles stretched from tree to tree about 7 feet from the Ground and covered with the Rind of the Birch Tree. A large fire right in the Middle served as well to warm the inhabitants as to dry their Fish, vast quantities of which where hung to the Poles and spread round the Rocks near the Hutt: This Family consisted of an old man, 3 of middle age and two young ones, and they had Each a Wife seemingly Proportioned to their own ages, which with 4 Small Children composed the Group. The Men where all quite naked: nor did they appear to Show the least attention or delicacy towards the Women, but would set down on their Hams before them, or lay wallowing in the filth & Dirt before the fire—the Women where very different, altho' their Skins where covered with dirt yet no small share of unaffected modesty appeared both in their manners and Dress—

We now expressed our desire to see the Sea otter skins when to our mortification we found they had only two newly killed and not dressed. The Indian pointed to the dead seals and made Signs that they were the skins he meant. We should on this information immediately *have* returned to the Ship and sailed but as it was late in the afternoon and the wind foul for getting out upon, the Natives telling us that they would have the Skins dressed ready for Sale by Sun Rise the next morning we resolved to wait—two women instanly set to work on the Skins which where just taken off the otters. They began by first laceing sticks round the Edges of the Skin, after which a square Frame larger than the Skin was formed of Stout Sticks and the Skin spread taught in it. The spreading of the Skin being compleated it was placed against a tree when the women with a mussel shell notched round the edge like a saw skraped it for about two hours frequently wetting it untill the Skin became as thin as Parchment: when all the Blood oil &c being clean off it was laced quite tight to the Frame and Placed over the Fire where we soppose it remained till next morning—when they brought them off and we Purchased them very cheaply together with a good dress of the Sea Otter Skins,—we continnued however to Proceed up the Harbour with the boat, one of the Natives accompanying us, in hopes to see more Indians or to Procure some Wild Fowl: several miles, and Passed through many fine Basons and Coves: but tho' we saw a great deal of Geese and Ducks we only got one, it being the Breeding Season they where wild in the Extreme. We Shott a Wite Bodyed Eagle which was as big as a hen turkey, and a Small Bird of the size of a thrush whose wing and tail Feathers where a fine blue on a Brown Spotted Body: and it had a tuft of Feathers on its head. It was near a Run of Fresh water and we take it be a species of the Kingsfisher—[1]

At 6 oclock this morning we weighed the Anchor and it being Calm the Boats towed the Ship out of the Harbour (which from the Quantities of seals we saw in it we called Seal Harbour) Intending to Proceed round the South End and examine the East shore having had information from the natives of a Tribe whose chiefs name is Shakes, living some-

Tuesday 23ᵈ:

Its Latt:
53° 18′

[1] Probably the osprey, *Pandion haliaëtus*, and the belted kingfisher, *Megaceryl alcyon* (information from I. McT. Cowan, University of British Columbia).

53° 13′ N   where in the Sound, formed by Bank's Island and the Main,
who the Indians said had plenty of Nickees. At noon the
Latt. was as per Margin South End of Bank's Island bearing
ESE 7 miles—

Wednesday   Last evening we came abreast of the South End of the Island
24th:
and saw several openings formed by many small Woody Isles
and Rocky Islets: but as it was nearly calm, we stood off
and on for the Short night and at daylight stood in with a
moderate Breeze from the South*ward* and under an easy
sail with a Boat ahead Sounding to get within the Island.
Having passed through between several Isles and apparently
in a fair way at 9 oclock being in the narrowest Strait,[1]
through which the Ebb tide run very rapid, the Ship
Grounded on a Sunken Rock in the middle of the Channel
and hung on the rock abreast the Fore chains: all the Guns
where immediately run from Forward close aft there being
seven fathems water under her stern, the Long Boat hoisted
out and sent with an hawser to an Island near us: the tide
leaving the Ship fast she had s*l*ewed two feet forward and
her stern Proportionally sunk in the water: owing to the
strength of the tide it was half an hour before we could get
the Hawser fast: when heaving a few minutes she launched
off, appearing not to have recieved the Least damage. The
Sudden transision from Gloomy Prospects to this Joyful
event may be better concieved than Expressed. Had she
remained fast a short time longer (in all Probability) the
vessel would have Been lost: as it blew fresh all the afternoon
and at high water had increased to an hard Gale which blew
right on the rock. With Grateful hearts, we thank God, it is

---

[1] Bishop evidently had survived Calamity Bay to enter Otter Passage
which 'may be navigated by any handy vessel but either local knowledge
or close attention to the chart is necessary as the strong tidal streams,
the large number of islands in the passage, and the lack of aids to navigation may be confusing to a stranger' (*British Columbia Pilot* (Ottawa,
1961), II, 223). In a Protest of 22 April 1796, the relevant passage of which
is not reproduced in the text (see below, p. 159), Bishop told the more
exact truth: 'Just before the Ship Struck, the wind died away almost to a
Calm, and the boat was desired to take hold of a Rope and tow the Ship
through, so that literally She was not sounding at the time though she
had been before.'

not so, for we are now lying in a snug haven, ALL WELL—
to be cast away on this Wretched, Savage coast, would
probably end a Life with misery! indeed.

Having sailed up the Sound about 20 miles to the N West Thursday 25th:
and it coming on thick rainy weather we run in to a Cove on
the NE side and anchored at 6 oclock yesterevening in
15 fathems over a muddy Bottom, and made an Hawser fast
to the shore to steady the Ship.[1] Fearful we might pass in this
thick weather, Smokett Shake's Tribe: we saw many Islands
where Indians have been but not lately:—

In the Morning at 6 oclock not seeing any Natives we got Friday 26th:
under weigh, Sailed along the East Shore with the Ship
sending a Boat well Man'd & arm'd along the opposite, to
look into the Creeks and Inletts for Natives. At Noon we
where nearly abreast the North Point of Bank's Island when
we hove too to wait for the Boat: the Latitude by an In-
diff*eren*t observation was 53°: 36' N[2] with a Large sound full
of small Woody Islands opening to us to N E*ast*. As soon as
the boat was on board we made sail for the North shore of
this Sound,[3] fireing a Gun frequently to alarm any Indians
near of the Arrival of a ship—

At 4 oclock in the afternoon being near the N. W*est* Point of
the Sound we bore up and Passed several small Islands and
Rocky Islets and running in about 2 miles came to a snug
Harbour formed by Islands and land locked all round Except
a small opening in N E*ast* where we anchored in 24 fathems
on the N W*est* side over a muddy Bottom.[4] The Wale Boat
well man'd and Arm'd was dispatched under the charge of
the 1st: officer through the opening in the N E*ast* with orders

---

[1] Bishop was in Principe Channel, between Banks and Pitt Islands.
[2] In fact 53° 38' N.   [3] Beaver Passage.
[4] In speaking of the 'N. W*est* Point of the Sound' Bishop seemingly
implied that he had entered it. But he meant the north-west point *of the
entrance* to the sound, that is, the south-west point of South Spicer Island,
at 53° 44' N. The *Pilot* indicates no likely anchorage in the area. Shakes
Islands, no doubt named after this chief, lie between Dolphin Island and
the southern side of the eastern extremity of Goschen Island.

to return before Dark, and myself went to haul the Seine, but without Success. At 9 oclock the Boat returned when Mr. Williams the Officer gave an acc*ou*nt of his having fell in with a Cannoe full of People after he had rowed three miles up in an East direction. They informed him they belonged to Smokett Shakes and that they had Quan Nuckee's (Plenty of Otter Skins) and would be down alongside tomorrow.

Saturday 27th. A Cannoe was seen this Morning Paddling through the opening, when they landed on the Point and after waiting Some time began to Hoop and hollow. A Boat was dispatched to them with Proper Peace Offerings, and conducted her aboard bringing the Chief in the Boat. He was an Old infirm man and appears to be the third in Power from Shakes, his name Eskinnia. They brought several Skins of the Sea Otter and the Chief himself was dressed in a Cottsack[1] composed of 24 beautiful small Skins, a shinning brown mixed with yellow and tails like Foxes, but with the Skin, much Smaller. He came avowedly to Examine the Ship, her Crew and the Articles of trade, sent by the Great Smokett, (Shakes). After Breakfasting with us he Asked my Name, then throwing off his dress at my Feet Said Tinkasta, (I give it you) Smokett! Our Presents of course where Suitable, the rest of the skins being purchased. They took their departure highly Gratified Promising to bring the Huen Smokett (Great Chief) down to the Ship—

In the Afternoon, Shakes in a large Cannoe Paddled by 20 men with his two Wives, his Son, and Several Other chiefs, Attended by 2 Large cannoes full of Arm'd Men, and the Cannoe which had been with us in the Morning, came Paddling down to the Ship, Singing, with Great Melody, in which every voice but the chief joined, the Song of Peace. Being arrived alongside they lay on their Paddles some time viewing the Hu'en Clue, (GREAT SHIP). Shakes appear'd to be about 40 years of age and was of a respectable Figure, but the

---

[1] A cloak. The word is variously spelled; R. Brown insists that *Kootsik* is the proper form (in *The Adventures of John Jewitt* (London, 1896), 76 n.).

Small Pox with which he was Covered, though it appeared
to be in the latest stages of the disorder, rendered him a
Piteous object: nevertheless after some invitation he came
on board and Giving me a Fraternal Embrace, (a ceremony
I thought Proper not to decline) Presented a dress of those
Skins I have before spoke of—a Laced Hatt and a Silver
hilted sword where Presents suitable in return, and highly
Gratifying to the Chief, who after being regaled with Biscuit
and Butter and a few Glasses of wine retired to his Cannoe,
and the Trade commenced, an old good Humered Blind
(but cunning Man) conducting the whole of it, for all the
Cannoes, who whould sell nothing, till the Goods had been
put into his hands, and his Assent given. It was matter of
astonishment to us, to see how readily he would find a Flaw
in the Iron &c and by feeling the Furs, the Price they ought
to fetch. But it being late in the Evening before we began
trade, it was dark before we got more than 20 Skins when the
Cannoes left us Promising to return next day. In retireing
they Sang a differ*en*t Song than they did before but Equally
agreeable to the ear: the Old Blind Man standing up and
giving the Burthen or Chorous. They where answer'd from
the Ship by nine loud cheers which the Sorrounding hills
re echoed to each other.—

About 10 oclock Shakes with his attendants came on board   Sunday 28th:
but with less state than he did yesterday, and we Purchased
many Prime Skins and dresses and without Clamour, the
Trade being conducted by the Blind man as before to the
Satisfaction of the Indians and ourselves. At noon the
Cannoes went away very peaceably having Sold all their
Furs. In the Afternoon there being no Indians near the ship
a Party consisting of 9 People went to Hunt the Bear or to
kill Deer having seen many tracks of these Annimals near
the Watering Places, but after Traversing the woods o'er a
considerable Space returned without meeting any Success—

These Indians are the same in their Dresses, Manners and
Ornaments with those of Queen Charlotte Islands, but not

having been visited By Ships often they are not so knowing and Clammorous and of Course the skins purchased proportionally cheap. The Women here have the same horrid practice of disfiguring the under Lip with those of the Islands. We have shott several Eagles, who are about the Size of a Turky, and do not Eat disagreeable. Their skins are covered thickly under the outside Feathers with very fine Down, and I found it highly pleased the Chief to give him the skins: it being reckoned an uncommon fineness in their Dress to have it together with their hair, strew'd over with the down of Birds.

July–
Thursday 9th:
This month began, with us, with wett uncomfortable weather and Gales of wind and has continnued with intervals of Moderate Breezes and Calms to this time. We remained trading with Shakes and his People till saturday the 4th. when having increased our Stock of Furs considerably and bought all they had we Sailed for the next Tribe whose chief is Kinnieu. Shakes and his People where not a little Glad when we made them sensible that we should return in 2 months and visit them again and we parted with some degree of Friendship, mutually satisfied with Each other. This Harbour bearing no name in our charts we call Port Teast. Its Latt is 53°: 42′ N Observed in the Entrence. From what we could understand from the Natives no Ship had ever been there before us, but they knew a Captain Ingream who had traded in 1791–2 on this Coast, from Boston.[1] As Shake's dominions are very Extensive and Contain many good Harbours and inlets, the Principal buisness is to look out for one near the residence of the Chief as in that Situation you are shure of Procureing the Furs of the whole Tribe, and in this respect the Season must be consulted, for they shift their Habitations often, we having fell in with several evacuated villiges. In the Spring and Early in the Summer the natives are found near the outside coast for taking the Hallibut and other Ground fish, but when the Salmon go up the Freshes to Spawn they shift to the narrows and falls for Procuring their winters Stock of this delicious food.

[1] Captain Joseph Ingraham of the *Hope*.

On Saturday afternoon being quite Clear of Port Teast with a Fresh Gale from the S E*ast* we where going very rapidly to the N W*est*. At the distance of three miles from the shore we passed close by Several Sunken Rocks seen only in time to Steer the Ship clear of them, and having run about seven leagues we hauld in to the N E*ast* and got within a Chain of Islands,[1] and as thick weather came on fast upon us we anchored off a Sandy beach in 10 fathems water within the Islands dist*ant* from the Shore ¼ mile—this weather continuing we did not get under weigh again till Monday, dureing which time we hauled the Seine and caught some good Fish. We where visited by a cannoe beloning to Shakes who where hunting the otter and had taken two whose Skins we bought.

Monday at 10 oclock we got under weigh with a light breeze but before we had proceeded 4 miles to the N W*est* it came on thick weather with a Calm and having observed several Reefs and Rocks about the Sound we anchored again near a woody Island, and sailed again with Moderate breezes and clearer weather Early Tuesday Morning and having Proceeded about six leagues to the NNW passing several Islands we came over to the North Shore of the Sound[2] and it falling Calm with the flood tide against us the Ship was towed in to a fine Sandy bay where we anchored and the next morning the wale Boat was dispatched to look for natives, having observed many places lately visited by them: at 8 oclock they came onboard bringing a Cannoe with 4 men in her beloning to Smokett Kinnieu's tribe who having recieved some trifling Presents left us to go and inform the Chief of the Arrival of a ship, but just as they where gone from the Ship an otter appear'd near them which they persued a Considerable distance and at last took it. Meeting with this Success and getting into the Spirit of the Chace, they continnued their Game Without side the Ship 'till late in the Afternoon, when

---

[1] Bishop presumably had come round the north-west of Porcher Island into Chatham Sound. Certainly the southern portion of the latter must be 'the Sound' mentioned without introduction in the following paragraph.

[2] Probably the south-west coast of Digby Island or thereabouts; the Kinahan Islands, perhaps named after 'Kinnieu', lie south of Digby Island.

they came along side with two large and three small otters besides several Seals the whole of which was offered for sale, but the skins being raw, we made signs to them to take them up to their women and let them dress them, and bring these together with their other Furs in the morning & we would

Thursday   purchase them all.—But this morning we were not a little mortified to find that they had only landed a little way from the Ship, to dress those Skins which they offered yesterday and which was brought alongside this Morning cured. We should now have Sailed if there had been any wind and the natives seeing this, made signs very fervently not to go, and Paddled away with great haste promising to bring down (Quan Nickees) Plenty of skins. In consequence of this, I have resolved at all Events to lay here till tomorrow morning. Wherever we land we find the tracks of the bear the Wolf and the Deer but are never so successfull as to fall in with our Game altho' we hunt with no small degree of Spirit. We get plenty of Fish with the Seine and now and then shoot Wild Fowl, but no vegetable worth Eating.

Friday 10th   We waited for these People 'till 10 oclock and not seeing them
54° 19′ N   got under weigh with moderate breezes and Serene weather and made all sail to the N West keeping in the middle of a Range of Islands to the S West[1] and the Land to the N East and at noon where opening a Sound which bears the Name of Stephen's Sound in Captain Mears Chart:[2] our Latitude was at noon as per Margin—This day Adam Peterson a good Seaman, was taken ill of a slight feaver. This was the man who hurt himself in the Gale of wind mentioned in Page 35.[3] He had repeatedly complained of a tenderness about the Part in his head where he recieved the blow, but the Surgeon could not discover that any thing was materially affected by it. The few fine days we have are embraced with Pleasure. The People dry their cloaths, and the ship is hung round with the Skins, and we have the satisfaction to find none damaged in those Chests we have pack'd.

[1] From north to south, Rachel Islands, Alexandra Bank, and Lucy Islands.
[2] Chatham Sound north of Brown Passage.
[3] See above, p. 47.

In this Evening it blowing fresh with thick weather coming on we bore up to the North*ward* and run 5 or 6 miles up Stephens Sound and anchored in 30 fathems close to the Rocks to which we fastened an Hawser, and this Morning a Boat well man'd was dispatched to seek for Natives, and at noon she returned when Mr Williams gave an Acco*unt* of seeing many places where Indians had been, Some of them lately. This induced us to Proceed with the Ship up the Sound in hopes of finding out their habitations, and we run up about 10 miles farther when it fell calm and continnued so all night: we could not Procure Soundings with 100 Fathems of Line altho' within 200 fathems of the Shore and the boat had 60 fathems up and down with the Rocks. The amazing high mountains hanging over us, their Tops covered with Snow, and the water gushing down in Perpendicular streams formed a Cold, rude, and unpleasent scene.

In the Morning at daylight we got a Breeze from the N W*est* with fairer weather, and an Arm of the Sound taking that direction we resolved to beat up it, and try to find Anchorage in a Sandy bay about 5 miles from us.[1] Having nearly reached this place a Cannoe was observed close in with the Rocks having three men in her: we called and beckoned to them to Come on board in vain. They appear'd wild and fearful in Extreme. A Boat was dispatched to them, and desirous of giving them confidance to venture on board no Arms where Put into her. As she approached them they keept waving their Paddles not to come near but seeing the boat persist they landed on the rock and arming themselves with Spears Stood ready to recieve them as an enemy. Upon seeing the defenceless state of the boat, they became less fearful and the chief embraced the officer, but no inducement he could offer was sufficient to get them to venture onboard: they made Signs however if we would Anchor in the bay that they would come tomorrow. This we did and moor'd as before with an Hawser to the Shore.

[1] Bishop was in the area between Revillagigedo Channel and Portland Inlet. Wales Passage, on the eastern side of Wales Island, would seem to have been the sound he entered.

Monday 13th: This morning being very fine and we having discover'd that the upper deck was becoming very leaky it was embraced to caulk the deck after which we payed it all over with Tar and Rosin: at noon a large cannoe containg 15 People came off to us and Sold many fine skins and Cloaks of Fur. It is a doubt with us, wither these People had ever seen a vessel before. They wore, by far, the most savage wild appearence I have ever seen. The variety of articles of trade on board the ship made them difficult and fickle in their Barter: the Place they came from was called by them Nash and we believe it is about 10 or 12 miles up a River which appears to be fresh water lying in N E*ast* direction from the Ship.[1] These People did not sell all their Furs but left us in the Evening and went on Shore in the bay where they Slept.

Tuesday 14 Early in the morning these Indians came off and haistily sold their remaining skins, and then left us with a Promise to return the next day with more. Our People where variously Employed: the Carpenters making new topmasts, dureing the rest of this fine day. Peterson is very ill: the Fever has left him but he has been delerious this two days, and we have great apprenshions for his life. We get some fish here, but not in abundance, and Procure among the woods some Pleasant Berries, much like those in England, commonly called uckle berries.[2]

Wednesday 15th: The weather is warm, calm, and pleas*ant*. We saw no natives to day and should have sailed had a Breeze sprung up being desirous of getting on to the North*war*d before the NW Winds set in—

Thursday 16th This morning we where about sailing when a Cannoe came up the Sound and shortly afterwards a nother made its

[1] The Nass River empties into Portland Inlet at Nass Bay; the settlement in question might have been there or nearer the present Nass Villages, five–six miles upstream. Bishop's remarks about physiognomy obviously are subjective, although, in contrast to the southern tribes, the Tsimshian were 'extremely broad in face with small, often concave noses' (C. D. Forde, *Habitat, Economy and Society* (London, 1963), 72).

[2] A huckleberry did grow on the coast, *Vaccinium ovatum* (Brown in Jewitt, 14).

appearence. They came alongside with a great deal of confidence and the Chief presented me with a Curious carved wooden mask. These where indeed a very different people[1] from those who where on board Tuesday, possessing a Gentleness of manners as conspicuously as the others where noted for their wild and Savage appearance. From the chief we learned that they where in a State of Hostility with these People and that they Eat their Captives. This was spoken with such an air of detestation that I believe this chief does not join the Horrid Feasting: altho' the mask he presented is adorned with teeth:[2] Dureing the day we carried on a brisk trade to the mutual satisfaction of BOTH Parties. These People appeared to have seldom seen a Ship by their curiosity and suprize at the various movements Exibited. They however understood the use of Powder and Arms. These articles formed the Principal medium of our Barter.

At 8 oclock not seeing any Indians we sailed with light Friday 17th: breezes from the South*war*d and proceeded up this N W*est* Branch about 4 miles when we came into another Sound lying in a South and North Direction. We where ashured of finding a Passage either into the Great Sound called Bucclughs' or out to Sea, the Ebb tide taking its course through the N W*est* Branch.[3] We had proceeded above two miles to the South*war*d when those People who had been with us last

[1] Bishop was just about at the junction of the territories of the Tsimshian, the Haida, and the Tlingit peoples. If this group came from the Tlingit, it was Bishop's only contact with those people on his way westward to return to the northern Haida.

[2] The question of cannibalism among the British Columbia tribes which so engrossed Bishop is difficult to elucidate. Cannibal rites bound members of one category of the secret societies which existed generally among the tribes: but just when which tribes had such a society is impossible to say (Boas, *R.B.A.A.S.* (1898), 674–8). Moreover, at least among some societies, human flesh was eaten not in delight, but in horror (R. Benedict, *Patterns of Culture* (London, 1949), 128–9) and this might have explained the reactions of Bishop's informant. Undoubtedly the Europeans exaggerated, if they did not invent, evidences of cannibalism; the Indians would seem to have realized this fear, and to have played upon it.

[3] If earlier identifications are correct, Bishop now entered the southern end of Pearse Canal, which runs south-west to north-east. He then sailed south-west between Wales Island and Fillmore Island. Bucclugh's Sound was the expanse between the mainland and the southern end of Prince of Wales Island.

Tuesday over took the ship in two Cannoes laden with Furs. This was too valuable a Prize not to stay for. We therefore Anchored in a Fine Sandy bay on the S E*ast* Shore, and dureing the rest of the day and Saturday we traded with them, when in the evening they took their departure, having sold all the Furs of any Value.

We caught young Salmon with the Seine and Hallibut with the Hook and line. Some of the latter weighed upwards of 100 lbs. We also shott two large Birds of the Size of a Hen turkey. These had a long Neck, legs, and very large Wings. The bill was like a Woodcocks (Proportionably larger) and they had over the top of their heads a covering of red rough Skin without feathers on it: they have a very small Swallow and makes a noise like a Buck in the Rutting Season. These Proved very Excellent eating.

Sunday 19th This morning at 2 oclock, Adam Peterson died regretted by the whole crew. He had been delerious for the Last 6 days, but became Somwhat Sensible a few hours previous to his dissolution. At 11 oclock a Grave having been provided his remains where Put into a Coffin and Carried to its last home with every respect and Ceremony our circumstances aforded. A Bottle with a Piece of written Parchment closed up in it was deposited near it, and after the Grave was filled up, a Fire was made over it to Prevent the Indians discovering the Spott 'whose cold Turf hides our burried Friend'.[1] To dispel the Gloom which such an event naturally raised in the Crew, after the Ship was cleaned, Prayers where read, which produced the desired effect, and in the Evening it being Calm, hauling the Seine and other divertions took Place.

We have found these Sounds by no means so healthy as the Sea Coast. They are very cold, and damp, the Land being very high and covered with snow, which at this season, from the heat of the Sun, being melted, pours down the Rocks with great violence and causes a Continnual fog and mist to

[1] William Collins, 'Ode Occasion'd by the Death of Mr. Thomson 1749' (properly 'the', not 'our').

arrise out of the Woods. Hence Cold Chills and Sore throats
are frequent amongst us.

It was not 'till this morning that we got clear of that Desolate   Saturday 25ᵗʰ:
and intricate sound. We came out through a multitude of   54° 39′ N
small Woody Islands and rocky Islets, (our Passage at the
Entrence not being 150 yards wide*) about 9 miles to the   *its Latt:
N West of the Arm we entered into it.[1] At one of the coves   54° 48′ N
we anchored in, we caught, at one Cast, of the Seine, upwards
of 450 fine Salmon. They where in such Abundance in the
Shallow water near a fall of Fresh, that scarce a Spot of the
Ground could be decerned but we saw no Indians since last
Saturday. We are now Endeavouring to get to Haine's cove
in Port Mears, where are a Socciable Tribe of Indians whose
Chief in 1793 was Kowe.[2]

Sunday morning after a night of Light variable Winds we   Sunday 26ᵗʰ.
found ourselves between Cape Farmer (the S East Extreme of   54° 42′
Bucclughs sound) and Petries Island (the N West Isle of Earl
Chathams Range).[3] There are many rocks and rocky Islets lying
off Cape Farmer, some of them 4 or 5 Leagues out and we
Experienced a diversity of Tides, which cannot be wondered
at when Several Sounds and rivers Empty themselves into this
Extensive opening. Cape Farmer appers to be about 8 Leagues
from Cape Murry (the N West Extreme of this Sound).[4] The
People, all in good health, attended Prayers this Morning.

[1] Presumably Bishop had come into Nakat Bay at Port Tongass, skirting
Tongass reef, the northern extremity of which is at 54° 47′ N., 130° 44′ W.
If so he was much closer to due west than north-west of the entrance to
Wales Passage. But he *was* north-west of the entrance to Portland Inlet, to
which he probably referred. Bishop had passed into modern Alaska.

[2] Port Meares was the area between Long Island and Dall Island. It is
difficult to tell what Bishop and/or William Douglas (whose directions he
now followed) meant by several locations given in the following paragraphs: Haines Cove is the first such problem. Bishop no doubt learned
of Kowe through Baker. J. W. Adamson likewise had followed this lead;
Kowe had slept on his ship and helped him collect many furs (Howay and
Elliott, *Oregon Historical Quarterly*, **30**, 205).

[3] Cape Farmer was one of the northern points of Dundas Island;
Bishop meant by it the westerly one, Arniston Point. Petries Island was
Zayas Island. 'Earl Chatham's Range' is vague, but obviously Dundas
Island was the central constituent, for Bishop if not for Douglas.

[4] Point Nunez or Cape Chacon, probably the former.

Monday 27th
54°

Yesterday in the afternoon it fell light winds and an ugly swell setting in on the Land together with a very thick fogg, rendered our Situation very unpleasant and dangerous. However at Sunset it clear'd away when we saw several Rocks on which the Sea broke with raging violence and which providentially we Passed clear of in the Fogg. Driven by the Current, for there was not sufficient wind to Command the Steerage of the Ship, we continnued plying all night to the West*ward* with Gentle breezes from the South*ward*, and at daylight this morning where close over to the West Shore of this (sea like, Sound).[1] At 9 oclock we heard the Report of a Gun and shortly afterwards heard the noise and Saw the Smoke of a Second: when we observed with a Glass a Cannoe Paddling out from under the High Western Land. The ship was tacked and we Stood towards her when very soon after the Cannoe came alongside. She was Paddled by 3 men, and a Forth with a great Coat and round Hatt on sat in the middle: He came on board with Confidance and taking me by the Hand Said 'How do you do Sir.' 'Cluto (ship) be England King George Cluto.' 'He be Boston Cluto.' When answer'd it was an English ship He expressed great Satisfaction. He now told us his Name, Illtadza, said He was chief, Equal to Kowe 'and lived at the same place at a nother villige'. He also informed us of Capt*ain* Moore's having been there: but had Sailed a good while ago: he also mentioned another Captain. He promised us a Large Quantity of Furs: In the afternoon the breeze Springing up Fresh he ordered the Cannoe away being fearful of having her upset by the voloscity of the Ship through the water! Staying on board himself to accompany us to Port Mears, his place of residence: dureing the Evening and all night it blew Fresh from the S W*est* with Thick Foggy weather: and altho' we keept Plying pretty close in Shore we did not see the Land till Daylight when it Ceas'd up. We found we had gained but little Ground, owing to a South Easterly Current, Port Mears bearing West 4 or 5 Leagues.

[1] I.e. the east shore of Prince of Wales Island.

Illtadza knows Captain Adamson of Mr Teast Ship the Jenny, and Counted 12 moons since he was at Port Mears, where he got 'Quan Nuckees'.[1]

As we where beating accross the Sound to get within Cape Irvin[2] where the Chiefs Kowe and Illtadza has their Summers residence a Cannoe under Sail full of People boarded us. The Chief was the Person mentioned in Mears voyages to the N West America who Exchanged names with Captain Douglas when he first discovered this Large Tribe.[3] Upon his approaching the ship he called out 'Douglas Con nee ha', 'whats' YOUR Name'. Upon being answered he said he had no skins to sell but that he was going to Shakes upon a trading Expidaton. Being presented with a trifling Present he took his departure. Illtadza told us Douglas Con nee ha was chief of the whole district, and that himself and Kowe where the next but where all united under the command of the 'Huen Smokett' Douglas Con nee ha. At six oclock in the Evening we anchored at Port Mears in 26 fathoms water distant from the shore ½ mile Cape Irvin bearing SEbE ¾ mile. Kowe and his Family came off in a Jolly boat which a Captain 'Hubbuts' (Roberts) had given him. The Chief instantly Presented me with 2 Rare Furs of the Sea Otter, and the Jolly Boat. Said Captain 'Moore' and Captain 'Lukwanny' (Lewberry)[4] had been there before us and he had Sold most of his nuckees, but nevertheless, when we had bought all that was at 'Cye Ganny' as he called his Town,[5] he would conduct the Ship to where we should get Plenty of Trade. Kowe sleept on board, and the next morning and dureing the whole day we carried on a Brisk Trade for some of the best Furs we had hitherto seen.

Tuesday 28th:

Wednesday

[1] Adamson was in fact in this region in August–September 1794, and, as noted, did have much success.
[2] Cape Irving, i.e. Cape Muzon.
[3] For an account of how Douglas's name survived, see Dawson, 160. The original contact is described in Meares, 366–7.
[4] These three names in brackets are written above the originals, having been inserted at a later date. Roberts was master of the *Jefferson*, Moore of the *Phoenix*, and Newbury (not 'Lewberry') of the *Despatch*.
[5] Kaigani. The present Kaigani Harbour is on Dall Island almost directly opposite the southern tip of Long Island, that tip itself now being known as Kaigani Point. The village was at the Harbour.

Kowe staid on board and Enforced the trade to our advantage. He also informed us that Comswa (mentioned in Page 46)[1] had Cutt off a Brig beloning to Boston the Captain's name Paulin or 'Pullen' (Berleig)[2] and Killed all the Crew but one man, a Sailor, which he keeps at his house, that as soon as they see a ship apper they Put him in a cave in Irons. Indeed we had Observed when we where there and at the Sound before we came there, that these Indians where uncommonly Bold and Impudent, their large cannoes full of Fire arms and Spears, and where ready no doubt to snatch any advantage over us that might offer. As it was we where on our Guard, but had we known this Event it would of doubled our vigilence and after they had disposed of their Skins should have availed ourselves of the favourable opportunity of seizing this bloody Chief as he staid on board some time after the rest where gone on shore, and keept him 'till they brought off the Poor Sailor, whose heart no doubt must have Sunk within him when we fired Guns as signals for trade.

Thursday 30th

This morning Kowe informed me that had sold all their Furs at Cye Ganny and advised that we should get under weigh and Proceed up the N W*est* Branch of the Sound. This we did with a Strong Breeze from the S E*ast* and in the afternoon having run about 35 miles up we sailed into a Snug Bason Landlocked all round on the S W*est* Shore, and moor'd to the trees on Each side the Cove.[3]

This large tribe, in the summer is divided into distinct Familys the head of Each being a Petty Chief, and reside in seperate Coves and Creeks where they procure their Winter food, all of them at this season being full of Fine Salmon, and for their winter Quarters I am Informed that several Families uniting look out for a Small Island near the Main where they build their houses on Stages formed by the fell'd Trees.[4] This

---

[1] See above, p. 64.
[2] In fact, one supposes, Burley or Burleigh. The ship was the *Resolution*; see below, p. 97.
[3] Bishop had proceeded up the east coast of Dall Island.
[4] This account was essentialy corect: see Forde, 72–4.

is their Strong hold. They here defy the Attack of their Enemies. We have seen many of these Islands which appear like so many Forts, and there are two in the N West branch of this Sound, one beloning to chief Called Clush Keese.

These Indians are the most Sociable Quiet Honest and cleanly we have before seen. Kowe is about 36 years of age, an hansome Robust Figure. His Actions bespeak him an affectionate Husband and Father, and tho' Gentle and Easy with his Friends, not wanting in Spirit to commit the most horrid Acts of revenge upon his Enemies. From his living with me on board and sleeping in the Cabbin, I have learned much of their manners and mode of Life. It appears that when a Chief dies his children do not inherit the fathers office, but his brother and so on till they are all Dead. It then takes its right through the Male Issue of the Eldest sister[1] and on in Succession through the Family, and in Case of default an Election takes Place in another Family. They mostly have but one wife, however the Chiefs tread out of the Common road and Kowe has his Trio. The women seldom have more than four children, scarcely ever five and Six is a Prodigy. When told that the Queen had borne 16 they would hardly credit the assertion,[2] and being informed that myself was one of eleven they surveyed me with great attention repeating the account to each other for some time. There women as well as those at Charlotte Isles and Shakes Sound have the under lip perforated, some few of them Excepted, and there where Generally Ladies of Easy access, but this Tribe both Men and women possess more native modesty than we have hitherto met and are infinately Superiour to the Southern Tribes both in Manners and Persons. They are very numerous, and where much more so before the small Pox which raged here a few years since, and by Kowes Account, swept off two thirds of the People, scarcely any that where affected Survived— They understand the use of Fire Arms well and Kowe himself is reckoned the Best Marksman among them. Of this we

---

[1] Bishop correctly described matrilineal descent.
[2] Charlotte Sophia, wife of George III, in fact had fifteen children.

had a Proof. He shott 2 Large Geese at a single shott: leaving only one Flying. Kowe informed us that as soon as Trade was over and the 'Huen Clews' great Ships where all gone and they had Provided their winters Store of Fish, that the whole tribe united where going to attack Comswa in a fleet of Thirty War Cannoes and requested if we should touch there not to Sell them Powder Musketts and Ball. The Cause of this Expidition is Kowe sometime since sent a Cannoe in which was his brother and one of his Wives on a trading Errant to a tribe near Comswas and while they where there, comswa attacked these People and subdued them. He also seized Kowes cannoe and Killed his Wife Brother and the Crew. Kowe has been at some pains even dureing the time he has been on board of us to rouse the Chiefs to Revenge, and Douglas Con nee ha (the great Smokett) is gone to Shakes as well to trade as to win him over to join them, or to stand nuter. These People Kowe ashured me are not Cannibals, but that they Cut the heads of their Enemies and Scalping them. When cleaned the Sculls are deposited in their great houses as trophies of their Prowess and Victory.

We cannot help wishing him success and victory over Comswa and his Bloody Tribe. Kowe seems confidant of it and Promises to take care of the Poor Sailor if they find him alive, and we even made him ashure us that altho' Comswa should oblige him to fight against Kowe, He should not fall in cool Blood.

Friday 31st: This day we carried on the briskest trade and Procured more good Furs than we have in any one day since being on the Coast. Nor was it attended by that noise and uproar which in general we have found. We where mutually satisfied with each others Exchange and for this we are much indepted to Kowe who easily settled all the trifling disputes which arise on Such an occasion

I am confermed in my opinion that there are no Human beings without an object of religious adoration. I have Seen many and various. These People know nothing of the Immortality of the Soul. They think when they die they cease to be, or to express it in their own words they are 'Illewe', ALL gone. Yet they believe there is a God which is Called by them Eds-wee, that He is very good, lives in a Great House and that he never dies.[1] I remember to have heard one of their Songs of which Eds'wee was the Burthen. This is all we have heard of their Religion and as Kowe is an intelligent Fellow I took some Pains to inform him what our conceptions where in this respect. He seem'd much delighted and heard me with Great Attention when I said that If He was good and died and I was also and died, that we should meet and talk and live in Gods House, but if we where 'Pee shae' bad, God would throw us in fire where we should be 'Illewe'

Yesterday and to day we have continued trading and I believe have pretty well Stripped them of their stock of Furs. Kowe told me this Evening there was no more. In consequence we Prepared to sail, hauled the seine and caught about 300 Fine Salmon. *Sunday 2^d August*

Yesterday we sailed from the Cove and beat down about half way the sound and then Anchored on the West shore for the night and this morning Proceeded again being off the N East Branch.[2] Kowe who continued to accompany us, advised that we should proceed up this arm to a Cove where he said we should get some trade, the only place that had not disposed of their Furs. At 6 in the Evening we run into a snug Bason on the N West shore and moor'd to the trees. Kowes Family *Tuesday 4th:*

---

[1] Dawson affirmed that the Haida believed in both a supreme deity, and a happy after-life for those distinguished in battle. Boas spoke of their worship of the sun and the moon, but distinguished between this and the worship of a god, such as that practised by the Tsimshiam. Moreover, both authorities maintained that the Haida believed in the transmigration of souls from the deceased to the new-born (Dawson, 121–2; Boas, *R.B.A.A.S.* (1888), 241). Bishop was probably right about 'Eds'wee', but perhaps incapable of grasping the concept of transmigration. Alternatively, the Kaigani Haida might not have shared this latter concept with their southern fellows; possibly, again, such versions of Christianity as Bishop propagated helped to develop the notion and also that of an after-life.

[2] By the 'north-east branch' Bishop presumably meant the channel between Sukkwan Island and Prince of Wales Island.

met him here, they it seems had been busily Employed since we left Kye Ganny in preparing the Rinds of the Fir Trees for to cover their Winters Habitation, making Matts &c and had got a very large cannoe loaded with these materials

Sunday 9th: Kowe has been as good as is Word. We have Procured a nother lot of very fine Furs. Hitherto this Chief has never deceived us: he yesterday took his Farewell and was saluted with three Guns, accompanyed with three loud cheers which every person onboard most heartily joined in. Kowe when leaving the ship Embraced me and could hardly refrain from tears. His Friendly Manners awakened very affectionate sensations in the minds of the whole Crew, and even the sailors where Eager to bestow some mark of their regard upon him, while He lamented only that he had nothing to return.

At 3 oclock this morning we weighed with light breezes from the N East and as we where Proceeding out a Cannoe boarded us, and haistily sold 12 Sea Otter skins and then left us. One of her People concealed himself in the Ship and was not discover'd 'till the Cannoes where Gone on shore. Being Questioned with respect to his intent he said he wanted to go and see 'King Georges England'. However as most likely we shall winter to the South*ward* and not leave the coast this season, *and as* there is a Trafic in those Parts which it is our Interest these People should not know, as well as the People to the South*ward* should not be informed of the Exchange we make here, I thought Proper to decline keeping him on board and it appears a Policy of some extant in his Brother Illtadza in sending him, as I had before told Illtadza that we should not leave the Coast this season and when to Expect to see me here again. And in the afternoon it Came on to blow hard from the S East, we run into a snug Bay on the West Shore and Anchored mooring her as usual to the trees.

Tuesday 11th: It blew an heavy Gale all yesterday accompanyed with rain from the S East. A cannoe came into the Cove and we took this Opportunity of sending our volenteer away, who could not be perswaded to go before we made a Promise to ship him next year when homward bound. It moderated in the night and this morning at 4 oclock we sailed with Gentle Breezes and fair Weather from the North*ward*—this day is embraced to dry our lately Purchased Furs and the Ship is hung round with upwards of 300 Excellent Skins.—

It may not be amiss to observe here that the Russians From Kamtschatka are gradually extending their commerce to the South*ward* along the coast of America. The Natives of Port Mears where visited by one of their Hoys this season but they, accustomed to the Liberal and Spirited manners of Brittish Ships, treated them with the utmost contempt and would not sell a single Fur to them. Indeed one of the Indians Frankly said, that if she had not so many men and musketts in her, some of the Tribes would have attacked her.[1]

Wednesday 12th:

We have had fair Weather this last 24 hours with the wind from West*ward* and have now Sea Otter Sound open to us towards which we are standing[2] and at noon Cape Irvin bore EbN dist*ant* 7 Leagues & N W*est* Extreme of Queen Charlotte's Islands SSE 9 Leagues.

Yesterday we had very unpleas*ant* weather heavy rains and Squalls of wind from the S E*ast*. We run along the Shore to the North West 'till 4 oclock in the afternoon when we hauld off to the S W*est* to Procure an offing before night. At 6 it suddenly clear'd up when we found our selves about $1\frac{1}{2}$ miles from a dangerous ledge of Rocks situated between douglas Island and Cape adamson.[3] There being a very heavy swell

Friday 14th:

---

[1] Under Alexander Baranof's direction the Russians were exploring southward with vigour at this time. Such expeditions as this preceded the establishment of a base at Sitka in 1799. The Russians did treat the Indians roughly: see McCracken, *passim*.

[2] It is difficult to determine what either Douglas or Bishop meant, but the latter's words suggest Bucareli Bay, or possibly Meares Passage.

[3] Bishop had sailed through Dixon Entrance into the open sea. Douglas Island was Forrester Island. Again, Douglas's location of Cape Adamson presents a difficulty, but for Bishop it probably meant Cape Felix or Cape Bartolome. The feature took its original name from the master of the *Jenny*, Douglas's erstwhile colleague.

the sea broke over them with dreadful rage. The breeze coming from the Westward enabled us to steer clear of them with a flowing Sheet. This may be reckoned one of those Dangers which a Ship is liable to encounter in a voyage of this Discription. The night was one of the most unpleasant we have met with hitherto. The wind veering in sudden Gusts from one Point to its opposite, an heavy swell from the Westward with a cross chop of a Sea occasioned by these contrary winds rendered our situation very uncomfortable. Nor did daylight at 4 oclock bring with it any alteration of weather for the better: it was so thick and rainy that we could not decern the Land in any Quarter and we had been driven about by currents and Contrary winds that we where not able to judge accuretly the real position of the Ship.

At 8 oclock however it clear'd up and the wind veering to N East brought with it fair weather: and at noon we Entered Sea Otter Sound. It fell Calm about 5 oclock in the Evening, and the boats towed the ship up, but as we could not get to an anchor in safty before it was quite dark, we lay too in the middle of the Sound all night and in the morning towed the ship within an Island on the East Shore and anchored in 26 fathems over a muddy Bottom, mooring her to the Trees with an Hawser

Saturday 15th.

We continnued in this Position 'till Tuesday morning the 18th: without seeing a single Native beloning to this Extensive Sound, altho' every where we landed Fires and Wigwams, some of them lately made, where seen. Sunday night a small Cannoe beloning to Kowes tribe, came up the Sound from Port Mears. They had been hunting the otter and had taken two, the skins of which we purchased. We also bought from them a young bear newly killed, which Served the Ships Company a fresh meal, the Flesh of it Eating like venison. These People told us that the tribes where at this Season of the year, divided into distinct Families and resided in seperate branches of the Sound for procuring their winters stock of Salmon and other Food. Kowe had before told us we should get

Tuesday 18th.

little trade to the Northward and indeed our own observations agreeing in this Particular Induced me here to close our Rout To the Northward for this year, intending to Proceed to Port Teast where our Friend Smokett Shakes Promised to await our return with a Large Quantity of Furs, and thence trace the coast to the Southward touching at Nootka, Port Cox and other places to Deception Bay where I Propose to continnue dureing the severe winter months, and get Early to our Northern Station in the Ensuing year.—At 4 oclock this morning we sailed with moderate Breezes from the N West and at noon the Land bore as follows. Douglas Isle EbS½S 12 miles, Flatt Island with its Rocks SSW 3 miles, S East Extreme of Land EbS½S 6 or 7 Leagues, and distant from the Nearest Land in N East 3 Leagues. Observed the Latt: 55° 00′ N—standing to the S East with Gentle Serene Weather, under all Sail[1]

We Where becalmed two whole days between Sea Otter Sound and Port Mears and this morning a Breeze springing up from S East which being foul to Proceed to Port Teast, we hauled in to Hains Cove and Anchored there. Some natives came on board but brought no skins of any consequence. We however learned that Douglas Con nee ha had returned from his voyage to Shakes. One of his people informed me that they did not get a single Fur from Shakes, that chief reserving them for us. He, also, said, he had a large Quantity. Of course this information made us more anxious to get thither and early the following day we sailed with a favourable Breeze from the Westward. As the night came on it became very foggy. We had sailed on an East course per Compass about 25 miles from Cape Irvin, but had not seen any Part of Queen Charlottes Islands.[2] The course was altered at 8 oclock to ESE sounding every hour. At 11 oclock at night we found

Friday 21st:

Saturday 22d:

---

[1] A baffling location; almost certainly Bishop's pen has slipped somewhere. Perhaps he meant to give 'Forrester Island' at south by east, half south (or east). If so he could have been at about 55° 05′ N., 133° 40′ W. Flatt Island is presumably the ledge of rocks he described earlier, and the south-east extreme of land either Cape Augustine or Welcome Point.

[2] Bishop meant not that he had sailed due east from Cape Muzon, but that he had made this distance east on a south-east course. The subsequent manoeuvres brought him into the north end of Hecate Strait.

ourselves in 25 fathems on an hard sand. The Ships head was Pointed to the North*w*ard and having run about 6 miles the water had deepened gradually to 75 fathems when we bore up again and Sailed ENE 2½ miles then sounded in 30 fathems.—It is to be observed that the only knowledge I have of this coast is collected from the single observations of Captain Douglas in the years 1788–9: and as these, however correct they may be, to sail round cape Rose[1] and its Shoals in fair weather, when the land can be plainly seen, are of little assistance to us now. We had not any sight, as I observed before, of Cape Rose, or any Part of the Islands and could not judge with accuracy our distance from it, having experienced a Rapid various tide. Of course this night was not passed without anxiety—after Sounding in 30 fathems, we hauled off NW and NNW and continnued under an Easy sail 'till daylight when we where in 70 fathems. It was very thick weather, but concluding we must be to the North*w*ard of the Cape by the Soundings, we sailed till 7 oclock ENE when it suddenly clear'd away and a Rocky Islet Surrounded with Breakers was seen a Short distance from the Ship bearing ESE. We Passed close by them. The Island was cover'd with Hughe Sea Ellephents which made a mournful noise as we sailed rapidly Past them. We discovered here that we where close over to the main and of Course clear of Cape Rose and the Shoals. It continnued very foggy to 11 oclock. We however Sailed with Confidance on a S by W course keeping a Good lookout and sounding frequently which we found to be various from 40 to 70 fathems. At noon we obs*erve*d in Latt: of 54°: 00′ N, the Weather having become quite Clear & Pleas*ant* with a Moderate breeze from WNW. A small Rock was seen bearing N E*ast* 10 miles. This was the only land in sight.

Sunday 23ᵈ:

Monday 24ᵗʰ. At 4 oclock in the afternoon Beresfords Isle[2] which lies to the South*w*ard of Banks Island was seen SEbE 6 Leagues

---

[1] Rose Point is the north-east point of Graham Island, the northern of the Queen Charlotte Islands.
[2] George Dixon called one or more of the westward Scott Islands 'Ber(r)esford('s) Island'. Bishop obviously did not mean to designate this. He probably saw Bonilla Island, which stands in about the same relationship to Banks Island as do the Scott Islands to Vancouver Island.

and soon afterwards the Entrence of Port Teast. The Breeze died away to a Perfect Calm till sunset, when it freshened up from WbSW and blew a Fresh Gale all night. We stood off and on till daylight when we made sail and at 8 oclock anchord in Port Teast all Well.

About 8 oclock this morning Shakes attended by 5 Cannoes   Tuesday 25th
came singing their Song of Peace alongside, one Person in his cannoe standing up and bearing a Green Bough. The Chief with is Brothers and children came on board and Embraced me very friendly. He however shewed no inclination to make me any Present as before. They brought only 4 skins which he wished to exchange for the Jolly boat which Kowe had given me but as this appeared to be matter of trade I demanded ten which after some debate and shewing him the use of her Sails he agree'd to bring tomorrow. He having shewed a great desire for an old Brass Blunderbuss which lay in the Cabin Presented me a very fine skin and was gratified with this object in return. It coming to blow hard from South East with rain, at noon He left us followed by the rest of the Natives.

From some observations this day we have great reason to believe these People are cannibals, for on Mr Williams the chief officer asking some of them for Salmon which lay in their Cannoes, saying 'Lux Tekeeda' (good food) they Said 'Come, Esskie Lux Tekeeda' (no, this is good food) taking hold of his hand and making a sign of eating it.[1] Indeed it appears plainly that however Friendly these Savages may be while they see us so well on our guard and arm'd, yet, no doubt, would eagerly seize any advantage over us which we by Accidents or neglect to our Safty, might leave in their Power and this is not a small oppression on the minds of the Crew: who look with anxiety to the day when we shall take our departure from these Barberous coasts. It seems the Small Pox is raging among them and altho' shakes is quite

[1] The Europeans surely were being teased. Their susceptibility and suspicions showed the strain of the business.

recovered, yet his Family are much affected by it and he has burried one of his Wives lately. His Eldest and favourite son is now ill of this terrible desease.

<p style="margin-left:2em;">

Wednesday 26th:

The Chief with his Brothers & People came on board accompanyed by some strange Cannoes about 8 oclock, but brought few furs and them, newly killed. This day these People altered their Friendly disposition towards us, and became so very impudent that it in some measure alarmed us. Shakes having requested me to fire a shotted Great Gun, I thought it a good opportunity to show him how well appointed we where for Defence—and first drawing the shott, we opened the cannister and to his Supprize shewed the Contents which was about 60 Pieces of Broken Cast Iron, nobs of Potts, pieces of Coged mill weels &c and then fireing it—it Scattered in such a manner as to tear 20 Cannoes in Pieces in that Direction. Shakes immediately requested I would give him one to shew the Women. The hint struck us, directly, that the Eannas had been urging them to attack the Ship, more especially as when we where here before we where crouded by them, several wishing to sleep on board, whereas we had seen but one of Shakes Wives since we arrived. We also learned that these People knew of Comswas success, which seems to have opperated not a little, as Comswa is but a little Tribe compared to Shakes. At noon they left us & seemed more Friendly disposed than when they came on board.

The remainder of this day was Employed in examining the Arms and Putting the Ship in the best posture of Defefence we could, being Determined should they attack us to Scatter them, and not to suffer but two out of the Cannoes at once—

Sunday 30th

Since Wednesday last we have had rainy blowing weather which is a reason we believe that Shakes has not visited us as we parted on that day, as I have said before, in a Friendly manner. We have however been visited by a Single scout Cannoe every day, and each day with different People in her. They stayed an hour or two, perhaps, sold a sea otter Skin or two, and always said that the Huen Smokett would be with us the following day, with Plenty of Skins. However if we do not see him tomorrow, I shall sail if the Weather will permit—Prayers where read to the Crew to day who are all in good health.

From the cannoe that has visited us lately, we have learned that Douglas Con nee ha is expected by Shakes and that Hydee, the chief of a Tribe to the South*ward* of this is now at Shake's House.—

This has been a remarkable fine day, and being in hopes of seeing Shakes we did not Attempt Sailing 'till it was too late for the favourable Breezes died away to a Calm. We where visited however by the scout cannoe as usual with Promises that he would come tomorrow,—TOMORROW (Peeshae).—We are at a loss to account for this behaviour of Shakes as in no instance have we afronted him, and must conclude that he ether has no Furs or to a worse Motive, that of detaining us in this manner till Conneehau with is People join him with a view of attempting the Ship— Monday 31st

We waited yesterday till ten oclock but seeing nothing of the Natives, we sailed and proceeded to the S E*ast* between Banks I: and the Main. At 7 in the evening the Weather being Bad with the appearence of a Gale from S E*ast* coming on we run into a Cove on N E*ast* side and Anchored in 10 fathems about $\frac{1}{4}$ mile from the shore and 6 miles Within the N W*est* Cape of the Island.[1] At 4 oclock this morning it come on to blow excessive hard with rain. The Jolly boat which was astern of the Ship brok adrift while we where letting go another Anchor to secure the Ship and in a few minutes was dash'd to Pieces. It blew at 6 oclock in such heavy Gusts that the Ship rode very hard altho we where Sheltered by the Land within $\frac{1}{4}$ mile of the Ship. Some sunken rocks where seen at lowwater within $\frac{1}{2}$ Cable length of our Stern. The ground however where our anchor laid was a good Stiff Clay. Wednesday 2d September

[1] Deadman Inlet would seem the probable location.

At noon it moderated a little, and the wind veer'd to SSE, and before night the Gale had quite abated: when we Prepared to Sail should the wind veer to West*ward*, a wind to which this Cove was open to, otherwise Land locked all round.

Monday 6th:
52° 31′

Owing to Baffling winds and Dirty weather we did not reach the S. E*ast* end of Banks Island, 'till this morning, and where often necessiated to anchor in our Passage through. With a Fresh Gale from N W*est* and Clear weather we are sailing, swiftly towards Nootka Sound, and expect to get there if this fine Breeze continnues tomorrow noon.

Near one of the coves we Anchored in coming through between Banks Island and the main and situated near the middle of the Island is an evacuated villige built on a Round Perpendicular Rock, with a Fighting stage, all round. There was only the shells of two Large Houses, each Capable of containing about 400 natives—This is one of Shakes' Strongholds in War, and errected with no small degree of military skill. From its resemblance to a fort it was Named Fort Charles.[1]

Friday 11th

It was not till noon this day that we arrived in Freindly Cove[2] at the Entrence of Nootka Sound, owing to two Calm days between Woody Point[3] and this Place.—We find the Snow Mercury of Providence in New England[4] here preparing to Sail for Canton. The Spaniards have evacuated this Place and gone to the Straits of John De Fuca where they have a Fort. This took Place by the natives Account two months ago.[5]

The Chief 'Maquinna' (or as Capt*ain* Mears calls Maquilla) came on board to Welcome the Ship, altho' extemely ill of

---

[1] Various big outcrops occur in this area.
[2] An indentation in the north head of the entrance. Bishop now met the Nootka people.
[3] On this occasion anyway, Bishop located Cape Cook properly.
[4] Providence, Rhode Island. Barnett's forename was William.
[5] For British and Spanish proceedings at Nootka, see above, pp. xx–xxiv.

an ague and mutual Presents passed on either Side. He had two Letters one Addressed in English the other in Spanish and seemed lately written to Capt*ain* Broughton of His Britt: Majestys Ship Providence. Hence we conclude that the Spaniards have given up this Place and that Captain Broughton is Expected to settle it. We told the Chief So, and him and his People expressed much Satisfaction on hearing it, and where very Ready to 'Peeshae' the Spaniards, who had killed their Favourite 'Canningham' or as Mears Calls him Callicum and many others.—'Wacush—Wacush Englies'. 'Peeshae—Peeshae Hispannia—cocksuttle Canningham'. 'PEESHAE HISPANNIA.' Freinds Friends the English. Bad Bad the Spaniards. They killed Canningham. BAD THE SPANIARDS.—We find only a Fishing Party beloning to Maquinna resides in the Cove. The Chief with the Principal People are at Malvinna a Place farther up the Sound.

As this American vessel is the only one we have seen Since leaving falklands Islands, it awakened in our minds a civility and good humour which had been sometimes interrupted by the savage disposition of the people we have been dealing with. Captain Barnett the Commander and Mr. Gardin the Supercargo came on board and welcomed our arrival, and partaking of our Common fare gave us the following Particulars of other vessels and themselves on the coast this season.

Captain Moore whom I have mentioned in Page 41[1] arrived in a ship on the coast last summer but not getting a sufficient Quantity of Furs, wintered in Deception Bay, and Sailed early off the coast this season, with a very large cargo of Skins. His Boat was attacked while watering at Comswas and one man killed. Capt*ain* Moore hauled in the ship close to the villige and fired on the Natives, which they returned so smartly that They where glad to get out again—

Captain Lewberry arrived on the coast near Norfolk Sound[2] Latt 57° N in May last from Boston: and trading the Coast

---

[1] See above, p. 57.   [2] Sitka Sound.

along to Port Mears anchored there on the Evening 19th July. His Friend the Chief Illtadza was sitting in the Cabin with him, and Snapping a Pistol which was not known to be loaded, and which Captain Lewberry had given him, it went off, and shott Poor Lewberry Dead. The confusion which such an Event through the ship in may be concieved. Lewberry had just life to say it was an accident, and Prevented any Bloodshed with the Natives, who to a man, expressed a deep concern for his ill Fate, and assisted at his Funneral with their Death Songs and meloncholy orations. The ship staid and made good trade there afterwards—and then Sailed in *Company* with the Mercury to Comswas, to try and Catch that Chief, and redeem the Poor Sailor—this was executed with the desired Success, for on the Evening of their arrival they seized Scatts Eye the Chiefs Brother, his Family, and a son of Comswas. In doing this there was several Lives lost, on the side of the Natives and the Women fought with a degree of Desperation unequalled. Having secured their Prisoners, they demanded the Sailor, whose Existence was denied by every one for a long time, but at last on a Promise that their lifes should be sacred and Seeing the Humanity of their conquorers in dressing their wound &c one of the Women confessed that he was chained to a tree in the Woods. —The man who owned this Poor Fellow as his slave, was Brother to the only Native that was killed in the attack of the vessel, and when a Division took Place of their Booty, He was decreed to him as a Sacrifice to the manes of his Brother—This Native demanded all the accumulated treasures of Sacctseye to redeem him, and which was Paid the next day, when the Sailor was brought on board the Mercury by two Women in a Cannoe.

It will naturally be sopposed that his Joy on this occasion would exceed all bounds. It was not so, he was in fact insensible to it, so worn down by Grief and cruelty, he had scarce strength to assend the side of the ship, and sitting down on the deck on his hams like the Natives, expressed his feelings in a broken manner with a mixture of his own

and the Natives Language and it was not for some days
afterwards that he was enabled to give any Account of his
captivity, &c—

[1]It appeared that the vessel they cutt off and that this man
belonged to, was a Schooner, consort of a Captain Roberts
in a Brig beloning to Boston. She was manned with 11 men
and anchored at Comswas sometime in July '94: the Natives
came off in great numbers and before the Crew could putt
the vessel in a Posture of defence they rushed in and killed
them in an instant. This man was filling Powder into cartridges and before he had time to look on deck the Shout of
the Savages anounced his misfortunes. He hid himself away
in the Hold, while they where removing the Dead Bodies on
Shore, and then they fell to work in riffling the vessel and
which they did effectually By the morning. Amongst the
latest articles that they removed in the Hold they discovered
him in a Cask—Instant death was what he expected and
what, he said, he wished. They however took him on deck
and then a long debate took place wither he should live or
die. At length it was settled as I have before related, and he
was carried on shore in Irons, where he beheld, his headless
companions and the Savage North West American women
Cutting off their privities and throwing them in wantoness
at each other. That night they made him lay on their heads
which they had Scalped, and in the morning Drag the dead
bodies on board the vessel which they set Fire to and she
Sunk at her Anchors, with the ashes of her unfortunate Crew.

To write this Man's misery dureing his Captivity would fill
many Sheets. Suffice it to Say, that in every respect he was
treated as the Slave of THEIR SLAVE. He was stripped Quite
naked and keept so while with them, not even a 'maro'[2]
about his waist, if he twisted one up of rushes, it was torn
from about him with that Savage inhumanity which dis-

---

[1] Howay prints a bowdlerized version of the following two paragraphs,
Canadian Historical Review, **6**, 299–300. He gives the man's name as
Bears.
[2] The Polynesian term for a girdle.

tinguish these People from the race of Human Kind. Whenever a Ship appeared in Sight he was draged into the woods and chained to a tree.—The winter, the only one, he has the Happiness to spend amongst them, was remarkably favourable (but the most serene is Cold). Duering this time, he was forced to Cutt wood, make their fires, and then driven from the Sight of it, outside the Hutt, and not even Allowed to approach the Slaves fire, but to bring them what they wanted.

The Redemption of this Poor fellow, has been not only an act of Humanity, but Policy, he has given an account of their manners, and designs, which could not have been obtained but by his SAD Experience.

Their Wars are frequently begun, even amongst them selves by opportunities of striking the first blow with Advantage, and a stranger coming amongst them unless especially well appointed, is in danger of an attack, as the Jarring Factions always unite on such an occasion, although they Fight often about the Division of their Booty.—The sailor was taken and placed always in the front of the Foremost Cannoe, when going to Battle, & a muskett Put in his hands. He was at several, where the Modes of Attack where various, but the Principal Battle he saw, was last June, when Comswa with 11 Arm'd Cannoes went to fight Skeet e skeetes, a tribe a little to the North*war*d of his. They Arrived, with great Parade, before the villige when a long Palaver Ensued between the contending Parties—at last it was resolved to Draw a Line on the beach, the Passing of which by ether Party Should be considered as the first blow. It was agree'd also that they Should fight with Knives and Spears, and the sailor was not to Join the contest—as musketts where prohibited. A Chief of Skeet e skeetes now Drew the Line in the Sand, and retired to the villige Side where the whole tribe stood Arm'd with a short Knife like a Dagger, and a Spear, with their leather war Dresses on. Comswa with his People landed and drew up in good Order with the Same arms, on the other side the line, keeping the Cannoes in the rear ready for a retreat—The two Parties stood more than an hour within the throw of a Spear, Provoking each other to begin. At length Comswa's Brother crossed the line and threw a spear and was follow'd by the whole with their horrid yells of war. The spears once thrown, where not resumed, but for the Space of 10 minutes they fought hand to hand with Daggers, and 11 soon fell on Comswas side and 8 on the other. Comswa gave way and retired with Precipitation to the Cannoes, leaving Skeet e skeetes master of the field of Battle, together with the killed and 8 wounded Prisinors

A Snow was seen in July by the Mercury Steering to the South*ward* between Q Charlotte Isles and the Main, who did not Speak or Shew Colours—in July. This vessel I think is a Spaniard, as the Natives told us of one having been to the North*ward*[1]—

1 2 0 2 5 0

Capt*ain* Boyd in a Sloop of 80 tons and man'd with 11 men exclusive of 6 Sandwich Islanders, arrived at S*outh* end of Queen Charlottes Islands in June, from Boston. The Natives, Koyer or Cower the Chief,[2] attacked Capt*ain* Boyds vessel, but was defeated with some Slaughter without loosing a man from the Sloop—it is surmised that he winters on the coast, and most likly it will be in Grey's Harbour, or what is Called by Mears, Shoal Water Bay.[3] He was at Nootka about 6 weeks

[1] Howay (1930–4) does not name the 'Spaniard'.
[2] Rendered as Koya, this chief's name distinguishes several geographical features of Moresby Island. His allegedly intended victim was John Boit of the *Union*, author of 'The Journal of a Voyage round the Globe' (Massachusetts Historical Society, Boston). The *Union* had sailed from Newport, Rhode Island, with a crew of twenty-two, 28 August 1794. She kept about the time-table which Bishop and Teast had hypothecated: it is tempting to see in the respective histories of the *Union* and *Ruby* voyages a paradigm of the forethought and shrewdness which won the trade for Yankees over British. Boit's clash with Koya was on 21 June. Fearing an attack, Boit seized three Indian leaders: 'one of them drew his dagger on my 2d Officer, and I immediately despatched him with a bayonet'. The other two he ransomed for furs. The journal makes no reference to suspected aggression at Nootka Sound, but does speak of 'a vast many Canoes' and the *Union* sailed in and out on the same day (18 August). Boit did not winter on the coast, but sailed in September for the Sandwich Islands, thence for Canton (see below, p. 173).
[3] Gray's Harbour (Light at 46° 53′ N., 124° 07′ W.) and Willapa (formerly Shoalwater) Bay (Light at 46° 44′ N., 124° 05′ W.) are not identical.

before we arrived, and not finding any vessel there, sailed with Precipitation, when Wiccannanish a Chief to the Southward of Nootka arrived in Friendly Cove with 6 large Cannoes—

The Mercury sailed from New Providence to Faulklands Islands to kill Seals—and remained there a year, when Mr Gardin arrived in another Ship beloning to the Same Employ, with Instructions to Proceed to N West Coast of America and with a Cargo Suitable to Purchase sea otter Furs. They sailed from Falklands Isles in the Severest time ★ July of the year★ to double Cape Horn and which by a constant Perseverence they had nearly affected in about 3 weeks, the Cape bore South East 60 leagues, when the rudder gave way and broke off in two Pieces. It Providentially happen'd to be calm, the first cecession of a Gale of wind Since leaving the Islands, and enabled them to get with some difficulty and danger the two Pieces in on Deck, where they Clamped them together with Plank and the next morning where ready to ship (Hang)[1] it again—and which they did before a Gale of wind, which came on from the North West Just afterwards, and Drove them round the Cape, when they Steered for Falklands Islands and Putting in there, refitted in the best manner they could, this essential article in navigating a vessel

But has the rudder was still in two Pieces and clamped together by Planks, it was determined not to attempt Getting round Cape Horn in this inclement Season, but to Proceed East about to Bottony Bay[2] where they procured a new one and thence by the Society Isles to N West America where they Arrived in Latt 57° N last May. Amongst the many difficulties this vessel has encountered in her lengthened Passage

---

[1] 'Hang' is in brackets above the original line, being no doubt an afterthought improvement.

[2] Botany Bay was the first intended site for the settlement of New South Wales; Governor Phillip abandoned it after brief inspection and took his fleet to Port Jackson, twelve miles north. But the alliteration struck into popular consciousness, and long remained a term for the settlement. The *Mercury* was at Port Jackson 7 October–7 December 1794.

to this coast the loss of most all the Crew at the Sandwich Islands may be considered the most Severe. These People tired with their voyage, too easily, sunk into the Lap of Pleasures which these Islands hold out to thoughtless Seamen and they all left the ship to live with the Natives Except two officers and two or three men, they had brought from Bottony Bay, transports whose time was expired.[1]

To Proceed to this Savage coast in so weak a state would have been the Sacrifice of the vessel at the first Port they entreed. It was determined to seize some of the Islanders in place of the crew, and which they did confining them below till the Ship was out of sight of their Native Land—and these fine Fellows has been the Guard and Protection of the vessel at all Places while the others have been Employed in the trade.—

We also learned the following Particulars of a Captain Brown who sailed in a Large Ship called the Buttersworth having two smaller vessels in Company, from London in 92.[2] The first season they where on this Coast owing to great

[1] I.e. convicts who had served their sentences.
[2] See R. S. Kuykendall, 'A Northwest Trader at the Hawaiian Islands', *Oregon Historical Quarterly*, **24**, 111–31. William Brown was master of the *Butterworth* and was accompanied by the *Jackal* and the *Prince Lee Boo*. His role in Hawaiian affairs was important; Bishop gives the gist of it, but telescopes and distorts the detail. In traditional Hawaiian politics, chiefs had power in more than one island without necessarily being supreme in any. Brown first wintered at the islands in February 1793 when the great division was between Kamehameha of Hawaii, already advanced in his historic role of creating a united kingdom, and a group of hostile chiefs in the western islands. Brown traded in weapons with both parties, but favoured the latter. In particular he established a compact with Kahekili, who in return granted the mariner nominal title over Oahu and Kauai. During 1793 Kahekili's rule was challenged in Kauai, and when Brown returned late in the year he again assisted that chief. During 1794 Kahekili died and was succeeded by his son Kalanikupule on Oahu and his brother Kaeo on Maui and Kauai. Late in 1794 Kaeo invaded Oahu, just as Brown returned again. Brown aided Kalanikupule, who defeated and killed his rival early in December. After this victory occurred the death of Kendrick, as Bishop relates. Kalanikupule expressed his thanks to Brown by granting him property rights, the precise nature of which are unknown. Similarly obscure is the cause for the rift which soon developed between the two, and which led to the seizure of the *Prince Lee Boo* and the *Jackal*. Brown evidently practised similar tactics on the North-west coast. He had been associated with Baker in the alleged shooting of Indians in Clayoquot Sound (Anderson, 111–12).

opposition they did not procure many Furs. They wintered at the Sandwich Islands and returned Early the Ensuing Spring 93—they had better success this 2ᵈ year and at the close of the Autumn, Capt*ain* Brown dispatched the large Ship to Proceed round Cape Horn and take in a Party of People he had left at Staten Land, with the Seal Skins they where expected to have Procured,—going himself in the Prince Lee boo with the collected Furs of the three Ships to Canton. He returned in the Summer of 94 to the N W*est* coast with refreshments &c to meet his concort the Jackall but as he did not arrive early enough to make a voyage that season, he determined to try the Events of the Pres*ent* year, and for this Purpose he sailed last autumn to the Sanwich Islands to Procure Provisions and Pass the Winter months, both vessels in Company with a Captain Kendrick in a large sloop beloning to Boston—[1]

When Captain Brown wintered at these Islands before coming to Wahoee* an Island, adjacent to Owhyhee,[2] the Principal one of the Group, he found a Strong Factious Party in opposition to the reigning Chief, and having himself recieved Some affront from the King, he landed 18 or 20 of his People and joined the opposing Party, who took the Island and Killed the King. They then Putt on the throne the Son of their former chief, who did Homage to Brown and Subjected himself and Subjects to His Will and Pleasure. The Island itself became Browns and his People took Hogs or any thing they wanted, no one dareing to oppose them.

* Woahoo

These vessels arriving there last Autumn, The King came off and did Homage to Brown as before, and at his return was Saluted by one of the vessels, one of the Guns happened to be shotted, which Pierced the Cabin of the American Sloop and killed Poor Kendrick at his table.[3] His Sloop soon

[1] John Kendrick was master of the *Washington*: see Howay (1941), *passim*. John Howel, Bishop's defrauder, was then aboard, and took command after Kendrick's death.
[2] Oahu and Hawaii respectively.
[3] Kendrick died 12 December 1794 (Howay, (1941), 489).

afterwards Sailed for Canton, and Capt*ain* Brown remained
with the Prince Lee Boo and Jackall, Killing and salting Provisions 'till about Christmas (94). He had such an entire
confidance in the Natives that, the whole of the Crews would
be on shore out of the vessels at a time Except the commanders
their Cooks and Stewards. It happened at one of these times
when the officers and Crews where busy on shore cureing
Salted Provisions that the natives came off, took the vessels
and killed both Captains. Another Party seized the Crews on
shore, put them in confinment and killed all the officers—
after some days had elapsed it was resolved by the Chiefs to
Putt all their Arms and Amunition on board the ships and
sail to Owhyhee to Attempt taking that Island from Tom
homy Haw,[1] and the Crews had the offer of Dying or to
conduct the vessels there. The latter of course was excepted,[2]
and every thing being in readiness they where to sail the
ensuing morning. The People of Woahoo where sacrificing
and regaling themselves after their Fashion before going to
Battle in the night. By what means I do not know, the English
Sailors got all on board the Ships and in Dead of night Cutt
the Cables and steer'd to sea. It is to be hoped they will reach
Canton altho' it is not known that either of them understood
Navigation[3]

These Particulars I have related as they came to me from
Captain Barnett and Mr Gardin the Supercargo of the
Mercury who when she touch'd at Owhyhee in her Passage
to this Coast heard the circumstances from an Englishman
of the name of — Isaac, who was mate of an American
Schooner which Tom Homy Haw cutt off in Winter of 93[4]—
CB—

These Gentlemen also informed us that a Large Ship[5]
sopposed to be English and to belong to London, Putt into

---

[1] Kamehameha.   [2] I.e. accepted.
[3] They did reach Canton (Howay, *idem*).
[4] Presumably Bishop referred to Isaac Davis, of the *Fair American*,
seized by chief Kameeiamoku early in 1790! But Davis was befriended
by Kamehameha immediately afterwards. See Kuykendall (1947), 24–5.
[5] Unidentified.

a sound at South end of Queen Charlottes Islands, some time last winter with the loss of some of her masts: the Natives for several days traded very Peacably with them, but from the Distressful Situation of the ship, several of the Crew Sick, and others on Shore Providing new masts: they took their opportunity and Cutt off the vessel, Killing the whole Crew. The Chiefs Name 'Kouyer'. He had been successful before in an attempt on an American Brig commanded by Captain Metcalfe,[1] which he carried, killing the Crew,—This is that Impudent Chief mentioned by me in Page 45,[2] and whose intent was made known to us by the Sailor redeemed at Comswas tribe to be to attack this Ship in conjunction with Comswas tribe. Our knowing this is enough to Prevent it happening. In our rout next year to the North*war*d I will most ashuredly avail ourselves of the Power we have to Punnish this Bloody villian, if he should dare offer the least insult

Thursday 17th:   We continnued in Friendly cove untill this morning when we Sailed with a Favourable Breeze from the N W*est* and clear weather for Port Cox or as the Natives call it Cloaquoit, the Residence of Wiccannanish. The Mercury also came out after us. That vessel having a Quantity of Copper left, it appears they are bound thither also, altho' from the shortness of their Provisions their stay cannot be long—at noon we passed Breakers Point[3] at Distance of 4 miles, the breakers appear to lay about 1 mile & ½ Westerly of the Point—

Saturday 19th: We have been baffled with light variable winds 'till this morning when a Fresh Gale sprung up from E S E*ast* with the Appearence of a Storm coming on and at noon finding our selves 4 Leagues Direct to leeward of Claoquoit, induced me to bear away again for Nootka to secure that Harbour before it should become thick Weather. The Mercury also bore up & followed us. At 8 oclock we Anchored saftly in

[1] Simon Metcalfe, probably aboard the *Eleanora*, mother-ship of the *Fair American*, when the latter was attacked in the Sandwich Islands.

[2] If Bishop meant 45, the passage is at p. 63 above, but the obvious cross-reference is to p. 99 above.   [3] Estevan Point.

Friendly Cove where we had scarcely moor'd the Ship when an heavy Gale came on and continnued to blow hard all the Night with rainy, thick weather—

The weather has continnued unsettled, a circumstance not to be wondered at at this Particular Season, when the Sun crosses the Equator '& Phoebus in the North declines no more'.[1] We where visited to day by the 2d Brother of Wicannanish, his Name Tatootche Tatticus, 'Thunder & lightning'.[2] A fine bold Warlike Person, and of very agreeable manners, he speaks a little English, and on every Subject we discoursed on, was very ready to undersand, and Expressed himself in such a manner as to be easily understood by us. He invited us to go to Claoquoit as soon as the weather would Permit telling us his Brother had a good many Furs at his Maghettie (House). After dining on board he left us to visit his Friend Maquinna who continnues very ill of an ague, which will probably, soon dismiss him to the shades.—The Spaniards have left a good deal of Plank behind which we have taken the liberty of shipping for the Purpose of making a Roof over the Decks when we get to Deception Bay to Winter—

This morning we sailed with a Fair N West Wind as did also the Mercury, on board of which vessel we put our letters,[3] Mr Gardin the Supercargo having Promised to Forward them by seperate vessels keeping 1 sett himself to his return either to America or Great Brittain—at noon Breakers Point WNW 6 or 7 miles Latt observed 49°: 14′ N. Its latt. will be 49°: 18′, 3 miles to Northward of what Captain Cook laid it down in[4]—

In the Evening Wiccannanish came off in a swift six handed Cannoe, but as it was nearly dark the chief would

---

[1] Unidentified.
[2] Surely a better rendering is 'Tootoocheeticus', as in Howay, 1941. See references there, *passim*, for allegations that he too planned attack.
[3] See below, p. 153.
[4] The Light on the south-west extreme of Estevan Point is at 49° 23′ N., 126° 33′ W. Cook put the position at 49° 15′ N. (Cook & King, II, 264). So again Bishop was more accurate than Cook, but himself not exactly right.

not come on board, but Presenting his Cottsack of two otter Skins, Ricieved in Return a Beautiful Great Coat and a Hatt, when he took his leave on our Promising to go into his Port, where we expect to arrive tomorrow—being only 6 Leagues to Westward of it—

Port Hyhocus N West corner of Bearkleys Sound Monday 28th

Last night we anchored at the Entrence of this Place thinking it to be Port Cox.[1] Nor where we undecieved 'till this Morning when the Chief came out to us, in a Large cannoe attended by many Smaller ones. He said his Name was Hyhocus, & was Subject to Wiccannanish at Cloaquoit about 3 Leagues to Westward of this Place, but that if we would go into his Port, he had 50 skins and would sell them to us, and would also send a Cannoe to Claoquoit to inform Wiccannanish of our situation, who he said would come to his Place with Skins— the wind being unfavourable to go to the residence of that Chief, we weighed our anchor and run into this snug Haven, formed by many small Woody Islands and the West shore of Berklys Sound and anchored in 15 fathems, muddy Ground—

Friday 2^d October

We where under weigh this morning, and Proceeding out of the Port when Wiccannanish came off, and beged we would Anchor again, and trade with him, and that moreover he would visit us again in two days if we would stay: accordingly we anchored in our former situation and in a short time Purchased many good Furs from that Chief. The trade being done Wiccannanish with his two Brothers Partook of some refreshments with us, when we where Suprized by his demanding to know if we would sell the Ship, and for which he offered to Procure a Cago of Furs, obseving that the American Snow would carry us together with the Skins to China, that vessel having gone into a Cove on the East shore

---

[1] Bishop had thought himself in Clayoquot Sound, 49° 06′ N., 125° 53′ W. In fact he was some 10 minutes south probably in an anchorage on the ocean coast of Uclith Peninsula, the northern head of Barkley Sound. At first glance, he could have been anchored off the inner coast of the Peninsula, i.e. in Ucluelet Inlet (in which Hyphocus Island lies), but the manoeuvring necessary to reach thither would surely have told him he was not at Clayoquot Sound.

to clean her Bottom previous to her Sailing off the Coast—
and this was done in so serious a manner that I have not a
doubt but he meant has he said: However he was of course
answered in the Negative: but not without a Promise that
when the ship returned I would bring one out agreeable to
his Wishes.[1] By his Brothers desire I took the dementions by
measuring this Ship: she is to be 54 feet in length and 16 feet
Beam: 6 Carrige Guns & Schooner Rigged with a Gigg
Wale Boat. The agreement was made for a very ample
Quantity of the best Skins—

Hyhocus has sold but two of the Fifty skins he Promised us
and to day frankly acknoledged that he had before dispos'd
of them to his Sovereign, Wiccannanish.[2] Hyhocus is an
agreeable looking young man, but his mind forms a striking
contrast to his Person. That he is a liar we have experienced
as well as some Petty Thefts, committed by him and his
People. He went out to day in a War Cannoe, and fell in with
a Small Fishing cannoe beloning to some of the Poor People,
under the command of a Chief to the North*ward* named
Clahoamas and which Wiccannanish is at War with. They
took these Poor Fellows and after riffling the Cannoe, cutt
off their heads and then Sunk her with the boddies, coming
alongside of us rejoicing at this victory, that is 9 to 2. He had
however the modesty to tell us, that he had only riffled them,
and then let them go. Of this we had our doubts and observing
a matt containing somthing that was Curiously rapped up,
we desired to see the contents but could not Prevail, as they
Pushed off the Cannoe directly. We however learned the
whole affair from one of Wiccannanish's People the next day.

Yesterday Wiccannanish sent a Cannoe to tell us the reason   Monday 5th.
of his not returning immediatley to trade with us again, was
His Friend Maquinna had died and that he had gone to

[1] Wickanninish's desire to obtain a vessel no doubt prompted him to
plan attacks on European visitors. For his designs against the *Columbia*
early in 1792 see Howay (1941), 268–70, 388–90.
[2] 'Sovereign' is an extreme term, yet the Nootka were particularly
conscious of rank (G. M. Sproat, *Scenes and Studies of Savage Life*
(London, 1868), 103).

Nootka on the occasion. This morning the Chief came on board and we bought 36 good Furs.—Wiccannanish is one of the most easy People to deal with I ever knew: He Prides himself in having but one Word in a Barter: he Throws the Skins before you, these are the Furs, I want such an Article: if you object, they are taken back into the Cannoe and not offered again. A Stranger not knowing this Whim of his, would loose many skins—

As soon as the Trade was done Wiccannanish took his leave of us with a Promise if the weather would Permit to visit us again in a few days, a fresh Gale with rain having commenced from the S East. Several of our People where ill to day from Eating the Large Pearl Muscles which line these shores in abundance, Some of them being 9 or 10 Inches long. However with an early application to Emetics they soon recovered.

Saturday 10th: This day we made our third attempt to sail either for Cloaquoit or to the Southward as the winds might suit when clear of this Sound, but it so happened that each time the ship was scarcely underweigh, when the favourable Breezes died away to a Calm and foul Winds followed and it being now near the Change of the Moon, a Period when the S. West moonson in the China Sea and on the Coast of Japan changes to the N East and Generally attended with Bad weather as I am informed on this Coast of America, determined me to remain here in Safty till the Change should be over, and then Proceed to the Southward—on Thursday last we where visited by two Chiefs from the East shore, their Names where Yapasuet & Annathat. They made some trade with us, and Promised to return again in two days—I believe these People are independant of Wiccannanish, but speak the same language and are of the Same Manners and Persons—we Procure some delicious Berries here and catch Plenty of Salmon, but they are not so fine as we have been accustomed to take.

Being now quite at leisure, and concieving that if an accident was to happen to me, that the Person who would succeed me in the Command would in a great measure be unaquainted with my intended Plan of Proceeding, the Events of which I have confidance to think, will Prove it to be the best I could adopt, I thought it a Duty in me to attatch an account of it in writing to the instructions given by Mr Teast,[1] & which is as follows.—

★ ★ ★

'Ship Ruby, at the Port of Hyhocus in Berkleys Sound. Saturday 10th October 1795'

'To Mr. Joseph Williams, or who ever should, in case of my Death succeed me in the command of the Ship.

Sir,
'With a mind arm'd with Fortitude and Resolution to Persue the good of the voyage I have undertaken to Perform, the conduction of which was so liberally intrusted to me By our spirited Employer, I consider it a matter of Duty in me to write while in health, and, far as Human, in Stability, the Plan of my intended future Proceedings, and which you will find to be nearly the Same as Mr Teasts instructions in that Part denominated, "Farther Orders"

'From Mr. Robert Gardin of the Mercury I am informed that Skins do not average more than 20 Dollars at Canton. To Proceed there then with only 1000, the Quantity which we nearly have at this time, would render the voyage unsuccessful, as I am sensible, that we could not arrive on the Coast again, before the end of July, a Season, you are well acquainted with, too late to Procure a 2d Cargo

'I have therefore resolved to Winter on the Coast, and mostly in Deception Bay, where I hope and Expect to get at least 150 Leather War Dresses, I also Propose going to Port Sidenham to Procure that valuable article and if Possible

---

[1] See above, pp. 10–16.

to find that Port said to be in the Latitude of 42° digrees North[1] where no doubt many are to be Purchased

'Should I find the scurvy or any Sickness reduce the Number of our Crew, I shall in the latter end of January, Proceed to the Sandwich Islands, to Procure refreshments, and also intend shipping six Islanders. But I intend not to Anchor amongst them, as I am sensible of the Danger, of not only loosing Perhaps Part of our Crew who whould too easily sink into the lap of Pleasure these Islands hold out to thoughtless Seamen, but too many sad Examples are furnished of the Success with which these People have attacked vessels. Our Stay amongst them of course will be short, and that mostly at Oneehow.[2] 10 days or a fortnight will be the utmost of our continuence there, to Procure Yams, which will be done to the utmost extant, as our Bread will be short and that article will not be served while Yams are in the Ship not even at the Cabin Table...

'I expect to Sail from thence by 1st: March and to steer direct to Douglas Island in Latt 54°. 43′ N[3] and Proceed into Kowes Sound. We shall, most Probably, sell here the whole of our Southern Articles and Perhaps much of the European Goods, in a short time.[4] I Propose afterwards either to Proceed up the W.N.West Branch, into Sea otter Sound, or go through between Douglas Island as we did before, at all events expect to reach Norfolk Sound by 1st May.[5] The Quantity of good skins to be Procured here, I have Good information is VERY CONSIDERABLE, and 'tis here I expect to sell the WHOLE remains of our EUROPEAN Cargo

[1] 'Said to be' presumably by the Americans aboard the *Mercury*, but perhaps by Baker. The possible anchorages between the Umpqua River area and Point St George were (north to south) Coquille River, Port Orford, Hunter Cove, Mack Arch Cove, and Chetco Cove.

[2] Niihau.

[3] The southern tip of Forrester Island is at 54° 45′ N., and islets run south.

[4] 'Southern' goods meant those purchased from Indians in the south.

[5] I.e. Bishop meant to reach wherever Sea Otter Sound was either by sailing between the main and Dall Island, or after sailing into the open sea between Forrester Island and the main.

'As Provisions will by this time become an object of consideration from their Scarscity, it will be of the utmost importence that no time is lost in accomplishing that desireable Event, of leaving these Savage Shores, with a large cargo of Furs, and no remain*in*g Goods—we shall then Proceed with all Possible dispatch to Sandwich Islands, our stay here will be so regulated as to enter the China Seas, after the change of the moon in October, a Period when the S. West moonsoon changes to the N: East and which is Generally attended by Typhoons, Tempests Fatal to many ships. On Entering the China Sea, we shall Proceed direct to Canton. There is nothing to be done any where else, every vessel that has tried, has failed of Success:—

' I have thus Pointed out the Tracts I Propose Persuing and which *you* will find Pasted after Mr Teasts instructions. For although not in the least apprensive of meeting my Fate in these savage climes, Yet we are Human, and you know well that if ever these savages dared to attack, they would not attempt 'till the commander became their victim. Death has many ways of making his sudden approach, by accident many, Poor Lewberry and Kendrick are sad instances, and in an event of this kind, you would, without this, be unaquainted with my intentions so Particularly, although the General outline is Given as I have before observed by Mr Teast in his instructions to which I must always refer you for your General course of Proceeding

' But besides this, I have somthing concerning my Private affairs, which I can impart no where so Proper as here. I believe from my own feelings & conduct, you, as well as every one in the ship, have a Friendship towards me, and would in a case of this kind do me every Justice, boeth with respect to my Character and Property—and the following are my wishes for you to Proceed in that Respect —

' By a Will left in England I have apointed my Affectionate Brother William Bishop of Basingstoke my sole Excutor, and

III

he would expect an account of the Sales of that Part of the Cargo Procured by me and which I must beg of you to keep in Such manner as you may think Proper, to prevent doubts as to what might be my due at the return of the Ship to Bristol. And this is Principally what I have to say with respect to my self, for as to what I have on board the ship, I give the whole away, in following Manner. My Quard*ran*t I give for your use 'till the Ship returns to England when you will deliver it to Will*iam* Raggett. My Gun, Trunk, and such of my linnin & Cloths as you choose to accept I give to you, my Watch to Mr Hunt, My Books to the Doctor,* this *Journal* excepted, which I beg may be Sealed up and delivered to my Brother William. My Log is Mr Teasts. Give Miles 1 Guinea and 1 Pair Boots. Raggett is to have my Blue Great Coat, the other keep yourself as the TOKEN OF A WARM FRIEND. The rest dispose of to those who most need cloths. Remembring my Bags, those Few curiosities I have Procured, after Mr Teast has taken his choice, I beg may be delivered to my Brother: also the Gold Ring in my Trunk—

'But trusting In the Providence of Almighty God, that this will be rendered of none effect, by the whole of us returning in health, to the happy land we sailed from, I subscribe myself your Sincere Friend

　　　　　　　　　　　　Char*le*s Bishop
(Copy) CB

*Except Charts and Books of Navigation, which I certainly leave to the use of the Person who may command. CB.'

★　★　★

Wednesday 14th:

This Moon has changed without any alteration as yet of the Weather, and this morning at daylight we sailed with Gentle Breezes from N E*ast* intending to Proceed direct to Deception Bay, where we intend Passing the Severe Winter months.

In no climate have I found more fine Weather in the Autumn, than this season on the Coast of America. We have not had a Serious Gale of Wind since 2^d of Sep*tember* and rain only 6 days in a Period of 42. Indeed we have found it by far the Pleasentest time, we have been on the coast, Warm, Geneial & Clear, and but for the vague and unfriendly discriptions given of the Autumnal Equinox by others, our minds would have enjoyed it in a Greater degree—for the least alteration was the forboding Storm amongst us, and of Course rendered our minds less capable of enjoying the Present fair Weather—

Without any thing material happening we sailed in over the Bar of this harbour last night at Sunset, but the wind blowing fresh out and with the Ebb tide we where obliged to anchor just within the Bar in 5½ fathems: the Ebb by our Log running 3 miles & ½ per hour. At 2 oclock in the morning the wind veer'd to S West with which we weighed and run safe in and at 4 Anchor'd within the Bluff called by Captain mears Cape disapointment, from his sopposing the Harbour to be inaccessible to ships, the breakers appearing outside the Bar to Extend from Shore to Shore, but there is a very good Channel, which at ¾ flood has not less than 4 fathems water, and soon deepens to 5-6-7-9 & 10 fathems close to the Bluff. It is to be observed in coming in you give the North Sand head about ¾ miles Birth without the outmost Breaker and then you have 4 fathems which soon deepens to 5, then haul in right for the Bluff, keeping well over to the North Breakers. If the wind is Northerly or Westerly, the South Sand being much shoaler give the Bluff a Quarter of miles Birth, there is no danger. But go not to the Eastward of ¾ mile from it, for there is a Shoal almost dry at Low water Spring tides lying nearly North and South, along by the Bluff and the Bay.

Deception Bay Sunday 18th.

The ship was scarcly anchored in Safty when it came on to blow strong from the Southward with thick Foggy weather. Of course we where not a little happy that we where So comfortably situated to avoid it. At daylight two Natives where Seen on Shore who hailed for us to send a Boat but as we where so busily Employed in mooring the ship—getting the Guns out of the Hold &c that we could not attend to them and after waiting a little time then went away to the Northward:—

Sunday 25th: For the most Part of this last Week the wind has been blowing Fresh from the East North East, with a Clear hard Sky, which has given us a favourable opportunity of unbending our Sails dry, and unrigging the Ship to Examine the State of our Cordage and render it fitt for the Ensuing Season—Since Wednesday we have been constantly visited by Natives who daily resort hither with Articles of Trade amongst which they bring Quantities of Excellent Cranberries and Dried Salmon—we learn however that Taucum who resided up Chinnook River when we where here before, is gone with his tribe a good way to the Northward up Woolquet River.[1] This Change took Place in Consequence of the Salmon not going into Chinnook River this year, Probably from the ravage there was made amongst them the last at that Place.

There are meriads of Large Pelicans fishing in the Stream, many of which we shoot, and they Prove very good Eating. They are exceeding Fatt, we Procured from one only, three half Pints of clear clean Greese when rendered down. They have that monsterous Bag attatched to the beak and Neck, the Same as the Affrican Pelican.[2] But I think these are larger, being full as big as a Swan, the Beak from 17 to 19 Inches long and their wings, when Extended, Spread from eight to nine feet. One of these Bags, when Stuffed, contained 6 Quarts of Saw Dust and Sand. They come down the Rivers in Swarms, fish for two or three days and then return for nearly that time, when I soppose their Stock being Exausted they Return again to the Sea in Succession. We shoot a variety of Ducks Teal & Snipes in a marsh[3] not

[1] Wallacut River. This and several following notes draw heavily from Elliott, *Oregon Historical Quarterly*, **28**, 258–80.
[2] The North American pelican is *Pelecanus erthrorhynchus*, which, as Bishop said, is very similar to *P. onocratulus*, which he would have seen in Africa.
[3] Behind Mackenzie Head, on the ocean side of Cape Disappointment.

far from the Ship, but there is another Marsh about 3 miles
to the North*war*d of us Situated between the Mouths of
Woolquet or James R: and a Small River to East*war*d called
by the Natives Ellemechs,[1] that is covered with Wild Geese

Upon the full of the moon last Tuesday the tides rose to
an amazing heigth, and floated trees that appeared to have
been half Berried for some years in the Sands. It was followed
by very tempesteous weather and a Continnual rain from the
South*war*d which has continnued without intermission untill
this Morning that it is *now* moderate and fair with light
breezes from the North East. The ship from her being too
far out was severely tossed by the late Weather and the
Cannoes where not able to come off to trade with us altho'
a Cables length within us it was quite smooth. If the weather
is favourable tomorrow we Purpose Shifting farther in.
Several Cannoes came in this afternoon and we have a
Prospect of Good trade. Prayers where read, as usual, in the
morning to the Crew who are all in Pretty good health, and
after Dinner the Wale Boat well manned was sent up to the
great Marsh to kill Geese. They found them in the greatest
abundance, but rather shie and owing to their being but
Poor Marksmen, they Procured but few.

November
Sunday 1st:

The Weather being favourable, the Ship was unmoored and
warped farther in, and then moor'd again with three Anchors,
securely landlocked all but two Points of the Compass, from
EbS to SEbE, the Bluff of Cape Disapointment being in the
Latter Possition at the Distance of one Cables length and the
North Point of Chinnook River in the Former,[2] at the Distance
of 3 miles—and Distant from the beach about 1½ Cables
length, in 3¼ fathems at Low Water.

Monday 2d:

The month of November is Passed, we have not Experienced worse weather than is known in England at this Period.
From the 1st: to the 4th day, we had moderate Breezes &

December
Tuesday 1st:

[1] Chinook River.
[2] The site of Fort Columbia, suggests Elliott. This is seven miles east
of Cape Disappointment.

Pleas*a*nt serene W*eathe*r with the winds in N E*ast* Quarter. From the 4ᵗʰ: to the 14ᵗʰ: we had almost a constant Succession of Gales of Wind and rain, winds Prevailing in S. E*ast* Quarter. The two following days where fair, the winds being in the North, and thus we have had it since. When the wind was to the North*war*d of East it was clear and frosty. When it veer'd to South*war*d rain and Gales of wind succeeded till it had blown round to South West, when Calms and fair for a Day or two was the consequence. Yesterday was the first Day we had the wind in N W*es*t since the day we came here but last night it veered to NE and now blows a Strong Gale with Dry frosty Weather. We have had hail but no snow, and have seen snow only once on the Tops of the High mountains over Chinnook River.

On the 10ᵗʰ: we where visited by Taucum the chief of the Chinnook Tribe, with several inferieor chiefs. We have hitherto been successful in trading with the Natives and which has been conducted with the greatest Harmony. Their Former disposition to theiving is much abated. We have lost, nothing, but when any of the inferiour people contrived to perloin a Knife or any article, upon aquainting the chiefs we generally have had it restored the next day. One of the Rubys People stole an Arrow, and upon its being Discovered, he was tied up and got a severe Flogging, this and several other circumstances has given these people great confidance in us. A trifling Present now and then gratifies their Desires, and which is generally returned by a Present of Fish or Cranberries, nor do they withhold their Daughters, some of whom are well Featured young Women.

Shelathwell, chief next to Taucum, has a Child by one of his Women Slaves, which he ascribes to Mr Williams, the 1ˢᵗ: officer, who was here four years ago in Mr Teasts ship the Jenny. We have not been able hitherto to Prevail upon him to bring it onboard, Perhaps fearful that the Father would claim his right to have it.—I have ventured from the Ship several times up to the Marsh to get Wild Geese and always with Success. We have Scarcely for the last month Eat salt Provisions once in the Cabin, and the People has had three fresh Dinners in a Week, with the addition of Cranberrie Puddings on Sundays. The Natives never interfere with our Boats or People on shore, and when they know I am out of the Ship, but few of them go on board, Perhaps fearful of causing an alarm.

But tho' I write thus of these People now, I am sensible had I acted so when we where here before, they would have eagerly snatched the advantage which the absence of half the crew gives them. The Buisness is I was then a Stranger, and a Stranger with them is always accounted an Enemy, till known by time or a 2ᵈ visit, in fact 'till they have confidance in him

The chiefs tell me of three Masters of vessels that they are at war With, if ever they come there again. These, for we only hear a lame account from them, as to the cause, was Induced to fire on the Natives no doubt in their Defence of Lives & Ship, for if one falls the other inevitably follows. Several of the Chinnook people where wounded but they say none where killed. In short you have to expect in these People all the Wiley guile ascribed to the Savage race, as a Stranger or an Enemy, and a Generous hospitality in their Friendship and confidance

We have compleated a Roof over the Decks which enables us to overhaul the Rigging &c always in the Dry, besides the comfort it gives the People in their Watches. Nevertheless we are making every thing ready to Proceed to sea should any disturbance take Place, a Circumstance we are careful in guarding against. We have finished the Rigging, and cutt our Sea Stock of Fire wood, and shall fill our water up when the weather Permits Boats to go on that Service, as I nitend to be ready to sail 20ᵗʰ January and Expect to be clear of this coast by the last day of that month & steering for the Sanwich Islands, our Bread begining to turn out but Indifferant and a Gradual dimunition in Quantity. The People are all in tolerable good health, one excepted whose emmaciated situation gives me some alarm, that I shall not have the Pleasure of returning him to his Native country.

Shelathwell and Comcomally[1] the two chiefs next to Taucum have come and fixed their residence near the Ship. They are both very good Friends to us, but the latter who is a little one Eyed man has endeared him Self to every one on board. He often sleeps in my Cabin and gives me many Proofs of his disinterested kindness. I have had a Jackett and Trousers fitted for him, and this day he first Putt them on to his great delight. They are going on a trading Expidition tomorrow for 10 days and Promise to Bring good trade. It seems to me that they are not on the best terms with Taucum as they never visit us when that Chief is here. I believe the cause arises from Shelathwell recieving an afront from one of Taucums People and the Latter will not avenge it by cutting off the offending head. Taucum however suffered him to be teid up While Shelathwell fired 5 arrows at him, all of which took place but niether proved Mortal.—

Monday 7th: Owing to a Constant Gale of wind and continnual rain, it was not till yesterday that Comcomally & Shelathwell took their departure on the Expidition before alluded to. They where in a Single cannoe Paddled with 10 men, each arm'd with a muskett. Comcomally had one of his Wives and a Child, and we dressed him in his Jackett and trowsers and other appurtenances of European cloathing. Their mode of trade is somwhat curious, and afforded us an hearty laugh has he more curiously discribed it.[2] They go up the River Chinnook two or three hundred miles and come to Strange villages, where they land and offer trade with some trifling

[1] Concomly, as the name was usually spelled, appears to have been or to have shortly afterwards become the dominant figure, and certainly looms largest in the literature through to his death in 1831 (V. F. Ray, 'Lower Chinook Ethnographic Notes', *University of Washington Publications in Anthropology*, 7, 58).

[2] 'A thorough-going occupation with commerce dominated Chinook life', *ibid*. 99. The Europeans' advent strengthened, but did not create, this situation.

Pieces of Copper or Iron. The Strangers naturally demand more. The chief then gives the Signal and they all discharge their Pieces laden with Powder, into the Air. These People never having heard or seen such a Strange Phenomena throw off their Skins and Leather War Dresses and fly into the woods, while the others Pick them up, and leave on the Spott the articles first offered. They then Proceed to other Places in like manner. And thus for the Quantity of goods we Pay for one of these dresses they get somtimes twenty, but we soppose this mode cannot last long, as they will naturally be aware of a Second visit of the kind. I have been twice on the Marsh lately but not with our usual Success. The Geese are become extremely wild. I shott 8 Woodcocks and many Snipes, which are in large flocks there. One of the People killed upwards of Seventy at once fireing—there are several kinds of these Snipes one of them not bigger than a Lark and of this discription are those in large flocks.

As the weather is pretty fine, we are filling our Water up, and Prepareing to Caulk the Ship.

This afternoon a small cannoe, with a Chief and two Slaves in her, came alongside, with two leather War Dresses to sell. He came on board with great confidance, said his Name was Bucquoinuc and lived at Queenhythe, adding that the Queenhythe People where good, very good. The circumstance of the Imperial Eagles Boat, cutt off, the officer and People killed and Eaten by the savages of this Place, struck myself and the whole crew of the Ruby with that horror natural at the sight of those cannibals who had glutted their infernal appitites on the flesh of our countrymen.[1] Being charged with the fact with all the severity my imperfect knoledge of the language would admit, he Said that he knew of the Fate of Mr Millar, whose name he Pronounced with great Propriety, as the chief, but said it was not done at Queenhythe, but at Queen-en-uett, a villige a little to the North*ward* of the Former. *He* told us that Mr Millar, having been invited, had

Tuesday 8th:

---

[1] See above, p. 58.

landed on the beach with the boats crew and began to trade with them for Skins, and that the Queen:en:uett People suddenly seized them, and cutt them to Pieces which was sent all over the country, to the differant tribes that where at Peace with them. Having ended his story But not to our satisfaction, for both the Chinnook Peoples Testimony and our own knoledge of this Maloncholly event Proved him a liar. I ordered him to be Seized and put in Irons, intending, at this time, to keep him in confinement untill Shelathwell and comcomally returned from their Expedition. I was the more induced to this, as the Chinnook People had thought lightly of us, in not avenging the fate of our countrymen before, for revenge with them is their dearest delight and Glory. He submitted to his situation with great manliness, & being told that we intended to carry him, as a Present to Mr Millars Father and Wife, he exprssed but little uneasyness, and seemed quite reconsciled to be putt to death. His cannoe Paddled away with great haste and in about an hour brought Shelathwell and comcomallys wives with several of the Chinnook People on board. These People acknoledged the fact to have happened at Queenhythe and said that Parts of these Poor Fellows with their apparel had been sent to them who not being cannibals had refused accepting any thing but their Cloaths or Arms, with some of their hair as curiosities. They told us that this Man was but a Small chief, and that at that time he did not live at Queenhythe. Indeed from his appeerence he must have been a young Boy at that time (87) as he does not appear to be more than 20 years of age now. Shelathwells wife was very urgent to have him set at liberty, telling me he was come on a Marrige treaty with one of her Daughters, and considering the matter altogether, that we had thus an opportunity of shewing these People how we would act if Driven to desperate measures, I became glad of this Excuse of letting him go, making him Promise, which I am Pretty shure he never will Perform, to come on board when Shelathwell returns, and I keept his two Leather War Dresses has his hostages. He was visibly delighted when set at liberty and hastened into the cannoe, fearful We should repent our Clemency—

In the Evening, Comcomally returned and came along side Sunday 20th
the Ship, having left Shelathwell with one of his Wives, at
her Fathers house up the River Chinnook. In their Passage
from thence an heavy sea upset the Cannoe and he lost two
Guns, two Leather dresses and a Moose Deer intended for
us. He had another in his cannoe, which he offered to give us
but we soon found to our Mortification that it was only fitt
for the 'DELICATE' venison Eaters in England. Disapointed
at our refusal of this Present he offered one of his Leather
War Dresses, and Several Bows & Arrows. The latter articles
I accepted: and bought from him the Former: For I was too
well Pleased with his Generosity to take the other without
bestowing an Equevilent Article.

We have had Some very blowing rainy Weather lately and
Snow and Hail often, but it is now Moderate with clear
Frosty Weather, and I was on Shore to day and visited the
Houses of the Absent Chiefs. Shelathwells Wife Gave me a
curious wrought Hatt, made by herself. The Women ascribed
the late Bad weather to us, Several of the Chinnook People
being on board, when the New moon was first seen and
Pointed at with our Fingers, these People immediately caught
hold of our hands, saying it was 'Peeshae' that we should
offend her, and we should be punnished with Bad Weather.
This led to an Enquirey if they Worshipped this Lunar
Goddess, and we find they do as well as the Sun[1]—but we
could not learn if they used any Particular ceremony towards
these Objects

Shelathwell returned to day, and we find they have not met Monday 21st:
with their Expected Success, each of the chiefs having got
only five Dresses, and I am sorry to add that two of them
where obtained at the Expence of the lives of the wearers.—
For like the Savage Hyhocus (Page 86)[2] they fell in with a

---

[1] This would seem to be a case of informants answering 'yes' to whatever they were asked. The Chinook worshipped not the sun and moon,
but guardian spirits originating from animals, birds and natural phenomena
(information from V. E. Garfield).
[2] See above, p. 107.

Cannoe with two men which they took and upsetting her killed the Poor Fellows in the Water. This Discovery was made After we had bought their Leather War Dresses, upon Observing them Pierced with Muskett Balls, and which unknown to the chiefs was related to us by a Brother of Comcomally

The Weather being very fine, I went on the Marsh to day in hopes to find Geese for a Christmas Dinner but killed only two. The Natives Bring us a Small kind of Wild Potatoes,[1] which Prove when Boiled, an excellent PILOT, to our Stale Salt Provisions.

Friday 1st January   We have passed thus much of the winter without feeling the Climate so cold as the *South* of England! is—we have had a good deal of rain and heavy Gales of wind, and our main deck from being almost continnually Wet, has be-come leaky, and on surveying it, it was found absolutely nescessary to shift most of the Planks in it. Accordingly a Party of Sawyers are set to work this day cutting new Planks for that Purpose.

Thursday 7th: Taucum and Chinini visited us to day and made considerable trade. The latter is just recovered from a state of Insanity, which has afflicted him this two months Past, and dureing which he gave away to his brother Chiefs, all that he was possessed of—Wives, house, Cannoes, skins and bows and Arrows, and which to their honour they have returned to him again now that he is in health.—

Thursday 14th: The main deck being finished and made good and tight, we struck the house, and Prepared to haul out of the Cove into the middle of the Bay, and we where the more induced to do this, as this evening a Muskett Ball was fired by the Natives, which Passed close over our heads. Comcomally wrestling or Playing with one of the officers, had recieved a blow in the

---

[1] If Bishop's subsequent comments are accurate, this was the wapato, *Sagittaria latifolia*. The plant was scarce in Chinook territory, so the gift was generous (Ray, *ibid.* 119–20).

Mouth, slight indeed to an Englishman, but to an Indian chief an Act sufficient to rouse him to revenge. He complained to me of it, but as I could not see any thing amiss I laughing told him, it was our manner of Play and where nothing ill was meant, with us, nothing ill was taken. He left the ship yesterday in apparent good humour, and this morning his wives came off telling me he was ill and desired I would go on Shore to him, which, our being very busy, was objected to. Comcomally had always discovered a very fickle disposition, & I do not know what ill might have been intended had I gone.—

Early Friday morning we hauled out and moor'd the Ship in the middle of the Bay, a little beyond the reach of a Muskett Ball from the shore, and since which we have been Employed in reeving the Rigging and Prepareing to sail. Comcomally came on board Friday Morning. Said he fired the Ball at the Ducks and did not intend it near the ship—as it was nearly dark: we gave this story (in our minds) the credit it deserved. Nevertheless as I ever have determined to avoid as much as possible, committing any hostility amongst these Savage nations, we appeared satisfied with it and a small Present was mutually exchanged—he is going tomorrow in his cannoe up the River to kill Wild Geese and Procure Some Fresh fish for us previous to our Sailing—and Shelathwell is going away to get 'Wapatoes' (wild potatoes) as his Parting gift— Sunday 17th

The ship now, is all ready for sea, every thing on board, and waiting only for the leading Breeze to Proceed for the Sandwich Islands. Shelathwell returned this evening and brought about 3 Bushells of Potatoes which he gave us. I cannot help mentioning here a circumstance highly to his honour. He had been Poorly and the Doctor gave him medicines which opperated with success. He had scarcely recovered before he set out on this expidition for 'Wapatoes'. The Surgeon lent him an excellent great Coat simply on his Promise of returning it in 4 days. He returned to an hour with it, and it was presented together with a Bushell of Potatoes to the Surgeon. Friday 22[d]:

This Chief has ever deserved our warmest Friendship and Praise. His Pacific manners, Truth and honesty are Seldom met with in Savage life. Comcomally also gave us 15 Couple of Wood Cocks, and severl dishes of Salmon Trout. They all express Sorrow at our going away, and very anxious to know the time when they may Expect our returning to them again.

We learned from Shelathwell that Bucquoi nuc the chief from Queenhythe that was stopped on board this Ship (page 99)[1] was sitting by a Fire where Powder was laid to dry, which going off, Blew him to Pieces. This accident it is to be feared happens often from their carelessness of that article, and here, as I forgot it before I cannot help mentioning for our credit, that Shelathwell was Paid for his two leather War dresses, with those Articles Bucquoi nuc had desired he might, while in confinement and which Shelathwell recieved the day he returned from his Expidition with comcomally—21st: December.

Wednesday I took a Party of our People and clear'd a Small Island, which we Called, Tree Island Posession and made a Garden, planting Indian corn and Sowing Reddishes, Mustard, cresses, salery, Cabbage and Turnip seeds, on the Same ground we did in the Summer (page 42).[2] On our return in October we found the Potatoes, abundant, large and good, the Redishes had gone to seed—there was several beens, but no appearence of Pease, mustard or Cresses, or selery. The latter we ascribe to the troop of small Birds which then inhabited this Islet and the former to the Pease seed having been kiln dried, as the soil every where here is rich and Good.

Saturday 23d: The Wind last night blew hard from the North West but this morning veer'd to North East with clear serene Weather, and I resolved to embrace this opportunity of sailing, notwithstanding from the noise of the Breakers we must Expect to meet a very rough Passage over the Bar. We unmoor'd, the

---

[1] See above, p. 119.   [2] See above, p. 58.

boats where hoisted in, and every thing in readiness to sail at 2 oclock, the time when the tide suited for sailing over the Bar—the Natives crouded round the ship With Expressions of Friendship and sorrow, and the Women seemed Emulous in bestowing Fish and Potatoes, and they where each of them gratified with a Present in return. At $\frac{1}{2}$ *past* 2 oclock we weighed the last anchor and in Quarter of an hour came in sight of the Bar on which the sea raged, in large white sheet Waves, with fearful violence, extending Quite from side to side without the least appearence of a channel. It was too late to recede, we where in the strong Ebb tide, with the Wind right out. Every thing was well lashed on deck, and Secured from being washed over board, and every man had his station with a good rope in his hand for the like purpose.—At 3 oclock we came on the Bar and altho' we had 21 feet water at the Shallowest cast the Sea was tremendeous beyond discription, and so fast and so Fierce did it roll that before one had Passed, another would insult the head of the Ship, several Breaking over us half way up the masts. Nothing remained but 'to hold Fast'. The boats from being well lashed and Secured to the Deck where Preserved from being washed away, and in a Quarter of an hour, we had Passed the worst of it and in a short time got into smoother water, All Well.

The Natives where seen on the hill[1] viewing the ship and as soon as we where Safe out the Guns where discharged as a Farewell Salute to them and a Course shaped towards the North End of Owhyee the Eastmost of the Sandwich Islands.

Had I known the Bar had been so bad, we certainly should not have attempted getting out to day, not from any fear of striking on the Bar over which I had sailed three times before, but there is too much danger of Pitching away the Masts from the Sudden rise and fall of the Ship in these hollow seas, and in case of such an Accident the Ship would fall right athawrt, and be in great Danger of Foundering overwhelmed by the sea.

[1] The site of Cape Disappointment Light.

As these People we have now left, differ very little From the Natives of Nootka so amply discribed by Captain Mears & also in the Account of Cooks voyage I have but few original circumstances to mention here. Their Infants have their heads pressed more flatt I think than the Nootka people do theirs, and this in a side veiw gives the head a most distorted appearence resembling an human face carved out of a Flatt Piece of Plank, the thickness of the head from the Black Part to the Eye Brows being often seen to be not more than half the Breadth of the face. In a front view it gives them a fine open countanance and Preserves them to great age from wrinkles about the Eyes. The men Pluck out their Beards. The Ears are bored as well as the Septem of the Nose, to which are fastened beads and other trinketts. The men are commonly below the Middle Size, but Active and Strong. The Women are shorter, and all of them full and lusty about the Waist. Some of them have their Thighs and legs tattooed. They wear a short Petticoat reaching down to the knees, composed of the inner rind of the Birch tree splitt into strong Fiberes and Placed over a Strong Sinnew of the Wale, which ties round their Waist, but not Plaited. This with a few small Skins Sewed together or a loose Piece of Cloth thrown over their Sholders form the Whole of their Dress. They are fond of rings of Brass round their wrists and fingers, and the young Women Daughters of the Chiefs have a load of Copper ornaments and beads about their necks,—the Women are very modest and reserved in their Manners, and are keept in great Subjection by the men who Sometimes beat them unmerciffully, and are considered as much their Property as their Cannoe, and this arises from the men, who Purchase their Wives from the Woman's Father. Telemmecks a Chief bought while we where there, the Eldest daughter of Shelathwell, one of the hansomest young Woman I have seen amongst them. He Paid the Father twenty Slaves, twenty Sea otter Skins, a Cannoe and twenty Leather War Dresses. His next Daughter who is also beautiful, is Exibited for Sale to a variety of Chiefs who occasionally visit for the Purpose of Alliance with Shelathwell. Bucquoinuc was one

who came on this treaty, and the mother told me it was
expected he would Pay the Price demanded and obtain her.
I jocusely asked 'Sitelnayoe' for that is her Name to accompany me in the Ship, and was told to ask her Father. The old
man Damanded fifty Sheets of Copper and twenty fathems
of Cloth and that the Chief officer should Stay with him as a
Pledge for her Safty. These People have as many Wives as
they can Purchase or Provide for, thus Taucum has ten. They
seem to live contented with their Share of connubial Felicity,
and live in harmony with each other. Their buisness consists
in cooking, making the houses, dressing and cureing the
Skins and Fish, and Paddleing their husbands in the Cannoe
&c—such is the degrading situation of the Fair Sex in this
Quarter of Globe. Compare it, ye Beauties of Albion! with
yours.

These People carry their wars, sometimes, to a great
distance from their home. About six years ago, the Chinnook
tribes united, went with 100 large War Cannoes, and near
100 Smaller ones, twenty days travel up that River, when
they came to some great Water fall, up which they Dragged
their Cannoes into a lake, over which they Paddled ten days
more and in the night came unawares on a large tribe inhabiting the farther shores of this lake. The men where
totally distroyed, and the Women and Children made Slaves
and brought to Chinnook in Triumph. The cause of this
distructive Expidition, I never could rightly understand, and
wither they where urged on, or By Avirice or Revenge
remains unknown to us.

The Chiefs and the free People, when they die, are put into
a Box or Chest, placed with their knees up to the Breast, with
their Back upwards, and wrapped up in the Best Sea Otter
Skins, and then Placed upon the top of some high tree. If he
is rich in Slaves they kill a certain number accordingly and
Bury them round the foot of the tree—but their Slaves when
dead are thrown out into the Woods and left to rott or to be
Eaten by Wolves &c—

The Men have here, as well as every where else along this coast, that indelicate mode of Sitting quite Naked amongst the Women, in the houses and are filthy to a degree, both in their manners and food. It is no uncommon thing, for them, while talking to another Person, to squat down upon an occasion, which nature Points out, even to some of the brute race, a retired spott for, and they, both men and women are to be met with in this situation close to the Door of the houses.

Nevertheless, they where hospitable, and kind to us and we never entered their houses, but fish and that of the best quality they had, was cooked and placed before us, and they seemed to feel a disapointment if we did not eat heartily of it, and would also delight in feeding, even, our Dogs and rendering every assistance or amusement to the People Employed on shore. Thus we passed upwards of three months, mutually pleased with each other

The Sea otter skins procured here, are of an Excellent Quality and large size, but they are not in Abundance and the Natives themselves Set great value on them. Beaver and two or three kind of Fox Skins, Martin and River Otter are also bought here—but the best trade is the Leather War Dresses, articles to be disposed of, on other Parts of the Coast, to great advantage. We Procured such a Quantity, that at the least Estimation is Expected will Procure us near 700 Prime Sea Otter Skins. These dresses are made from the Hide of the Moose Deer which are very large and thick. This is dressed into a kind of White leather, and doubled, & is when Properly made up, a compleat defence against a Spear or an Arrow and Sufficient almost to resist a Pistol Ball.

As none of us are acquainted with Bottoney, I can offer nothing on that head, but what is discribed in the Account of Nootkan Productions, in Cooks voyage, we found here— Except the Wild Potatoe called by the Natives 'Wapatoe' which we have seen nowhere else. They in general are of the Size of a Pidgeons Egg, and appear to grow like an onion or

Turnip, above the Surface of the Earth, are found in Swampy grounds, and when boiled or roasted, Eat not unlike Potatoes, but it is observed that if they continnue boiling longer than necessary they harden in the room of disolving to a flour or Paste. We observed that the Potatoes we Planted in the Summer and found grown to Perfection in November, that altho' they where flourey rich and good, had aquired a sweetish taste, Probably owing to the Situation in which they where Planted, which was a very warm one. Also Excellent Cranberries where brought us in abundance, and which we met with nowhere else.

Deception Bay is Pretty well sheltered from all winds except those from the East and South East, when it blows from thence it comes down the Sea Beach of the Great River Chinnook and blows right into the Bay and causes a considerable Sea to heave in, but a Ship of not more than 16 feet water may moor close into the Cove under the high Bluff and be well secured to avoid these winds, the Ground being every where a stiff blue clay. There are two small Rivers empty themselves into the Bay,[1] Besides Chinnook from whence Issues a most Rapid Stream & causes that terrible Sea on the Bar. This latter River must take its rise a great way Back in the Country, as the Natives go twenty days before they come to the falls, as I have before related, and we cannot allow less than 30 miles a day, as we know they Sometimes go much farther in that Period.[2] About its Entrence there are many Shoals, over which the Sea breaks at low Water or in rough Weather & it would not be Prudent to Sail out with the Wind to West*war*d of North; as the strong Ebb tide meeting a Rebuff from the North sand, and the Cape, takes a Direction over for the Southern Shoals

[1] Wallacut River and Chinook River.
[2] The Columbia winds for 1200 miles. If the Indians penetrated as far as Bishop suggests then they must have reached the present Grand Coulee Dam area and Lake Franklin D. Roosevelt. Alternatively they might have gone only to Priest Rapids and/or to Lake Chelan.

III

TO THE SANDWICH ISLANDS

We are out of sight of New Albion and at noon North Point of Owhyhee bore South West 2207 miles. The Weather is fine and the winds fair that am in hopes of reaching it, in twenty Days. We have the mortification to find the Ship makes considerably more Water than we did, and this unpleasant circumstance we ascribe to the rough Treatment we met coming over the Bar.

Sunday 24th:

We have had fair Winds and a Good Passage hitherto and begin now to feel the trade Winds.[1] The North Point of Owhyhee bore at noon South West By West half West, distant 303 Leagues. This afternoon a Leek was discovered about 1 foot below the Bends in the Wake of the Larboard fore Channal, through which the Water gushes in fast, and is, we Soppose, the Cause of the Ship making So much more Water than Usual. At Present it is impracticable to do any thing to it, there being an heavy Swell, and the leek So much below the Water mark

February Sunday 7th. 26° 26′ N 140° 52′ W

Last night in Examining the leek, we discovered two others, of less consequence indeed! at Present, farther forward and one of them seems to be lower down. This morning it being Moderate we hove too on Larboard Tack, to try and stopp the first leak but found it too far down to do anything to it at Sea. From its having increased Since we first discovered it, it gives me some Alarm that I Shall not be able to Proceed direct to America but forced to go to Canton, as there is no Harbours at Sandwich Islands, even if there was no fear of the Natives, where the ship might lay in Smooth Water, to Careen, and come at these Leaks.

Tuesday 9th.

Nothing in Particular occurred till this day, save that the Ship has continnued makeing more water, and when it Blew Fresh, keeps one Pump almost continnually going. This morning at daylight we Saw the Sandwich Islands, Morotoi[2]

Friday 19th:

[1] Which prevail north-east early in the year.
[2] Molokai.

in the Direction of SBE 10 or 12 Leagues distant and Woahoo South West, 14 or 15 Leagues. We kept our wind and Stood for the former in hopes of Procureing refreshments to day and by 3 oclock had Passed the North West Point at the distance of two miles and Came into an Extensive sandy Bay on the West side the Island, our Soundings being 26 fathems with a Bottom of Sand and shells at the distance 1¾ miles from the Shore. Several Houses where observed near the Beach and three Cannoes where lying off, but as we drew near them with our Colours hoisted they Paddled haistily to the Shore, and halled their Cannoes up among the Bushes. We keept Plying in the Bay untill Sunset, when perscieveing they did not intend coming off, we bore up for Woahoo, running under an Easy sail all night, and the Breeze dying

Saturday 20th: away almost to a Calm, at daylight we where not nearer than 5 Leagues to the Island: at 11 oclock we Passed the S. East Point and at Meridian Anchored in Why, tee, tee[1] Bay in 14 fathems, Sand and Shells, and found riding here the Snow[2] (formerly the Sloop, Meares) Washington, Capt*ain* Roger Simpson, who sent an officer onboard to inform himself if we where in want of refreshments, and finding we had not yet received any from the Shore, very Politely sent an Hog with a Quantity of vegetables, accompanyed with a Message that himself would come onboard the Ruby in the afternoon. Several of our Countrymen who Reside with, Tim Hamy Haw, the Soverign of all the Islands, Except Attooi[3] and Oneeheehow, had come off to us as we run down towards the Bay. They came Paddling off like the Natives and seemed to Possess a degree of command over them, ordering them with great authority to Stay in their Cannoes. They Informed us briefly that Tom Hamy Hau had taken all the Islands lately except the above mentioned and that he was Prepareing his Forces to Attack them: adding also that it was a Taboo day and that the King would not come off till

[1] Waikiki.
[2] The *Washington*'s current rigging won her description as a brig, a brigantine, and a snow (see Howay (1941), 239 n.). Obviously she had two masts square-rigged, and, if Bishop was correct, a supplementary mast behind the mainmast.   [3] Kauai.

tomorrow. Nevertheless they dispatched a Cannoe at my request to desire the King to send off some Provisions to us and which soon after we anchored returned with two Large Hogs and vegetables Fruit &c with a request on the Part of the King to see one of the officers on Shore. Captain Simpson as well as our Country men ashureing me there was nothing to apprehend the Docter readily accepted the Commiseon attended by one of the White inhabitants, the Particulars of which will be related hereafter. Captain Simpson was Recieved onboard the Ruby with that Attention his Politeness deserved and was in our Power to bestow. He informed me They had Sailed from Canton last July, but meeting with a Dreadful Typhon, on the coast of Japan, in their way towards the North West coast of America, Which blew away some of their Sails, and Suffering other distresses from Contrary winds, and want of Provisions, was necessiated to bear up for the Sandwich Islands, & give up the thought of reaching America 'till the Ensuing Season. They passed most of the winter in Karakakooa¹ Bay at the Island of Owhyhee in Company with the Prince William Henery, Captain Wake, who sailed about 6 Weeks ago for the Coast of California. 9ᵗʰ: January Captain Broughton in His Maj: Ship Providence arrived there and Sailed for Attooi the 14ᵗʰ: of this Present month. This Information naturally awakened in me a desire of seeing Captain Broughton, from whom we might derive great assistance in Stopping our Leaks, and being in Company with him could Allow the Ship to be Careened and put into disorder without fear of the Natives. Hence I resolved to Sail for that Island tomorrow. Captain Simpson after chearfully partaking of our Fare returned to his Ship. It blew Fresh in Squalls dureing the night and both vessels drove considerably, but the wind being along the Shore, did not approach any Danger. In the Morning many Cannoes thronged off from the Shore with vegetables, but Brought very few Hogs, and for those, nothing but Powder was demanded, and a middle sized Hog could not be got under a Quart of that article.

¹ Kealakekua.

Sunday 21st: At 8 oclock the King, Tom Hamy Haw, came off in a Large double Cannoe attended by Several others, having Previously sent off 4 Large Hogs and a Cannoe Full of Taroo Yams Potatoes &c. The King brought with him his chief Counseller and Particular Friend John Young,[1] a native of England, who was an officer beloning to an American Schooner cutt off by the Chiefs of Owhyhee, and who being on Shore at the time his life was saved by the King, who, from his honesty and worth, is very kind and Indulgent to him and the rest of the Whites who have put themselves under his Protection. This man told me that in consequence of the War, and the Large Army amounting to near 10,000 men that the King was obliged to feed dureing the Expidition, together with the Distruction to all annimals and Plants by the conquored previous to the Islands being taken, had rendered these Plentiful Islands almost to a State of Famine, and he sopposed that 20 Hogs Includeing the Kings Present, would be the utmost we Should Procure here, adding that there was none to be got at any of the Islands Except Owhyhee, the King having drawn off all their Stock to feed his Troops, and he said even at Owhyhee I must not expect more than 40 or 50 from the great Supplies given to Vessels lately, and the Ravage a Civil War rageing now in that Island would make among their Stock

This I must confess was no pleasing intelligence and the Rest of the Whites together with Capt*ain* Simpsons Testimony and the existing circumstances before recited, left no room to doubt the Truth of it, and began to give me some alarm that I should not be able to accomplish fully the Purpose of our visit to these Islands. Nevertheless has I had prede*ter*-mined to Sail to Attooi in hopes of seeing Capt*ain* Broughton, and the wind blowing fresh into the Bay with Squally un-settled weather, we got underweigh, and stood off and on to Pick up any Provisions that came in their Cannoes, the King staying on board. At Meridian the 2d officer going into the

---

[1] Young and Isaac Davis were Kamehameha's chief lieutenants, and figures of considerable significance: see Kuykendall (1947), 25, 43.

after Hold, was alarmed with the noise of water rushing into
the ship, and soon discovered a very serious Leak extending
about 18 Inches from the End of a Plank, the 2ᵈ below the
Bends under the Starboard main Chains through which the
water gushed in very fast. It appeared also that the water
ouzed in considerably farther along, but there being a good
deal of okam in it, Prevents for the Present the water coming
in very fast. Situated thus, I did not hissitate to bear up
directly for Attooi, the Washington also Accompanying us.
The King Having recieved several Presents of Powder Ball
a Pistol and two Bottles of Rum left us well satisfied,
Promising to do me every good thing he could when We came
back to him again. His Majesty was saluted with 3 Cheers
from each vessel with which he appear'd much delighted, and
by the directions of John Young his People returned them
very properly.

We continnued running under an Easy sail all Sunday   Tuesday 23ᵈ:
night and the next morning where off the N E*ast* Point of
Attooi at the distance of 3 Leagues, but the wind veering to
South East and South Blew Fresh in Squalls with very unsettled Weather: hence we did not reach Whymoa¹ Bay
untill this day at 2 oclock in the afternoon. We anchored in
26 fathems muddy Bottom, the Entrence of the Little River²
being in the direction NBE½E 3 miles Distance. The
Washington also Anchored close to us. We soon learned that
Capt*ain* Broughton had sailed from hence 18ᵗʰ: for Oneehehow and that he had left that Place Monday morning, bound
for the North West Coast of America. I felt a great disapointment in not Seeing him, and equally anxious on account of
the serious situation of the Ship. We have Examined the
Leaks we know of, and they appear to be too general to
Expect they will not in a little time become worse, and a Gale
of wind would I have no doubt accelerate that unpleasent
event. To stop them amongst these Islands is Impracticable,
(as the ship must be lightened and Careened) as well from the

¹ Waimea.
² The only river flowing into the Bay is the Waimea.

Concourse of Natives as from the want of a vessel or Place of Secureity to depossit the goods taken out. On the other hand, where we to attempt going to America, and to find, on Entering those seas in this Tempesteous Season, the ship unable to Proceed, which we have great reason to Expect she would, we should then be too late to Reach Canton, before the North East Moonson ceased and the South West commenced, and of necessity must linger out five months, dureing the Continnuence of the Latter,[1] before we could attempt Entering the China Sea, amongst these Islands, or in fact I hardly know to what determination such an event would drive me to. The Crew, already Poisoned by the false Pleasures and Idle life, of their countrymen residing at these Isles, exibit signs of discontent, and no less than 4 sent a message to desire being informed wither I would discharge them, and being told I certainly would not, and moreover that if they got on shore, I would to the amount of their wages due, Present goods to the King to return them back to the Ship, and to convince them that I would by no means relax in what I considered my duty, on one of these People being rather Insolent to 2ᵈ Mate, He was tied up and the Boatswain was ordered to begin, and give him 12 Lashes, but some circumstances appearing at the instant, in his favour, upon a Promise of their going to their duty, with the Same Attention and good Order has heretofore, he was cast loose and Peace and Harmony again restored.

Wednesday 24ᵗʰ   I hisitated long, and felt much anxiety, and concern, in relinquishing my Plan of Proceeding to the North West, with such a Prospect of a Successful trade before us. But the circumstances before recited, together with the Hope that we shall be able to refitt at Canton, time enough, to Sail (with the first of the South West moonsoon) again for the Coast of America, induced me to resolve upon bearing away, as soon as we can Procure a few more refreshments, immediately for China and secure the Present cargo we have collected, and

[1] The south-west monsoon begins in April–May, the north-east six months later.

refitt with all possible dispatch to accomplish the other Part of our Voyage, leaving a Letter N° 7[1] with Capt*ain* Simpson of the Washington in case of Accident before we reach China. In consequence of this determination a brisk trade was carried on with the Natives for Hogs and other refreshments. The People Appeared in good Spirits and it was made known to me that the cause of their wishing to Leave the ship was the fear, that we should go to America in the present Leaky State of the Ship.

Dureing the whole of yesterday we where Employed in Friday 26th: the trade and Procured altogether 77 Hogs and a considerable Quantity of vegetables. The Washington having broke an anchor Stock, Capt*ain* Simpson requested the Assistance of our Carpenters in replacing it which was readily complyed with. He is an Englishman, and appears to be a Gentleman, and having given me a good deal of information together with Several Letters of introduction to his Friends at Canton and Macao, I yielded to his Solicitations and spared him a few necessarys which I am ashured of replacing there, taking his Bill on the owners of the Washington for the Same—we Sailed Early this Morning for Oneehehow to compleat our Stock of Yams, and as we Passed that vessel they gave us three Chears which was of course returned on our Part. In the After noon we where busily Employed in Killing and Salting Hoggs following the method proscribed by Capt*ain* Cook,[2] and in the Evening hove too for the night off the S E*ast* Point of the Isle of Onnehehow.

At daylight we made sail and Passing the South East Point Saturday 27th hauled up to the North*war*d for Yam Bay.[3] In a short time

---

[1] See below, p. 156.

[2] Cook & King, III, 11–12. King related Cook's continuing interest in the question and described the technique his captain evolved. After hair, large bones, and entrails were removed, the meat was butchered into pieces of four–eight lb. This was cleaned and salted while still warm. It was pressed for one day, and then pickled for six, being carefully examined throughout and defective parts removed. Only then was it barrelled, well interleaved with salt.

[3] Probably at Kamolino, four miles north of the south-west point of the island (information from Miss A. Conrad).

the Cannoes came off and a brisk trade was Carried on for vegetables. At Noon it being nearly Calm we anchored in 26 fathems over a Sandy Bottom about 2 miles South from Yam Bay and about that distance from the Shore.

Those Islanders I had seen on board the Mercury at Nootka came off, and seemed happy to see us, bringing Presents of Matts and Yams. One of them had a 'Paula Paula' Letter[1] written by Mr Gardin the Supercargo of the Mercury, recommending them to the Attention of Strangers, and containing a Brief Account of the Natives having killed and devoured Capt*ain* Barnett, in Berkley Sound a few days after they Parted company from us. He was on shore with a Party consisting mostly of these Islanders, cutting Fire Wood, when the Natives in great Numbers rushed out af the Woods, and dispatched him in an Instant, in Sight and close to his own Ship. One of the Islanders was also wounded through his Arm, but Saved themselves by a Precipitate Flight to the boat and Escaped to the Ship. Mr Gardin fired at them but without Effect, they sheltering themselves behind the Large trees. The vessel in the utmost Confusion cutt her Cables and Pushed out to Sea, leaving these Infernal Cannibals rioting on the Flesh of their unhappy commander. This was described by the Islanders in so Pathetic a manner that their tears affected every Person around them. Hearing som bustle behind him he was examining his Piece to see the Priming was good when two spears where thrown into him. He fired and the natives rushed out and beat out his brains, instantly ripping up his stomack, scooped up his Blood and drank it with Savage eagerness. They followed the People to the Boat, but where not Active enough to catch the Sandwich Islanders —The Mercury passed these Islands about 3 months ago in her way to Canton

Sunday 28th. We continnued trading 'till noon, when having Procured a Sufficiency of yams, which are by no means Plentiful at this

---

[1] Presumably an open testimonial. 'Palapala' is the Hawaiian word for anything written (Miss Conrad).

time, to last us to China, we weighed and made all sail for Canton. Many Islanders wanted to go with us to 'Pretannee'. A youth who had rendered himself familiar by his great good humour was after much Solicitation received on board. His Sister (by no means an unhansome young Woman) pressed much to accompany her Brother, and had actually got on board, and it was not without a Present and some harsh words we could Perswade her to return to her cannoe. Their Parting was like Brother and Sister. It was affectionate nor could they refrain from Tears. She continnued to follow us 'till the Breeze Freshening they found the Ship haistily leaving them, when with seeming reluctance they paddled slowly back towards their Native Isle

We continnued on Course all night under a Press of sail, and in the Morning our Horrison was bounded only by the Sea. It may not be improper here, to give some Account of the Political Situation of these Islands one with another, and which I had an opportunity of collecting from the Information of Capt*ain* Simpson and the whites residing on the differant Islands.

Soon after the Deaths of the English Captains at Woahoo, and the Recapture of the vessels by their Crews, as related in Page 82,[1] Tom Himmy Haw the King of Owhyhee, having had intelligence of the Proceedings and Intentions of the People of Woahoo, and also of the vessels being retaken, By the desire of his chiefs, and advice of his White Friends, Prepared a most formidable army of at least 10,000 warriors, with a Fleet divided into four Divisions, each consisting of three hundred Cannoes, for the purpose of Subjecting Woahoo, and the intermediate Isles, Mowee, Rani[2] and Morotoi, and as the English say to revenge the Deaths of Capt*ain* Brown and his Officers. This Formidable fleet Set Sail from Owhyhee last June, the King having left Nimitahaw

---

[1] See above, p. 103. For a scholarly account of the episode he described, see Kuykendall (1947), 44–8. Except as noted, Bishop presented a generally true picture.

[2] Maui and Lanai respectively.

(the Brother in law of Tianna)[1] and Isaac Davis an Englishman,[2] who was chief Mate of the American Schooner cutt off at Owhyhee. He is of Great repute and worth, and much beloved by the King and his subjects. These two where to act as Co Regents, dureing the Kings Absence from Owhyhee: In addition to their other Force they had this Schooner, who was loaded with the Train of Attillery, consisting of twleve Guns, from three to Six Pounders, Powder, Shott, and Military stores. This Part of the Force was under the Direction of John Young, assisted by Six other English, beside which, there was one or more English in the vanguard of Each division, who are Esteemed good Warriors even by the Sanwich Islanders! They met with little or no opposition in conquoring the Isles of Mowee, Rani and Morotoi, and having thus subjected them, and appointed a Chief of his own to the Government of each with directions to forward Provisions for the use of the Army, The Army Proceeded towards Woahoo and Arriving about the Middle of August they Landed in three different Parts of the Island meeting at First with little opposition. Tianna (so well known in Captain Meares voyage) was a Principal Chief in one of these divisions, who having concieved some cause or affront from the King, went over to the Enemy with as many of his followers, has he could persuade to Rebill.

They had various skirmishes with the Enemy in which the Latter was always routed, but no general Battle. The King of Woahoo, Tom hoa moto, finding it impossible to hold out any longer, fled in a single Cannoe to the Island of Attooi,[3] leaving his followers to shift for themselves, who finding this, surrendered at discression to Tom Hummy Haw, except Tianna who being rendered Desperate by his haughtiness of Soul and the forlorn situation to which he was reduced,

[1] Namekeha and Kaiana are the modern spellings; they were brothers.
[2] See above, pp. 103, 136.
[3] The major enemy was Kalanikupule, who in fact remained on Oahu, hiding from his conquerors, for some months before Kamehameha captured and killed him. His full brother, Koalaukani, fled to Kauai after the battle (Miss Conrad). Bishop was strangely confused.

deserted by every one, he withstood, on a hill near Why tee tee Bay, the attack of near a hundred asailants, catching their Spears in his hand, and hurling them with resistless force back on his foes, for a considerable space. At length a Spear was thrown into his Bowels, and while endeavouring to Pull it out, two Islanders came up behind and clove in his scull. He fell and with him fell all opposition to the Sovereignty of Tom Hummy Haw. The Whites bear ample testimony of Tiannas courage, but (with what Truth I will not pretend to say) they charge him as being the Leader in cutting off the Schooner, and also of a meditated Attack of another vessel which was prevented in the Instant by the Arrival of the King on board, who dismissed the Natives with a severe Rebuke to Tianna, nor did the People onboard the vessel know the situation in which they had stood 'till the King himself informed them. On the other hand Tianna having rendered himself odieous to the King by his desertion, and the whites desireous of rendering the King beloved by their countrymen might be induced to throw the blame on a Chief, who is not now capable of refuteing them. I have mentioned these Circumstances from his being a Character well known in Captain Meares voyage, and spoken of there in such glowing colours of worth—

The whites discribe the King as exerciseing his Power with great moderation, and indulgence to the conquered. Some of the Principal leaders however has been Putt to Death. They soppose, that in the different Skirmishes not less than five hundred of the Enemy fell, whereas they have not lost more than twenty men dureing the whole Expidition.

Immediately on the King being in full possession of Woahoo, in a Council of war, it was resolved to Attack Attooi for giving refuge to Tom hoa moto, but first to build two vessels one of Forty five and the other of Thirty Tons, the Schooner having become Leaky, and her Bottom Eaten much by worms. The whites have been busy on this buisness and the two vessels are in a great state of Forwardness and will

BISHOP'S VOYAGES   [February

be ready to Launch in two months: they say it was by their
advice that they are built and which they purpose, if the King
should die or alter his disposition towards them, to Escape
with from the Islands. I believe there are near twenty English-
men here, with the King, beside two or three with Davis at
Owhyhee, who by Accounts lately brought from that Island
is quelling a Rebelion in that Island under the Faction of
Nimitahaw, who it seems is resolved to share the Fate of his
Relation Tianna, or become the Soveriegn of the Island.
I asked the King if he was not alarmed for the Situation of
Owhyhee, 'No' says he, 'I Expect Davis will send me the
head of the Rebell in a day or two'—He has constantly a
Guard of Thirty men with loaded musketts and Bayonets
fixed, attending his Person on shore and if in the night he
finds them off their Guard or asleep, if it is the first time, they
are severely Flogged, but caught in that situation again they
are instantly putt to Death. And this seems necessary, has no
doubt he has many Enemies. He is very kind to the whites,
and they are one and all, resolved to be faithful to him, and
to Punnish those who are not. It Seems his chiefs are averse
to Attacking Attooi, but the King tells them it was by THEIR
advice he took the Islands and now by HIS advice they SHALL
take Attooi and Oneehehow. He had lately a Child born with
only one hand caused as THEY SAY by his Queen eating some
Fish that was Tabooed, and to appease the Deity, it is resolved for six Moons that the King and all his Subjects Shall
not wear any Cloth over their boddies except the Marro Tho'
the Taboo allows them to carry their Tappor or Cloak in their
hands, and this is Strictly observed, even by Tom Himmy
Haw, himself—

It appeared the only reason the King had of seeing one of
our officers on Shore, was to see if we had confidance in his
Honour and hence that he might ashure himself we where his
Friends, for on the Surgeon's arrival he was conducted by
one of the Guards to His Majesties Taboo House, where he
found him inclosed by Pales, in a small Square, Naked all
but a short feather'd cloak over his sholders. He advanced to

the Fence and the Guard stopping the Docter at about 2 yards distance, the King only asked my Name, said he had heard the ship and every one in her was 'mytie' good and that as soon as the Taboo was over, he would come off, and Giving the docter his 'Horooha' a word expressive of Farewell or good betide you, left him to stay on shore, or go back immediately to the Ship has he pleased, having ordered a Double Cannoe to attend him. Agreeable to the orders he had received he staid not Long on shore,—saw quantities of a Tarro groing in a swamp, walked through the Town which he sopposes is near two miles in Circumference, composed of Detatched houses, without any attention of order, some large others not much bigger than a Common Dog house, the Natives very civil, bidding him 'Horooha' as they Passed. Several Ponds of Fresh water where observed full of Fish. *He* was entertained by one of his Countrymen residing here for the Purpose of collecting Pearls, and recieved from him an account of those circumstances of the War &c as before related.

On our arrival at Attooi, the chief of the four Islanders I had seen on board the Mercury at Nootka came off, and did not forget the Present I had made him there, of two yards of Baze for a Maro. It was now in his power he thought to return the Favour. And he did it most gratefully by Presents of Hogs yams &c, and was otherwise of much service to us. This Island is the Pleasentest by far we have seen but his now torn to Pieces by the distractions and civil War reigning at this time — Taheo' the late King dying, left a Son called King George, a youth of about 17 years, whose Mother had bourne several children before she became the wife of Taheo, by a Principal Chief, the Eldest of which is Named Teeavey, and also Rerowee—they Both claim the Soveriegnity of the Island and sopport it by the Sword.[1] Teeavey, has got Posses-

[1] Keawe (Bishop's 'Teeavey, and also Rerowee') succeeded to his father's chieftaincy in 1779. His mother soon after married Kaeo (Taheo), and had by him a son, Kaumuali (King George). Kaeo succeeded in supplanting Keawe with Kaumuali, and thus himself enjoying further power, before being killed on Oahu, December 1794 (see above, p. 101 n.). Then Keawe fought back, as Bishop relates, and triumphed by July 1796. But he died soon after and Kaumuali returned.

sion of the West side and by far the best and most Numerous Part of the People in his cause. The other has the East side, and altho' not so strong in Numbers, his Party is Resolute and Firm to his cause. While we where here two Battles or skirmishes had happened in which Teeavey tho' much stronger had no reason to boast a victory. A small stream of water in a valley seperates the Encampments of the two armys, and I am told it requires the utmost force of the Taboo to Prevent the armies rushing on to Death or Victory and which the contending chiefs Politically exert, for as Soon as the Taboo is Proclaimed in one camp, for one, two, or three days, it immediately takes place in the other for the like time. In this time, these intervals of war, they sit on the opposite banks of the stream converseing with each other as Friends.— Teeavey was several times onboard. Has a bold Hansome Person and is himself a Renowned Warrior. He told me he meant to join Tim Himy Haw if he came down to that Island before he had conquered King George, but should he be Successful before he came He purposed opposing the King of Owhyheee with the whole Force of the Island. On his leaving us, the most grateful Present I could make him was a Quantity of Powder and Ball in return for several large Hogs and Yams &c and Directed one of his chiefs to accompany us to One hee how, and to see his subjects behaved well, and to order us as much Yams has we wanted.—

Saturday
26th
19° 55′

Since leaving Oneheehoow, we have had in general very Pleasent Weather with fair and moderate Breezes, and have Made nearly two degrees of Longitude daily. Our time has been passed in airing and repacking the Furs, all of which turned out sound and dry. The ship continnues leaky and we observe she makes more water in a Calm than when there is a Press of Sail set which Probably contracts the open Seams

This morning at 1 oclock the Northmost of the Ladrone Isles was seen West by South 6 Leagues, and at daylight we

Passed on the North side of it at the distance 7 miles. It consists of 4 Cragged Islets close to each other, and appears pretty Steep too. Of a tolerable heigth *they* may be seen in fair Weather 8 Leagues off the Deck—they occupy a space of three miles each way, of a Barren Rude appearence, & its only inhabitants I believe are Birds. The Latitude of its Center is 20°: 01′ N.[1] By our Chart we should have seen two other Islands, over the situation of one there Placed, we passed with the Ship, the Longitude of the above, Reduced to several setts of Distances of the Sun and moon.

Yesterday at 3 oclock in the afternoon with Gentle Breezes   Thursday 31st:
we where persuing our Course, the People being all Emp*loy*ed on Deck—a Dangerous Reef of Rocks was discovered bearing from WbS$\frac{1}{2}$S to S.S.W. distant only two and half miles from the ship. The course was immediately altered to the North being apprehensive, as it was almost Calm, that a Southerly Current we had experienced from Tuesday, would set us down upon it and found Indeed we receded from the shoal very slowly for at Sun set we where only six miles distant—

This Shoal which was now Called the DANGERS Reduced to the meridian Observation of the sun three hours before lies in Latitude of 20 degrees 18 min*utes* North, and its East End in 223°: 07′ W*es*t Reduced from the Result of 5 setts distances of ⊙ ☾ the next Morning.[2] Extends in an East by North and West by South direction about Six miles and appears to be 1 mile Wide with Breakers all over it, and on its West End there is a Single Rock, which From our situation appeared like a Boat under Sail, and is the only one we Saw above Water. The only Chart we have that bears any mark of this shoal, is that in Captain Meares Voyage to N W*es*t

---

[1] In fact, Pajaros is the northern of the Marianas Islands, at 20° 32′ N., 144° 54′ E. Bishop probably saw Maug, 20° 01′ N., 145° 13′ E. Maug has three islets; birds are its only residents.

[2] I.e. the observations were taken from both sun and moon. The longitude might otherwise be given as 136° 53′ E., i.e. 360° minus 223° 07′. The reef was apparently Parece Vela. Bishop doubled its length, perhaps partly because the sea breaks off the reef itself. It is at 20° 20′ N., 136° 00′ E.

America—but is there placed thirty two miles to the North of the Place we find it in—Sad Error!—for I had noticed it, and concluded we where passing it very Safly to the Southward—had it been night the consequences might have been Fatal. We keept a North Westerly course all night, the winds being light, and in the morning where out of Sight *of* it—

IV

MEMORANDA CONCERNING
RUBY VOYAGE

First letter to Teast, off Lundy Island, 3 p.m. 11 October 1794:

It is with the greatest pleasure I write, that we are proceeding to Sea all well. The wind at pres*en*tt is south, blowing a fresh double reef Topsail Breeze, and the ship bears her canvass tolerably well. The Pilot is of the same opinion with myself that she Sails much better than when we came home, with this wind we shall be able to get well to the west*ward* and keep clear of the French

The sight of you, yesterday awakened in my mind the many Instances of kindness and Friendship I have recieved from you and I trust my conduct will ever be such as to leave no doubt in your mind of the gratefulness of my heart—Mr Williams and the Crew give me every satisfaction, and are all well and in spirits.

May God bless you Sir with health and happiness and bless also the property you have intrusted to me, that my return may equal your most sanguine wishes...

* * *

Second letter to Teast, from Lundy Road, 2 p.m. 20 October 1794:

Has taken shelter from westerly gale, and spent £1. 15s. on stock feed.

* * *

Third letter to Teast, from Praia, São Thiago, 11 November 1794:

Progress to date satisfactory; sight of the supposed enemy frigate and contact with the Nancy.

* * *

Fourth letter to Teast, from Rio de Janeiro, 15 December 1794:
Satisfactory progress to date.

We are now compleated for sea, and are getting under-weigh with a fair wind. As it is very probable we shall not stop any where untill we arrive on the North west coast of America, I have given the people every refreshment, and I trust you will not be displeased at my expences—I have taken up from your Corrospond*e*nt Thirty Six pounds, and have given a bill on you for Forty seven Pounds four Shillings, the Amo*u*nt of the money recieved together with interest and Brokerage and the rate of Exchange here (77)[1] payable at 30 days sight.

Good performance of ship, especially in outstripping the two
Americans seen near the Equator.

There is two ships going to sail for Lisbon the 20th: so that I hope our letters will reach your hands at an Early date— I shall particularly esteem it a favour if you will drop a line to Mr Bishop, Attorney, Basingstoke, when hereafter you may hear from me, as in many instances I may not have time to write them, and I have a very Affectionate group of relations there anxious for my welfare—I would also wish you to inshure 300£ for me to China, or Indeed! to inshure my Commissions in the same proportion you do your property. I have taken the Liberty to trouble you with these requests, being not more Anxious on any subject, than to deserve your approbation and Esteem. The anaxed bill is an account of my expences here and at St Jago's...

	£	S	D
To Anchorage at Isl*a*nd St Jago	1	1	0
Fruit at D°. 400 Oranges, 1 D*ollar*	0	5	0
Anchorage here at 1 Milrea[2] p*er* Day, 7 days	1	13	9
Pilot and Harb*our* Master	7	4	0
½ Pipe Port wine	9	0	0
1 Roll Brazil Tobacco	0	18	0
1200 Bill*e*ts Fire wood, 2/2 p*er* Cwt	2	4	0

[1] Presumably this meant that English bills carried only 77 % of their face value. If so, Bishop paid only a few shillings for interest and brokerage.
[2] Milreis.

	£	S	D
1 Whip Saw	0	12	0
Poultry	2	6	0
Linguist	1	1	0
Corn for Stock	0	15	0
Fresh beef, vegetables, fruit &c, 11 days	9	0	0
	£36	0	0

★ ★ ★

Fifth letter to Teast, from the Falklands, 13 January 1795:

Satisfactory progress to date, despite ill weather.

The People and officers are all well, and behave much to my Satisfaction, except the Cook, who is a worthless fellow, and has been an useless burthen to me. By his own request I have discharged him anongst the Spaniards, from whom I have recieved very kind treatment—

★ ★ ★

Sixth Letter to Teast, from Friendly Cove, 27 September 1795:

Sketch of passage to Baker Bay, where wood and water sought.

Our Stay in this Harbour was not longer than absolutely necessary to procure those articles, having learned from the Natives that two ships where before us, and taking the advantage of a spurt of wind from the South*ward* we pushed on to Queen Charlottes Islands, in hopes to pass these ships and secure the winter Furs to the North*ward*. We arrived at South End of Q:C: Islands 12th June, but had the mortification to find not only these but an additional vessel had preceded us. We however continnued to collect Furs daily, but mostly newly killed. On the 20th: with favourable winds, I determined to stretch over to the main and trace its coast up to Port Meares. This we did and collected a good many Skins. Arriving there, your Friend the Chief Kowe (shurely the best Indian on the coast) helped me to 360 Good Skins—I made him well acquainted with your Name and from him gained much valuable information—

153

It was now the latter end of August and we experienced much rough weather in getting into sea otter Sound. We did not see a Single native here, the buisness is, they leave the Sea Coast by the end of July, and go to the Freshes, to procure their winters Stock of Salmon. Finding I could not dispose of more than half our Cargo, I determined to return and trace the coast to South*ward* and buy up those articles, with which you are aquainted,[1] and sail Early to the North*ward* in the spring. After touching at various ports we arrived here the 11th Instant and found the Mercury preparing to leave the Coast, bound direct to Canton. From her I have learned there has been Six vessels including our Selves on the Coast this season, all of which are off but one, an American Sloop (uncertain). We have a fair prospect of making a good account next Season, and hope ZA (2500)[2] will be the Consequence of our staying on the coast—

I propose leaving this place the 1st: fair weather and proceed to ports Cox, Effingham and Hahazard,[3] and lastly to deception bay, where if the scurvy does not attack us which at present we have no reason to fear, to remain there untill middle of Feb*ruary*, and then Sail to the North*ward*. But should that dire desease attack us, I certainly must go to Sandwich Islands to recruit not only health and provisions but men. These barbarous Savages have been too successful, and have carried three vessels without a defeat (last season) and they even came off to attack this ship, but was detered with out Bloodshed on either hand.[4] Afterwards we made good trade with them. —

You will most likly be made aquainted with the fate of Capt*ain* Brown and his squadron. The Captain and his officers where all killed last winter at the Sandwich Islands, but the vessels sometime after retaken by the Crews, and

[1] Leather war dresses. This oblique phrasing evidently meant to conceal information from any prying eye.
[2] In the originals, no doubt, the code was not translated.
[3] Unidentified.
[4] The reference must be to Koya's and Cumshewa's alleged intentions.

sailed for Canton, and a large ship sopposed to belong to London, put into Queen Charlottes Islands about the Same time, in distress, was Cutt off and the whole Crew perished

Our present purchase stands thus. 1ˢᵗ Qual*ity* Da4 (454), 2ᵈ Qual*ity* is Ba3 (253). These are all prime good Furs, and 3ᵈ Qual*ity* including Pieces equal to Skins is Aa25 (175). Other Furs equal to a (50) Otter Skins. I expect by the end of October to make the Acc*ount* K (1000) good—

Believe me, dear Sir, that I will do the utmost to make a good voyage. I feel not only my interest in it, but my honour engaged, and trust my Conduct Shall ever merit your approbation and Esteem—Both officers and men behave exceedingly well and deserve my Esteem and regard. Mr Gardin has disinterestly given me all the information he knew. I mention this, if you should See him while I am out. He will have two duplicates of this Letter which he has promised to forward by seperate conveyances.

I somwhat expect to hear from you in my return from the North*ward* next season by your ship, as I understand every where that the Jenny made good trade, and Sailed lastly from Port Cox for Canton, in October. There is nothing to be done, as far as I can hear, any where else. Every vessel that has tried it has failed of Success. I hope should your ship be under the command of a Stranger to the Coast, that she will be well appointed, and on their Guard. The Natives every where are turning out such bold Pirates, that it is become absolutely necessary to trade with them Arm'd. We have been onshore once, but did not as far as I know recieve any damage, the Sea being smooth, and we hove off in half an hour,—

★ ★ ★

Seventh Letter to Teast, from Kauai, 24 February 1796:

Unhappy state of ship, which has forced change of plans.

23ᵈ January we sailed from Deception bay, intending to proceed here for provisions, having only 6 Casks of Bread and 8 tierces of Beef, and expected to have arrived at S*outh* End of Queen Charlottes Islands by 15ᵗʰ of April. We had purchased dureing the winter 200 Leather War Dresses, which without doubt would have returned 700 Prime Sea Otter Skins. Immediatley after getting over the bar we discovered the Ship made more water than usual...

As this letter will be left in the hands of Capt*ain* Simpson of the American Snow Washington, who is bound to the Coast, it is not necessary for me to detail the proceedings of the Ship in this letter, as you will perceive that it is only in case of Accident in our passage to China, that it can be of any Service. You will read the Prime Sea O*tter* Skins number I (900) Inferiour Ba (250). I am sorry to add I hear an unfavourable account of Sales at Canton. I expect to arrive at Macao by 1ˢᵗ: April, when I shall embrace every opportunity of writting of my proceedings, Letters that of Course must reach your hands before this...

★ ★ ★

MANIFEST OF SHIP RUBYS CARGO, GOING TO CHINA MARCH 1796, *prepared 13 April 1796 and submitted to Henry Browne and select committee of supercargoes of the East India Company:*[1]

9 Chests ⎫ Nᵒ 1. a ⎫ Containing 864 whole Sea Otter
              ⎬   ⎬ Skins, 47 large Cloaks of Sea Otter
              ⎪   ⎪ Fur, 169 Pieces of Furs, 483 Sea
1 Puncheon ⎭   10 ⎭ Otter tails—

[1] Bishop's correspondence with the supercargoes is recorded in the East India Company Papers, 'Factory Records—China'. Browne was currently chairman of the committee. The work of the committee is detailed by Morse.

1 Cask N⁰ 11 Containi*n*g 104 beaver Skins and Pieces, 25 Silver grey fox, 38 Martin, 20 Rackoon, 1 Lynx Catt, 20 River otter, 4 Wolves, 12 black fox and 14 deers Skins—

2 Boxes N⁰ 12, 13 Containing 150 Marmot skins.

L N⁰ 1 a 6 ⎫
4 Butts ⎬ Containing 192 Leather war Dresses, and 40 or there about dressed deer Skins
2 Punch*eon*s ⎭

European Goods remaining

vizt: 16 half Barr*e*ls Gunpowder, 4 Chests containi*n*g 125 trade guns, 23 Pistols, 5 thousand flints, 34 Copper Rods, 2 Cop*p*er Tea Kettles, 32 brass Guinea Kettles, 16 Quart Cop*p*er Potts, 18 Cop*p*er sauce Pans, 75 Cop*p*er neck Maneillas,[1] 20 brass D⁰, 4 Pewtor screw Juggs, 10 D⁰ Tankards, 7 Dozen Pew*t*er Spoons, 197 three lb Pew*t*er Basons, 83 Cutlasses, 122 bars swedes Iron, 90 bars steel, 9 Boxes tin Plates, 3 Cwt: 1 : 21[2] block tin in bars, 10 Iron Potts, 13 Pye Pans with covers, 10 Cwt : 2 : 0 Lead shott and ball, 5 Tinny bound Hatts, 379 yards fine striped Cloth, 352 yards broad brown Cloth, 70 yards Baiz, 54 Gall*on*s Rum, 14 Cwt Old Iron, 24 Pairs Bellows, 24 Grindstones, 150 stone Jars, 26 Coop*e*rs Adzes, 40 Hatchetts, 45½ dozen Razors, 23 Dozen Fire Steels, 1 Trunk, 14½ dozen Files, 14 Looking Glasses, 31 Doz*e*n Mane Combs, 1 Dozen Scissors, 9 Dozen tin Japan Pow*d*er Flasks, 6 Leather Spring D⁰:, 6 Leath*e*r shott Belts.

Ships Stores.

5 Coils spare Cordage, 3½ bolts Canvass, 8 Casks beef & Pork, 5 D⁰ bread, 2 Casks flower, 2 D⁰ Peas, 2 D⁰ Rice, 4 D⁰ Sea Coal, 1 Punchen Malt, 1 Punch*eon* containing 3 Cwt loaf Sugar.

★ ★ ★

[1] Manillas.
[2] I.e. 3 cwt., 1 quarter, 21 lb. In detailing accounts Bishop normally gives the price of goods in such quantities as so much per cwt.

Bishop to Browne and the select committee of supercargoes, from Macao Road, 15 April 1796:

In compliance with the letter of Licence obtained from the Honourable English East India Company, I have to inform you of the arrival of the Ship Ruby under my command from her trading voyage on the North West coast of America and Sandwich Islands (direct). I had purposed to have continued on the coast of America untill next Autumn, but in our passage to Sandwich Islands, for provisions, the Ship became so leaky, as to render it necessary to bear up for this place immediatly, and secure the Cargo I have already collected and to refitt the Ship, which now at her Anchors makes 23 Inches water per Hour. I purpose waiting here a few days and shall Esteem it a favour, if you will give me advice, wither it will not be better to refitt here, or at Canton—also I am much distressed at a report here of the death of Mr Teast, my Employer, the doubt of which I hope you will be enabled happily to remove.

* * *

Browne to Bishop, from Canton, 17 April 1796:

I have been favoured with yours of 15th Instant advising the arrival of the Ruby at Macao, In answer to which I can only Say, that if you mean to sell the Sea Otter skins you have on board, it will be necessary for you to come to Whampu'[1] as you may occasion great inconvenience to the East India Companys Affairs, by attempting to sell at Macao, but if your object is only to repair, you had better remain at Macao in which case, it will be necessary for you to Apply to the portuguese Governor for leave to go into the Typa,[2] and repair there, as you will by so doing save the Charge of

---

[1] Whampoa was the anchorage at Canton (see map in Morse, II, 1). Bishop's odd sign over the 'u' is much more like an apostrophe or a grave accent than the commonly used circumflex. He regularly imposed his orthographic idiosyncrasies when transcribing other peoples' letters.

[2] The Taipa was the channel-harbour between the two islands (known by that name) four miles south-south-east of Macao (see map in Morse, I, 192). Macao is sixty-five miles south of Canton.

measurage: which must be paid if the ship comes to Whampu'.
I am sorry it is not in my power to give you any information,
relative to Mr Teast, but I inclose you a letter, Received by
one of the Companys Ships, which will probably be more
Satisfactory.

Endorsement:

Immediately on Receipt of this Letter we proceeded up to
Whampu'—CB—

★ ★ ★

Protest, dated Canton, 22 April 1796:

*General outline of the voyage, stressing especially the disabilities
suffered by the* Ruby, *and tracing the voyage through to Baker
Bay.*

Dureing her stay there *she* was caulked all round above the
bends, and Six Standard knees set up in the between decks,
the ship having opened the waterway seams of the upper
Deck in a Gale of wind near Queen Charlottes Islands—
That on the 23ᵈ January 1796 she sailed from Deception bay
with intention of Proceeding to the Sandwich Islands to
procure provisions, after which to return, and trade dureing
the Summer months on the coast of America—that before
her Sailing from Deception bay, the ship did not make more
water than she usually had done, at most 2 feet in 24 hours—
That her passage out over the bar of Deception bay, was
Exceeding rough, and the ship was found to make considerably
more water on leaving the Land than She usually had done—
That on the next day, Sunday 24ᵗʰ January it had increased
3 or 4 Inches per hour—That on Monday 8ᵗʰ February a leak
was discovered about 1 foot below the bends in the wake of
the Larboard fore Chains, and was then Sopposed to be the
principal cause of her making water—That on the day following the Ship was Careened for the purpose of stopping it, but
without effect, it being too low down, and on the same day
two other leaks where discovered below the bends on the

Larboard bow, which we ascribed to the Straining of the ship in passing the bar of Deception bay.—That on 19th february she arrived amongst the Sandwich Islands, and that by this time the Ship made from 19 to 22 Inches water per hour, according to the weather or sailing on an even keel or with the Tacks on board, on an even keel she was found to make most water,—That on Sunday 21t February a very serious leak was discovered through 2d Seam below the bends in the wake of Starboard Main Chains, Extending from a Butt of the Plank one foot and half forward and the water ouzed in much farther,—That at Several Examinations of the Hold, the Sceiling[1] of the Ship was found to be wett almost fore and aft, so as not to leave a doubt in the minds of the undersigned, that the Leaks in a very short time would become worse— That the ship being off the Island of Woahoo, had been informed by the Natives, that Captain Broughton in his Majestys Ship Providence, had sailed from thence for the Island of Attooi seven days before, And that in consequence of this Information we sailed immediately for that Island in hopes of seeing Captain Broughton, and deriving great assistance from his Carpenters, and beside which the Ship being in Company with the Providence, could have been put into disorder and Careened without fear of the Natives, a Circumstance otherwise not practicable with Safty.—That on Wednesday 24th: February, the ship arrived in Whymoa bay in the Island of Attooi, and found there, that the Providence had Sailed for Oneheehow, and from that Island for the coast of America 22d February,—That being thus deprived of this Expected Assistance, the ship making near three feet water in 4 hours, with every probability that it would shortly increase, if the Ship met with bad weather, she continnued purchasing and procureing Provisions and Refreshments untill Sunday 28th february—when she left the Island of Oneheehow, and bore up for Canton in China—That the undersigned Master will attest to the truth of the following reasons, when, or wherever it may be required, for his

[1] Ceiling—'the inside planking of a ship's bottom, carried up to the lowest deck' (O.E.D.).

adopting this plan—1st: The ship has commenced leaking in an Extraordinary manner since she sailed out of Deception Bay, and continnued increasing to the time she left the Sandwich Islands—2dly Those leaks that have been hitherto discovered were considerably below the bends, and where not to be come at without lightening and Careening the Ship, and putting her in a situation, as before said, not Practicable, with Safty, amongst the Sandwich Islands.—3dly. it was then the latter part of the N. East Monsoon, and required the utmost dispatch to reach the coast of China before it ceased and the South West, commenced, which generally takes place in April or beginning of May, *so* that had He attempted going to America, and found on Entering those seas in this Tempestous Season, the Ship unable to proceed—her passage to Canton would have been rendered very precarious, and dangerous, by being necessiated to Pass to the South*war*d of Luconnia,[1] through the Sea of Celebes and Sooloo[2] Sea, and have entered the China Sea by a passage unknown to any person on board, and which was understood to be repleat with danger, and also a Navigation forbidden us by the Hon'ble East India Companys licence, unless forced by stress of weather.—4^{thly}. That the North West coast of America is without Friendly Ports to Refitt in, without the Company and assistance of a nother Ship, and thus the undersigned Master considered it good and proper for the Above reasons, to repair with all possible dispatch to Canton, and Secure the Cargo of Furs already collected, without risquing a total loss, notwithstand*ing* He is sensible, that 700 Prime Sea Otter Skins, at the lowest calculation will be lost to the adventure, should He be able to Refitt and regain the coast of America by 15th August, and be ever so successful at that late period of the Season in Procuring a 2^d Cargo—The undersigned Master has thought proper thus to make a Statement of the voyage, and his proceedings, as he had written to Sidenham Teast Esq*uire* Sole owner of the Ship and Cargo, from Nootka Sound, dated 27th: Sep*tember* 1795 stating the Quantity of Furs then collected and of his intention of remaining another

[1] Luzon, the northern of the Philippine Islands.   [2] Sulu.

season, with the Expectation that he would be able to Procure ZA or 2500 Prime Sea Otter Skins by the 10th October 1796, and which the undersigned has not a doubt on his mind, but that He would have Accomplished it, Had the Ship Continnued free from Leaking or Accidents— And In witness here off the Said Master hath Signed his Name and Seal—

Signed Charles Bishop— (Seal)

Signed and Sealed in the presence of us the officers Ship Ruby the day of the date hereoff

Signed: Joseph Williams—Chief Mate
Thomas Hunt—2 D⁰
Thomas Moon—3^d D⁰
John Booth—Surgeon—

★ ★ ★

An Account of Goods expended in purchasing and procuring 864 Whole Sea Otter Skins, 47 large Cloaks of Sea Otter Fur, 169 Pieces of Skins, 483 Sea Otter tails— 104 lbs: Beaver Skins and pieces, 25 Silver grey fox Skins, 38 Martin Skins—20 Raccoon Skins—1 Lynx Catt skin— 20 River Otter Skins—4 Wolves skins—12 Black Fox and 14 deers Skins, 150 Marmot Skins.[1]

	£	S	D
*23 Half Barrells Powder @ 72/6	83	7	6
64 Musketts @ 15/-	48	0	0
15 Pistols @ 8/-	6	0	0
5 Thousand Flints @ 6/-	1	10	0
54½ Sheets Plated Copper	136	5	0
8 Rings Brass Wire	18	11	3
25 Copper Tea Kettles	9	9	0
6 Brass Guinea Kettles @ 6/6	1	19	0
5 Brass Neck Mannilas @ 3/-	0	15	0
7 Pewtor Screw Juggs @ 7/6	2	12	6

[1] The careful reader will note that Bishop's arithmetic sometimes erred. These notes ignore minor errors.

	£	S	D
1 Pewtor Quart Tankards @ 2/8	0	2	8
3 Pewter 3 lb Basons @ 2/6	0	7	6
2 Hangers @ 3/6	0	7	0
2 Silver Mounted Dᵒ @ 10/6	1	1	0
95½ Bars Swedes Iron @ 5/-	23	15	0
82 Large Iron Potts @ 3/4	13	12	10
2 Pye Pans and Covers @ 5/4	0	10	8
†95 Small Iron Potts @ 1/6	7	2	6
55 Gallons ½ Punchen Rum @ 3/-	8	5	0
1 Cwt Lead shott and Ball @ 28/-	1	8	0
12 Dozen & 9 Common Hatts @ 1/1 each	7	15	9
1 pair Indian Shoes @ 5/-	0	5	0
857 yards of Cloth @ 4/6	192	16	6
334 yards of Baiz @ 9d	12	10	6
71 Blanketts @ 4/6	15	19	6
150 Stone Jars @ 7½d	4	13	9
19 Dozen Looking Glasses @ 3/-	2	17	0
79½ Dozen Knives @ 2/6	8	13	9
11 Dozen mugs @ 1/6	0	16	6
8 Leather War Dresses @ 7/6	3	0	0
7 Leather Trunks	10	11	6
8½ Dozen Files @ 4/9	2	0	4½
3 Dozen & 10 Gilt Framed L. glasses @ 1/6 each	3	9	0
16½ Dozen Mane Combs @ 1/6	1	4	9
225 Dozen Buttons @ 9½d	8	18	1½
1 Dozen Scissars @ 8/6	0	8	6
1 Dozen Tin Powder Flasks @ 10d	0	10	0
6 Leather Spring Dᵒ @ 3/9	1	2	6
6 Leather Shott belts @ 3/6	1	1	0
3 Coopers Adzes @ 3/-	0	9	0
8 Hatchetts @ 1/6	0	12	0
136 Copper Rods @ 1/-	6	16	0
32 Dozen Ferretts bells @ 7d	0	19	6
10 pair Pairs Buckells @ 9½d	0	8	0
7 Tincil Bound Hatts @ 13/-	4	11	0
17 Dozen Pewter Spoons @ 15d	1	1	3
	£658	12	4

Errors Excepted Charles Bishop

* It is to be observed that only 11 half Barrels where sold to the Natives The rest, part of it was lost in the Magazine owing to the ill state of the Casks, Part used for the Ship, making Signals &c and Some in filling up the rest—CB

† By mistake there was only ONE hundred Small Iron Potts shipped. CB—

★ ★ ★

An account of Goods expended in purchasing and Procureing 192 Leather War Dresses, intended to be traded away again to the Northward and reckoned, equal to Purchase 677 Prime Sea Otter Skins of 1st: Quality.

	£	S	D
10 lbs Powder @ 1/6	0	15	0
4 Musketts @ 15/-	3	0	0
314 Copper Rods @ 1/-	15	14	0
73 Tea Kettles (276 lbs) @ 2/-	27	12	0
16 lbs sheet Copper @ 1/2½	0	19	4
24 Sheets Sheathing Copper			
8 Quart Copper Cupps @ 3/-	1	4	0
6 Copper Lipped Sauce Pans @ 3/6	1	1	0
1 Pewtor Screw Jugg @ 7/6	0	7	6
8 Silver Hilt swords @ 10/6	4	4	0
4 Common Dº @ 3/6	0	14	0
62 Bars Iron @ 3/6	10	17	0
0 Cwt. 3. 0 Muskett Ball @ 28/- per Cwt	1	1	0
4 yards Cloth @ 4/6	0	18	0
8 Blanketts @ 4/6	1	16	0
8 pair Copper Buckells @ 9½d	0	6	4
7 files @ 6d	0	3	6
3 Tin Powder Flasks @ 10d	0	2	6
6 yards Baiz @ 9d	0	4	6
2 Brass Guinea Kettles @ 6/6	0	13	0
30 Dozen Buttons @ 8d	1	0	0
	£72	12	8

Errors Excepted Charles Bishop

★ ★ ★

An Account of Goods expended for the use of the Ship Purchasing and Procuring Provisions &c

	£	S	D
24½ Bars of Iron @ 3/6	4	5	9
2 Cwt. 3. 0 Lead Ball & Shott @ 28/-	3	17	0
12 half Barrels Powder (Charged in Page 18)[1]	c	c	c
2 Musketts @ 15/-	1	10	0
17 Dozen Pewter Table Spoons @ 1/3	1	1	3
39 Dozen Buttons @ 7d	1	2	9
11 Dozen Knives @ 2/6	1	7	6
1 Dozen Looking Glasses @ 3/-	0	3	0
2 Punchens Rum (216) Gallons @ 3/-	32	8	0
4 Dozen Ferretts Bells @ 7d	0	2	4
6 yards Cloth @ 4/6	1	7	0
18 Pairs Buckells @ 9½d	0	14	3½
15 Copper Rods @ 1/-	0	15	0
8 yards Baiz @ 9d	0	6	0
10 Dozen Scissars @ 8/6	4	5	0
4 Dozen Files @ 6/-	1	4	0
10 Jars @ 6d	0	5	0
6 Razors @ 3d	0	1	6
2 Cwt. 0. 0 Old Iron @ 10/-	1	0	0
6 Bars Steel @ 6/-	1	16	0
	£57	11	4½

Errors Excepted Charles Bishop

★ ★ ★

[1] See above, pp. 162–3.

An Account of Goods served out to the Crew as Slops—

	£	S	D
116 yards Cloth @ 4/6	26	2	0
71 yards Baiz @ 9d	2	13	3
14 Blanketts @ 4/6	3	3	0
37 Hatts @ 1/1	2	1	0
1 Tinsel Bound Hatt @ 13/-	0	13	0
2 Gilt Framed Glasses @ 1/6	0	3	0
18 Knives @ 4d	0	6	0
11 Pairs Shoes @ 5/-	2	15	0
1 Pewter Tankard @ 3/-	0	3	0
	£37	19	3

Errors Excepted Charles Bishop

★　★　★

An Account of Goods disposed of at Faulklands & San'wich Isles:

	£	S	D
5 yards Cloth @ 4/6	1	2	6
1 Fowling Gun @ 15/-	0	15	0
2 Hatts @ 1/1	0	2	2
2 Dozen Knives @ 2/6	0	5	0
3 Razors @ 3d	0	0	9
3 Looking Glasses @ 3d	0	0	9
1 Half Barrel Powder @ 72/6	3	12	6
	£5	18	8

Errors Excepted Charles Bishop

★　★　★

Defisciencys and Brokage:

	£	S	D
1 Large Gilt Framed Glass @ 9/-	0	9	0
20 Stone Jars @ 6d	0	10	0
3 Dozen Muggs @ 1/6	0	4	6
2 Pistols (burst) @ 8/-	0	16	0
1 Muskett D° @ 15/-	0	15	0
2 Hangers @ 5/6	0	11	0
100 Small Iron Potts not shipped @ 1/6	7	10	0
	£10	15	6

Errors Excepted Charles Bishop

★　★　★

Captain Roger Simpson, Snow Lady Washington in Account with Ship Ruby, 26th February 1796:

Debtor—

1 Coil Cordage @ 20 Spanish Dollars—	20
1 Half Barrel Powder @ 30	30
6 Gallons Rum @ 8 Dollars	8
1 Puncheon Bread @ 38	38
Spanish Dollars	96

per Creditor

By Bill 96 Spanish Dollars on Messrs Bargmin and Bosman, owners said vessel[1] at Macao, Payable at Sight.

Charles Bishop

★ ★ ★

Remains of the European Cargo, going to Canton March 1796:

	£	S	D
16 half Barrels Gun Powder @ 72/6	58	0	0
127 trade Guns @ 15/-	95	5	0
23 Pistols @ 8/-	9	4	0
5 Thousand Flints @ 6/-	1	10	0
35 Copper Rods @ 1/-	1	15	0
2 Copper Tea Kettles (16 lbs) @ 2/-	1	12	0
32 Brass Kettles @ 6/6	10	2	0
16 Quart Copper Cupps @ 3/-	2	4	0
18 Copper Sauce Pans @ 3/6	3	3	0
75 Copper Neck Manillas @ 3/-	11	5	0
20 Brass Dº @ 3/-	3	0	0
4 Pewter Screw Juggs @ 7/6	1	10	0
10 Pewter Tankards @ 2/8	1	6	8
7 Dozen Spoons @ 1/3	0	8	9
197 (3 lb) Pewter Basons @ 2/6	24	12	6
45 Hangers @ 3/-	6	15	0
38 Dº @ 5/6	10	9	0
122 Bars Iron (38 Cwt. 2. 14) @ 23/6	45	7	8
90 Bars Steel (9 Cwt. 2. 0) @ 60/-	28	10	0
9 Boxes Tin Plates @ 62/-	27	18	0
3 Cwt. 1. 0 Block tin Bars @ 95/-	16	6	7
5 Large Iron Potts @ 3/4	0	16	8
13 Pye Pans & Covers (4 Cwt. 2. 0) @ 15/6	3	9	9
5 Small Iron Potts @ 1/6	0	7	6
10 Cwt. 2. 0 lead Ball & Shott @ 28/-	14	14	0
5 Tincil bound Hatts @ 13/-	3	5	0
379 yards fine Striped Cloth @ 4/6	85	5	6

[1] John Howel claimed, in May 1795, recently to have bought the *Washington* (Howay (1941), 490). An East India Company record of mid-1797 says it was Howel's property, but that he was 'engaged in a House of Agency with Mr Bagman third Supracargo of the Dutch house', i.e. the Dutch East India Company at Canton (Morse, II, 285).

	£	S	D
352 Dᵒ broad Cloth @ 4/6	79	4	0
70 yards Baiz @ 9d	2	12	6
54 Gallons Rum @ 3/-	8	2	0
14 Cwt Old Iron @ 10/-	7	0	0
24 pair Best Bellows @ 3/-	3	12	0
24 Grindstones 1 Ton. 14. 0. @ 32/-	2	18	5
150 Stone Jars @ 7½d	4	15	0
26 Coopers Adzes @ 3/-	3	18	0
40 Hatchetts @ 1/6	3	0	0
45½ Dozen Razors @ 2/4	5	6	2
23 Dozen Fire Steels @ 1/3	1	8	9
1 Trunk @ 31/6	1	11	6
14 Dozen & 7 large Files @ 9d	6	13	6
4 Looking Glasses @ 2/4	0	9	4
3 Dᵒ Gilt @ 1/6	0	4	6
3 Dᵒ Dᵒ @ 1/10	0	5	6
4 Dᵒ Dᵒ @ 1/1	0	4	4
31½ Dozen Mane Combs @ 1/6	2	7	3
14 Pairs Scissars @ 8½d	0	10	1
9 Dozen Japan Powder Flasks @ 10/-	4	10	0
6 Leather Spring Dᵒ @ 3/9	1	2	6
6 Leather Shott Belts @ 3/-	0	18	0
	£608	15	11

Errors Excepted Charles Bishop

★ ★ ★

per Contra Creditor

	£	S	D
By amount of goods sold Purchasing Furs	658	12	4
By Dᵒ Dᵒ Dᵒ Leather Dresses	72	12	8
By Dᵒ Purchasing Provisions &c	57	11	4½
By Dᵒ served out as Slops	37	19	3
By Dᵒ Sold at Faulkland Islands	5	18	8
By defficiencys and Brokage	10	15	6
By Amount of goods remaining	608	15	11

Total Creditor £1452   5   7½

Debtor to Goods as per Invoice £1444.   1.   7
Total Creditor   £1452.   5.   7½

Creditor by over charge in small Articles £8.   4.   0½

Errors Excepted Charles Bishop

★ ★ ★

Upon the Receipt of Mr Brownes letter (see page 13)[1] we proceeded immediatly to Whampu' where we arrived the next evening 22ᵈ April. The following morning, I waited on

[1] See above, p. 159.

Mr Browne at Canton, and after explaining the buisness of the voyage, and the situation of the Ship, I requested him to recommend to me a Person, to whom I could with propriety consign the Sale of my Cargo to, alledging, very truly, that I was a perfect Stranger to the Chinese and of Course liable to much imposition—Mr Browne gave his advice, that I had better certainly do so, but declined recommending any Person in particular—

I brought two letters to Canton, from Captain Simpson of the Washington to a Mr Howel, whom I had heard of at Macao. To this Gentleman's house I repaired, and found him a Person of very genteel address—and after talking over some Circumstances of the voyage, I found he did buisness as a Broker. I thought it best to consign the Sale of the Cargo to him, which he accepted at $2\frac{1}{2}$ per Cent, urging, at the same time, that as the cargo was not a large one, he hoped in a few days to settle the buisness and in the Mean time, considering that I had no Cargo of China goods to take in return, it would be very expensive to me to have a Factory, and therefore at my request permitted me to take part at his table. He accompanyed me to Whampu' the next morning with some Chinese Merchants to Examine the Cargo, who all agreed it was by all means, for the number of Skins, one of the best collections they had seen—Mr Howel returned to Canton and I staid on board to forward the repairs of the ship, which as may be seen by the Log was carried on with all possible dispatch—

On Thursday 28th: April I wrote to Mr Howel to know how affairs went on with respect to the Sale of the Cargo, and Received in Answer the following letter.

★　★　★

John Howel to Bishop, Canton, 28 April 1796:

At the moment your letter and Mr Williams arrived I was settling for your skins, on farther enquiry I found it was impossible to strike with Ponqua, or Poiqua,[1] as the latter would not give any thing near the Price, and the former was in too ticklish a state to be trusted, and could not raise the Money to make prompt payment

These last two days I have found the Merch*ant*s COOLING, and this day as the Hoppo[2] goes to Whampu' tomorrow I thought it best to Conclude for sixteen Thousand Dollars for the sea otter skins and tails with SUNQUA, on terms of the most perfect security, as I shall explain to you on board the Ruby tomorrow.

If you had been at hand I should have consulted you on the step I have taken, but you will find it has been for the best. If your vessel had not been Secured to day,[3] she could not have been measured, your Skins could not have been taken out, untill she was measured, and it is probable the Hoppo would have delayed it untill the Arrival of some other vessel. Your repairing would therefore have been impeded, untill the season for returning to the Coast was so far advanced, that you would have encountered the same risks Capt*ain* Simpson did last year. These circumstances infleuenced my Conduct.

[1] Morse gives frequent information concerning the merchants operating at Canton. His orthography differs slightly from Bishop's. The times were particularly strait for these merchants: see E. H. Pritchard, *The Crucial Years of Early Anglo-Chinese Relations, 1750–1800* (Washington, 1936), 370.

[2] 'The superintendent of Maritime Customs for Kwantung...was the Emperor's financial representative at Canton. He was known to the English merchants as the Hoppo, this being a corruption of the Chinese name of the department of government under which he served, the *hu-pu* (Board of Revenue). The Hoppo caused the foreign merchants at Canton continual trouble by his rapacity and high-handed actions' (Cranmer-Byng in Macartney, 8).

[3] On arrival at Canton a vessel had to be 'secured' to one or other of the merchants, forming the society known as the Hong. 'He is then termed the security merchant, and every trading transaction, relative to the vessel over which he is placed, entirely depends upon his controuling pleasure.—With this extraordinary authority, he possesses the power of arranging the trade of the cargo which he superintends, in any shape that may best answer his private advantage' (Meares, lxxvi). A merchant's credit with the Hoppo had to be good, before he was permitted to 'secure'.

Chunqua, and Conseequa, made no offers worth Attending to. In the Morning I shall be with you and will then inform you respecting your Stores &c.

★ ★ ★

Bishop to Browne, Whampoa, 26 April 1796:

I shall esteem it a favor if you will Inform me wither, Transfer on the Hon'ble Companys books, will answer the Same purpose as Cash, for bills on the Hon'ble Court of Directors in England, and be esteemed the same in value...[1]

★ ★ ★

Browne to Bishop, 26 April 1796:[2]

I have just recieved yours of this date, and in return have to inform you, that provided the Merchant you mean to sell to, has credit in the Companys books, Transfer will be considered in every respect the same as Cash.

★ ★ ★

On Monday 2d May the Hoppo came down and measured the ship by a line from the Centre of the Mizen to the centre of the Fore Mast calling her length 38 5/10 Cubits, and her breadth, from Gunnel to Gunnel before the Main Mast 15 2/10 Cubits—we Embrace all the fair Weather we can to get the ship Caulked, but find some of the bends so bad as to be under necessity of shiffting it. On the 14th May finding an unexpected delay in the delivery of the Furs, I wrote to Mr Howel the following letter

★ ★ ★

[1] The technique of transfer was adopted in response to the shortage of specie. Thereby a merchant in credit with the Company could ask the Company to pay (in bills drawn on the London Directors) part of that credit to a third party (Morse, II, 143–4).
[2] The place of writing is not indicated, if obvious from context.

Bishop to Howel, 14 May 1796:[1]

Feeling as I do for the interest of my friend and Employer Mr. Teast, you will not, I trust be displeased when I desire to know the reason of this delay in the delivery of the Furs. To the point, if an apology is necessary I'll make it afterwards.

Is Sunqua to take the Skins, if not, is the Ernast money Secured, Should Sunqua forfiet his deposit, will he be nevertheless the Security Merch*ant* and what differ*en*ce will it make in the Sales to another Merch*ant* his being so...Pray write me the particular situation in which we stand, as I am very desirous to conclude the buisness. You know as well as any person the necessity there is of my Sailing immediatly we can get ready, and which will be empeded now by the Furs not being delivered, that is so far as relates to my intended plan—

Send me, if you please 50 Dollars, 20 Gall*on*s Spirits and if Permitted by the Customs, one doz*en* Wine. Those orders you may recieve Signed by me, I beg you will honour, and I will thank you to inform me what is the usual p*er* Centage charged on Monies advanced to Seamen—

And now my friend, I have to intreat your attention to the particular Situation in which I stand, and I trust at the Same time, you have too much Candour, to soppose I mean anything derogatory of the opinion I first formed and which led me to consign the Cargo to you. I wish only for the Necessary Information, to give the Gentleman who Employs me, as well as a fair—an open and honourable account of my Proceedings, and which, from his conduct to me, He has an independant right to Expect.

Pray give my Comp*liment*s to Mr Davis, and that I shall expect him on board the Ruby, on Monday or Tuesday I shall be in town, by which time I hope affairs will be in a fairer way then I have reason to soppose they are at Present.

★　★　★

[1] On this period, see also pp. 183–5 below.

Howel to Bishop, 15 May 1796:

You feel as every honest Man ought to do, and which you convey to me by your letter of yesterday...There was no delay in the SALE of the Rubys Cargo, and the difficulties that have since arrisen, are of that nature which are remediable and far less troublesome than those which continnually arise here on winding up a transaction of a similer kind. It is easy enough to SELL a Cargo of Furs, but the difficulty consists in Selling them WELL—The price I sold yours for, I know to be the highest that any has produced this year, of which I can shew you convincing proofs when I have the pleasure to See you at Canton.

The intrigue here yet continnues. Last Evening Ponqua and the Linguist called here, at the Same time Sunqua Sent for me. I took Captain McNamara with me and we searched his Hong, but he Had thought proper to be out of the way. The Hoppo is at the bottom of the whole buisness which you will see here exemplified. Ponqua renewed his offer for the Skins, the Linguist assured me the Hoppo would not grant Sunqua a Chopp. The advice they gave under the specious cloak of friendship, was, that I should so sell to Ponqua. 'When will you pay me'—'Ten days'—'No'—'If you will bring four thousand five hundred Dollars here, (which on his securing the vessel, would be the ballance or thereabouts of the Eight Thousand Dollars Cash) and procure Eight thousand Dollars Transfer on the East India Company, I will sell you the skins immediatly'—'How can do so, what for you make afraid'—the Conversation of Course ended there—

In Reply to your question, wither if Sunqua forfiets his deposit, he will be the security Merchant for the Ruby, I inform you, that it is only from his inability to Secure the vessel, that the delay has arisen—of Course, should he forfiet it, he will not secure the vessel. A nominal eleven hundred Dollars I have recieved—but the deduction on Gold, and

the light dollars[1] returned will reduce it to about one Thousand
Safe in my possession, the remaining Six hundred I can
Secure you, as Capt*ain* Boit[2] owes them about that sum.

The Linguist is arrived whilst I am writing. He says that
Sunqua (that is, Saoloo) is gone into the City this morn*in*g
with Ponkequa the rich Hong Merchant, who will secure the
duties and then the difficulty will be done away. At 4 PM he
will give me a finall Answer, when a boat Shall be dispatched
to you

The usual p*e*r Centage charged in the Companys ships in
time of War is 70 p*e*r C*en*t in time of Peace 40 p*e*r Cent. The
Americans charge according to agreement. . . . I transmit you
50 Dollars. All your Orders shall be duly honoured. I have
a Doz*e*n of wine for you. There has been more trouble to get
that Leagar of Brandy, part for you, than you can well concieve, the Coolys are now gone for it, and I detain your boat
only 'till its arrival—

Talking about apologys, my good Friend, is quite out of
the Question. I know your motives for your Conduct, they
do you great Credit, and I doubt not but the whole affair will
be settled much to our mutual satisfaction. When Mr Teast
recieves the account of Sales, he can compare them with the
Jenny's, and if acquainted with Alderman Curtis[3] he may
enquire what the skins brought here in the Jackall being the
Cargo's of the Buttersworth, Jackall and Le Boo on their
first voyage, and of the latter two vessels, after their recapture,
where sold for, there will be a difference in his favour of
(Shall I say) 30 p*e*r Cent—

I feel myself honoured by your confidance and remain with
all Esteem. . . .

★ ★ ★

[1] I.e. literally light.
[2] John Boit was earlier mentioned as Captain Boyd (see above, p. 99).
[3] Sir William Curtis, 1752–1809, one-time Lord Mayor of London and
Member of Parliament, had extensive business interests, notably in the
Greenland fisheries (*Dictionary of National Biography*).

About this time, the ship Ceres arrived from Botonay bay. Captain Headly, her Commander, informed me of two American vessels having left that Place, to proceed to the North west coast this Season, and also, of the Prince William Henry and another vessell having sailed from England for the same purpose—that I could now count Six vessels on the Coast,[1] and Percieving that we could not possibly get away before the middle of June, and allowing 10 weeks Passage it would be the latter end of August before we could arrive on the Coast of America, a Period to late to Expect more than half a Cargo of Skins—I therefore was Induced to give up the Idea of Proceeding there,—therefore wrote the following letter to Mr Browne.

★ ★ ★

Bishop to Browne, about 18 May 1796:[2]

As I am desirous to render the ill success of my voyage, as little felt as possible, I beg leave to offer the ship Ruby, to the Hon'ble East India Company, for a freight of China ware to England. The state of the vessel will not admit her being laden with Teas, or perishable goods, without the highest probability of loosing much—

I shall be much favoured by your answer, as Soon as convenient, that I may regulate my conduct accordingly.

★ ★ ★

Browne to Bishop, 23 May 1796:[2]

In answer to yours of this date, I beg leave to inform you, that China Ware is not part of the Hon'ble Companys investment to England.

★ ★ ★

[1] The *Ceres*, Thomas Hedley, was at Port Jackson 23 January–3 April 1796. The Americans then in port were the *Otter*, Ebenezer Dorr, and the *Abigail*, Christopher Thornton. Howay (1930–4) lists seven ships on the coast in 1796, including the *Otter* and the *Prince William Henry*.

[2] Bishop's and Browne's letters were both dated 23 May, but the context shows that Bishop knew Browne's answer by 20 May.

In consequence of the Preceeding Letter, I began to consider seriously, how unprofitable, and with what loss, it would be Attended, to Carry the ship home, whose worth on her Arrival, must be Small indeed! for in opening her Side between the Main and Mizen Chains, to Shift some plank, that would not bear Caulking, it was with difficulty we could Shutt her up again. I began to Calculate the Expences attend*ant* on a Voyage to North West coast and also to England. The following is a Copy.

★ ★ ★

De*bto*r Ship Rubys voyage from China to N. W*est* Coast of America.

To Amo*unt* Wages from 10th June 96 to 10th February 1797 is 8 mo*nths* at 63£	£504
To Expences in Riv*er at* Canton (4000 Dollars)	1000
To Expences victualing &c 8 months at £32 : 10 per M*onth*	260
To Wear and tear and Expence of refitting the vessel for Engla*nd* or as she is now	700
To Interest of 1400£ for 8 Mon*ths* at 5 per C*ent*	46
To Insure*nce* of D° 8 Mo*nths* 8 per C*ent*	112
	£2722

per Contra C*redi*tor	Sp*anish* D*olla*rs
By a Collection of 700 Prime Sea otter Skins at 12 D*olla*rs Each	8400
By D° 350 Otter Tails a*t* 1 D*olla*r each	350
By D° Land Furs	100
	Sp*anish* D*olla*rs 8850
	5/- per D*olla*r being £2212. 10
	2722. 0
	Ball*ance* lost £509. 10

De*bto*r Ship Rubys voyage to England in Acco*unt* with her Arrival there.

	£
To Wages 7 months at 63£ per M*onth*	441
To Victualling &c £32 : 10—7 Mo*nths*	227. 10
To Interest & Insure*nce*	106. 0
To Wear and tear	350. 0
To diff*erence* in Exchange Gained by remitting on 3000 Sp*anish* D*olla*rs	75. 0
	£1199. 10

per Contra *Creditor*   £
By freight to England   £000000
By Value on her Arrival in England   300
               —————
               1199. 10

           Ballance lost 899. 10
      Errors Excepted Charles Bishop

★ ★ ★

Hence it appears, that to Carry the vessel to England, whose State is highly precarious, and should She arrive Safe, whose worth must be trifling, and her present Sails, Rigging Cables, and Provisions, worn out and Expended, That I cannot but think, that in writing the following letter to Mr Browne, I consulted the Interest of my Employer by sacrificing my Command, Pay, and the comforts I enjoyed on board the Ship, 'to render the ill success of my voyage as little felt as possible'...Charles Bishop—

★ ★ ★

Bishop to Browne and Supercargoes, 20 May 1796:

Finding by a Calculation made, and which I beg leave to submit to your perusal, that the Ruby, in consequence of the low price given for Skins at Canton, must make, in all probability, a sinking voyage by proceeding to the North west coast of America, even to admit we may meet with no Accident but that the collection of Furs equalled my most Sanguine expectations, on the one Hand, and that by proceeding to Europe, with a Rotton vessel, whose original purchase, four years ago, amounted only to 300 or 350£, on the Other, I think it a Duty I owe to Mr Teast, my owner, although I have no Specific Orders, other than to DO, what I shall consider MOST ADVANTAGEOUS to him, to Sollicit your permission to discharge the crew of the Ruby, into the Hon'ble Companys Ships, and Sell her together with her remaining European Goods, and materials, and remitt the proceeds of the Sales, together with that of her present cargo of Furs, by this fleet

I beg pardon for the intrusion I make on your time, but shall be happy of a personal interview when you are most at Leisure...

★ ★ ★

Upon my waiting on Mr Browne, he said He thought I was right in my Application, that the Select committee where willing to comply with my request, provided the purchaser was a brittish Subject trading under the protection of the Hon'ble Companys licence, but that it was not in their Power to grant it on any other terms and that they would write me an official letter to that Effect.

★ ★ ★

Browne and George Cuming to Bishop, 23 May 1796, granting permission in these terms. This is followed by a copy of a declaration signed William Jones, Commercial Resident of Amboyna and Banda, 22 December 1796:[1]

This is to Certify whom it may concern that the within written Copy of Letter of Permission, by the Select committee of Supercargos for the Hon'ble English East India companys affairs at Canton addressed to Captain Charles Bishop, respecting the Sale of the Ship Ruby is a faithful transcript of the original Letter

★ ★ ★

Being in want of some necessary stores, to go on with the repair of the Ship, I wrote to Mr Howel to procure them for me, and also for information respect*i*ng the sale of the Furs &c and Rec*eive*d in Answer, two letters, nearly of the Import, 1st:

★ ★ ★

Howel to Bishop, 26 May 1796:

By Mr Davis who visits you tomorrow, you will recieve 150 D*olla*rs and what other Sums you are in want of draw on

---

[1] Jones presumably was appointed to this post following Rainier's capture of the islands (see above, p. xxxiii and below, p. 201). The entry shows how long after the event Bishop wrote up the journal.

me for the Same. The buisness of the Skins is not yet finally settled, but you may be ashured your Cargo will fetch Sixteen Thousand Dollars, the depossit included, and I hope to Send for them the day after tomorrow

* * *

(2ᵈ:)

Mr Davis will be with you tomorrow, by him you will recieve the news and the needy, or necessarys. Every thing is in a fair train, and I am pleased with the complexion of affairs here. Being now called to a Meeting of Monquas creditors, I have not time to enlarge, which Indeed would be needless, as Mr Davis will see you so soon

P.S the Money intended for you yesterday was sent here

* * *

VOUCHERS RESPECTING PRICE OF PROVISIONS:

Captain *William* McNamara of Honble Companys Ship Deptford; to John Howel Esquire, *from Canton, 22 May 1796:*

Agreeable to your request of yesterday, I have to inform you that the average price of Beef and Pork, when we left England was from £7 to seven Guineas, and that the usual charges from one ship to another in the Companys service, as settled between the owners, is 50 per Cent added.

Captain *George* Saltwell, H: Company's Ship Kent, to John Howel Esquire: *from Canton, 25 May 1796:*

The average Price of Provisions when we left England was Seven Guineas, and has been Sold here amongst our Ships at 50 per Cent advance on the above price.

* * *

About this time it appeared that Sunqua the merchant who had bargained for the Skins for 16000 Dollars and had paid a Thousand deposit, as a Security, was not able to get the Ship Secured by the Houng Merchants and consequently take out the Skins. Of course according to the agreement the bargain became void, and he forfieted the deposit money. The fact was, he was indepted to his Government, the duties of a former contract: and they would not Suffer him to purchase my Cargo.—Things thus Situated, the Hong merchants would not make any offer for the skins worth attending to, and prevented others from doing so, by not securing the Ship.—The arrival of 2 English trading ships brought the Hoppo down to Whampu' to measure them, and the opportunity was taken to give him the following Petition, which by the Assistance of a French Gentleman (my Particular Friend Mr. Aqie) was translated and read to him.

★ ★ ★

To His Excellency the Hoppo of the province of Canton:

Being Obliged to represent to your excellency the conduct of Sunqua, a Copy of whose agreement is enclosed, and which he never has fulfilled. I beg leave to State the following circumstances

That in the first Place he made a false Chopp★. Secondly he has detained me by various Excuses, in consequence of which I have Suffered great inconvenience and loss. 3dly. that since he has forfieted his agreement he has prevented others, from purchasing my Cargo, and in consequence of which I shall be necessitated to depart from Whampu' unless your Excellency will order the Hong Merchants to Secure the Ship or Oblige Sunqua to fulfill his agreement with me.

★False chopp / a warrant or official order is called so.[1] Sunqua had Forged a false order to the Custom Officers, to deliver him the Skins but was detected, and 'tis Sopposed He'll be made to pay dearly for it

★ ★ ★

[1] This was the definition of a chop(p), not a false one.

About 10 days after this representation was made, an order came from the Hoppo, for the Hong Merchants to be assembled and for me to make Choice of either, to Seecure the Ship, and Ponqua was the one we fixed on.

The fleet had been ready to Sail by the 1st: June but did not proceed till about 23d: I had waited in hopes of being able to transmit the Proceeds of the sale home, but in vain. In consequence the two following Letters No: 8, 9, to Mr Teast where written in haste when the fleet was about Sailing.

★   ★   ★

Eighth Letter to Teast, 20 June 1796, sent per Deptford:

If I should not be able to close my accounts before the fleet Sails, I write this to inform you briefly, that your ship[1] turned out So leaky in our passage from the Coast of America to the Sandwich Islands for provisions, in February that I was obliged to bear up for Canton. We arrived here 14th April and to this hour I have been deluded with the Idea of getting 16000 dollars for the Furs, and have now at length settled to take 11,000, which with the one thousand forfieted by the party who where to have given 16,000, will make 12,000. I am also about selling your Ship and have an offer of 1300£ for her and the remaining European Goods.—The whole of my papers and proceedings shall appear the first opportunity— I feel much distressed on this occasion, that it is not in my power to send them now but am so situated that I do not know positively how my buisness Will End.—I trust you will have confidance in my integrity and honour, rendered, perhaps, suspicious by these untoward events. There is nothing I must confess ever gave me equal concern, day after day I have been put off with the expectation that the TOMORROW would close the buisness—and now the Companys treasurey is closed, and no bills will be granted 'till the arrival of more ships from Europe. The Supercargoes go to Macao 22d: on

---

[1] Now Bishop does not equivocate: the faulty ship is wholly Teast's (see above, p. 8 n.).

which day 'tis Expected the fleet will Sail for England. The companys Paquets close to day, which is my reason for writing this hasty letter, fearful I may not be able to inform you more fully before they Sail. The Crew will be settled with, partly in Bills on you and Partly in Cash I borrow, unless I shall be able to get a sufficiency of the Latter to settle wholly with them—as I am resolved every circumstance of my conduct shall appear before you in unadorned Truth, I will now conclude.

PS. we brought down to China 1100 Sea otter Skins and 200 Leather War dresses.—The Ship sells for 700£,European goods 300, Land Furs 50: and Leather war dresses 250 Pounds Sterling, in all 1300—In this circumstance I trust you will acquiesse with me, that I have acted right, for considering the Expence in wages wear and teare, there would be in carrying the Ship to Europe, who on arrival could not be worth 300£ will I trust reconcile you to the Step I have taken, and the more Especially as you may remember telling me to act always for your Interest and in the Same manner as if the Property with which you invested me, was my own—This I pledge myself always to do, not being so zealous in any thing as Concious rectitude of Conduct.

★ ★ ★

Ninth letter to Teast, 21 June 1796:

Not being able to sell the skins as yet and consequently not to pay off the People in Cash, and as the fleet is about Sailing, I am induced to give the following persons bills on you, as they have entered into an agreement with me that if I would discharge them before the fleet Sails, that they would not demand any Extra pay, which otherwise they would be entitled to, for being discharged in this Foreign Port. I beg you will accept them and charge them to my Account. The Names and Particulars are as follows.

	£	S	D
Mr. Thomas Hunt—2ᵈ officer	53.	16.	7
Mr. John Boothe—Surgeon	36.	19.	4
Thomas Symonds—Boatswain	52.	13.	6
Richard Evans—Armourer	47.	11.	0
Richard Bounds—Carpenter	11.	16.	0
Lewis Miles—Seaman	56.	1.	7
John Norton—Dᵒ	42.	4.	9
Richard Greene—Dᵒ	46.	13.	9
James Ricketts—Taylor	37.	16.	9
John Black—Seaman	36.	8.	0
	£422.	1.	3

NB. Mr Hunt: this sum includes his wages and his commission on the Cargo taken at 10£: Thirty five Shillings monthly pay deducted from his wages for 20¾ months. C.B.

NB. John Black is a Seaman shipped 13ᵗʰ December 1794 at 3£ per Month: in room of William Croker who on Account of ill health and at his own request was discharged. CB.

I trust Sir, that by the next ship for Europe, I shall be enabled to transmitt to you, an open and fair account of my agency in this unfortunate Expidition, and that after perusing my papers, you will find I have wanted nither zeal nor integrity, but hope you will with me ascribe the failure of Success to the right cause, The state of the vessel I commanded, who in her voyage had to encounter the stormyest Latitudes of both Hemispheres. Had it been only a voyage to the coast of Africa, no doubt but she would have performed it and returned all well to Bristol long ago, but in this voyage even before we had passed Cape Horn, we had been obliged to put into Falklands Isles and caulk the upor works all round, and the copper sheathing was almost totaly washd off her bows to the Fore Chains before we reached Easter Island. The frequent Gales of wind we met with on the coast of America, every thing had its effect to prove the Ruby was ill calculated for an expidition of such length

The skins are not yet sold, the People whom we had bargained with for 11,000 Dollars having declined, and I believe that 2000£ will be the utmost they will neat clear of the Duties.—The Scarcity of Cash has been so great in China since the war, that skins sold only for 9 Dollars last December...Mr Howel has informed me he will write you fully on this Circumstance, hence there is no necessity for me to enlarge on the Subject. I had heard on the coast they would not fetch more than 15 dollars, hence my resolution of wintering on the coast as I wrote you from Nootka (N° 6) 27 Sep*tember*. If the fleet does not sail tomorrow, and we should sell the Skins to day which I have some hopes of, I will write you again.

★ ★ ★

The following is Part of the Copy of Letter N° 10 dispatched by same fleet. It was written deliberatly from time to time on board the Ship at Whampu', which as I was laid up with sore Boiles at this time I could not get it up, before I had previously dispatched the 2 Preceeding Letters.

Tenth letter to Teast, begun 1 May 1796:

General review of expedition's troubles from September 1795 to arrival at Whampoa, where the market for skins soon proved weak.

As I felt myself a perfect stranger to the manners and customs of these imposing Mandarines and Chinese, I have consigned the Sale of the Cargo to a Gentleman of respectability here of the Name of Howel, who it seems, does a good deal of buisness here, in this way for the Country Ships. He is to have 2½ *per* C*ent*. In this I hope you will aquiesse with me that I have acted right, for you will hardly Concieve the difficulties and impositions a Stranger has to encounter... and while Mr Howel is attending this buisness, I am getting the Ship ready to Careen, we find the copper sheathing almost totally off the bottom before the main Chains, but in a few days we shall be better able to See what repairs she will want.

Friday[1] 6th May. N° 10 Continnued,...

Monday last I recieved a letter from Mr Howel, at Canton (vide Page 23)[2] and the next morning he came down to

---

[1] Properly, 5th. [2] See above, pp. 168–70.

Whampu', and gave me such reasons for striking the bargain that perfectly Satisfied me that more could not be got. Sixteen Thousand Dollars is four Thousand more than I was before offered for the Sea otter Skins, and Tails. As for the Land Furs they are in no estimation here and will hardly pay the Duties, for which reason I purpose not to sell them.—As all the necessary papers relative to Mr. Howels agency and the Sale of the Furs will accompany this, it will not be necessary for me here to say more, but proceed to state the situation and equipment of the Ship. For this few days past we have been Employed in giving the Ship a Partial Careen, and ripping the Sheathing off the bends and what is left of the Copper on the 1st and 2d streak below them...I am sorry to add I feel it necessary to Call a Survey to know wither the ship can be repaired, either for a passage home or for the N West coast of America, and what those repairs must be. We are now cleaning the Starboard side, which as soon as it is done, we Shall go on with the other, and then hold a Survey, the result of which you shall be informed off

Wednesday 10th May. No 10o Continnued.

Before I proceeded as was intended, I sent for Captain Headly of the Ship Ceres of London, and Captain Wattleworth of the Ship City of Goa of Bengal. The former was of opinion that the vessel might be repaired for a passage to Europe, and concluded by saying if Called on by the Survey he could not condemn her Especially as we where in Company with a fleet of Companys ships where stores and Plank could be bought to refitt her:—the other, Captain Watteworth, who is an old India trader and well acquainted with its Navigation and winds, declared he would not leave the Port in So rotton a vessel. This being what I thought of her myself, as well as the opinion of Several Carpenters and Mr Hunt, I declined calling a Survey for this reason, that if Condemned no person would buy her by reason of its hindering inshurence to be made, whereas I might be able to get a good Price for her, and in which case, if Permitted by the Companys

Supercargos, I shall think it my Duty to Sell her and in the mean time we went on refitting her in the best manner we could, to be ready to sail at all events, should I not Succeed in disposing of her to advantage.

Thursday 25th May. N° 10 Continnued.

    Capt*ain* Headly having informed me that a Capt*ain* Dorr, in a ship from Boston had sailed for the N W*est* coast from Bottony bay, and that Capt*ain* Barbor from Bengal had Sailed also sometime before,[1] I could count Six vessels on the coast this season, vizt. the Washington, Prince Will*ia*m Henry, Capt*ain* Barbers Brig, Capt*ain* Dorrs Ship, & Capt*ain* Erwan consort to Prince W*illia*m Henry,[2] who traces up the coast of Mexico and His Majestys Ship Providence.—The lateness of the Season before we could arrive on the coast, the probability of our not getting more than 400 Skins, if so many, induces me to think it wrong to attempt going again. It appears by the Calculation which I inclose (vide Page 29)[3] that even 700 Prime skins must loose near 400£ to the adventure. Impressed with this Idea I gave up the thought of returning to the coast, and applyed to Mr. Browne and the Select committee for freight of China ware to England (vide Page 28).[4] As for Teas, it would be the highest imprudence in me to take them in, even if the committee thought proper to give me a freight, and the impossibility of your being able to inshure against damages, which would most likely exceed the amo*u*nt of the freight—China ware is not part of the Comp*an*ys investment this year.—From the same motives, which influenced my mind in declining to go to the N W*est* I applyed to Mr Browne and the select committee for permission to sell the Ship & remain*i*ng European goods, & Rec*eiv*ed in answer the inclosed copy (vide Page 31).[5]

---

[1] The *Arthur*, Barber, from Calcutta, left Port Jackson 3 April 1796. It is obscure why Bishop now omitted the *Abigail* from his calculations.
[2] From the listings in Howay, 1930-4, this might have been the *Sally*, Joseph Pierpont.
[3] See above, pp. 175–6.
[4] See above, p. 174.   [5] See above, p. 177.

Whampu 15th June. Letter N° 10 continnued:

Situated thus, I could not find any person to bid for her that stood within the discription of their permission, consequently I was necessitated to go on with the repairs to be ready to sail for England with the Hon'ble companys fleet in full confidance that the Skins would have been Sold by this time. By the 6th of this Present month the Ship was already, and Equipped for Eight months in the best Manner we where able. On that day I recieved an offer, and to which I at length acceeded—Captain Robert Pavin a free merchant of India, under the Companys Licence, is to give 700£ for the Ship and materials, 300£ for European Goods, 50£ for Land Furs, and 250£ for the Leather war dresses, in all 1300£. This I hope you will think with me, is better to accept than to be at the Expence of carrying home a vessel, which when she arrives her rigging and Sails worn out, her provisions and Stores Expended can be of little value. She is now fitted, or I believe no one would give 300£ for her here.

N.B...The remainder of this letter I had not time to Copy from the reason given in the beginning of it, and it was dispatched after the Ships where under weigh beating down the River

★　★　★

On 6th: July the long Expected Sale was made of the Sea Otter Skins and Tails for Thirteen Thousand dollars in Cash and on the 9th: they where delivered and the money Paid, Five Thousand of which according to agreement, was Paid to Ponqua the Security Merchant for the duties of the Skins and Custom and admeasurement of the Ship. I am told he gained nothing by this but having So much ready money put into his hands, he was not necessitated to pay to the Government till the China new year, which is somtime in March.—

★　★　★

SHIP RUBY'S accounts. CANTON.

Howel & Company Bill of Disbursments

Debtor Ship Ruby and owners, to John Howel and Company, Canton:

	Dollars	Cents
23^d April—To Cash paid the Pilot	30	o
24th—D° paid to Captain Bishop	40	o
25th—Boat hire to Whampu' to Examine Furs	2	50
29th—Cash advanced Captain Bishop	20	o
Sundry necessaries, vizt: 10 Caddy Tea, 4 —2 Caddy Pepper, ¾—China ware for Ships use, 16	20	75
2^d May—Cash advanced Captain Bishop	50	o
2¾ Gallons Linseed Oil & Jar	4	50
8th—Cash advanced Captain Bishop	24	o
11th—6 Dozen Bottled Porter @ 1¼ D per Dozen	7	50
15th—9 Gallons Brandy @ 1	9	o
Cash advanced Captain Bishop	52	o
19th—D° D° D°	119	50
2 Piculs Damar[1] @ 5	10	o
Duty on D°	2	o
24th—Cash advanced C.B	3	o
25th—13½ Gallons Brandy & 3 Jars	14	o
27th—Cash advanced Captain Bishop	150	o
D° Paid the Hoppo Man, per order Captain Bishop	23	o
2^d June—paid ship Warren Hastings, per Bill	2	12
11th—Advanced Captain Bishop	100	o
15th—Paid Captain Foy as per Bill	483	o
17th—Paid Captain McNamara as per Bill	241	50
Paid Captain Dundas as per Bill	3	50
22^d—Advanced Captain Bishop	621	o
3–6th July—Boat hire delivering Furs	8	o
6th—Cash advanced Captain Bishop	621	o
D° D° D°	100	o
Charge of Linguist 177¾, House Comprodore 100, Ships Doctor 200.	477	75
To Expences of Factory Provisions &c from 23^d April unto 6 July	350	o
Shroffage on 1400 Dollars @ ½ Dollar per Month	7	o
Cash advanced Captain Bishop	594	o
To Amount Bill of Disbursments	3611	62
To Cash paid Ponqua the Security Merchant being for the Duties of the Furs & the Rubys admeasurement	5000	o
To our Commissions on 14000 Dollars @ 2½ per cent	350	2
To Cash Paid Captain Bishop	400	o
D°	100	o
D°	100	o
D°	100	o
D°	500	o
D°	100	o
D°	65	o
Debtor Spanish Dollars	10326	64

[1] Dammar.

per Contra Creditor Ship Ruby.   Dollars Cents

	Dollars	Cents
By Cash received from Sunqua, a deposit forfieted 1100, Less by Expenditure on 50 Johannes:—48, Light Dollars returned—48	1004	0
By Amount of Sales of the Sea otter Skins & tails	13000	0
Of Ship Ruby Stores &c	2800	0
Of Sundry European Goods on board her	1200	0
Of 197 Leather war dresses	1000	0
Of Sundry Land Furs	200	0
Captain R. Simpsons Deficit on us	96	0
Total Creditor	19300	0
Debtor	10326	64
Credit Ballance Due ship Ruby Dollars	8973	36

Canton 10 July 1796:
E.E. Signed John Howel & Company

★ ★ ★

EXPENCES AND DISBURSMENTS OF SHIP RUBY
AT CANTON 1796

Macao	Spanish Dollars	Cents
13 April—Pilotage to Macao roads	12	0
√Refreshments for Crew at D°	3	0
15th—√D° D°	3	0
16th—√D°	3	0
√Writing letters, Postage	1	50
17th—√Refreshments	3	0
18th—√boat hire	1	50
√Tea & ½ Dozen Fowls	2	50
√Pork & Greens	3	0
√Oil for binnacle	3	0
20th—√fowls and Greens	3	0
√Lamp for Cabin	0	50
√Bill at Tavern, refreshments to self & boats Crews at Several times 26 Dollars half	13	0
22d—Pilots Chop to Whampu'	10	0
√Postage letters to and from Canton	6	0
√2½ Cwt Buiscut @ 4 Dollars per Cwt	10	0
√Fresh meat and Greens	4	0
23d—Boats assisting to Whampu'	1	0
Whampu'		
√Pilotage to D°	30	0
24th—Expences to Canton	6	0
Broad Axe and Adze	4	0
29th—√8 lbs Tea	4	0
√3 lbs Pepper	0	75
√China ware Cabin use	16	0
1st May—√3 Gallons paint oil	4	50
Fresh beef, Greens &c for Ships Company	49	0
3d—Boat hire and Expences to Canton	6	50

	Spanish Dollars	Cents
6th—Sheaves and Pins for blocks	4	0
Boat hire to Canton	2	0
√6 Dozen Porter @ 1¼ Dollar per Dozen	7	50
√9 Gallons Coniac brandy @ 1 Dollar per Gallon	9	0
9th—Fresh beef and Greens &c 6 days	26	0
2 Gallons oil for Pitch	4	0
Brooms and Loybins[1]	3	50
√2 Piculs Damar	12	0
14th—Paid Caulkers	16	0
Do Carpenters	5	0
Do Carpenters of the Osterly	5	0
28th—Fresh beef Greens &c 19 days	114	0
√13½ Gallons Brandy	14	0
5 lbs Sheathing Nails	2	50
June 1796—√15 lbs large Nails. Warren hastings bill	2	12
√Captain McNamaras bill for 2 Tierces ⎫		
3 Barrels Pork, 1 Tierce Hams, ⎬	241	50
1 Whip Saw ⎭		
√Captain Foys bill, for 10 Tierces beef, ⎫		
16 feet 2½ Inch Oak Plank, 36 feet ⎪		
Deal Do, 2 Cords Fire wood & 4 Cwt ⎬	483	0
Junk ⎭		
24 lbs Sheathing Nails	3	50
2 Pickels Damar (226 lbs Country Pitch)	12	0
2d—Paid Caulkers	23	0
Do Carpenters	24	0
4th—1 Picul Damer (133 lbs Country Pitch)	6	0
10th—Paid Carpenters & Caulkers	23	0
21st—Paid Mr. Hunt 2d Mate on Account of wages	75	0
Do Richard Evans, Armorer	57	0
Do Mr Booth Surgeon	256	25
Do Richard Bounds, Carpenter	14	0
Do Thomas Symonds Boatswain	77	0
Do Lewis Miles Seaman	50	0
Do John Nortin Do	63	25
Do Richard Greene	53	0
Do John Cornew	26	50
Do James Ricketts	50	0
Do John Black	17	0
Do James Cheard	9	25
Do James Norman	28	75
Do George Beaven	8	0
Do John Learne	8	0
Do James Jinkins	8	0
9 July—Do Mr Moon 3d Mate	403	75
Do Mr Williams on account Wages & Commissions	535	0
Do William Raggett	154	60
√Boat hire delivering Skins	8	0
Fresh Beef Greens &c for Ship Company and ⎫		
workmen, 36 days, & 2 Dozen Wine for the Sick ⎭	227	0
Paid Bonnars bill: for refreshments to boats ⎫		
Crews, 10 Caddies Paint, 3 Cwt Buiscut ⎭	42	25
√Expences of Factory Provisions &c from ⎫		
23d April to 9 July ⎭	350	0

[1] I.e. most likely bins for containing lye.

Spanish Dollars Cents

	Spanish Dollars	Cents
July 9—√To John Howel & Company their commissions ⎫		
(cont.) for Selling the Cargo 2½ per Cent on 14000 ⎬ 350	350	2
Dollars ⎭		
√Charges of Customs to Linguist	117	75
House Comprodore	100	0
Ships Comprodore	200	0
√To Ponqua the Security Merchant for the ⎫		
duties of the Furs and admeasurement of ⎬	5000	0
Ship ⎭		
Total Spanish Dollars	9595	74

NB articles Mark'd √—are taken from Howel & Company's bill

★ ★ ★

The Charges of the House and Ships Comprodore 300 Dollars being so unjust, as I never had either one or the other, I was led to hope that by representing the matter to the Hoppo of Canton he would direct that this imposition should not be levied on me. I there-fore sent the Following address to His Excellency the Hoppo of the Province of Canton

★ ★ ★

Bishop to Hoppo, 2 July 1796:

I am sorry to trouble your Excellency with complaints against two of the Linguists, who refuse to undertake the buisness of the Ship Ruby under my command, unless I pay them 300 Spanish Dollars for the House and Ships Comprodores which people I never Employed, or could procure, by reason of the Smallness of the Ship and her Crew they said it was not worth their while.[1]

I am well convinced your Excellency will not suffer this imposition when it is made known to you therefore I humbly pray your Excellency to interfere therein

★ ★ ★

[1] 'From the outset [of British trade with Canton] a host of minor functionaries had also taken their share of the spoils...there were the linguists who were supposed to act as interpreters, but in fact were low-grade clerks who spoke a smattering of pidgin English, and the compradores who supplied the ships and factories with provisions. The services of these and other minions of the officials were compulsory' (Cranmer-Byng in Macartney, 8).

This was presented into his hands but I was afterwards told by one of the Houng Merchants that it being Customary for all Ships to pay these fees to the Linguists he did not choose to alter it in the present Instance

The People beloning to the ship having hinted to the officers that If I discharged them here they would expect four months additional pay to find them a passage to Europe, and upon inquiry I found they where intitled to get it unless they entered in a Specific agreement not to demand it. I therefore drew out the following which all except the officers signed[1]

★ ★ ★

Ship Ruby at Whampu' in River Tigris 15th June 1799.[2]

It is agree'd between Charles Bishop Master and Consigner of the ship Ruby of Bristol, on the one Part, and the undersigned, being Seamen and mariners of said Ship on the other Part, Witnesseth,

That if the Said Charles Bishop, Should sell the said Ship Ruby at this Port, that we will not demand or claim any Sum or Sums of money to find us a passage to England or as Extra wages for being discharged in a foreign Port, or other cause, save and except the ballance of our wages due to the day we shall be So discharged, and in witness whereof we have Each affixed our marks or Names in the Presence of the Officers of the Said Ship Ruby the 15th day June 1796.

Signed—Thomas Symonds, boatswain
   Richard Evans armorer
   Richard Bounds Carpenter
   Lewis Miles Able Seaman
   John Nortin D°
   Richard Greene D°
   John Cornew $\frac{3}{4}$ Seaman

[1] But why did the men thus renounce their rights?
[2] The Boca Tigris was an anchorage at the mouth of the Canton River (see map, Morse, II, 1). The year should read 1796.

John Black   D°
James Ricketts   Taylor
William Raggett   ½ Seaman
James Norman   D°
James Cheard   D°

Signed in the Presence of us, the Officers of Said Ship

Signed, Joseph Williams   1ᵗ Mate
    Thomas Hunt   2ᵈ D°
    Thomas Moon 3ᵈ D°
    John Booth Surgeon.
           Charles Bishop

★ ★ ★

Debtor Sidenham Teast Esquire Owner of Ship Ruby, in account with Charles Bishop Master thereof, in a Voyage to N. West Coast of America &c:

	Spanish Dollars	Cents
20ᵗʰ October 1794—		
Lundy Island To Corn for Stock at Lundy Island	7	0
10ᵗʰ November—Anchorage at St Jago	4	0
St Jago Fruit: 400 oranges	1	0
15 December—Pilot and Harbour Master at Rio de Janario	28	80
Rio de Janiro ½ Pipe Port wine	45	0
1 Roll Brazil Tobacco	3	60
1200 billits Fire wood	8	80
1 Whip Saw	2	40
3 Dozen Poltry	9	20
Linguist	4	20
Corn for Stock	3	0
Fresh beef, Fruit, vegetables &c for Ship Company 11 days	36	0
Difference of Exchange between London & Rio on a Bill 36£	44	80
Falklands Islands—To 4 Bullocks at Faulklands Islands bought with Tobacco	—	—
13 April 1796—Pilotage to Macao roads	12	0
Maco Refreshments for Crew &c while there	70	0
23ᵈ—Pilotage and Boats to Whampu	31	0
Whampu'—Expences of Provisions, Stores, refreshments from 23ᵈ April to 9 July 1976 at Whampu &c per Disbursements	1656	62
9 July		
Expences of Carpenters & Caulkers repairing the Ship	96	0
Boat hire delivering Skins	8	0

	Spanish Dollars	Cents
Whampu'—Howel & *Company* their commissions for selling the Cargo, 2½ per *Cent* on 14004 Spanish Dollars	350	2
July 9		
To the Charges of Customs at Canton	5377	75
To Wages of Mr Joseph Williams Chief Officer from 29th of *September* 1794 unto 9th July 1796 ie 21 Months 10 days at 20 Dollars per *Month*	426	67
To Wages of Mr Thomas Hunt 2d Mate 20 Months 22 days @ 19 Dollars	395	54
To Do Thomas Moon 3d Mate 21 Months 10 days @ 18 Dollars	384	0
To Do John Booth, Surgeon, 20 Months 22 days, @ 20 Dollars	414	67
To Do Richard Evans, Gunner, 20 Months 22 Days, @ 16 Dollars	331	74
To Do Thomas Symonds Boatswain 20 Months 8 days, @ 18 Dollars	364	80
To Do Richard Bounds, Carpenter, 20 Months 22 days @ 5/6 per Week	96	30
To Do Lewis Miles, able seaman 20 Months 22 days @ 16 Dollars	331	74
To Do Adam Peterson Do 9 Months 6 days @ 16 Dollars	147	20
To Do Richard Greene Do 20 Months 22 days @ 16 Dollars	331	74
To Do John Norton Do 20 Months 6 days @ 16 Dollars	323	20
To Do John Cornew ¾ Seaman 20 Months 22 days @ 12 Dollars	248	80
To Do James Ricketts Do 20 Months 22 days @ 12 Dollars	248	80
To wages of John Black, 18 Months 10 days @ 12 Dollars	220	0
To Do William Croker cook 3 Months 16 days @ 12 Dollars	42	40
To Do William Ragget ½ Seaman 21 Months 10 days @ 8 Dollars	170	67
To Do James Cheard, ¼ Seaman 20 Months 22 days @ 4 Dollars	82	94
To Do James Norman ¼ Seaman 20 Months 6 days @ 5 Dollars	101	0
To Money & Slops advanced to John Learne apprentice	32	60
To Do Do Do George Beaver Do	26	0
To Do Do Do John Jinkins Do	31	0
To Commissions of Chief officer, 1 per Cent on 9827 Dollars the neat Sales of the N. West Cargo	98	27
To Commissions 2d officer 7/6 per Cent per 100£ on Do	36	95
To 4 months additional pay to the Chief officer to procure a Passage to England	80	0
To Do Do 2d Officer Do	76	0
To Do Do 3d Officer Do	72	0
To Do Do Surgeon Do	80	0

	Spanish Dollars	Cents
15 August 1796—To My Wages commencing 29 September 1794 to 15 day August 1796 ie 22 Months 16 days at 24 Dollars per Month	540	80
To my Commission on the neat Sale of the Sea otter furs 8627 Dollars at 3½ per Cent, 2½ being deducted to pay agentcy	301	25
To my Commission on the Sale of the Land Furs & Leather war dresses amounting to 1200 Dollars at 6 per Cent	72	o
Spanish Dollars Debtor	13828	27

15 August 1796   Errors Excepted   Charles Bishop

★   ★   ★

Creditor Sidenham Teast Esquire owner of the Ship Ruby in account with Charles Bishop Master thereof in a voyage from Bristol to the North west Coast of America and China—1794-5-6.

	Spanish Dollars	Cents
Lundy Island: 19—By a bill in favour of…for corn &c October 1796	7	o
By 2 months advance wages to Chief Officer @ 20 Dollars	40	o
By 2 months advance wages to 2ᵈ Dᵒ @ 19 Dollars	38	o
By 35 Shillings per Month advance to 2ᵈ officers wife in England for 20 Months 22 days	145	13
By 2 months advance wages to 3ᵈ officer @ 18 Dollars	36	o
By 2 Dᵒ Dᵒ Dᵒ to Surgeon @ 20 Dollars	40	o
By 2 Dᵒ Dᵒ Dᵒ to Gunner @ 16 Dollars	32	o
By 2 Dᵒ Dᵒ Dᵒ to Thomas Symonds @ 18 Dollars	36	o
By money advanced Richard Bownds, Carpenter	32	o
By 2 Months advance wages to Lewis Miles @ 16 Dollars	32	o
By 2 Dᵒ Dᵒ Dᵒ Adam Peterson @ 16 Dollars	32	o
By 2 Dᵒ Dᵒ Dᵒ John Nortin @ 16 Dollars	32	o
By 2 Dᵒ Dᵒ Dᵒ Richard Greene @ 16 Dollars	32	o
By 2 Dᵒ Dᵒ Dᵒ John Cornew @ 12 Dollars	24	o
By 2 Dᵒ Dᵒ Dᵒ James Ricketts @ 12 Dollars	24	o

	Spanish Dollars	Cents
By 2 D° D° D° William Croker @ 12 Dollars	24	0
William Raggett did not Exchange his shipping note	0	0
By 2 D° D° D° James cheard @ 4 Dollars	8	0
By 2 D° D° D° James Norman @ 5 Dollars	10	0
By Amount of Slops, Cloth, Hatts, &c served out to Crew	468	83
By Amount of Hospital Money deducted from Crew's wages	68	40
By Amount of bill drawn at Rio de Janira £47.4	188	80
January 1795—By a Fowling Piece & 6 Razors sold at Falklands Islands	21	0
February 1796—By Amount of Stores sold to Captain R Simpson	96	0
May Canton—By the forfeit of a Bargain in sale of Sea Otter Skins	1004	0
July By Sale of Sea Otter Skins	13000	0
By Sale of the Leather war dresses	1000	0
By Sale of the Land Furs	200	0
By Sale of remaining European goods on board	1200	0
By Sale of the Ship Ruby stores &c	2800	0
By Amount of Bills drawn in favour of the Crew	1937	45
14 December—By 10 per Cent on 10000 dollars Amboyna allowed by Howel & Company on a Bond of Respondentia from Macao to Amboyna	1000	0
By amount of interest become due on the discharge of Bond of respondentia	475	0
Creditor Spanish Dollars	24083	61
Debtor	13828	27
Ballance Creditor Spanish Dollars	10255	34

Amboyna 14 December 1796   Errors Excepted   Charles Bishop

★ ★ ★

Copy of Bill of Sale of the Ship Ruby.

This indenture and bill of sale, made at Canton in China 15th day of August[1] in the year of our Lord one Thousand seven hundred and ninety six, between Charles Bishop master and consignee of the ship Ruby and the Cargo thereof,

[1] The chronology becomes so confused that it is uncertain whether this is the correct date, or whether Bishop meant July.

13-2

wherof Sidenham Teast Esquire merchant in Bristol is owner and consigner, on the one part, and Captain Robert Pavin, a free mariner trading under the licence of the Hon'ble English East India Company on the other part.

Witnesseth, that for and in consideration of the Sum of Thirteen hundred pounds of good and lawful money of Great Brittain in bills of Transfer credited on the Hon'ble English East India Companys Books, paid by the aforesaid Robert Pavin unto Charles Bishop for the sole Benefit of Said Sidenham Teast Esquire, the Said Charles Bishop by and with permission of the select committee of Supercargos intrusted with the said Hon'ble Companys affairs in China, do hereby sell and deliver up the Ship Ruby, burthen per Certificate of Registry, one hundred and one Tons, together with the Leather war dresses, European Goods, anchors Cables, boats Provisions, stores and every thing there unto beloning or appertaining to Said vessell, unto the aforesaid Captain Robert Pavin, to and for his sole use and benefit, Renouncing by these presents as Consignee, all right and tittle to the same for himself and Sidenham Teast Esquire his heirs Executors and administrators, for ever,...and in witness hereof the Said Charles Bishop afixeth his Hand & seal the day and year above written and in the presence of the Subscribing Witnesses—

Witness Present   Signed Charles Bishop
     George Madagon
     J Howel   ☺ seal

★   ★   ★

Thus having disposed of the Ship & Cargo and Mr Howel having passed his receipts for the Amount, Mr Pavin was put into possession and loaded her with an assorted Cargo of China Goods for Amboyna. The agreement respecting the purchase having been made 6th June, and Mr. Howel ashuring me he had the purchase money in his hands ready to settle with me, I gave him possession on the 9th of July reserving her papers untill a final settlement—on the 14th July I called on Howel to come to a settlement with me, which he appeared ready to do but as the English supercargos were gone down to Macao, he desired me to write to the Select Committee informing them I had such a sum of money in Transfer bills, and to know what manner I should dispose of it for bills drawn by them on Hon'ble Court of Directors in England, in consequence of which I wrote the following letter.

★ ★ ★

Two letters consequently written to the Supercargoes, dated 14 and (no reply having come) 22 July 1796.

★ ★ ★

Richard Hall, G. Cuming, and Samuel Peach[1] to Bishop, from Macao, 28 July 1796:

We this day received your letter of the 22^d instant addressed to our president, that which you inform us of your having written on the 14th has not yet reached us

We have carefully refered to the proceedings of the late committee, under date 23 May last and find by a letter to your address that permission was then granted to sell the Ship Ruby under certain limitations—but no mention is anywere made of an Engagement on the part of the committee to accept transfer for the amount—It is an indispensable preliminary that we should know what Merchant has granted a transfer before we can pledge ourselves to carry any sum to acc*ount* and if, after we are posession of that information it should be convenient to give the credit required, we can only engage to grant you bills, on the Hon'ble court of directors at the rate of Exchange we may hereafter settle when we open the Treasury for the present Season

---

[1] These men comprised the new select committee, which re-formed each summer at the end of the trading season. Hall was President; Bishop mis-spells Cuming, 'Cumming'.

It will be more convenient to the Committee that you should post from the presentation of your Transfer untill we arrive at Canton:—it is necessary every merchant at the time he has credit given him should grant his reciept to us for the same as it appears in our books in the form of a payment.

★ ★ ★

I shew'd this letter to Howel and begged he would give me the Name of the Merchant the transfer had belonged to. He said that he had not compleated the whole Sum, that the merchant he was going to get the remainder from, was in the City and would not be out again that day. At same time advised my answering the committees letter and inform them the ashurence I had recieved from Mr. Brown late President of the Select committee respecting transfer &c.

★ ★ ★

Letter from Bishop to Supercargoes, not dated:

Quotes letter from Browne, bearing date 26 May but actually written 26 April.[1]

Impressed with this Idea I sold the Ship to Captain Robert Pavin together with her European goods for 1300£ in transfer and her Cargo of Furs principally for Cash, but which I have paid away in duties Expences and wages to the Crew, all but about 3000 Dollars—

I must solicit your attention Gentlemen to the unfortunate situation of my voyage, and as I have hitherto acted to the utmost in my power to render the loss has little felt as possible by my owner, I must hope you will not throw any obstacle in my way of getting as early as possible through my buisness as I purpose leaving China in His Majesty's Brig Amboyna, should I be able to compleat it before her Sailing—and should you Gentlemen resolve to recieve Transfer from me has Cash

---

[1] See above, p. 170. Bishop's copy does not indicate the error in dating.

I shall thank you for your determination as early as convenient, & I will immidiatly forward the Names of the Merchants and their Reciepts.

★   ★   ★

To this letter I received a short note from Mr. Hall dated 4th August informing me Mr. James Drummond one of the supercargos would be at Canton in a few days who would be ready to settle any Accounts of Transfer I had with the Company.

On the 10th August I wrote the following letter for Mr Teast meaning to leave it to be forwarded by the first ships for Europe.

★   ★   ★

Eleventh letter to Teast, 10 August 1796:

General review of matters reported in eighth, ninth, and especially tenth letters.

Mr Hunt who is gone home in the Brittannia with most of the Crew will be able to give you any information you want not contained in those letters, to whom I refer you, for altho' we did not latterly after our arrival here agree So well has we had done before, yet I have confidance to think he will not assert any thing but Truth, which is what I charged him to do upon taking his leave of me...I have now to inform you of particulars since the departure of that fleet. With a great deal of difficulty, and not without waiting personally on the vice Roy,[1] we got the ship secured by one of the Houng merchants of the Name of Ponqua, who in a few days brought us a merchant that offered 13000 Dollars for the sea otter Furs, including the duties to be paid by us— It was 1000 dollars more than had been offered since the forfieture of the 1st bargain and as I was pressed for the money

---

[1] Bishop surely confused the Hoppo with the Viceroy, of course a far superior officer.

I had borrowed for disbursments and without probability of getting more, it was taken, and Ponqua the Security Merchant took on himself the duties of the Ship and Cargo for 5000, hence the Eight thousand remaining together with one thousand and four Dollars, forfieted in a former contract with Sunqua for 16000 makes the whole neat produce for the Sea otter Skins & tails 9004 dollars. Mr Howels bill of disbursments and accounts current together with my own will be inclosed in this letter.

The companys supercargos being at Macao no buisness will be done by them respecting the granting of bills untill they come up to Canton, which will not be perhaps this 2 months. Nevertheless the select committee has permitted me to pay the ballance of my expences and disbursments into their treasury which they are to grant a reciept for, to give bills in your favour as soon as they come up to Canton, at the rate of Exchange they may open their Treasury at, which last season was at 5/3 per old mexican dollars. Probably it will not be higher this. This reciept, I purpose to leave with Mr Howel, to get three setts of bills drawn in your favour and to inclose a sett in each of my 3 Letters and Accounts duplicates of each other, to go by different conveyances

And now Sir! I come to the buisness of my not returning immediately to Europe, to give you personally an account of my agency in this unfortunate Expidition, and in the first place I declare I have neglected doing nothing that seemed to me to favour your interest throughout the voyage, as to my accounts I have vouchers for them all Except a few small sums where no bills passed on the occasion, and in perusing my bill of disbursments, I must beg you to consider, that on my arrival I fully intended to refitt and Sail again for the N West coast of America but on hearing of the many vessels gone to the coast this Season, and for reasons given in my former letters, I gave up the design, but at that time not seeing any probability of selling the vessel, I was still necessitated to go on refitting her, to be ready should I not get an offer for her to Sail for Europe. Consequently my Expences are great, but great as they are, I cannot but think they were judiciously laid out, for I belive no one, had I not refitted her would have given 200£ for the Ship. The Arrival of His Maj*esty's* Brig Amboyna from Admiral Ranniers[1] squadron at Amboyna, brought us the intelligence of the Capture of the Spice Islands,[2] and I am informed by her commander that officers are much wanting in the fleet, and he had no doubt on my going round with him that the admiral would soon give me an appointment from the length of My Naval Services—you will Consider Sir! I served 13 years in the Navy without any reward but the respectable certificates from my commanders of my behaviour and of course have Some reason to hope for Promotion, to loose then this opportunity, by returning to Europe, would I concieve from your friendly manners and liberal behaviour to me, incurr even from you, the only person that my returning can possibly concern, a degree of censure—I think it will make but a few months difference, as the admirals station is nearly Expired wither I stay here to sail in November, or go with the fleet. A year in all probability will bring me to England, when I hope to see you in health, and clear up personally any unfavourable impression you may have concieved of my conduct—my own Expences has been so great together with the possibility of being keept in India longer that I expect, Induces me to draw my wages and Commissions to the full, and on my departure shall have about 400 dollars in my chest, not having any other known Friend in India—you have a shurty in hand more than Equal to any possible Error in my accounts, which should any be found I have no Objection to consign to the clearing away, when I come home—and believe me ever to be, dear Sir! with Esteem & Gratitude...

★ ★ ★

This letter in triplicate and accounts also, where all ready to seal, soon has the bills could be obtained from the Select Committee, but alas! an Event of which the following are the

---

[1] Rainier (see above, p. xxxiii).   [2] Banda.

particulars rendered the writing of them lost time, and created for me a world of unhappiness and anxiety.

It was on 13th: August Mr. Drummond arrived at Canton, he sent me word he should be ready to do buisness with me on the morrow at 11 oclock,—I told Mr Howel of it who said he should take care to be ready, we breakfasted together and at 9 he parted from me to go and get the bills, as he said, but never made his appearence again that day. I called on Mr. Drummond, told him the circumstance, adding that I had no doubt but that Mr Howel would be ready with his accounts that evening, or tomorrow early. Mr. Drummond replied, with a significant shake of the Head, I wish for your sake Captain Bishop, he may. I began now to be Alarmed, and when Howel came home in the evening (which he did not do 'till 10 oclock) I taxed him in warm terms for his suspicious conduct. He heard me with great composure and by some plausible Excuse or other put me off 'till tomorrow, (tomorrow! tomorrow!) damnation! and so on 'till the 18th: when I received the following Notes from him.

* * *

Howel to Bishop, 18 August 1796:

Unless I procure Transfer for you before 12 oclock this day, I shall be under the necessity of going down to Macao with you in the Ruby, where the Sum now due can be Settled, with the Hon'ble Companys Select committee there on terms more benifical than any I have under the pressure of opposition, from a powerful Source, hitherto been able to procure...

* * *

To this note I replied that I should not suffer the Ruby to depart from Whampu' untill I was settled with, or a Sufficient security give, that I should be paid immediatly at Macao.... In the Forenoon of that day I recieved another note from him...

* * *

Howel to Bishop, 18 August 1796:

I do not think it consistent with your duty you should suffer the Ruby to leave China, without a full settlement of her affairs, but going down to Macao, whilst you have all her papers, bill of sale &c as well as my person for security I think is a different case

The sum of Transfer has been several times agree'd for, but on my being informed that if the Hong Merchants would Call on Mr. Drummond, that he would inform them of Mr Halls determination, they have after the visit always retracted, from what reason I pretend not to state. If you wish evidence of this, you may recieve it from their own mouths.

I have ever found you inclined to oblige me in every particular—and I could never Surmise, either, that Such impedements would arise, as have arisen to the discharge of the contract here, under the circumstances of the case. However I trust you will, when done with perfect Security to yourself, and owners, which may be effected by my giving you a bill of sale of the Cargo, and your retaining the Ships Papers from Capt*ain* Pavin (worth trebble the amount due) shew the Same disposition to serve me as has uniformly Characterized you.

To Mr Hall it may be said that supposing money would be more acceptable than Transfer, from the tenor of his letter: and finding that you could pay it in at Macao, you had adopted that mode—Money is so acceptable that the offer of it will be no sort of offence.—On the consideration of these circumstances which appears to me a proper statement, I think it will be preferable to adopt my proposal, as at this critical time the least delay would baffle your Expectations, and Ruin the Rubys voyage

I will make another attempt this morning and at 12 oclock will see you on the Subject—If you suppose my dear Sir!

that I have thus long delayed, with any improper view, the Settlement with you for the Ruby Cargo &c, you will recollect the innumerable difficulties I have had to Struggle with, and that they were principally created by a Scandalous exercise of a Superiour power. I hope nothing will arise either in action or intention, that may tend to lower me in your opinion, which would be still more mortifying to me than the Loss of any property could be...at ½ past 12 I will inform you of the result of my Exertions.

★　★　★

To which was added the following Note.

I have written to you on the subject of the inclosed because I thought it more satisfactory—the americans want three per Cent for their money per month, I can get it at Macao for 1¼ per Cent.—Do not mention I mean to go down with you—By and bye I will Explain to you the reasons of my not succeeding here.

★　★　★

It was plain now I could not be settled with here, and the only way I knew of Secureing the Property, was by insisting on having a bill of sale of the Ruby's Cargo, and the snow Lady Washington now on the N West Coast, and which I then understood Mr Howel was sole owner of[1]—The Rubys bill of sale, and papers I still held in my possesion. All of which Mr Howel readily acceeded too. Anxiety, and the great heat at Canton unrefreshed by sea breezes, caused me much ill health about this time, and I felt a sensible decline every day. I was therefore Glad, soon as I had made every thing as Secure as I could, to sail with the Ruby to Macao, where we arrived 23ᵈ August—Mr Howel and Captain Pavin

---

[1] Yet earlier Bishop had otherwise described the ownership of the vessel (see above, p. 166). Presumably Howel had told him that 'Bargmin and Bosman' were his agents, which indeed was true at least in part. Perhaps not they but yet further parties were the other owners to whom Bishop now alluded.

went immediately onshore, being determined myself to remain on board untill I should be settled with. The vessel had
no Crew in her but 1, 2 & 3ᵈ officers who where Attentive and
Obed*ient*. On the 3ᵈ day Mr. Howel wrote me word he should
be ready on the morrow to settle with me and disired I would
come on shore rather than risque the loss of the money by
bringing it on board. Accordingly I repaired on Shore taking
with me my papers & securities—He left me at 9 oclock the
next morning to go and fetch the money, we where to meet
again at 12 oclock.—at 1, I recieved the following Note:

★ ★ ★

Howel to Bishop:

The Inclosed will shew you I am disapointed and can't
pay you in the manner I have promised, but you have
Sufficient security in your hands—sell then! the vessels,
and their Cargos, and pay your self—the Surplus you will,
I have no doubt, deliver to me—

★ ★ ★

Upon inquiry I found the Washington belonged to several
other proprietors and that Howel was only part owner & Ships
Husband. The Rubys Cargo had cost 10000 dollars, but if
put up to auction would probably at Macao not fetch 6000.
I had purposed to go to Amboyna, and has her cargo was
expected to meet with a rapid sale there, I thought if inshurence was made and a proper interest alowed, it would
be not very material to Mr Teast, if he recieved his Money
in bills from Amboyna in the room of Canton: I therefore
agree'd to the following bond of Respondentia

★ ★ ★

Know All Men by these presents, that we John Howel and
Robert Pavin, are held and firmly bound unto Charles Bishop
in the Penal Sum of nineteen Thousand Eight hundred dollars
current money of Spain, to the true and lawful payment

whereof we do hereby bind ourselves, our Heirs, Executors, administrators & assigns, firmly by these presents, in witness whereof we have hereunto set our hands and seals at Macao in China, this 29th day of August in the year of our Lord (1796)—

Whereas the above bound John Howel and Robert Pavin have taken up and recieved of the aforesaid Charles Bishop the full and Just Sum of nine Thousand nine hundred Spanish Dollars, which sum is to run upon Respondentia on the Ship Rubys Cargo, whereof Robert Pavin is now Master or Commander, from this Port or Road of Macao to the Molucca Islands and from thence else where unless a Sufficient Sum can be there procured to pay and discharge this bond, at the rate of 2 per Centum per Month interest, and in consideration of which the usual risque of the Seas, Rivers, Enemies, Fire, Pirates &c to be on account of the Said Charles Bishop,

And for the farther security of the Said Charles Bishop the Said John Howel and Robert Pavin do hereby consent and agree for themselves their Heirs Executors, adminstrators and assigns, to mortgage and assign over the Said Charles Bishop the several wares and merchantdize laden or to be laden on the Said Ship Ruby, which said wares or Merchantdize with their produce are thus mortgaged and assigned over and to be diverted to no other use or purpose whatever, untill payment of this bond is made with the premium that may become due thereon

Now, the condition of this obligation is such that if the above bound John Howel and Robert Pavin, shall well and truly pay or cause to be paid unto the Said Charles Bishop, His Heirs, Executors, administrators or assigns, the full amount of this bond, and the premium due thereon, at the Expiration of the voyage, or in manner above specified or in Case of the Loss of the Said vessel, which God forbid! such an average as by custom shall become due on the Salvage,

Then this obligation to be void and of no Effect, otherwise to remain in full force and virtue—

Signed John Howel—

Signed Rob*er*t Pavin—

Signed Sealed and delivered
where no Stamp paper is to be had
in Presence of us

Signed   Geo*rge* Madagon
            Will Hugh Dobbie.

★ ★ ★

Messrs. Howel and Pavin afterwards entered into a Private agreement with me, to allow 200 Spanish Dollars p*er* Month untill the bond should be cleared, for my detention and loss of time &c. Things being thus aranged, we sailed in Company of his Maj*esty's* Brig Amboyna and Store Ship Eliza 3ᵈ Sep-*tembe*r Having left the following letter to be sent to Europe the first opportunity in room of that written at Canton 10 Aug*u*st (vide Page 55).[1]

★ ★ ★

Second version of eleventh letter to Teast, from Macao, 29 August 1796:

I had expected not to leave China before the whole of your buisness was completely settled, and the bills Recieved and inclosed for you, but Sir! I am much disapointed. Mr Howel together with Capt*ain* Pavin who contracted to buy the Ship, depending on the arrival of a vessel of theirs, from the Isle of France,[2] have loaded the Ruby with a Cargo of China Goods and Stores for the markett at Amboyna and the Spice Islands, and disenabled themselves to settle with me, and I am necessitated in consequence to take a bond of

---

[1] See above, p. 199.   [2] Mauritius.

Respondentia on the Ship and Cargo for the sum of 9900 Spanish Dollars, which I beg you to inshure from Macao to Amboyna and the Moluccas Islands in and upon the Ship Ruby, Robert Pavin Master. I go myself in her, and expect to arrive there in six weeks perhaps sooner. The Ship is now tight having been hove down at Canton, as far as the 1st: Course and her leaks Stopped, and may be now considered in a safe and good condition, and fitted well for the voyage, man'd with 25 men beside the Master & Self and arm'd as before with 10 Carrige Guns—

Upon our arrival at Amboyna the Sale is to commence and I am to recieve the money untill the whole bond of respondentia is Cleared—there is no doubt but the Commander in Chief, Admiral Rannier will be glad to give me Governments bills for the whole, which you shall recieve together with my accounts

I must hope Sir! the unlucky events of my voyage will not deprive me of your confidance and Esteem. I have written fully on my proceedings and the misfortunes and disapointments I have encountered, in Confidance that I should finally settle my affairs here, but as this letter contains also those accounts unsettled. I must defer sending it untill I get bills on Government or India Company to inclose...

★ ★ ★

V

MEMORANDA CONCERNING
NAUTILUS VOYAGE

Twelfth Letter to Teast, from Amboyna, 23 October 1796:

I am happy to write by the companys packquet going to Madrass and now about sailing that we arrived here from China 15th Instant, and the Cargo is sold, so that on the 26th. Captain Pavin is to settle with me—and as I understand, Admiral Rannier will be glad to give me bills on Government at an Early date for Cash, so that I am in hopes of being able to forward one sett by the ship Eliza to Bombay who sails about 27th. from whence they will come to you by the Earliest opportunity—I am sorry I am not enabled to send on a sett by this vessel—my accounts &c will be inclosed with the bills, and brought up to 19th Instant. The ballance will be seen in the following short statement, Vizt.

	Dollars	Cents
Due you 29 August in Ballance of Bill of Disbursments	8485	—
Inshurence 10 per cent on 10,000 Dollars alowed by Howel & Company	1000	—
Interest 2 per cent per Month on 8485 Dollars 1 Month 20 days	282	36
	9767	36
N.B. $\{$ on Examining the Accounts there is found to be	294	more
and interest thereon 2 per cent 1 Month 20 days	9	81
Spanish Dollars	10,071	17[1]

I wrote to you three letters duplicates of each other from Macao informing you of the Necessity I was laid under, of taking a bond of respondentia on the Cargo of Goods laden in the Ruby for the purpose of having it inshured, 10 per Cent being allowed by Msrs. Howel & Pavin, and your account stands with him as above.

I write this hasty letter, has the pacquet may meet an earlier opportunity of forwarding it to Europe than the Eliza, to advise you of our Situation, and you shall find in my letters accompanying the bills my motives explained, for what I have done, and tho' it may lessen me in your opinion as a merchant, you will find they have tended to one general

---

[1] The N.B. was not in the letter: see below, p. 217.

point of good, namly, to render the ill success of my voyage as little felt as possible,—I ashure you Sir! my Anxiety on this subject has not favoured my constitution or health, and altho' I have been well ashured of your liberality, yet I cannot but feel anxious, to Clear up any unfavourable impression in Person, which my conduct, from the necessity of unforseen circumstances, may have given rise to

★   ★   ★

The 26th: arrived, the merchant to whom Captain Pavin sold the Cargo failed in his payment, consequently Pavin was not able to keep his promise with me. In a few days after He failed altogether and Pavin being his principall Creditor, took back the Cargo he had sold, and opened a store for himself— in the mean time Admiral Rannier was preparing to sail for India 1st: December. Therefore I was obliged to give up all thoughts of going with him, Pavin not having been able, to pay off 1/3d of the bond.

Situated thus! I gave up the thoughts of going in the Navy altho! Admiral Rannier had kindly taken me by the hand and promised to promote me the first opportunity, and Indeed! would have given me before He sailed an appointment to be 3d Lieutenant of His Majesty's 40 Gunship Resistance, if I had not told him my commercial concerns being so unsettled, I could not accept of any appointment what ever, untill they where finished—

The Nautilus, a beautiful little Brig, 4½ years old built at Calcutta, by Colonel Kidd[1] for a yatch, burthen about 80 tons, registered 65, Copper bottomed, arm'd and well found in Stores, was putt up for Sale. The merchant who had failed, had bought her from her commander, for 7000 Dollars, but not being able to make good his payment, she was again

---

[1] Alexander Kyd (1754–1826), Bengal Engineers, had been promoted Brevet Lieutenant-Colonel in May 1796. He was the son of a naval officer and the heir of Robert Kyd, founder of the Calcutta Botanical Gardens. One of the aims of the latter institution was to encourage the growth of teak for shipbuilding.

offered to sale—and having carefully examined her, I found she was well adapted to the trade on the N W*est* Coast, and concieving, IF I COULD ARRIVE IN TIME IN CHINA TO REBUY THE LEATHER WAR DRESSES, and European Goods, I had left behind, I should have funds Enough to make a voyage to the N W*est* and be in good season on the Coast, and, with the knoledge of the trade and information I possess, of being able to get a large Cargo of Sea Otter Skins, and thus make up for the losses sustained by the infirm state of the Ruby, impressed with a resolution to persevere for what I consider'd the good of my employer, I Purchased this vessel for 6200 dollars, or 4000 Star Pagodas, Madrass Currency, from Mr Charles Sheldon Timins[1] agent and Commander of said brig, 23ᵈ November 1796. The following is the Copy of her bill of sale.

★ ★ ★

This Indenture and bill of Sale made at Amboyna this 23ᵈ day of November in the year of our Lord (1796) between Charles Sheldon Timins, Master and Consignee of the brig Nautilus whereunto Major Alexander Kydd of the Hon'ble East India company's Engineer Service, is owner, on the one Part, and Charles Bishop agent and consignee for Sidenham Teast Esq*uire* Merch*ant* in Bristol on the other part.

Witnesseth that for and in consideration of Four Thousand Star Pagodas, Madrass Currency, payable upon the delivery of the vessel &c, I, the aforesaid Charles Seldon Timins, by virtue of Power of Attorney granted by the said Alexander Kydd, do hereby sell and deliver up the brig Nautilus, and the whole of her equipage and papers compleat, unto the aforesaid Charles Bishop, for the sole use and benefit of said Sidenham Teast Esq*uire* renouncing upon the payment of Four Thousand Star Pagodas, all Right and title to the said Brig, and my receipts for the said sum shall be considered

---

[1] For a note on the Timins family, see C. N. Parkinson, *Trade in the Eastern Seas 1793–1815* (Cambridge, 1937), 377. It is written to illustrate 'the close connection which existed between the Navy and the Maritime Service'—so strong a theme in Bishop's story.

as a total discharge of any claims the present owner, Major Alexander Kydd, his Heirs Executors &c &c hereafter make upon the Said Brig Nautilus

In Witness whereof I have hereunto set my hand and seal this Twenty third day of November in the year of our Lord (one thousand 796)

Signed   Charles S. Timins

Signed seal'd & deliver'd in the presence of us where no Stampt Paper is to be had

Signed   { George Smith
           { Robert Pavin

★ ★ ★

The vessel being rigged when I bought her, and wanting only ballast, water and Provisions, I began immediatly to equipp her for sea, to be ready to sail for Macao soon as Mr Pavin should have settled with me—on the 1st: December Admiral Rannier in the Suffolk with his squadron sailed for Madrass, by which opportunity I sent the following letter to be forwarded to Europe.

★ ★ ★

Thirteenth letter to Teast, from Amboyna, 30 November 1796:

In my last letter, N° 12 dated from this place 23 October, I informed you of our safe arrival here, and of the Cargo of the Ruby having been sold by Captain Pavin, but the merchant failing in his payments, he has taken back the whole, and is now selling off rapidly, by wholesale and retail, and has already accounted with me for near half the sum due, and in the Course of a fortnight will get through the whole I expect— Admiral Rannier being to sail tomorrow for the coast of India with the whole of his squadron except the Resistance, I am of course necessitated to give up the thoughts of going with him, not having anyone here with whom I could trust my concerns.—

214

Two or three days before our arrival here a beautiful little brig called the Nautilus built about 4½ years ago at Calcutta for a yatch, arrived with a Cargo of Madrass goods, and after the delivery of it was offered for sale for 7000 Sp*anish* Dollars, which after mature consideration and deliberation I bought for 4000 Star Pagodas Equal to 6200 Spanish dollars—and now having premised the buisness with the purchase of the vessel, I have to lay before you my motives for so doing—trusting to my good intentions and your liberality that you will acquiesse with me—In the first place the Nautilus is almost new, perfectly sound and good, copper bottomed, sails remarkably fast—Is registered 65 Tons but measures and Carrys near 80, armed with six three pounders Brass Guns with six brass swivals, pretty well found in Masts, y*a*rds, sails Rigging anchors and Cables, and very well calculated for the Fur trade on the North west coast of America, witer I mean to proceed with her, for you are to recollect that the Fur trade is not so barren yet, but that with the knoledge I have derived will be made to answer well, and had not the Ruby failed under us, I should most certainly have proved it to you in my last voyage

I shall sail from hence in a fortnight, and proceed to East-*war*d of the Peleu[1] Islands thru' the straits of Luconnia and Formosa to Macao, a passage most likly not more than six weeks. I expect not to be more than three weeks there, pro-cureing an investment, part of which, will most probably be the 200 Leather war dresses, I brought down in the Ruby, a Certain 800 Otter Skins of the first quality. I shall with these I hope have sufficiency of Cash to lay in an investment for 2500 skins and allowing myself no more than two months in so fine a vessel as the Nautilus to reach the coast of America, expect to be in Norfolk Sound Latt: 56½° N by 15th April, a period early enough to proceed any vessel from Europe or America.

I purpose the Establishment of the Nautilus to be with respect to myself and two officers, the same as in the Ruby

[1] Palau. One is left uncertain as to the precise route Bishop took.

with a crew of 10 Europeans and seven Chinese all at easy wages, and I declare to you Sir! that nothing in my life has ever been undertaken by me in which I was so sanguine and certain of success, as in my intended voyage—by the End of June I expect to have disposed of all my goods, after which I mean to fill up all my Casks with Salted Salmon which sell well and may be reckoned at 20£ per Punchen—Captain Pakenham[1] of His Majestys Ship Resistance, was with me when I proposed the plan of my voyage. He formerly commanded one of the men of war on the Newfoundland station, and is well aquainted with the fisheries and their value, and has laid open to me such a scene of Commerce and with such sanguine Expectations of success, that he immediately offered me 10000 Pagodas eaquel to 15000 Spanish dollars, to invest me with to purchase a Ship at Macao to go with the Nautilus to the NW. Coast and fill up salted Salmon—I consider it certainly as a great mark of his confidence & Esteem, but of course declined his offer, untill I should be able to hear from you—The experience I have derived has a trader and also as a Merchant, will I trust prevent me from involving myself in a speculation, that I am not certain of its Effect.—I am as far has HUMAN! Certain of the Fur trade, and purpose when I shall arrive with skins from the Coast at China, to sell them, refitt the Nautilus, buy up an investment again, and the remainder, amounting most likly to the sum I now hold of yours, to remitt in bills to you, and then proceed on a nother voyage to the N. West unless I should find express orders from you to the contrary. From China I will send home the Journal and accounts of the Ruby, and also in case of Accident to me, mean to appoint Mr. James Drummond, one of the Companys Supercargos at Canton my agent for your concern. He is a good Merchant and very much Esteemed, and your letters addressed to Him will Come to my hands safly.—

[1] Captain Edward Pakenham, R.N., had commanded the *Resistance* as she assisted Rainier's successful ventures. Thence he derived considerable prize-money, and no doubt this prompted his rather remarkable offer to Bishop. Pakenham had a North American background, but the examined records do not indicate precisely when he served in Newfoundland.

You know my licence will Expire next September. You may be able to get it renew'd, tho' I can answer for it in India it will not be asked for—The Nautilus being a Country built vessel is free to trade anywhere in India, but if you could get a free mariners Indentures for me, I perhaps could improve the voyage—If you have confidence in me, which I am determined to merit in the end, I must hope you will not damp my ardour and Zeal for this adventure by Countermanding my intentions—with respect to the 2^d voyage, I declare Sir upon my Honour—that if I do not find it will answer much to your interest, I will wind up the concern and return immediattly to Europe—But think Sir! what a Sacrifice I should make, of my experience information and opportunitys by returning now—I totally renounce the Navy, of course, my mind is zealously turned to mercantile affairs and determined to attend to every circumstance that may conduce to serve you—

The Nautilus is not inshured, you will act in this as you please. I think from hence to China it should not be more than a West India passage in Peace, and from China to the N. West coast and back again, not more than 8 *per cent*. There is no enemy to fear and the Navigation safe and well known.

* * *

On 16th De*cember* Cap*tain* Pavin finally settled with me, and I delivered up the Papers of the Ruby, and cancelled the bond of respondentia, when the ballance of the Rubys voyage remaining in my hands including the Purchase of the Nautilus was 10,255 dollars and 34/100 (vide Pages 49, 50, 51) but by a mistake in making up the accounts then, was thought to be 9960 dollars—and so written in Letter N° 12[1]—on the 27th De*cember* the vessel was compleatly watered and ready to sail on the morrow when it was found she had begun to

[1] The accounts cited are at pp. 192–5 and the letter at p. 211 above. In the accounts Bishop includes interest on the Bond (475 Dollars) while in the letter he excludes that but adds interest on the capital (282.36 Dollars) so that the sum named was 9,767.36 not 9,960 Dollars.

leak very suprizingly and on using the Pumps they where
become immediatly Choaked: so that we were obliged to
keep bailing out the water with bucketts untill we could get
the Pumps put to rights. Alarmed at the vessel thus suddenly
becoming Leaky, we serched Earnestly to discover the cause,
but in vain. It was found necessary to Start the water and
Clear the Hold, when has they worked aft the leak was traced
to proceed from a bolt hole in wake of the 2^d Rudder brace,
the bolt of the brace not having passed through a timber had
worked loose and fell out. The sceiling was opened, a Timber
put in and the Brace properly secured after which she made
no more water, but being ballasted with Sand & Shingle, for
fear of accident I thought proper to throw it overboard and
ballast her with Stone.—The vessel was all ready to sail by
4th January 1797, when the Carpenter caulking the wedges of
the mast discover'd a nest of white Ants which had eaten
near a third through in wake of the partners. A survey being
called it was found necessary to get the mast out and Cutt
3 feet off the heal to set its defecttive part below the deck.—
A Careful search was made everywhere but we could not
discover any other trace of these distructive animals being in
the ship—on the 6th the mast was got in again and on the
7th: six large Ships appearing off the Harbours Mouth who
where sopposed to be six French Frigates, the merchant
vessels where ordered to slip their Cables and run up into the
inner Harbour. The next day however the ships Came in and
Proved to be six English East India men from Europe bound
to China—having procured some Provisions and stores out of
them, and settled all my buisness at Amboyna we sailed
13th January, but in passing thro' the fleet the wind suddenly
died away, and before we could apply to the boats we drove
foul of one of the India-men and Carried away the main Boom
and a Top Gallant Mast.

The Ship Jane sailed in company with us untill 24th January
when being in the Latt: 0° : 36′ N she parted from us bound
to Madrass, by whom I wrote the following letter to be
forwarded to Europe. ★ ★ ★

Fourteenth letter to Teast, at sea 0° 36' N, 130° 20' E, 24 January 1797:

I embrace this opportunity of the ship Jane parting company bound to Madrass to inform you of my sailing from Amboyna the 13ᵗʰ January—and expect to arrive at Macao in three weeks—while we lay waiting the Change of Moonsoon at Amboyna, I took the opportunity of overhauling the Rigging Sails &c and Caulking the vessel, the condition & workmanship of which is certainly most excellent, the more I see of her either has a sea-boat, fast Sailer, or as a Strong vessel, comfortably accomodated, the more I admire her—In my Letter Nº 13 dispatched by Admiral Ranniers Squadron 1ˢᵗ December I informed you of my purchasing this vessel and my reasons for so doing—

The Commandant of Amboyna, Major McNeal,[1] desirous of forwarding my expidition, spared Me from the Companys stores 40 Excellent Musketts and 12 Barrels Gunpowder. I have got some Cutlery and shall get 1500 yards broad blue Cloth at China, which (tho' a little damaged, yet good as the best in the world, to tare up into short Pieces) was selling at the company stores in China 25 per Cent under prime Cost when we came away, beside which I hope to be able to gett the 200 Leather war dresses I brought down in the Ruby.

My Crew at present consists of 12 Seamen, 2 Officers and one Servant whose wages is full 25 per Cent less than was given to the same Number out of England—I have in bengal Cloth and bills and Cash about 3500 Spanish Dollars, which I trust will be fully sufficient for the remainder of the Provisions Stores and investment for 2000 sea otter Skins—a few days before we left Amboyna six sail of English East India

[1] Daniel MacNeile, Madras Infantry, was promoted Brevet Major March 1794, substantive Major June 1796, Brevet Lieutenant-Colonel July 1796. In that month he sailed from Madras to Amboyna with a reinforcing garrison, and remained commandant there until 1799 (these biographical notes on Kyd, Pakenham, and MacNeile were compiled in London by Lieutenant-Colonel M. E. Laws, R.A. (retired)).

Men arrived from England bound to China. These ships will depart again for Europe about Midsumer, and I shall leave With them my Journal accounts &c for you, which most probably will reach your hands soon as this—you may ashure yourself Sir! I will neglect no opportunity of writing to you of my proceedings...

★ ★ ★

We had a very rough passage to the Bashee[1] Islands and suffered a good deal in the article of sails, besides which I had the unhappiness to loose the Chief Officer and a seaman[2] overboard who were both drown'd, in Passing the Bashee Islands. I stoped at Grafton Island[3] which is settled by the Spaniards, to procure some stock with which they abound, thinking thereby to lessen the Expences at Macao, not knowing it was war with Spain[4]—the Spaniards behaved very civil at first and mutual presents where Exchanged, but soon has he found I would not leave the vessel and go on shore, They began firing Shott as fast as they could, from the fort. We where within about pistol shott of it and was necessitated to Cutt the Cable to prevent accident. As soon as we where under Sail we returned their Salute as long as our Shott would reach the Shore, and then bore up for Macao where we arrived on the 19th. Febr*uary*—on 23[d] I paid off the Crew agreeable to Articles and began equipping the vessel by re-shipping part of them again.

Following is the bill of Expences from Purchasing the vessel untill her Arrival at Macao.

★ ★ ★

[1] Bashi, i.e. Batan, the group of islands north of the Philippines.
[2] Subsequent references indicate that the chief mate was David Christie, the seaman William Dixon, and that they drowned 5 February 1797.
[3] The correct identification of William Dampier's Grafton Island is Diogo (High Round) Island; it is small, however, and Bishop evidently called at Itbayat Island.
[4] After some weeks of worsening relations the British government received Spain's declaration of war 5 October 1796. Certain news of the war did not reach Canton until 13 June 1797 (Morse, II, 292), and this garrison must have anticipated such information.

Costs and Expences of the Nautilus Equipping at Amboyna for Macao 1796, 7:

		Spanish Dollars	Cents
25 November 1796	27 Gallons Coniac Brandy @ 3 Dollars	81	0
Amboyna	6 Dozen Madeira Wine @ 6 Dollars	36	0
	9 Bags of Rice @ 3.60	32	40
	1 Chest of Bread	6	20
	3 Dozen Candles	2	25
	1 Table, 10 Panes Glass	2	50
December	1 Short set coarse China ware	17	75
	Paid Caulker of the Resistance	6	0
	4 Boat loads ballast	8	0
	1 Bolt Canvass	10	0
	Paid for wood and water	10	50
	Boat hire at several times	12	0
	4 Cwt Salt Beef @ 11 Dollars per Cwt	44	0
	2 Cwt D⁰—@12½ Dollars per Cwt	25	0
	Expence of People unmooring & mooring again	8	0
	Paid Sail Maker	1	50
	Paid Carpenters bills	22	80
	Master Foreman of Company Slaves Bills	129	35
	2 Cheese, 6 Jars butter, 3 D⁰ Sweet oil	37	0
	5 Bottles Mustard, 6 Dozen Bottled beer	38	50
	100 Gunny bags, 1 Bag Rice, 2 Dozen Spoons	17	0
	Expence of fishing & Getting in and out Mainmast	20	0
	5 Cwt Junk[1]	15	0
	40 Fowls @ 1 Rupee each	18	75
	30 days Markett Expences, fish Greens &c	14	16
	1 Bag soft Sugar	6	0
	1 Coil 2½ Inch rope, 4 Loglines,[2] 3 Glasses	15	0
	Expence of People refitting rigging & Cooper	4	50
	A Large Iron Pye Pan	2	75
	1 Bag of Rice, 15 lbs Tea, 2 Quart Potts	11	0
	1 Jar Pickells, 1 Bottle Soy	3	0
January 9th.	Expence of removing up to Inner Harbour	5	0
	2 Tierces Salt Beef and Pork @ 60 Dollars	120	0
	12 Tumblers, 1 Lanthorn	8	50
	Expence of Shiping a Crew	14	50

[1] In its specifically nautical meaning of old cable used for oakum and various miscellaneous purposes.
[2] Seemingly, although the word could be 'loybins' (see above, p. 189 n.).

	Spanish Dollars	Cents
February Bashee Islands — Ton of yams, 3 Hogs, 15 Sheep 2 Dozen Fowls 3 Cwt Sweet Potatoes and 4 Goats	53	0
To Wages of Mr David Christie, Chief Mate 23^d November 96 to 5 February 97 @ 20 Dollars per Month 2 Months 13 days	48	50
To D^o Mr Martin 2^d Officer 20 Dollars 1 Month 7 days	24	67
To D^o George Fowls Able Seaman 1 Month 8 days @ 12 Dollars	15	20
To D^o Samuel Reid Boatswain 16 Dollars 1 Month 27 days	30	25
To D^o William Clare—Seaman 12 Dollars 1 Month 8 days	15	20
To D^o William Sparks D^o— 12 Dollars 1 Month 24 days	21	60
To D^o Edward Conroy Gunner 13 Dollars 1 Month 8 days	16	45
To D^o John Bartlett Seaman 12 Dollars 1 Month 8 days	15	20
To D^o George McClay Carpenter 20 Dollars 1 Month 24 days	36	0
To D^o Jacob Rainhold Seaman 10 Dollars 2 Months 28 days	29	33
To D^o Robert Hinch Seaman 10 Dollars 1 Month 8 days	12	67
To D^o John Block Cook 8 Dollars 1 Month 8 days	10	13
To D^o John Baptiste Steward 10 Dollars 1 Month 15 days	15	0
To D^o John Ballon Landsman 6 Dollars 1 Month 15 days	9	0
To D^o Oneehehow Servant— 4 Dollars 2 Months 28 days	11	75
To D^o William Dixon Seaman 12 Dollars 23 days	9	20
To my wages from 23^d November 96 to 21^t February 1797 @ 24	70	40
To Pilotage thro the Lema Isles[1] to Macao	30	0
Total Cost &c	1279	46
	10255	34
Including the Nautilus then Remains	8975	88

Macao 21st: February 1797

Errors Excepted Charles Bishop

Musketts Powder and other articles bought at Amboyna will be found in the Invoice of the Investment for the N West

[1] The (four) Lema Islands lie west of Macao, running north-east to south-west.

coast—on our arrival at Macao, the English Supercargos being at Canton I dispatched the following letter to Select Committee—

★ ★ ★

Bishop to Hall and Supercargoes, 20 February 1797:

I feel not a little anxious Sir! and Gentlemen! that my Conduct should have been such as to leave me in doubt, of your countanence and protection. I am also sorry for the unlooked for occasion that let me to it, but with your permission, and if it may not *be* deemed too great an intrusion on your time, I will relate the circumstances of the unpleasant situation in which I had involved myself and my owners property has they occurred.

The Ruby's *troubles; Howel's first deception; Sunqua's failure; sale of the* Ruby; *Howel's advice to go to Macao; failure of negotiations there, and consequent move to Amboyna; meeting with Rainier; purchase of* Nautilus; *passage to Macao.*

And now Sir! and Gentlemen, being perfectly clear of any commercial conexion with any person but Mr Teast, I must hope you will favour my Exertions for his interest and my character by suffering me to refitt the vessel, and compleat the investment for the N W*est* coast, by granting me permission to return to China with the furs I may collect, and it shall be my studdy to attend to any particular instructions, I may recieve from you—

I beg pardon for having trespassed so long on your time, and which my circumstances only can Excuse...[1]

★ ★ ★

[1] The copy of this letter in the East India Company's 'Factory Records—China' (**116**, 124–9) differs not only in unimportant detail, but also in including a manifest of stores carried from Amboyna to Macao. Dated 14 February it runs:

'1 Chest—Containing 40 Dutch Muskets & fifty Cutlasses purchased out of the Hon'ble Companys Stores at Amboyna for trading, & defending the vessel on the Coast of America [*cont. overleaf*

This letter was inclosed in this Short one to Mr Hall the Chief supercargo.

★ ★ ★

Bishop to Hall, 20 February 1797:

I have the Honour Sir, to inclose to you a letter to yourself as Chief of the Hon'ble companys supercargos in Canton and the Gentlemen of the Select Committee, and at the same time beg leave to solicit your good offices for me, ashuring you Sir that my conduct shall evince my gratitude for any attention you may shew me...

★ ★ ★

On 26th. February I recieved the following letter from Mr Hall which I immediately answered.

★ ★ ★

Hall to Bishop, from Canton, 24 February 1797:

I have recieved your letter and inclosure of the 20th Instant, and shall submit your buisness to the decission of the com-

9 Barrels Gun Powder do do
1 Cask Lead Ball   do
1 Trunk—Containing 54 Pieces coarse Chintz   28 Pieces coarse Handkerchiefs
Iron Ten Cwt
1 Box Cutlery

11 Blocks Elliffee Wood for furniture

{ Nutmegs—1 small bag containing about twenty Pounds
{ Cloves—1   do   do   do   about Eight Pounds each
{ Mace—1 Small Box containing about Ten Pounds

* These Spices were the property of Mr. David Christie chief officer of this Vessel who was unfortunately drown'd together with one of the Seamen the 5th Instant & were taken on board unknown to me & contrary to my Directions.

Stores. 4 Bags Rice—4 Casks Beef & Pork—1 Cask Peas—3 Barrels Gunpowder—2   do   filled Cartridges.'

★ ★ ★

'Elliffee' wood is unidentified. Perhaps the correct reading is 'ellissee', which could be a corruption of aloes, i.e. eagle wood (suggested by J. S. Bastin, University of London). This no doubt is the wood which Bishop offered to Drummond. The note about the spices sought to exculpate Bishop from any accusation of infringement of the Company's monopoly over these goods.

mittee as soon as I have considered a little more of the Subject. In the meantime I request you will send me an Attested Copy of the Nautilus' Register, also the date of your Original Licence from the company to perform a voyage within their Limits in the Ruby, and the time that licence was to remain in force...

★　★　★

Bishop to Hall, 26 February 1797:

I have this moment recieved the favour of your letter, and have the honour to inclose to you, an Attested copy of the Certificate of the Nautiluss Registry—the Date of the Hon'ble Companys Licence, for me to trade under certain restrictions, within their Limits, is from the 17ᵗʰ. day of September 1794, until 17ᵗʰ September 1797, including three whole years.

The Period before I could possibly return here from the coast of America must exceed the time limited, and consequently it is not only my wish, but I am necessitated to submit it to yours and the other Gentlemen of the Select committee's decision, which I must hope will favour my Exertions to redeem my credit, and my owners Interest in the adventure.

I shall Esteem it a favour and be much obliged to you for your instructions as Early as convenient, it will stimilate my Efforts to be ready to sail if possible by 1ˢᵗ: April.[1]

★　★　★

[1] The copy of this letter in the East India Company's ' Factory Records— China' (**116**, 133–4) is accompanied by an attestation by William Jones of the sale of the *Nautilus*, and a copy of the register of the *Nautilus*. The latter is dated Fort William 12 March 1796; it describes the *Nautilus* as of 60 tons burthen, built at Calcutta, owner Major A. Kyd, master C. S. J. Timmins, bound eastwards, cargo sundries.

The minutes of the subsequent 'consultation' of the select committee refer to 'the Candour & we believe strict regard to Truth with which Captain Bishop has stated the unfortunate circumstances of his Case'.

On 4th March I received the following Letter

★　★　★

Hall and others to Bishop, from Canton, 2 March 1797:

Having duly considered the circumstances set fourth in your letter to the committee of date 20th ultimou, and inclosure and subsequent letter and inclosure to Mr Hall of date 26th Same Month, we have adopted the Resolution, of permitting you conformably to your request, to proceed on a voyage in the Nautilus brig to the Northwest coast of America, and to return to this port with the furs you may collect—

We must explicitly declare however that in other respects this Indulgence does not extend to the Abrogation of any restrictions or conditions contained in the original contract with the Hon'ble Company entered into by yourself and Constituents bearing date 17th Sep*tembe*r 1794 and which Contract therefore retains as full force, untill the period of your return, as if you continued to Navigate the Ruby.

★　★　★

To which I replyed,

Letter received; sincere thanks; the indulgence will win full respect.

★　★　★

Upon our Arrival at Macao, I found the Dragon Cutter of Bengal fitting for the N. W*est*—Capt*ain* Lay her commander had a short time previous, bought the Leather war dresses I brought down in the Ruby, and Cloth I found had become scarce and dear at Canton, so that it appeared pretty clearly, I should not be able to equipp the vessel with a proper investment, with my present funds, which where daily becoming more Slender—stores of every discription where also particularly scarce and dear, and the necessary alterations and amendments in the vessel would require a large proportion of the money yet remaining in my Hands, but on which hand to turn for assistance I did not know, and secretly wished I had not purchased the Nautilus and began the voyage— However having gone so far, I concieved it would be exceedingly weak and wrong in me to recede without trying every effort. James Drummond Esq*uire* one of the English supercargos, a man of very Extensive Knoledge and ability, universally respected and beloved by all discriptions, by the Portugeese, the Chinese and the Europeans of different nations visiting & residing in China, had shewn me some civilities when before at Canton. Influenced by admiration of his character and Gentlemen like manners, to him then! I wrote the following letter, which led on to a correspondence, wherein will be seen on his part, a series of unmerited favours and exertions to forward my plans, and alas! on my part nothing but barren, yet sincere and grateful acknowledgements.

★ ★ ★

Bishop to Drummond, from Macao, 13 March 1797:

I must frankly own Sir! that the delicacy of my situation is such, that I have been some time considering wither I ought or could with propriety address you on the following subject, being so little known to you, as to disposition, ability and circumstances, but the necessity of the application, will I hope plead its Excuse, and should you after perusing a fair Statement of the latter, adopt either of my proposals you shall most certainly find that you have not misplaced your confidence, as to my disposition, and I should hope after seventeen years active maritime life, you will not be disapointed as to my ability as a Seaman—

Teast's original plan; the misfortunes of the Ruby; *the forced passage from Sandwich Islands to Macao.*

The unpleasant situation in which I involved myself and my owners property, at Canton, by consigning the Sale of the Cargo, too haistily to a person, whom I then thought an

English Gentleman is not I presume a Subject you are un-acquainted with,[1] and it may be only necessary for me here, to inform you, that being unable to Settle with me after all his promises, I was necessitated to accept a bond of Respondentia, on the Ruby and Cargo, which was freighted with China Goods for Amboyna, payable out of the 1st: Proceeds of her voyage, and bearing Interest 2 per Cent per Month and 200 dollars per Month for my detention untill the bond should be wholly taken up—you may remember Sir! I expressed my intention, of remitting home the whole of my owners property, and rejoin the Navy, having served near 12 years of the first of my maritime life in it, with unsullied Character, has a Midshipman and Masters Mate, and Certainly felt myself intitled to promotion whenever I could meet a friend to procure it for me—but in this I was disapointed—The Rubys Cargo sold so slow, that there was not a sufficient sum raised to Clear half the bond, before the Admiral departed from Amboyna and with him, my hopes of Promotion fell. Finding this would be *the* case, a short time before the fleet sailed, I purchased the beautiful little vessel I now command, named the Nautilus, built by Colonel Kidd at Calcutta, and of a very curious construction. She is 57 feet long 22 feet broad, and 12 feet deep in the Hold and will carry about 80 tons, tho' registered 65 only. The Excellency of the workmanship and materials of which she is formed, and her construction and accomodation render her in every respect a vessel well suited to the fur Trade on the N. West Coast, where a heavy cargo is not required to be carried. For this purpose I bought her for 4000 Star Pagodas, and with the hope that I should reach this place in time to repurchase the Rubys remaining Investment and Leather war dresses, and in this case concluded that my funds, would have been sufficient, for the outfitt—but several Expensive circumstances occurring at Amboyna, together with a very rough passage here wherein our Sails and rigging suffered so much, that much of them must be replaced with new, the Loss of an Anchor and Cable, and

[1] A strange mode of expression, considering Drummond's inside view of Howel's deception (see above, p. 202).

finding that Cap*tain* Lay had bought the Leather war dresses &c I brought here in the Ruby, that I find to Compleat an investment for 2000 Sea Otter Skins in one season, and to put the vessel in a respectable State, as to her sails, Rigging, provisions and Stores, I shall have occasion for four thousand Dollars additional funds to do it.

And now Sir, Having thus premised the buisness of my application to you, by a faithful account of the Events which led to my present circumstances, I beg leave to sollicet your assistance, and offer on my part as Consignee and agent for Mr Teast to assign the vessel and cargo to you, either as part owner in the Expidition or on Respondentia, and have only to add that you will very much oblige me, by adopting either, leaving the Terms to yourself. The necessity there is of my having most of the articles I am in want of, from Canton or Whampu' gives me occasion for a very small proportion of Cash—I have also Bills for 1500 dollars, drawn by Mr Jones the commercial resident at Amboyna, on Mr Hall and the select committee,[1] payable at a short sight, one of which I inclose, and you will oblige me by having it presented,— Blue Cloth and Stores is principally what I am in want of— But if Sir! you please to accept my proposals, I will write you what I have now on board and Particularly what I am in want of, with the Number of Skins expected to be procured by the sale of each article—the Experience and Knoledge I have of the coast and trade together with the Excellent vessel I command, gives me I believe a Just Idea, that the Expidition will eventually prove Successful, if by your means I can be ready by the 15th April,—I must beg leave to add Sir! That if you should decline yourself in taking any part with me, you may have it much in your Power to recommend the Subject

---

[1] The East India Company's 'Factory Records—China' (116, 119–20, 122) show that the committee received and considered a letter from Jones, dated Amboyna 12 January 1797, on this matter. Jones reported that in consequence of his desire to retain all available specie in the island, Bishop had paid 1500 Dollars into the Amboyna treasury. Jones therefore had given Bishop bills on the committee for that amount. On 24 February the committee resolved to inform Jones that 'this channel may not be resorted to unless in cases of very pressing and unavoidable necessity'.

to any other Gentleman—so little known as I am in Canton, I must hope you will Excuse the Liberty I have taken and intrusion I have made on your time...

★ ★ ★

The following Reply was recieved 25th March.

★ ★ ★

Drummond to Bishop, from Canton, 22 March 1797:

I am favoured with your letter of 14th. and have delayed replying thereto for some days, with the expectation of informing you of the acceptance of your bill on the committee in which at first there was some demurr, but I have now the pleasure to acquaint you that it will be paid when due—

I much regret your being so disagreeably situated in respect to want of Funds, and equally sorry, that my situation in the Companys service, renders *impossible* the giving the assistance you require,—To be concerned in Ships or Commerce of any kind is in direct violation of the companys orders, and with regard to lending you money on Respondentia it is totally out of the question, as it is nearly the Same thing—I shall most willingly, however, give you every aid in my power, and having at all times heard you favourably spoken of I will endeavour, provided you send me a list of the articles you require, to procure them for you on Credit from the Chinese.

If you are desirous, of purchasing stores from the India men, it will be requisite for you to indorse the bill on the Committee, that I may recieve the money for you, in doing which or in any purchases for your account, I shall not think of charging you any Com*missions*—fully gratified if I can be of service to you—

★ ★ ★

On 24th March not having recieved then the above letter I had feared the letter 13th had miscarried and therefore wrote the following previous to my recieving Mr Ds Letter.

★ ★ ★

Bishop to Drummond, 24 March 1797:

I had the Honour to address you a letter on the 13th. instant respecting the outfitt of my intended voyage to the Northwest coast of America in the Nautilus, inclosing in it one of a sett of Bills for 1500 dollars Drawn by Mr Jones, the commercial Resident at Amboyna, on Mr Hall and the Select Committee, payable to me on Order at 15 days sight, and which I requested you would do me the favour to have presented for acceptation. I am fearful this letter may not have come to your hands, and therefore inclose you a Copy, and in perusing it I must hope you will do it Sir! with much Candour, for Sanguine in my Ideas, of bringing up what the Sailors call Leeway and of returning home with credit to myself and emolument to my owner, I did not bring into account of my purchasing the Nautilus, the disapointments and obstacles I should meet in fitting from Macao, or most ashuredly I should have declined it, but having now proceeded so far, it would be weekness in me to recede. Indeed! I cannot but by a very serious loss of Property.

I am therefore putting the vessel in a respectable State as to defence, and have had a new bulwark built up all round her with an high rail, as she was before open on deck with a low one. This and several other alterations, absolutely necessary has been done, adding strength and respectability to the vessel, armed with Six Brass 3 Pounders and 4 Swivals & 50 Stands of Arms, beside Cutlasses and Pistols. These with a good Crew of 22 in N° will render her too formidable, allowing us to be on our guard, for any tribe of Indians on the Coast of America, and the moore especially as great part of the Crew are old voyagers to that Coast, and know the consequence of admiting too great a familarity with the Natives—The vessel so far has respects her Hull and rigging will be ready, I hope, early in the ensuing Mo*nth* and if you Sir! will do me the fav*ou*r to accept my proposals, I have not a doubt of making a great voyage, as I should then be able to get away in the Space of 3 or 4 weeks—but I have another motive Sir! for wishing you to accept my Assignment, namly the Pleasure Mr Teast would feel on recieving my letters, in his property being so far secured—I write not this from concious defect in principle in my self, for there my mind ashures me all is well, but having made an hasty consignment before, without inquiring to whom, and thereby involving myself in much danger, and difficulty, together with the possibility of accident befalling me, he may naturally feel anxious on that subject.

I beg leave to add Sir! that should you adopt my plan, and wish to send a person in the vessel on your account, that he will be recieved by me, with pleasure, not only on that account, but as a Companion and assistant in the voyage, and if it should be Capt*ain* Simpson it would greatly heighten the pleasure I should recieve therefrom. I inclose herewith an account of what Stores I want for the Ship, and what articles are farther necessary to compleat the investment for 2000 Skins, together with an account of that part I have already on board, and the Number of Skins Expected to be procured by them—also the 2^d of the sett of Bills, trusting Sir! you will pardon the intrusion I make, when I inform you I do not know to whom else I could apply on that Subject. I shall esteem myself obliged by an answer early as convenient that I may regulate my conduct thereby.—

P.S. If on anticipation of my bills, you could provide me with 500 D*olla*rs at Macao it will be gratefully acknowledged—I have 7 or 8 blocks of curious furniture wood. If they are worth your consideration, they are at your service.

★　★　★

From Mr Drummond in Reply, *from Canton, 28 March 1797:*

I am favored with your Letter of the 25th: enclosing Duplicate of your former together with the list of goods required to fitt out your vessel for the N. W*est* coast.—I have already informed you that my Situation in the companys Service, will not admit my being in any manner concerned, in commerce, nor do I know any person at Canton, likly to enter upon a speculation, which has hitherto been universally unsuccessful

It will nevertheless aford me pleasure if I can render you any Service, and I shall immediatly sett about endeavouring to procure what your list specifies is positively required. In doing which, however, I expect to be unequivocally informed of your situation and connection with Mr Teast, and wither you are authorised to draw on him for any sum you may require. The stores may probably be procured for bills on him, provided you are positively certain they will be discharged.

I think I have heard it rumoured that this Gentleman is dead, if so you cannot shurly expect his successor to enter into a new Speculation, when nearly the whole of the former one has been lost—You will I trust excuse this freedom but it is necessary I should be informed on these points, If I step forward to be of Service to you and to obtain you credit.

Your bill on the committee is not yet paid. Whenever it is I shall try and send you 500 D*olla*rs to Macao.—Probably by an Application on your part to Capt*ain* Simpson,[1] he may have no Objection to be concerned with you. It is worth the trial and his Knowledge of the Coast, added to his presence at Canton may greatly facilitate your outfitt—The Blue cloth I think may be easily procured on Credit—but of this I shall inform you in a few days.

★ ★ ★

[1] For relevant correspondence, see below, pp. 251–7.

The following letter was written in reply to Mr Ds: of the 22^d instant, *28 March 1797:*

It was not till late yesterday evening, I was favoured with yours of the 22^d., and I ashure you Sir! I feel very much obliged by the attention and kindness you have shewn to my intruding epistle, altho' I declare I did not know untill now, it was contrary to the Hon'ble Companys orders, for the Gentlemen transacting their business to engage in any private commercial concern, and acting under this Idea I trust you will forgive the liberty I took in proposing it.

The Bill you have done me the favour to get accepted, was recieved from Mr Jones, for various coins, not dollars, current in Amboyna, and has Mr Jones aledged, he had no orders to draw on the committee, yet has it amounted to so small a sum he sopposed, they would have not much objection in honouring his bill—I had indeed supposed from my not hearing from you before, that my letter of the 14th had miscarried and was lost, and on the 25th I wrote you another, which doubtless you have by this time recieved. In it you will find a list inclosed of the various articles of ships Stores and investment, I am in want of and which are highly necessary for me, but I cannot pay for them immediatly, and consequently the offer you have kindly made to procure me credit, is very acceptable, and demands my warmest acknowledgement—and trust me Sir that for all you avouch for me on this Subject, I shall feel myself bound both by principle and Gratitude to perform.

I have heard of a Mr Perrone,[1] who owns part of a Cargo of Seal Skins brought from the Island St Paul in the American Ship Otter Capt*ain* Dorr. He is said to be disengaged and

---

[1] The reference is to Pierre Francis Péron, author of *Mémoires du Capitaine Péron sur ses Voyages*...(ed. L. Brissot-Thivars) (Paris, 1824). This relates the adventures of the *Otter* while hunting on the American coast in 1796, and so contributes a further item to the literature of that subject. For an accessible account of Péron's history, see J. W. Earnshaw, *Thomas Muir* (Sydney, 1959). The seals had come from St Paul Island (and Amsterdam Island) in the Indian Ocean, at 38° 43′ S., 77° 31′ E.

desirous of Entering on a Speculative voyage—if you have an opportunity of seeing him and think it Eligible, shall I trouble you to propose to him to taking part in my Expidition—in the course of 10 or 12 days the vessel will be in a very forward State as to her equipment in Rigging and Carpenters work, and if you think it necessary, I could be enabled to come up to Whampu' in McEvoys boat, when any stores &c you may have done me the fav*ou*r to secure could be sent down in her

I inclose you herewith the 3^d: of the sett of bills indorsed but alas Sir! it is like 1500 Corns to feed a Troop of Horses— I have so many wants, that where it not for the Encourage- ment given me in your kind letter, I should dispair of accom- plishing what I have so much set my heart on—you will oblige me Sir! by putting me in the way to recieve 500 Dollars of it, for my present necessities, and the other part I consign to pay for 8 or 10 Tierces beef, 2 Furkins Butter, a 7, 7½ or 8 Inch Cable—20 sheets sheathing Copper, 20 lbs Copper nails, and 10 or 12 bolts Canvass, N° 3, 4, 5, and 3 Cwt Cordage 1, 2, 2½ & 3 Inch.—Mr. Hammond purser of the Qu*ee*n Charlotte, told me I could have beef from him, the Canvass Copper and nails are immediatly necessary for Equipping the vessel.

I really am afraid I have by troubling you so much imposed on your good disposition towards me, and feel some anxiety, that my local situation, holds out no prospect at present to make any return for the Generosity you shew me—

★ ★ ★

Answer to Mr. Drummonds Letter 28th March, *31 March 1797:*

I was favoured with yours of 28th last evening, and in answer thereto, I beg leave to inform you, that I have no Athority to draw bills on Mr Teast, altho' I think he would duly honour them, yet on this doubtful consideration, I would rather adopt any other mode of obtaining the Credit necessary, and Should prefer that by way of respondentia, having no objection to allow a fair premium for inshurance on the gross sum as well as Interest *per* Month.

With respect to my situation with my owner Mr. Teast, I have to inform you that he Equipped the Ruby with every thing thought to be necessary for an Expidition to the NW. coast and China, and placed her under my directions—Instructed as I have before related, to act always keeping within the limits prescribed by the Hon'ble Companys licence, in the same manner I would where the property he invested me with my own.—But as it was impossible to forsee in England that the Ruby would fail in the middle of her voyage, there was no necessary instructions given in that case, How I was to act, either as to purchasing a nother vessel or returning home a passenger, and as I have hitherto consulted in the best manner I am able, the good of my employer, I consider that I have done and am still doing my duty towards him altho' I confess Sir! Had I forseen the difficulties I now feel in proceeding on in this Expidition, I should most ashuredly have a dopted the Alternative I held, of remitting home the whole of his property at Amboyna and returning to Europe myself, but having proceeded in it so far, I cannot recede without a great loss of Property, and which would sweep of with it, the Small hard earned Sum which composes my share[1]—I must therefore hope Sir! as my intentions are, and my Actions, hitherto have been directed by a mind disposed to fair and honourable persuits, that you will assist me with your influence with the merchants at Canton, and I ashure you Sir! it shall be my particular regard and Studdy, to act in such manner, that you shall in nowise regret having shewn me attention and assistance, at least so far has depends on my conduct.

It was indeed! rumoured at Canton when I was there that Mr Sidenham Teast was dead, but it arose from the Father

---

[1] A comment which suggests that the payment of commission was an incentive to rashness as well as to industry.

236

Sidenham Teast who died some time in 1790, and whose name I saw in an old news paper for that year.

I thank you most sincerely for the Trouble you have taken with my bill—I wrote to Captain Simpson 27th and have not yet been favoured with his answer—Consequa[1] the Chinese Merchant, when I was at Canton before, offered, if I would not go into the Navy, but get a vessel to go to the N.W. coast to assist me with Cloth &c but I have since heard he has been much troubled by the Mandarins, and is in the City.—I have mentioned this circumstance merely for your information—

★ ★ ★

Letter, To James Drummond 7th April 1797:

I am favoured with an immediate opportunity of writing to inform you that I have taken the Liberty of giving two drafts on you one to Captain Lenox[2] for 219 dollars, and the other to Mr Thomas Musgrave, Chief Officer of the Boddham[3] for one hundred and seventy six—Captain Lenox has been so good to take on board his ship 8 Blocks of curious furniture wood brought from the Moluccas Islands, aluded to in a former letter and which I must beg the favour you will accept.

I have procured the Canvass out of the Indiamen in the roads, also some arrack—I propose including in my voyage to the N. West to go dureing the winter into the South Pacific to Masafuera[4] where from good athority I find 20,000 seal skins may be procured in about 10 weeks.—I have had the misfortune to bruise my fingers, and cannot write for this day or two, but in great pain—I shall thank you to Excuse me writing more fully 'till I am better.

★ ★ ★

[1] In 1795–6 Conseequa had been punished for 'his extensive dealings with Europeans without the license of a Hong Chop' (Morse, ii, 283).
[2] Charles Lennox, of the *Woodford*.
[3] *Boddam*.
[4] See above, p. xxxiii.

Drummond to Bishop, 5 April 1797:

I have been favoured with your letter of the 31st. since which I have seen Consequa, who readily consents to become interested in your concern—I have no time at present to write you the particulars but shall have leisure so to do by Capt*ain* Simpson, who will proceed to Macao shortly in the City of Goa.

In consequence of this arrangement I shall proceed to purchase the Goods you require and send them if possible by the City of Goa—if you will apply to Mr Manoel De Souza,[1] I believe he can furnish you with 500 Dollars.

★ ★ ★

Bishop to Drummond, 10 April 1797:

Agreeable to your letter of the 5th. I have this day recieved 500 D*olla*rs from Mr De Souza. In your appointment of this buisness you have done me a great favour, as I am enabled thereby to get rid of those Harpies at Macao, to whom I owe Small Sums. Your letter also conveyed to me the happy tydings, of the arrangement you are so good to make for me with my friend Conseequa, and the bringing down the goods and stores for me in the City of Goa,—in consequence of which we have gone on with fresh Spirits in getting the vessel ready for Sea which is nearly compleat.

Since my letter 28 March some Chinamen have got me a Pickell of what they call Copper, (a composition of mettle)[2] which will answer to mend our Copper Sheathing, and has it is cheap I have adopted it knowing how scarce Europe Copper is, but should you before recieving this have brought any for me, it is good trade on the Southern parts of the Coast, in Exchange for Leather war dresses, and will as such be very acceptable

[1] A Portuguese resident at Canton, with extensive business interests (Pritchard, 185).
[2] Probably the Chinese white copper, which was an alloy of copper with zinc and smaller quantities of other metals (Macartney (ed. Cranmer-Byng), 258, 293).

I wrote you also 7th if thought Eligible, to proceed from Coast of America Early as possible in the Autumn to Masafuera in Latt 34° So*uth*[1] for Seal Skins—I am induced to propose this arrangement from the following Motives, 1st: allowing we sail 1st May from hence, we shall in so Prime a Sailor as the Nautilus be most probably not more than 2 months in our passage to the Coast. We have then, July and two following Months, to be on the coast, a Period with the Knowledge I have of it long enough to get 2000 Sea Otter Skins, if invested with proper articles of trade—leaving the coast of America the latter end of September, we shall arrive at the Sandwich Islands it may be Expected by 20th October— here I take on board Eight Islanders and 2 Cannoes and if I should be so fortunate to fall in with Capt*ain* Lay, or a vessel of my owners bound to Canton, I would freight the Otter Skins down to You, thereby securing that part of the voyage— of Course taking great care in a step of this kind, to prevent fraud in the person I intrusted them with and this is one reason I wish Capt*ain* Simpson to go with me for he could proceed here with the Cargo—Leaving the Sandwich Islands the End of October, it is a fair passage to arrive at Masafuera 10th December where I land at last 12 picked Men, who begin to kill and dry skins—I am well ashured after the first fortnight of taking off 600 dry Skins every day, which in collecting 20,000 the quantity I estimate the vessel to Carry will detain us no longer than two months, and leaving Masafuera 15 Feb*ruar*y may expect to arrive at Macao 15th April making a voyage altogether within the year. I am well informed as to the buisness and have several of the crew who have been sealing there—there is also this advantage attending it, that the wages of the crew will be reduced to one half, from the time of leaving the Sandwich Islands, and a Comm*iss*ion or Share of 1 *per* C*en*t allowed to each man has a Stimulus to work hard.—The Expence attending the voyage is so little, compared to an outfitt on purpose, and the advantage held out by the high price of Skins here that perhaps I am not too Sanguine in thinking you will accord with me in it—The

---

[1] To be exact, 33° 45′ S., 80° 45′ W.

Sandwich Islanders will serve to man to Cannoes to bring the Skins in small parcels through the Surf to the boat outside, which, man'd by 4 others, ply to the Ship with them

I have thus! Sir shewn you the additional plan of my voyage, and shall Thank you for your opinion on it when most convenient, and if has I do! you think it good and will tend to my owners advantage—with an active and perservering disposition of mind, I shall proceed accordingly, and propose to Captain Simpson the part he is wished to take in the buisness.

★　★　★

Drummond to Bishop, 14 April 1797:

I have been favoured with two letters from you, and shall use my endeavours to get the things down in the City of Goa—I am apprehensive however, that I shall not be successful, in obtaining permission for the China goods, but of this you will be informed by Captain Simpson, of the City of Goa, which Ship will, I think, leave Whampu' in 7 or 8 days, when I shall again write you...

★　★　★

Bishop to Drummond, 16 April 1797:

I am this day favoured with your Letter of the 14th and am still sanguine in thinking, as you have not mentioned anything of the subject, that on consideration, you will accord with me in the plan I wrote you, of going on our return voyage from the Sandwich Islands to Masafuera for 20000 Seal Skins— I ask your opinion as a Person capable of judging the Elegibility of the Plan.—I have Indeed written to Captain Simpson, on the subject, proposing the part he is wished to take in the buisness, but have yet no answers, as well as to a letter written him 25th: March, inclosing a list of some articles of Stores, I thought he might be able to Collect for me, not knowing then the City of Goa was to come down here. I am fearful he has never recieved these letters, for I know him to be punctual in his correspondence and therefore beg leave to trouble you to have the inclosed letter delivered to him— When from Captain Simpsons assenting to it you may be the better able to form an opinion as to the propriety of the deviation in the route of the voyage.—So far as it respects my crews or my own Exertion, and perseverance I am pretty certain of success, and the accounts I have, both from Carteret's voyage, and the Chief Officer with me in the Ruby, who was there in 92, as well as the testimony of several of my present ships company, convinces me, as the seals on that spott of land, so remote from any other are so abundant, that in filling up the Nautilus it would not lengthen our Voyage four months and allowing only one dollar per skin 20,000 dollars so obtained would add much credit and emolument to all concerned

I hisitate long and am indeed! much concerned in troubling you so with my buisness,—but to whom in my present circumstances can I apply.—It is my wish to obtain and continue in your esteem, and my conduct now is particularly circumspect, but I declare Sir! to you I am very sorry I undertook this expidition with Such slender funds, it has involved me in a world of anxiety, which I might have avoided but which now, having gone so far, it would be shame and weakness in me to relinquish, without trying every effort, and I must ask your Assistance to get me out to Sea.—The 500 Dollars you where so kind to remit me is Expended, in the Equipment of the vessel, and daily fresh Provisions, and I am now without 20 dollars. Attcheu and Chinqua, two Chinese, have offered to get up my dry Provisions and Stores for the voyage, if Mr Conseequa will secure to them the payment of their bill. They have also agree'd to furnish me with 4 Pickell of Brass wire and 2 Pickel of Beads, which I had omitted in the list for the investment—Advance wages to the Crew, and other Expences here will require near 1000 dollars cash, to discharge by the time of our Sailing—I declare I am much affected, by the necessity of innumerating these circumstances, and but that I know I am writing to a Gentleman who has Candour to reply in gentle terms at the least, I would not do it—ashure Mr Consequa I am willing to give him every security in my power, and in case of accident to us in the voyage the vessel can be inshured, which I could make over to you to recover and pay the respective shares.—I would give bills on my owner, but for the possible rejection of them, in consequence of my not having any order to draw upon him.— I must also trust you will pardon the intrusion I have made on your time and attention—and tho' I have already so much to be grateful for, suffer me to sollicet once more your freindly aid, by proposing a means of my getting off speedily with Comfort and Credit—

★ ★ ★

Drummond to Bishop, 24 April 1797:

Capt*ain* Simpson who goes to Macao in the City of Goa, will carry you some stores &c of which I cannot at present give you the list, but the Amount of these things together with the Cloth, will Exceed I imagine 6000 D*olla*rs, the whole of which will be carried to Consequas Debit. Previous to your Sailing I shall transmit you regular accounts, of all the disbursments, and then it will be necessary for you to draw up an agreement Specifying your several Shares, that Conseequa may know how far he is interested. I have informed Capt*ain* Simpson, that it will likewise be necessary to write to Bengal or Europe for inshurence; Specifying in your letter to either place, the amount to be inshured, and to lower the premium, I shall transmit a bill on Conseequas Account. Any part you deem proper of Conseequas advances, may be considered as beloning to Capt*ain* Simpson, to athorise his holding a Share—a Power of Attorney must be filled up to me, which in the event of Loss or accident to the vessel will enable me to recover the amount inshured, and pay the proportion to Each party concerned.—I have written to Mr De Souza to know if he can advance you 1000 Dollars, which I trust will be convenient to him.

It is impossible for me to decide on the Elegibility of your plan, they appear good however, and Capt*ain* Simpson approves of them, and most sincerely do I wish you Success— allow me to remind you of Conseequas Interest. He has stood forward very hansomely, for without I fear you could never have been fitted out, as it would have been impossible for me to have assisted you—The fleet will probably sail about 20th May, I think not before—The Cloth will be sent as soon as possible...

★　★　★

Bishop to Drummond, 8 May 1797:

I recieved your letter of the 24th ulti*mo* in due time, and Capt*ain* Simpson arriving soon after in the City of Goa, I have defered writing in hopes of being enabled to transmitt to you for Conseequa a Particular Account of the Costs and Expences of the Nautilus, but find I must defer it a few days, untill I have collected and paid all the bills I owe here. From a brief calculation I have made I find the vessel will, with that part of the investment on board cost upwards of 10,000 D*ollar*s—I propose soon as the whole costs can be Collected, to divide the whole adventure into hundredeths and Mr Teast, Consequa, and Captain Simpson, each hold his particular share to which their funds have contributed, in due proportion and I think the ballance should be equal between Capt*ain* Simpson and Conseequa. The Power of Attorney shall be filled up and transmitted to you, together with the letter for inshurence, soon as I know the sum it will be necessary to inshure.—I have to thank you for the receipt 1000 dollars from Mr De Souza 2d Instant—I declare Sir I have found you so ready in obliging me, that I am unwilling to suggest to you a plan I have concieved of getting the Cloth down from Canton earlier than I am afraid we must expect by any ships lest from not being acquainted with any impropriety attending it, you should think me forward and troublesome. Achie and Chinqua, two Chinamen have offered to bring it or any other goods down upon the bargain you may

243　　　16-2

make for Mr Consequa with them. Chinqua is now gone up to Canton—in adopting or rejecting this circumstance, you cannot but please me, being ashured that if it is convenient and proper, that you will favour my desires of a Speedy departure.—

The vessel is now ready, and I have a tolerable good Crew. Her state and appointment is certainly respectable for an outfitt at Macao. Captain Simpson with whom I am on terms of intimate Friendship agrees to go with me, and take an active part in the voyage. He is to have equal pay & Com-*missions* with myself, namly 60 D*ollars* P*er Month* and 4 p*er* C*ent* commissions—I shall take care to leave duplicates of all my accounts in this adventure in case of accident for Mr Teast, which I will trouble you to have sent to him...

* * *

Bishop and Simpson to Drummond, from Macao, 16 May 1797:

Inclosed we send you the power of Attorney filled up, we have mutually exchanged agreements with respect to the plan and execution of the voyage, a Copy of which together with our accounts we will trasmitt for the Satisfaction of Mr Conseequa, but in consequence of the enlargened Scale of the adventure, we are sorry to be under the necessity of troubling you again for Cash on acc*oun*t of Conseequa, and that too for the very considerable Amount of 2000 dollars, unless you will permit us to give bills on YOU for 1000 when in that Case 1000 Cash will be fully sufficient to pay the advance and clear the vessel for Sea

Achie has been with us this morning and informs us that he has got 609 yards Cloth to deliver us tomorrow morning. He brings also a Muster of Cloth, which tho' dear for pur-chasing Skins, will sell to advantage. We are both of opinion if Mr Conseequa can get for us 1200 yards more, making with 600 already brought down 1800 yards, it will be Sufficient to procure 1000 of the Primest Skins, and to make up the deficiency of the 2000 yards, *we* purpose taking 200 Chinese Blanketts at ½ Dollar Each, which we can buy here. We could put to Sea immediatly if we had all the investment on board, and the Peoples Advance paid. Anxious to proceed has the Season is so far advanced, permit us Sir! to sollicit your attention to our circumstances, and to request you will favour us with your answer, respecting the Cash as early as possible, and if you could forward the Cloth by these Chinamen it would enable us perhaps to proceed a week sooner than if we wait for the fleet coming down.

★   ★   ★

Bishop to Drummond, 20 May 1797:

This Evening Chinqua delivered on board 23 Pieces Cloth measuring 609 yards as by y*our* note 14th—and I have given him a reciept for Mr Consequa. He brought also 4 Pic*ul* Brass wire for which I am to pay 60 D*olla*rs p*er* Pic*ul*. Will you have the goodness to settle with him for it, and deduct it from the 2000 dollars Capt*ain* Simpson and myself wrote you to get for us from Conseequa, by Mr De Zousa—the Partner of Chinqua, Achie brought us a Muster of Cloth N° 2, and Said he could get any quantity of it at 2½ Sp*anish* D*olla*rs per y*ard*. We requested in our letter to you Conseequa would get 1200 yards—the vessel is now fitted at a great Expense and Cloth even at 3 D*olla*rs p*er* y*ard* would be preferable to going without a Suficient investment to purchase 1500 Skins at the least. I think, we have goods now on board equal to about 900 or perhaps 1000, and 1200 yards more would compleat a respectable investment

I declare Sir I am so sensible of the trouble you have, that it is with great reluctance, I address you on the subject of our wants, and can only add I am truly Grateful for your perseverance in Serving us...

★   ★   ★

Mr. Drummonds Note of 14th.

I am much concerned that all my endeavours to procure you more Cloth than what is now sent by Achune 609 yards in 23 Pieces, have proved unsuccessful—I am sending about the Shops to try if it is possible, and you will hear from me the result, tomorrow...

* * *

Letter from Mr. Drummond dated 21st May 1797.

I have been favoured with your letter, and am a good deal concerned, that your expences have so far exceeded your original estimate. Conseequa who has very large sums due to him from the company is so much embarrassed, that he cannot raise a dollar, and hitherto every charge has been defrayed from my own Funds,—which at the present moment, when money is so scarce is not a little vexing, however safe I may ultimately be, in procureing repayment,—I shall have no Objection to accept your bill, drawn on me for Conseequas account, payable in one or two months, and if by presenting the inclosed to Manoel Vicente De Barros you can engage him to Supply you with 1000 more, I will be responsible to him for its payment. I have not seen the person you mention who was to shew me the Sample of Cloth. I am Endeavouring to get you some of the 2^d Cloth, but it will come so enormously dear, that I fear it will defeat the Intent of your voyage, which ought to be oeconomy—

I have been and am so busy with the Companys and my own buisness, that I have really had no time to send you the Accounts. Should I be at leisure, however, previous to your Sailing, I will send them. At all events you will not omit writing for Inshurence, valuing vessel and Cargo at her original Cost.

* * *

Bishop to Drummond, 25 May 1797:

I was favoured with your letter and inclosure to Vicente De Barros yesterday. He readily supplyed me with the Cash, 500 dollars of which I have recieved this day, and have given him a bill at 2 months on Conseequas account for 200 more due him for sundry Stores we have recieved—

I shall pay the peoples advance immediatly, and then be able to transmit to you the accounts of the vessels costs and Expences together with a letter for inshurence—I think I ought also to bring into the account for Inshurence, the Expence of Fitting and bringing the vessel here from Amboyna, 1200 D*olla*rs, which sum tho' not coming into Conseequas and Captain Simpsons share in the adventure, yet it does in Mr Teasts, and the Premiums paid on this Surplus Sum can be carried to my Account.—

Capt*ain* Simpson has shewn me the latter part of your letter to him, respecting our touching at Port Jackson—If the Nautilus was large it certainly would be a good Plan, but filled as she now is with provisions stores and Cargo, it would not be possible for us to Carry a Cargo, the profitts of which would pay the Expences, beside the expenditure of Provisions not to be got there. This is also Capt*ain* Simpsons opinion, as well as mine— Indeed! I am Sanguine still of proceeding first to the Coast, the Natives have always skins by them, and the last vessel, when the cold begins to sett in, has as good a Chance of selling her investment as the first in the Spring—and I hope to be enabled to send Capt*ain* Simpson down from the Sandwich Islands with 1500 Sea Otter Skins in Nov*embe*r while I go on to Masafuera—we are both much obliged to you for your friendly Attention to our concerns.

★ ★ ★

Letter from Mr Drummond, 28th May 1797.

I am happy to find that Mr Manoel Vicente De Barros has been able to Supply you with the Cash you required. I have

endeavoured, but hitherto in vain, to procure more Cloth.
A few days will determine however wither it is possible to
gett any when you will be advised thereof—I received your
packquet of Letters and they will be forwarded by the
Glatton to Europe.

★   ★   ★

Letter from Mr. Drummond, 7th June 1797.

I inclose you Conseequas Account current, by which you
will Observe the sum of Head Dollars[1] 6039 advanced by
him as well on his own Account as Captain Simpsons. As
much risque may attend your future voyage, I begin to be
alarmed on his account and has he may consider me as the
Cause of involving him, I am anxious to Secure his property,
as far at least as depends on my self. You will therefore write
in duplicate by the Indiamen about to Sail ordering Inshurence on the Sum above specified, adding thereto to
Cover the premium 20 per Cent Tho' as the Spanish war is
positively declared,[2] it would not be matter of Surprize if the
Policy was declined altogether—you must state your intended
views in this letter, and if possible your positive track,—that
the underwriters may be the better able to judge of the
risque. These letters you will address in duplicate to Messrs.
Boyd Benfield & Company London[3] informing them the
Inshurence is on account of Conseequa, and on whose account
I shall take care to provide them with Funds. It will likewise
be necessary, that you leave coppies of your Accounts and
Reciepts of Cargo to prove the property on board.

You have now embarked in the voyage and ruin would
attend your relinquishing it. Great Prudence must however
be observed, and on no account approach near any Spanish
possessions—I think if you winter at any of the Southern

---

[1] Some Spanish Dollars had heads; others did not. Their value remained
the same either way (information from J. P. C. Kent, British Museum).

[2] An affirmation still slightly premature, it would seem (see above,
p. 220 n.).

[3] This was a substantial merchant firm of 14 Albemarle Street and
2 New Broad Street.

Islands a trip to Kamschatka, or the Russian Settlements on the American coast of which I believe they have several, might prove beneficial—

To which the following P.S. was added:

When I began my letter, I had not made up my accounts. Some things may be omitted, which you may notice. I have Since seen Conseequa, and the sum is so much less than I had expected that he leaves it to your own Judgement, wither you will inshure or not.

* * *

Letter to James Drummond Esq*uire* 9th June 1797:

I am favoured with your letter of 7th by McEvoy, as I was embarking and on my way to the Nautilus, with intent of sailing tonight, which if the wind continues favourable I purpose still to do—I inclose to you an Invoice of the Cargo now on board, also a bill of the vessels Costs and disbursments in fitting—This has so far exceeded my calculations that it gives me not a little distress and anxiety when I think of it, and but that I have confidance in my plans, and dispositions to pursue them I should almost shrink from the Idea of it. We send you also duplicate of the letter we have written for inshurence, and also I beg leave to trouble you with the triplicate letter for Inshurence to Mr Teast my owner to be sent the first opportunity that offers after the Sailing of this fleet.

I am obliged to you for sugesting the Plan of going to Kamschatka, but we are now full, and moreover without a dollar left, to furnish investment to make it worth our while to drop the Sealing Expidition—you will percieve by the inclosures, the Expence we have from Necesitty been at, and I hope Sir! you will Judge of them with Candour. Indeed I do not give them as Certain and true, because I have reason to think there may be Errors which from the Harressed State I have, filted in. I trust you will Excuse—I leave them thus! not having time to be more correct, in case of accident befalling us, But Trusting in Divine Providence that we shall return with Success and health, and that we shall have the happiness to find you So...

★   ★   ★

Letter for Inshurence, to Messrs: Boyd Benfield & Company, London, from Typa Harbour, 10 June 1797:

The Barque Nautilus built at Bengal about 4 years ago Estimated 75 Tons, man'd with 20 Seamen and Marines exclusive of the under Signed, carrying six three Pounders cannon, Muskettoons and Small Arms suitable to the Number of the Crew, having been fitted at great Expence at Macao for 12 months voyage, and now lying ready to sail, intended to proceed from hence in company with the Hon'ble English East India Companys fleet now about to sail, thro' the Straits of Luconnia and Formosa, into the North Pacific Ocean, and parting with them proceed direct to the North West coast of America, to procure Sea Otter Skins and other furs, and after finishing her trade there, to proceed about the Middle of October from the Coast of America, to Sandwich Islands and through the Pacific Ocean, passing to East*war*d if possible of the Society Islands direct to the Island Masafuera, which lies in 34th degree South Lattitude and 81st: degree West Longitude, for the purpose of Killing and Procuring Seals Skins, and after having got a Sufficient number to fill the vessel which it is expected we shall have done by 1st March 1798, to proceed direct from thence through the Society Islands to Macao, or Whampu' in River Tigris where the risque 10 days after Anchoring at Macao or 24 hours after Anchoring at Whampu' shall cease on acco*un*t of the Inshurers.

Now this is to request of you Gentlemen to have a Policcy of Inshurence done for the Sum of H*ea*d Dollars 8500 in and upon the Said Barque, with proviso, that if that part of the voyage, respecting her going to Masafuera shall be relinquished and the Said vessel return direct from the Coast of America to Macao that half the premium thereon is to be returned, the Inshurence to be made, as usual, against Ememies, Pirates, dangers of the Sea &c &c and the Expence Attending this inshurence to be placed to the account of Mr Conseequa part owner of said Barque as per Advice from James Drummond Esquire

★ ★ ★

The following Letter, and its Answer, relate to my Conection with Captain Roger Simpson.

★ ★ ★

Bishop to Simpson, from Macao, 17 April 1797:

I wrote to you the 10th: a long letter respecting a Plan I have formed of putting my otter Skins on board another vessel on leaving the coast or the Sandwich Islands, and proceeding with the Nautilus to Masafuera for Seal Skins, offering you, if you like to go with me, the Same Wages and commissions as myself, together with every comfort the vessel can bestow, and our Society mutually contribute to, my plan being for you to come down with the Skins and continue in pay untill their Sale Shall be compleat and by waiting a few months for our arrival, you would most probably get the Command of the vessel, as I shall be necessitated to part with her and proceed to Europe on the Expiration of thisVoyage.— My letter to you of the 10th: convey'd also in Some Measure the terms, vizt: 4 per Cent Commissions on the otter Skins. I am by my owner allowed 6 per Cent but as this Sealing Voyage was not thought on before, I give you 2 per Cent of my Commissions and Charge 2 to Mr Teast, which will be the same terms as Adamson and his supercargo Sailed on and Equal Wages—I have indeed! wished much for Mr Drummonds Opinion on the Subject, which on consideration, I am inclined to believe He would from his great Mercantile knowledge, acquiesse in, if you agree to Accompany me— By a letter from him to day he informs me you are to leave Whampu' in a few days in the Goa, also of the arangement he has made for me—I am certainly much obliged by his Attention and Generous Exertions in my favour, and as I am convinced he will recieve much Satisfaction in my voyage turning out Succesful, I would wish to Secure by your going with me that part of the Plan as above related.

The Captain of the Canton[1] informed me he should be able to Spare a 5 oar'd yawl. I saw the boat and think it would answer us if She can be procured for 20£ or thereabout. Will you purchase her for me and bring her down,—I hope to have the pleasure of seeing you Shortly, and if you go with me and have any Spare Cash to throw into the adventure, you may take the opportunity of Obliging yourself and me too— I mention this circumstance for I am really at my witts end to raise Cash to pay the Advance and leave Macao with Comfort and Credit—If you should not be about coming shortly, write me word,—This Letter I inclose to Mr Drummond, because I have reason to be Sorry I have not adopted some plan like it before, as probably my other letters to you dated 26th. March and 10th April are not come to Hand:

★ ★ ★

Letter to Captain Charles Bishop in Reply, dated 22d April 1797:

I am now about to Answer two of your Letters, one dated 26th March the other 17th—I hope e'er this you have got an officer in Mr Edes[2] Room—I was very sorry to hear my old friend Reid was ill, and happy to hear since that he is re- covered, it is very odd I have not had a letter from him, nor any answer to two of mine, which where of consequence. I soppose he has Sailed, He is a good fellow & Carries my best wishes with him,—not getting the Clemmons (Leather war Dresses) must have disapointed you, but I hope you will do well without them—I am glad to find you have improved your vessel, and that you have procured Canvass, if you have not

[1] Abel Vyvyan.
[2] The references to Ede and Reid in this letter obviously relate to uncopied letters from Bishop to Simpson.

enough I have Some half worn Sails on board the Goa—
I feel myself much Obliged by the good Opinion of me you
transmitted to Mr Drummond who has Spoken to me on the
Subject and offered me money to take a Share of the Nautilus
with Conseequa. If so I wish to know what kind of shares we
are to have, nothing less than a Third will make it worth my
while to go the voyage—not knowing that circumstance,
renders it impossible for me to determine, altho' I have told
Mr Drummond I was agreeable to go—in one of your letters
my friend, you mention 24 dollars a month, I hope you were
not in Ernest when you wrote that as it is only Servants wages
in the N. West trade—I must inform you I am willing to take
a third Share, and for our own Credit Sake we will hereafter
settle the 24 Dollar buisness.

I approve much of the plan of your voyage and your trade,
but when Mr Drummond set me off to procure the part of
the investment wanting, I had not your list up at Canton with
me and have ordered 200 Trunks instead 150—$\frac{3}{4}$ths of which
are to be red, Paper covered and varnished, my reason was
for that, when I was on the coast last year, they would not
give so much for a Leather covered black trunk as they would
for a red paper one, and red had the preference to any other
colour—50 are to be black leather trunks, the whole to be
delivered in the Typa in 20 days for 300 Dollars, I could
not possibly get them cheaper. I have ordered 1 Pic*u*l Beads,
red yellow and blue for the Sandwich Islands. I have likewise
bought and get on board the Goa, 7 Pic*u*l of fine Stout
Leaguer Iron Hoops as thick as Bar Iron almost—a Case of
Pickells and some Empty Water Casks if you want them.
I have bespoke 8 Doz*e*n Port wine, and a Cask of Ale, the
Cable I have look'd at, which is 9 inch, and meant to have
gone to Canton to have agree'd on the price for it, but was
taken ill this Morning. The City of Goa is already to Sail
and I am not able to go up and report it.—There is some
Jacketts here but I fear they are too dear, being 4 D*o*lla*r*s p*e*r
Jackett,—I dont see you have thought about small brass
bangles, which I sold very well, I believe I shall get a pickell—

I am not able to get any small Rope Indeed! rope of any Kind—I have rec*eive*d on board for you 10 Teirces of Beef to-day each weighing Gross 378 lbs and are in good order. I have likewise a good stock of fire wood—I shall collect everything you have indented for that lays in my Power and anything else that I think will be of Service...

Canton 22^d Ap*ri*l

A little recovered my health I recieved the favour of yours of 17th my dear friend this day—Mr. D– gave it me, with whom I had some talk again respecting the voyage. He observed to Me you could not have applied to a worse hand than himself, and asked my opinion. I told him, I approved very much of the plan of your voyage. He has given me a Power of Attorney to be signed by you & me, and requests we will write to Messrs: Colvins and Bassett,[1] for inshurence and Says he will cover the Premium with a bill on acc*oun*t of Conseequa, but says what ever we do must be jointly

Mr. D– says he can procure no Pork for you, if so my friend turn to and Salt for the voyage. I bought 244 lbs which I mean to Salt and if I have time shall Salt more—I have got some vingar and a few Coals—I have a deal of difficulty in getting down to Whampu' what I have already bought, and much wish I may Succeed at all.—I have bought the 9 inch Cable to day and the Cantons Jolly boat which I shall bring down with me—I believe I shall bring down with me 30 p*ai*r English Blanketts at 4 D*olla*rs p*e*r Pair. I have therefore as funds are low, proposed taking them and 2000 yards Cloth instead of Jacketts Trowsers and Chinese Blanketts. I shall bring one firkin Butter and part of another.

I can say no more than I have recieved my Grand Chop to depart and Pilot with orders to proceed down to Macao immediatly, but in Consequence of not having got such things down I have already agree'd for, I shall make an Excuse for

---

[1] A firm in Bengal, probably at Calcutta (see below, p. 260).

one night. But I shall possitively sail from Whampu' to-morrow so look out for us, and be careful to have a boat alongside us before we get into the Typa, otherwise some trouble may arrise to the Ship. I think you had better get McEvoys boat ready of Lintin[1] and then we shall be shure of being safe...

★ ★ ★

Capt*ain* Simpson Came down with the Goa to Macao, where he delivered her up 2ᵈ May to Manoel Vicente De Barros, and entered into agreement to accompany me in the Nautilus, in Quality of Factor or Trader, and in Case of Accident to me, he was to Succeed to the Sole command. He also holds half the Share, which Conseequas Funds, advanced in the Adventure, intitles him to, and for which He is accountable to Conseequa. Add to this, He is a Sober intelligent and honourable young Man, possessed of great Maritime and Nautical Ability, and an Extensive knoledge of the N. W*est* Trade &c.

The following agreement was mutually entered into between us the 10ᵗʰ May 1797.

★ ★ ★

This Indenture of two parts made and Entered into between Charles Bishop, Commander and Consignee of the Bark Nautilus, of Bristol in the County of Somersett, Mariner, on the one part, and Roger Simpson of London, Mariner, on the other part, Witnesseth, That the aforesaid Roger Simpson hath contracted and agreed, and doth hereby contract and agree to do and perform on board the aforesaid Bark a voyage to the North West coast of America, and such other places in the Pacific Ocean as it is usual or may be Expidient to touch at, for the purpose of procuring a Cargo of Furs, and that dureing the continuence thereof, he will truly and faithfully perform the duty of Trader and Factor on board the Said Bark, under the Directions of the Said Charles Bishop: and

---

[1] An islet-port in the Canton River estuary, twenty-two miles north-east of Macao.

255

should the Said Charles Bishop think proper to remit Such furs as may be collected in the Said Bark, to China in any other Safe vessel, at any time or place, then, and in that Case the Said Roger Simpson, doth contract and agree, and hath hereby contracted, and agree'd, to proceed at the request of Said Charles Bishop with the aforementioned furs in Charge, and the same to deliver to the Order of the Said Charles Bishop, or otherwise dispose thereof as he Shall be directed in writing

And Furthermore the said Roger Simpson doth contract and agree, and hath hereby contracted and agree'd that in case of the death or incapacity of the said Charles Bishop he will take the command of the Said Bark, and conduct the voyage aforementioned, as to him shall Seem most advantageous to the interest of all persons concerned therein, for the same Wages and Allowances as the Said Charles Bishop would have recieved for conducting the Same, Provided Always, that in Case of the death or incapacity of the Said Charles Bishop, His Heirs: Executors, Administrators or Assigns, shall be intitled to whatever wages were due, and Commissions on whatever Furs were collected prior to the death or in capacitation of the Said Charles Bishop,—And moreover the Said Roger Simpson, hath contracted and agree'd, and doth hereby contract and agree to give his opinion in writing, in a Book to be keept for that purpose, on any proposition of the Said Charles Bishop, for the furtherence & advantage of the Said voyage and in the said book all reasons shall be specified, if required by Either of the contracting parties of the other, for proposing, assenting to, or dissenting from, any plan, which, on the Said voyage, may be proposed,

And the Said Charles Bishop hath contracted and agree'd, and doth hereby contract and agree with the Said Roger Simpson for and in consideration of the premises, to pay, or cause to be paid unto the Said Roger Simpson, his Heirs, Executors Administrators or Assigns the Sum of Sixty dollars per Month, and Four per Centum on the amount of the Sales of Such Furs as may be collected, after such Duties or imposts as may be charged thereon shall be deducted, and also to furnish the Said Roger Simpson with good and wholsome food, water Spirituous Liquors and Medicines, together with Such accomodations as the Nature of the case will admit, and next in conveniency to those occupied by the Said Charles Bishop himself, dureing the Aforesaid voyage—And in case of the death or incapacity of the Said Charles Bishop, the Said Roger Simpson is hereby constituted and appointed Commander and Consignee of the Said vessel or Bark, with full power and Athority to persue the Said voyage, as in the Articles of Agreement made and Entered into between the commander & Officers and Mariners of the Said Bark is Specified and set forth, and furthermore the Said Charles Bishop hath contracted and agree'd, and doth &c &c—to give his opinion in writing in a Book to be keept for that purpose, on any proposition of the Said Roger Simpson for the Furtherence and Advantage of the Said Voyage, and in the Said Book all reasons shall be Specified if required by Either of the contracting parties of the other, for proposing, assenting to, or dissenting from any plan which on the Said voyage may be proposed.

Now Know All Men by these presents that we the aforesaid Charles Bishop and Roger Simpson, are held and firmly bound and do hereby firmly bind ourselves, our Heirs Administrators or Assigns, unto Each other in the Penal Sum of Ten Thousand Spanish Dollars, for the full and true performance of every Matter and thing, specified and set forth in the premises, In Witness whereof, We have hereunto set our Hands, and Seals at Macao in the Empire of China this Tenth day May in Year of our Lord One Thousand seven hundred and ninty seven.

Signed Charles Bishop

Signed, Sealed & Delivered
&c &c &c Signed Roger Simpson

Signed Robert Ogilvy
Stephen Bones

★ ★ ★

*Fifteenth letter to Teast, from Macao, begun 30 April and con-
cluded 5 June 1797, sent per* Glatton:

*Passage from Amboyna; loss of two men; disappointment at
finding war dresses sold.*

However with a persevering and determined disposition of
mind, we settt to work refitting the vessel, in which I have
made the following alterations additions and Amendments.—
Her rail, which was low and seemed rather calculated to chuk
People overboard, than to save them from falling, and had
been the cause of my loosing those 2 poor fellows overboard,
was only two feet high with painted Cavass. This has been
replaced with one four feet high, well Secured with Stantions
and boarded up with Inch board all round and a Barrocade
to the Quarter Deck.

Her channels which were too narrow, and the Chain plates
which were too Slight, with dead blocks to reeve the Ends of
the Shrouds thro', which is an unsafe, and consequently an
unseamanlike fashion, have been replaced with strong
Channels sufficiently broad, and new Chain Plates with dead
Eyes, to set up the Shrouds with Lanyards, the Puttock plates
for the Topmast shrouds the Same,—Her Main boom of
42 feet, having been twice carried away, is now laid aside,
and in the room of making a new one, we have turned her
into a Barque by stepping a Mizzen Mast, and by this means
enabling us to keep the boarding nettings up always under
Sail or at Anchor, a circumstance now become highly necessary,—Her tops, which before were only crosstrees with a
rim round them, are now properly made, and covered with
light board for the purpose of having two Swivals mounted
in each, when trading with the Indians on the coast or at the
Sandwich Islands.—The combings of the Hatches being too
low, have been replaced with higher ones fitted with loop
holes for Close quarters, and a Companion over the fore and
after Hatchways,—Her Bowsprit which was decayed in the
Partners and was condemned, has been replaced with a new

one—Her decks and upper works, which had been badly caulked by Malay Slaves at Amboyna, has been caulked alover again, and the vessel twice painted—Her Standing rigging well refitted, and where bad, replaced with new and new Running rigging almost fore and aft,—Her old Suits of Sails repaired, and new Courses and Topsails added to them. —A new Europe Cable and bower Anchor and a new boat.

And now Sir! I must hope when you consider what a Place Macao is to refitt, where the cheapest Europe articles bear an advance at least of 70 *per Cent* and where provisions are dear and scarce that you will inspect the inclosed bill of Expences and disbursments with Candour, as indeed I must hope you will do all my proceedings. Ashure yourself Sir! that my mind is disposed to fair and honourable persuits, and that in no Instance have I swerved to Charge what in my last moment I would wish to eraze. Indeed! I am confidant notwithstanding all my care and attention, to the Ships Expences, I am looser by the disbursments—but for most of them I have vouchers either in Shape of Bills, reciepts, agreements or the Log Book.

But in consequence of missing the Leather war dresses, and the great Expence of equipping the vessel here, I am necessitated to enlarge the scale of my funds—and which gave rise to the great obligations I am under to Mr: James Drummond, one of the Companys Supercargos, who as a Gentleman, and a Merchant, is in the highest estimation in this Quarter of the World—I at first wrote, informing him of the whole circumstances of my voyage in the Ruby, my instructions from you and further intentions, in hopes he himself would adopt a part in the Expidition, not knowing then, that by particular orders of the Company, their Servants are prohibited from concerning themselves in any private commercial conection— He andswered my Letter in a Friendly manner informing me of this Circumstance, at the Same time offered to procure for me, the credit I solicieted from the Chinese Merchants— (vide Correspondence.). The obligation he has confered on me I shall never forget.—

Negotiations with the Supercargoes.

Indeed! every person, With whom thro' buisness I am acquainted seems interested in my concerns and anxious that I may set off fair to make a good voyage, my conection with Mr Howel, of course, after the involved state he reduced your property to has ceased, and tho' at Amboyna every thing was fairly settled, yet I will never trust him again,—

I am under the necessity of informing you that in consequence of missing the Leather war dresses, together with the Expences of Equipping the vessel, that I am obliged to admit a Partner in the concern, in the Person of Mr Conseequa a Chinese Merchant, who gives half his share to Capt*ain* Roger Simpson, who goes with me in quality of Factor or trader, from his general Knowledge of the N. W*est* trade. We have jointly written for Inshurence to Bengal, and Mr. Drummond is so good to Cover it for Us—I am now making up the Accounts, and wait only for Mr Drummond to send me Conseequas from Canton, to Close them. The vessel is certainly Equipped in a very respectable manner, with 12 months provision and an able Crew of 20 men, with an investment sufficient to procure 1400 Sea otter skins probably 1600.

Having been detained here so long I have by and with the advice of the parties concerned, together with the opinion of those Gentlemen acquainted with the Riches of the pacific Ocean made, or intend the following arangement in the voyage—

The Nautilus now about to sail arrives on the N. W*est* coast the latter end of July, and proceeds to Certain Known Ports and points where skins are to be bought, and continnues there untill the investment is sold, or the 20*th* October arrives when she leaves the Coast of America, and unless there is a probabillity of falling in with a vessel, going immediatly down to China at the Sandwich Islands, proceed on to Masafuera where from good and certain information 20,000 Seal Skins may be procured, dried and Shipped in three summer months—but should on leaving the coast of America fall in with or hear of a vessel being at the Sandwich Islands, I would first repair there, and freight the otter skins down under the charge of Capt*ain* Simpson and consigned to Mr D— thereby secureing that part of the voyage, and taking 8 Islanders on board it would greatly facilitate my Sealing Expidition.

Seal skins are worth here now 1½ dollars each but allowing them only to be worth 1 Dollar when we arrive, 4 months Extra time, in a voyage were no difference of Equippment is made, is well Spent in gaining 15 or 20,000 Dollars.—As I have obtained permission to return here with the Skins and Furs I may collect, I must hope Sir! you will Sanction my Exertions to redeem the Rubys failure and as probably we shall be near 12 months on our voyage, I request you will favour me with a letter, by the first China ships that Sail after the Receipt of this, it being my intention to sell the Nautilus totally and remit home the proceeds to you, and return myself to Bristol and if anything could give me more pleasure than making a full flowing good voyage, it would be hearing from you, and that you have not lost that confidance in me, I was honoured with when in England. I ashure you Mr Teast, I value your good opinion so much, that I am very anxious on this Score, and my Zeal for your Interest will I hope Excuse my conduct in the deviations I have made.

I inclose to you a sett of the Rubys accounts and also a rough statement of my present expidition—the fleet is now about Sailing from Canton, and I am favoured with an opportunity of sending this up Immediatly—we shall Sail in a day or two, and if anything transpires before worth your Attention I will write you of it.

★ ★ ★

In consequence however of a different arrangement being made with respect to inshuring the vessel (vide Letter to

Messrs. Boyd & Company Pages 95–6)[1] I wrote the following one to Mr Teast in Triplicate by different ships of the Hon'ble Company's Fleet then about to Sail for England:

★ ★ ★

Sixteenth Letter to Teast, from Macao, 10 June 1797:

Advises Teast to insure vessel for 9970 Head Dollars; outlines plan of voyage.

The Nautilus is about 4 years old built of Tic Wood[2] at Bengal, and finished in most Excellent Manner, has been compleatly equipped here for the voyage, carries 6 three Pounders Brass Cannon, four Swivals, with small arms suitable to the Crew of 22 Seamen and mariners beside myself—has on board an investment reckoned equal to the purchase of 1500 Sea Otter Skins with 12 months provisions and Stores, and is Copper Sheathed—

In consequence of the news of a Spanish War great Care will be taken not to approach any Spanish settlement. I have written you a pacquet of Letters per Favour of Daniel Beale Esquire inclosing the Rubys ACCOUNTS,* and Captain Broughton has favoured me with taking Charge of the Journal of her voyage for you[3]

★ ★ ★

* on Particularly examining those Accounts, an Error was observed when they where found to be as stated in Pages 45–6–7 and 49–50–51.[4]

The following is the Articles of Agreement entered into by the officers and Crew for Performing the voyage.

★ ★ ★

---

[1] See above, p. 254.

[2] For the significance of teak construction see above, p. 212 n., and Parkinson, 1937, 324–5, 329, who stresses its excellence.

[3] For Broughton's carriage of the Journal, and Beale, see above, pp. xii and xx respectively.   [4] See above, pp. 187–90 and 192–5.

Articles of Agreement made and entered into between the Master officers Seamen and Mariners of the Bark Nautilus whereof Charles Bishop is at present Master, now bound from Greens Bay[1] in China to the North west coast of America, and thence to any Island or Islands in the Pacific Ocean, for the purpose of Procureing a Cargo of seals Skins, and thence back to China, That in consideration of the Monthly wages against Each respective officers, Seamans and mariners Name hereunto set, they severally shall and will perform the above Mentioned Voyage, and the said Master doth hereby agree with and hire the said officers Seamen and Mariners for the Said voyage at the Said Specified wages to be paid pursuent to the Laws of Great Britain—And they the Said officers seamen and Mariners do hereby Promise and oblige themselves to do their duty, and obey all lawful commands of the officers of the Said Bark or the boats thereunto belonging, as becomes good and faithful Seamen and Mariners, and that at all Places where the Said Bark shall put in or Anchor at, dureing the Said voyage, to do their best Endeavour, for the preservation of the Said Bark and Cargo, and not to neglect or refuse doing their duty by day, or by night, nor go out of the vessel on board any other, or on shore, on any pretence whatsoever, without leave first obtained of the Master, or commanding officer on board, That in default thereof, they will not only be liable to the penelties, mentioned in an Act of Parliament made in the second year of the reign of King George the Second entitled an Act, for the better regulation of Seamen in the Merchant Service,[2] but will farther, in case they should on any account whatsoever, leave or desert the Said Bark without the Masters Consent untill the aforesaid voyage be finished and concluded and the Said Bark unladen,

[1] Green Point is on the peninsula which forms the northern head of Deep Bay, on the eastern shore of the Canton River Estuary, near the entrance. Bishop may have referred to Deep Bay, the small inlet (Shak Wan) in the peninsula itself, or even Tai Shan Bay, north of the peninsula (information supplied by Henry Talbot, University of Hong Kong).

[2] 'An Act for the better regulation and government of seamen in the merchants service', 2 George II, cap. 36. For a comment see Fayle in Parkinson, 1948, 35 n. Such Acts were enforceable only in British territory; Meares, for one, often lamented the want of control over his seamen.

be liable to forfiet one hundred Spanish Dollars, with every their Wages, goods and Chattels on board, renouncing by these presents, for themselves, Their Heirs, executors, administrators or Assigns, all right and title thereunto, and it is further understood and agree'd to by the Said officers Seamen and Mariners, that 48 hours absence without leave, is and shall be deemed a totall desertion, and doth incur the aforesaid Penalty: and that any person, who shall Plunder or Embezzle the Cargo or stores of the Said Bark, or Trade with, or Recieve Presents, from any person or persons whatsoever, without permission first obtained from the commander, doth incur and become liable to all the penalties and forfietures herein before Specified   And furthermore the Said Master doth hereby promise and agree that on arriving at the Sandwich Islands, if the said Seamen and Mariners, shall choose to relinquish their Wages for the remaining part of the voyage, which is to be considered as concluding and Ending on the delivery of the Cargo of Seal Skins in China He will then allow to each such Seaman or Mariner a Commission per Centum on the sales of Said Cargo of seal skins, in lieu of Said Wages,

And the Said officers Seamen and Mariners do hereby contract and agree with the Said Master, that in case of his the Said Masters death or incapacity, they will well and truly obey, in manner and form, and under the Penalties herein before set forth, Roger Simpson, now Trader or Factor of the Said Bark, as Master thereof, the Said Roger Simpson, in such case becoming liable to the payment of all wages or other Just dues to the said officers Seamen and Mariners in like manner as the Said Charles Bishop hath hereby contracted to be—Now for the Due performance of the Premises, and in testimony thereof we the Said officers, Seamen, and Mariners have volontarily set our names or marks hereunto, in the month and day to the Said names affixed and in the year of our Lord 1797.

★　★　★

	Name	Date	Quality	Monthly Wages	
1	Charles Bishop	22ᵈ February 1797	Master	Sixty Dollars	Discharged Port Jackson 5 October 98
2	Roger Simpson	10 May 1797	Factor	Sixty Dollars	Discharged Port Jackson 5 October 98
3	Robert Sutherland	7 April 1797	Chief Officer	Fifty Dollars	Discharged Owhyhee 30 December 1797
4	John Harbottle	22 February 1797	2ᵈ officer	Forty Dollars	
5	Alexander Dobson	24 February Dᵒ	Boatswain	Eighteen Dollars	
6	George McClay	21 February Dᵒ	Carpenter	Eighteen Dollars	Discharged Port Jackson 5 October 98
7	Samuel Reid	29 May Dᵒ	Gunner	Eighteen Dollars	Discharged Owhyhee 2ᵈ January 1798
8	William Sparks	24 February Dᵒ	Able Seaman	Twelve Dollars	Discharged Port Jackson 5 October 1798
9	William Clare	24 February Dᵒ	Dᵒ	Twelve Dollars	Discharged Attoi 22 January 1798
10	John Bartlett	24ᵈ February Dᵒ	Dᵒ	Ten Dollars	Discharged Owhyhee 2ᵈ January 98
11	Robert Hinch	22ᵈ February Dᵒ	½ Seaman	Ten Dollars	Discharged Port Jackson 5 October 1798
12	John Block	24 February Dᵒ	Dᵒ	Ten Dollars	Run Port Jackson June 98
13	Thomas Reidson	7 April Dᵒ	Dᵒ	Ten Dollars	Run at Otaheite 6 March 98
14	Antony Harvey	22 April Dᵒ	Dᵒ	Ten Dollars	Run Port Jackson 20 May 98
15	James De loss	15 May Dᵒ	Dᵒ	Ten Dollars	Run Port Jackson Dᵒ.
16	Maheildo De Santos	15 May Dᵒ	Dᵒ	Ten Dollars	Run Port Jackson Dᵒ.
17	John Lewis	12 April Dᵒ	Steward	Twelve Dollars	Discharged Macao 12 June 1797
18	Owhyhee Cocos	22 April Dᵒ	Landsman	Six Dollars	Run Otaheite 6 March 98
19	Simon Rosa	30 May Dᵒ	Cook	Ten Dollars	Run Kamschatka October 97
20	Assancoe	30 May Dᵒ	Taylor	Eight Dollars	
21	Kowhowe	2ᵈ May Dᵒ	Landsman.	Six Dollars	Discharged Attooi 21 January 1798
22	One Cruiz	30 May Dᵒ.	Seaman.	Ten Dollars	Discharged Owhyhee 23 December 1797
23	Amowee	15 June Dᵒ.	Chinaman	Four Dollars	
24	Oneehehow	22 February Dᵒ.	Captain's Servant	Four Dollars	

ENTERED AT SANDWICH ISLANDS

	Name	Date	Quality	Monthly Wages	
25	James Stowe	5 January 1798	Gunner	Eighteen *Dollars*	Discharged Morotoi 1 February 1798
26	Samuel R. Chase	22 January 1798	Able Seaman	Twelve *Dollars*	Discharged Port Jackson 5 October 1798
27	James Cordell	12 January 1798	Seaman	Ten Dollars	Discharged Port Jackson Dᵒ—
28	Michael McDonald	23 December 1797	½ Seaman	Ten Dollars	Run at Otaheite 6 March 98
29	John Fergusson	2ᵈ January 1798	Landsman	Six Dollars	Discharged Port Jackson

The foregoing Letters, agreements &c will, I should hope, sufficiently explain my proceedings in Equipping the vessel, and the motives of my Conduct therein, and the following will be the account of the Expences and Disbursments From the time of her Arrival untill She Sailed from Macao for the N. West coast of America together with an Invoice of the Investment taken on board for the purchase of Sea Otters Skins on the N West Coast,—

★ ★ ★

Debtor Owners of the Nautilus in Account with Charles Bishop, Master, for Equippment of the vessel at Macao 1797.[1]

		Spanish Dollars	Cents
February 1797	2 Sheets Sheathing Copper	4	50
	2 Tierces Pork—@ 60 Dollars	120	0
	1½ Dº Beef—Dº	90	0
	1 Barrel Splitt Peas	30	0
	2 Iron Kettles	3	0
	1 Vase Lamp	7	0
	1 Pewtor Water Jugg	1	50
	1 Brass Stew Kettle	1	50
	7 Bottles Mustard	3	50
	3 Bottles Sweet Oil	3	0
	3 Bags Rice	9	0
	1 Barrel Pitch	18	0
	1 Barrel Tar	16	0
	1 Pair Ships Pistols	5	50
	Postage of Letters to Canton this month	4	0
	Daily Provisions as per Bill this month	32	0
	Boat hire bringing necessaries for Ship	4	50
	Wood for new Trusseltrees & Combings	11	50
	an Anchor Brandy, ½ Leaguer Arrack, 1 Picul soft Sugar, ½ Picul Sugar Candy, 12 lbs Candles (Chays bill)	64	50
	3 Dozen Madeira Wine	30	0
	Paid three China men working on board	1	50
	Expence of shiping seamen and boat hire	10	0
March 1797	Chinese Carpenters bill, for Rail bulwark &c	110	0
	44 hearts and dead Eyes for the Rigging	15	0
	Blacksmiths bill, sundry articles & work	30	0
	4 Cwt Iron @ 5¼ Dollars per Cwt	21	0

[1] Except where indicated by crosses, each item in the original account has a tick beside it in the left-hand margin.

		Spanish Dollars	Cents
	Boat hire and Postage of Letters this Month	26	75
	China men Employed this Month	4	0
	12 hearts and blocks for the rigging	6	0
	133 lbs Iron	10	0
	Compradores, Messrs. Peters & Company for Provisions &c	188	40
	Sundry Planks to Make chainwals	5	0
April 1797	Mr Mitchells bill for Cordage—	42	0
	11 Bolts Canvass—16 Dollars	176	0
	2 Leaguers Arrack—160 Gallons each	180	0
	5 Caddies fine Tea	2	0
	Expence of the Crew avoiding the impress[1]	10	0
	Planks for fishing Bowsprit, & new Tops	18	0
	20 fathoms 2½ Inch bolt Rope	1	50
	20 Inch and half Boards for Hatches & bulkheads	10	0
	5 Small Spars for Studdingsail booms	1	50
	1800 Assorted Nails	7	0
	New Binnacle, Goose & Hen coops, Companions &c	42	0
	½ Dozen Knives and Forks	2	0
	4 Coils China Rope	2	0
	4 Plates of Iron for Tops to mount Swivals	2	50
	6 Tumblers	2	0
	1 Gun Worm—50 Sail Needles	2	25
	Paid China man taking Care of Rigging &c on Shore	5	0
	Sea Store China ware	19	0
	Compradores, Peters & McEvoys bill Provisions &c.	285	20
× May 1797 Returned	Holmagrens bill Nº 1 14 Cheeses Pickells &c.	4̶8̶	0
	Manoel Vicentes Bill, for Caboose, Junk, Iron & Rope	237	85
	Doctor Vicelans bill surgical Assistance & Medicine	74	0
	Holmagrens bill Nº. 2. 7 Dozen⎫ Brandy, 2 Cases Gin, Jar butter⎭	94	0
	Coppers bills—Water Casks &c	72	0
	Sundry Rope and Junk from Captain Lay	41	0
Twice Charged ✓×	Hire of Chinese Carpenters to work on board	30	0
	Painting the vessel twice, inside and out	25	0
	Padre Moors Bill Bower Anchor	60	0
	Captain Simpsons Bill Sundry Stores &c	453	34

[1] An echo of the claim of impressment exercised in times of need by Navy officers to the vast trouble of merchantmen (Parkinson (1937), 49–50, 213, 380). But just where did the ten dollars go?

		Spanish Dollars	Cents
June —	Comprodores, Messrs. Peters & McEvoys bill	797	0
	Boat hire April & May, June bringing Provisions &c &c	91	50
	Postage of Letters April May & June	9	0
	Expence of shipping men, and avoid impress	12	0
	Paid Carpenter of Lady Washington for Sundry work	10	0
	Paid Caulkers for Caulking the vessel	36	0
	36 Fathoms Coir Rope for Topsail ties	3	0
	1 Pickel Copper Sheathing	62	0
	19 Caddy Copper nails	12	50
	Sail Needles and twine	4	0
	× Chinese Carpenter for sundry work on board	3̶0̶	0
	Spoons Steelyards and fire Tongs	2	0
	Expence of Straw breeming the bottom[1]	1	0
	Paid Chinese Picking Okam &c	5	0
	3 Compass Glasses	3	0
	a Topmast steeringsail	2	50
	× 1500 assorted Nails—not Received	8̶	0
	Cleaning and repairing Arms	7	0
	1 Picul Fine bread	9	0
	Cooking utensals	3	50
	Sea Stock of Pumkins	6	50
	Paid China men Packing Sugar & Jams &c	2	0
	7 Pickel soft sugar—@ 6 Dollars	42	0
	5 Pickel Sugar Candy, @ 12½ Dollars	62	50
	20 Pickel Ship Buiscuit @ 6 Dollars	120	0
	25 Caddy sail twine @ ½ Dollar	12	50
	30 Caddy Green Tea	20	0
	10 Caddy Shouchong	6	75
	65 Caddies Coarse Tea	17	75
	10 Picul Flour—4 Dollars	40	0
	1 Box Preserved Ginger	16	0
Cargo	× 24 Sealing Knives	16	0
	2 Dozen Drinking Mugs	8	0
	× 100 Tubs to stow Sugar in—(in Cargo)		
	30 Pickel Bengal Rice	112	50
	300 sail needles	1	50
	Boards for building a Sleeping Cabin for Captain S.	2	0
	2 Ankers Brandy	35	0
	½ Picul Candles	35	0
	Glass lights for the Compass	3	0
	6 China Hams @ 2¼ Dollars	13	50
	1000 nails	4	0
	2 Dozen 6 and 7 Inch blocks for Rigging	6	0
	Spare Paints	12	0
	10 Tierces Beef @ 50 Dollars	500	0
	a new, India mans, yawl	80	0

[1] Breeming means clearing a ship's bottom by burning.

		Spanish Dollars	Cents
Cargo	a new 10 Inch Cable 120 fathoms	350	0
	2 Furkins Butter	40	0
	1 Spare Topmast	10	0
	a Cabin Stove	12	0
	Armorers Forge and implements	20	0
	Wages of Samuel Reid boatswain Discharged	7	25
	D° of P. Hunter seaman Discharged— 1 Month 4 days	14	0
	Spanish Dollars	5554	50
	Less by Holmagrens bill No 1. Returned	48	0
		5506	50
	+less Chinese Carpenter twice charged	30	0
		5476	50

★ ★ ★

Account of 2 months advance Pay and other moneys Paid to the Crew and their Creditors previous to leaving Macao.

	Dollars	Cents	in Cash	
On Account of Mr Robert Sutherland, Chief Officer	117	25	114	25
On Account of Mr John Harbottle 2d Officer	50	0	40	0
Alexander Dobson Boatswain	97	25	78	75
George McClay Carpenter	116	50	116	0
Samuel Reid, Gunner	94	75	76	0
William Sparks, Seaman	74	50	53	0
William Clare Seaman	87	25	56	0
John Barlett Seaman	36	0	35	0
Robert Hinch Seaman	47	50	46	0
Thomas Reidson D°	39	75	36	0
John Block ½ Seaman	38	0	29	50
Antony Harvey Seaman	38	50	31	0
James De Los Seaman	30	37	24	50
Mahieldo De Santos D°	26	75	24	50
One Cruiz D°	20	50	20	0
Owhyhee Coco Landsman	19	25	12	0
Simon De Rossa Cook	27	0	20	0
Assancho Chinese Taylor	34	0	28	0
John Lewis Steward	24	0	24	0
Oneehehow Captains Servant	12	0	0	0
Captain Simpson	206	0	203	0
Spanish Dollars	1237	12	1087	50

NB. this List is only to shew the Expence I was at in Collecting and Keeping together the Crew but which Sums of course stands against their wages & includes the Slops I had let them have—but the Sums marked in the Margin was paid in hard Cash—amounting in the whole to 1087 Dollars 50 Cents.

★ ★ ★

Invoice of Sundry Goods laden on board the Brig Nautilus for Purchasing a Cargo of Furs, on Account and Risque of the owners thereof[1]

	Spanish Dollars	
41 Dutch Companys new Musketts, 4½ Pagodas each ⎫		
42 Dᵒ Dᵒ, new Cutlasses 1 Pagoda each ⎬ =	517	70
12 Barrells Prime Gun Powder 9 Pagodas each ⎭		
Cwt 3.2.0 Lead Ball and Shott—@ 8 Dollars per Cwt	28	0
55 Pewtor Basons each 3 lbs @ 1 Dollar	55	0
12 Hatchetts @ 1 Dollar	12	0
10 Coopers Adzes @ 1¼ Dollar	12	50
8 Dozen Files @ 3½ per Dozen	28	0
2 Dozen Plated Spoons @ 2 Dollars	4	0
4 Shott Belts @ 1½ Dollars	6	0
25 Leather Trunks, (Europe)—@ 3 Dollars	75	0
200 Canton Leather and Paper Trunks @ 1½ Dollars	300	0
60 Iron Potts	50	0
33 Tan'd Leather Hides @ 2 Dollars	66	0
4 Picul Brass wire @ 60 Dollars	240	0
40 Dozen Looking Glasses @ 1½ Dollar	60	0
1 Picul Beads @ 60 Dollars	60	0
609 yards broad blue Cloth @ 1219 Dollars ⎫		
299 Dᵒ Dᵒ Dᵒ Dᵒ 830 Dollars ⎬ =	2438	0
Duties on Dᵒ & Copper 389 Dollars ⎭		
650 old Keys	28	0
150 Looking Glasses	12	0
170 Jars for filling Powder @ 1 mace each	23	0
× 6 Jacketts and Coats—Not used in Cargo	0̸	0
1 Picul Beads	24	0
3 musketts @ 5 Dollars	15	0
5½ Dozen Clasp Knives @ 6 Dollars	33	0
7 Picul Stout Leaguer Iron Hoops @ 3 Dollars	21	0
1½ Dozen Pairs Scissars	5	0
× 4 Dozen Clasp Knives not used in Cargo—@ 2¾	1̸1̸	0
× 10 Caddys Thread not used in Cargo	8̸	0
100 Small half Tubbs	13	75
3 Picul sugar Candy @ 12½	37	50
13 yards Superior fine Cloth 3.17 Cents per yard—	41	21
Spanish Dollars	4159	75

Macao 10ᵗʰ: June 1797

    E: E: Charles Bishop
    E. E. R. Simpson

       ★ ★ ★

[1] Except where indicated by crosses, each item in the original invoice has a tick beside it in the left-hand margin.

Account of monies Rec*eive*d from, and Paid by Mr. Conseequa.

*Credito*r	By bill in favo*u*r Peters and McEvoy	908
	By D° in favo*u*r Achie and Chinqua	324
	By D° in favo*u*r Attack, Chinese trader	100
	By D° in favo*u*r John Lewis	172
	By Cash Paid Capt*ain* Lenox	219
	By D° Paid Mr Musgrave	176
	By D° Paid Quishang for trunks	200
	By D° paid Capt*ain* Vyeyan for boat	80
	By D° paid 2 bills Looking Glasses	36
	By D° paid Captain Palmer, Cable,	390
	*By D° Rec*eive*d from Mr De Souza	1500
	By D° Rec*eive*d Manoel Vicente	1000
	By Cash paid on acc*ount* Stores	200
	By Cash paid Capt*ain* Simpson	300
	By Duties on Cloth and Copper	389
	By Cash paid 609 yards Cloth	1219
	By D° paid 299 yards D°	830
	By D° paid 10 Tierces Beef	500
	By D° paid D*octo*r Vicelans	92
	By D° paid Paid Padre Moore, Anchor.	60
		8695
	* D*ebto*r to bill on Select comm*itt*ee	1500
	Ball*ance* C*arrie*d on Acc*ount* Adventure	7195

In the foregoing bill of Disbursments, there may be some
Deduction to make, from the bills of Mssrs. Peters and
McEvoy (the compradores) for money advanced, or Expences
of the People paid by my Directions, or Private Expences of
my own, or Servants, and which, as they are written in
Portaguese I cannot now clear up, untill an opportunity offers
of getting them translated,—whatever deduction there may
be to make, it will lessen the Expence of the outfitt, and of
course be deducted from my particular Share in it.

Char*le*s Bishop—

★ ★ ★

On 16th June we took our Departure from Macao Sailing
in Company with the Hon'ble Companys fleet bound to
Europe, and on 19th. met with an heavy Typhoon which
seperated the fleet, and in which we Sprung our Fore Mast
and Bowsprit as was Sopposed, for we did not discover it
untill 2 days after the Gale was over—

On 23^d June, having cutt up a Spare Topmast and fished the Foremast with it in the best manner we could at Sea, we fell in with part of the Hon'ble Companys Fleet, and from the Taunton Castle Captain Studd,[1] I obtained a Spar 52 feet long 12½ Inches diameter to serve us for a Foremast in case the present defective one should give way in our passage.— Captain Studd accepted my Bill on Mr Teast for the European cost of it, (10£ accompanyed with my letter of advice N°. 17) after which we parted Company and proceeded on our voyage. On the 30th. we anchored in a Bay near the South Point of Formosa for the purpose of getting our water filled up, 2 Casks having leaked out together with the long passage we have had across the China sea that near 2/5^{ths} of it was expended.—Soon as the Ship was secured at her Anchor, I went with 2^d officer and five men in the boat to find a watering place, which we did nearly abreast the Ship—but there being too much surf to Land the boat, we came to a Grapnal just without it, and about 20 yards from the beach, and the People swam a shore with the Casks and bucketts, myself and Boat Keeper staying in the boat. They had began filling the Casks when suddenly a large Party of Indians rushed out from behind some Rocks, and fired a volly of Shott, arrows and Darts amoung our people, who instantly fled, being totally unarmed, into the water towards the boat. The Indians following them close to the Edge of the Surf, gave the boatkeeper and my self an opportunity to discharge the loaded arms in the boat at them with Effect, and several where killed and wounded. However in the interval of Loading our musketts, two Indians more daring then the rest, rushed into the water to catch hold of Mr Harbottle who was the hindmost of our people, being wounded by an arrow in the back and his thigh bone broken by a Gun shott. Happily however he got within reach of one of the oars and we Saved him by timly wounding his assailants—except a few Shott holes in the boat together with loss of Casks and bucketts and the wounded State of the 2^d Officer, we got on board safe—and began to get underweigh but unfortunately the Anchor had

[1] Forename, Edward.

hooked a rock, and the weather looking very unsettled we where under the necessity of loosing the anchor and putting out to sea as fast as possible.

On 3ᵈ July we met with another very heavy Tphoon or Chinese Storm, which did us considerable damage and made the vessel leaky in her upper works, from that time[1] to 4ᵗʰ August we had a series of Light baffling winds and Calms, with dry Sultry and hott weather, when being in Latitude only 35° 54′ N and Longitude 150° 19′ East with not more than 18 or 20 days water in the Ship, together with the leaky state of the upper-works, and defective condition of her Fore-mast & Bowsprit it was judged most prudent to repair to Harbour of St Peters and Paul[2] in Kamschatka and refitt the Condition of the vessel. We accordingly steerd for that port and on 25ᵗʰ arrived there, having then not 2 Gallons of water on board.

It was not untill 9ᵗʰ: October that the vessel was put into a fitt state of Proceeding to sea. The season for going to the N West coast of America having elapsed, it had become the Intention of Mr Simpson and myself as the best plan to persue for the Interest of all Concerned to repair to the Sandwich Islands and on to Masafuera to procure Seals Skins dureing the winter in Northern Hemisphere and return to the N West coast in the Spring of the following year. The following Letters where left in the hands of the Russian Governor who promised to forward them with the Anual dispatches to Europe in November.

★　★　★

[1] A passage, not here reproduced, from Bishop's subsequent 'Protest' (see below, p. 283) delineated the period as from 5 July, when the *Nautilus* was at 22° 30′ N., 126° 00′ E., to 1 August, when at 31° 00′ N., 147° 00′ E. Another non-reproduced passage (from the letter to the East India Company supercargoes, 5 September 1799, see below, p. 315) describes the vessel's position on 3 July as about thirty leagues north-west of 'Botol tobago' (Botel Tobago, i.e. Hungtow Island, 22° 03′ N., 121° 33′ E.).

[2] Petropavlovsk, 53° 00′ N., 158° 39′ E. In the non-reproduced passages Bishop refers to 'Awatska', i.e. Avacha Bay, on which stands Petro-pavlovsk.

*Eighteenth[1] letter to Teast, from Petropavlovsk, Kamschatka,
8 October 1797:*

*Will explain why the vessel is so situated and not making for
America; troubles which drove the* Nautilus *to Formosa; the
landing there.*

I took also with me a few Knives, beads and looking Glasses,
to give any Natives we might meet and induce them to bring
us fresh Stock with which the Island abounds. Amicably
inclined to do them no harm whatever we landed at a good
watering place without percieving any Natives and began to
fill the Casks, when Suddenly our people were fired upon by
a large party of the Natives 'till then concealed behind the
rocks close to the boat—Altho' out of the boat and on my
way thro' the surf to the beach, I regained her again immediatly and with the Boat Keeper kept up so smart a fire with
the ready loaded arms upon the Indians that our people
reached the boat in Safty all except Mr John Harbottle 2ᵈ
Mate who was dangerously wounded in the back knee and
his thigh bone broken—we recovered him from the Natives,
however, altho' they disputed the Point with us till several
fell and others retreated evidently wounded, and we regained
the Ship. The Cause of this unprovoked attack arose as we
immagine from the conduct of a Certain Capt*ain* Browne,[2]
who committed some depredations amongst these people in
the year 1793, and which I did not know before, But poor
Harbottle was one of his officers at the time—we had another
misfortune attending our anchoring in this bay, our Anchor
got so entangled with foul ground that we could not possibly
get it, and we lost with it 20 fathems Cable—disapointed at
not filling up our water, we went to an allowance of 3 Pints
p*er* Day, Each man. A violent Typhoon arose soon after
quitting this bay, and our Starb*oar*d fore Channel was broke
down by a sea, nevertheless by wearing the vessel we Saved
the Foremast,—for near 30 days after this we had a succession

---

[1] Bishop omitted letter seventeen, for which see above, p. 272.
[2] William Brown of the *Butterworth* might well have behaved so, but
Bishop does not identify him.

of Calm or Light baffling winds, so that on the 4th August being then only in 30 degree North 150th: degree East, we found it necessary to keep a direction for this place, for the purpose of getting water and securing the mast—we had little or no rain all the time, or we had hoped to have catched enough to make out at 3 Pints *per* man 'till we reached the coast of America—but the tottering state of the Foremast and Bowsprit, placed us in so precarious a situation to encounter the stormy and savage shores of America, that being nearly in the Meridian of this Place, we bore up and got safe in 24 August, having when we anchored only three gallons of water on board—I must beg Sir you will not concieve it arose from any improvidence in me, in not furnishing a proper quantity of that essential article, before we left Macao. We had Then, 70 days water at 1 Gallon *per* Day each man, but to those who are acquainted with an outfitt at Macao, it will not be strange to hear, the villian Cooper, had so ill prepared the Casks, that one third of our whole Stock was lost. Disapointed, also, at not filling up our water at Formosa and not Catching any rain water, we had spun it out to the last Cask and the last Gallon of that cask before we could get in to anchor here.

The Russian commander, the same Hospitable Captain Shmalleff so highly spoken of in Cooks voyage,[1] recived us in a most Friendly manner, and has assisted us in fitting out with every assistance in his power.—Pine Spars do not grow here, but he let us have a Kingships mizen Mast, an Anchor and new 12 Inch Cable (118 fathems) requiring only a Certificate from us *that* we where in distress for those articles, and

[1] Cook and King, III, 210, 218, 220. At that time Schmaleff was second-in-command. Bishop's non-reproduced passages refer to him as Major and 'Chavalier'. The letter of 5 September 1799 said further that Schmaleff's promotion resulted from his courtesy towards Cook's expedition, and elaborated on his continuing kindness: 'He readily offered us every assistance, the settlement could aford. The artificers and People where ordered to do any thing for us we requested and our wounded officer was placed by his directions in the house of the 2^d in Command whose Wife and daughters were his kind nurses and Attendants. We daily received presents of fresh Salmon & milk and often Wild fowl and vennison, the Chief & 2^d in Command each gave us a Bullock...'

that he recieved no payment or recompence for Supplying us.
His people worked for us, and we daily recieved refreshments
from him. Our wounded officer has been taken care of on
shore and is now recieved on board much recovered. The
Fore mast has been securely fished and hooped and we have
a new Bowsprit.

But now Sir, having lost our season on the coast this year,
I beg leave to inform you of our intended plan. We sail this
Evening or tomorrow for the Sandwich Islands to get a few
of the Natives and proceed on to Masafuera to get Seals skins
which are valuable in China—our stay there will be so regulated to arrive on the N. West coast by 31st May, 98, a period
with the goods and knoledge we have of the coast, early
enough to accomplish the otter skin part of the voyage so has
to return to China by november, when I hope to Accomplish
my arduous undertaking with Success and Credit, and to
return with such information and Knowledge of these seas,
that you may be Enabled to derive benefit from a future
undertaking and with surer prospects of success than when
I set out in the Ruby.

I Inclose a Protest made out on our arrival here as to the
necessity of our coming, and the good Major Shmalleff under-
takes to forward our letters this winter to Petersburg from
whence I hope you will recieve them safe.—I take the Liberty
to inclose a pacquet for my Dear Friends in Hampshire which
I trouble you to forward.

★ ★ ★

A letter to the same Effect, relating the particulars of the
voyage and its disasters, together with our farther intentions
was written to Mr. Drummond, for the information of
Mr Conseequa, and Addressed to him in English, Russian
and Chinese.—

On Tuesday 10th October we set Sail, and on Saturday 14th
we met with the heavyest storm the oldest seamen on board

ever knew. Other Gales of wind and Typhoons were but squalls compared to this tremendous Blow

★   ★   ★

COPY OF THE REMARKS IN THE LOG BOOK SATURDAY 14th OCTOBER 1797.

'Heavy Gales and severe squalls and Gusts of wind with constant rain, veering round gradually from S East to South and west, with the most terrible sea the oldest seaman on board ever knew—10 PM the Mizen staysail splitt and blew to ribbons,—3 a.m. an heavy sea struck us and broke in the rail, and Bulwark from the fore to the main Rigging on the Larboard Side, which splitt the shear plank, and caused us to make a good deal more warter, 1 Pump being kept constantly going—5 a.m. shipped another very heavy sea, that intirely washed away all the rail and Bulwark on both Sides before the main mast, swept the Caboose overboard and 1 Brass three Pounder, 2 other guns were swept off the deck but saved by their breechings—at 6 a.m. Fore staysail blew away—

'From the damages done by the sea in rending the gunwalls open, and constantly deluging the deck, the vessel leaked so much that both Pumps would hardly keep her free: in this situation it was Judged prudent to cutt up the Spare Spars and throw them overboard and to Clear the decks. The Small Bower anchor being loose over the bows by breaking of the Stantions, and the seas now making a Clean Sweep over the deck, it was impossible to save it, and it was Lost— the Spare Pump Geer having been brought upon deck to be at hand, was lost overboard too. However the deck being cleared and leather nailed over the worst parts in the Gunwalls, our Pumps constantly going, kept her free again. At noon no abatement of the storm, but clearer weather.'

★   ★   ★

The next day the Storm abated a little, when from the wrecked state of the vessel, it was judged most prudent to endeavour to regain the Harbour of St Peter and Paul, distant only about 60 Leagues. The loss of the spare pump Geer was irreparable, we thought, any where else, without giving up the voyage and returning to Macao. We therefore beat against an almost continnued Gale with snow and sleet untill 24th: when the cordage, from its frozen state, gave way so often, in Clewing up the Sails, that finding it impossible to regain our wished for Port we bore up for the Sandwich Islands, to endeavour to refitt the vessel there.[1]

In the severe weather off Kamschatka much of the Cargo was damaged and Spoiled, Particularly the Trunks and Sugar. On the 2[d] December we arrived off owhyhee and on the 8th: Anchored in Karakakooa bay, where by the Assistance of the Europeans resident on the Island, we began our repairs, which we compleated in the best manner we were able by the 2[d] January when having purchased 2 Cannoes *and* shiped several European seamen, in room of some discontented we discharged, together with 4 additional Islanders, we sailed for the Leeward Islands[2] to compleat the stock of Provisions, which having done in the best manner we where enabled we finally left the Islands 30th January 1798 and made Sail towards Masafuera.

★ ★ ★

Costs and Expences of the vessel at Kamschatka.

Repairs	Dollars	Cents
1 Iron Pott @ 1 Dollar	1	0
2 yards Mazarine Cloth @ 321 Cents	6	42
20 Catty Sugar Candy @ 12½ Cents	2	50
5 Looking Glasses @ 12 Cents		60
8 Pewtor Basons @ 1 Dollar	8	0
Spanish Dollars	18	52

[1] For elaboration, see below, pp. 284–5.
[2] Subsequent references (see below, p. 285) indicate that Bishop meant the western Sandwich Islands proper, not the chain extending still farther west, now known as the Leeward Islands. These references give the date of departure thence as 31 January.

Provisions	Dollars	Cents
5 yards Mazarine Cloth @ 321 Cents	16	5
192 Catty Sugar Candy @ 12½ Cents	24	0
8 lbs Powder @ 25 Cents	2	0
6 Trunks @ 150 Cents	9	0
2 Cutlasses @ 131 Cents	2	62
Spanish Dollars	53	67

Costs and Expences of the vessel at Sandwich & Society Islands

Repairs	Dollars	Cents
5 Musketts @ 7 Dollars	35	0
35 yards Mazarine Cloth @ 321 Cents	112	35
14 yards Worcester Cloth @ 243 Cents	34	2
6 lbs Powder @ 25 Cents	1	50
3 China Trunks @ 150 Cents	4	50
50 Catty Beads @ 42 Cents	21	0
Spanish Dollars	208	37

Provisions &c	Dollars	Cents
15 Musketts @ 7 Dollars	105	0
49¾ yards Mazarine Cloth @ 321 Cents	159	70
52 yards Worcester @ 243 Cents	126	36
100 lbs Gun Powder @ 25 Cents	25	0
10 lbs Sugar Candy @ 12½ Cents	1	25
95 Penknives & Scissars @ 37 Cents	35	15
545 Looking Glasses @ 12 Cents	65	40
90 Files @ 30 Cents	27	0
8 China Trunks @ 150 Cents	12	0
17 Cutlasses @ 131 Cents	22	27
20 Pewtor Basons @ 1 Dollar	20	0
150 lbs Lead Ball @ 7½ Cents	11	25
150 Catty Beads @ 42 Cents	63	0
8 Hatchets @ 1 Dollar	8	0
10 Coopers Adzes @ 125 Dollars	12	50
7 Picul Iron Hoops @ 3 Dollars	21	0
Spanish Dollars	714	88

	Dollars	Cents
Repairs Kamschatka	18	52
Dº Sandwich & Society Islands	208	37
Invoice Price Spanish Dollars	226	89
Provisions Kamschatka	53	67
Dº Sandwich & Society Islands	714	88
Invoice Price Spanish Dollars	768	55
Total Expences Spanish Dollars	995	44

Errors Excepted   Charles Bishop

★   ★   ★

Nothing material happened (except that in setting up the Lower rigging, we carried away Three of the main Shrouds, and was under the necessity of cutting off 10 fathems of the new Cable to convert into Main Rigging) untill 25 february when a serious leak was discovered about 10 feet below the main mast in wake of a timber below the bends. This with two others caused her to make 18 inches water per hour, and the break of her deck and three Butts in her sides coming near together the vessel worked much in those parts.

On 6th March we Anchored at Otaheite.[1] We was induced to Stopp here to Recruit our stock of water and Provisions as well to get two Strong pieces Timber, to bolt along the Gunwales, to the beams over the break of the deck. On the evening of this day the Sandwich Islanders deserted from us, all except 2—

On the 10th: we sailed for Huhaine,[2] to compleat our stock of Hogs, and Yams, not being able to procure a Sufficient quantity here—having Careened the Ship and stopped the leaks, filled up our water, and procured two strong pieces of Timber to bolt over the break of the deck, by the assistance of the brittish Missioneries[3] resident on this Island, with whom I left the following letter for Mr. Teast.

★ ★ ★

Nineteenth letter to Teast, off Tahiti, 12 March 1798:

The Great Storm; passage to Sandwich and adjacent islands; concern to waste as little time as possible.

In our passage to these Islands we found the vessel leaked again—these leaks have been discovered and we anchored in Mateavy bay[4] on purpose to stopp them, which we have in a

---

[1] Tahiti. [2] Huahine.

[3] For the mission, see above, p. xxxiv. Henceforward the Introduction significantly expands Bishop's story. The text itself adds some details (see below, pp. 286–7).

[4] Matavai Bay is on the north coast of Tahiti. For a note on its exact eighteenth-century location, see Beaglehole in Cook, I, xciii n.

great measure done, but here we lost 5 of our crew by desertion and found it absolutely necessary to get out again which we did last night.[1]

The situation of the vessel is such now that if any more misfortunes occur, I am much afraid that we shall be obliged to relinquish the Expidition—Harressed and oppressed as I have been with anxiety and distress, I have only to add at present, that when a favourable opportunity offers I will write you a more particular account of all my proceedings, and the Journal and Accounts of the voyage shall be carefully conveyed to you

I leave this letter in the hands of the Brittish missioneries resident on this Island who have been settled about 12 Months here. They behaved exceedingly kind to us, and have been the means of preventing the villian King and his people from attacking us while in the bay Kareening

Should any more misfortunes overtake us, we shall proceed to Port Jackson, where everything I can possibly do for the good of your concern shall be done—but hoping that I may be yet successful enough to procure 15000 or 20000 Seal Skins...

★　★　★

On the 24th March we anchored again in Mattavy bay, Otaheite, having been driven from Huaheine by a strong Westerly Gale of wind, without accomplishing the purpose of our going there, in which time several of our Sails were splitt to pieces, the leaks opened afresh, and the weak state of the vessel became so apparent, that it appeared absolutely necessary to go to some port, where she could be repaired, and Port Jackson was deemed the most proper place for that purpose. The Crew Indeed! was unwilling to proceed so far with her, and two of them stole off in the night with our only boat.

[1] Probably because of the natives' hostility, but perhaps to halt further desertions.

[1]The King having meditated a plan to Cutt off the Missioneries, for the sake of their property, soon as we should sail, and had already committed hostilities on part of them who went to endeavour to recover our boat and People, they all met in Council and the Majority resolved, if we would take them on board, to leave the Island and go with us to Port Jackson, agreeing to draw bills on the directors of the Missionery society, for the Expences which would arise for their Passage, and it having been our intention, previous to leaving the Society Islands to lay in such a stock of Provisions, as would prevent the necessity of our purchasing much at Port Jackson, where of course we Expected it would be dear, we agree'd to take them on Condition they should pay the difference of Price between buying them here and at Port Jackson and work their passage down in the vessel. And on 29th March we recieved on board 11 men 4 Women 4 Children with all their Cloths and Effects, and on 31st: we got under way and sailed. Our Anchor being hooked to a rock we unfortunately parted the Cable and lost it, and put to sea, Harressed and opressed in mind with a Leaky ship & with only one Anchor—on the 8th: April a Rupture of a blood vessel in my stomach which continnued, with intermissions of a few hours, four days, had very nigh put a period to my sufferings and life together. However it happily stopped on the 12th: and in the course of a few weeks I became pretty well,—on the 14th May we arrived Safe at Port Jackson, the vessel making about 2 feet water per hour.

The next day being 15th May, I signified to Richard Atkins[2] Esquire deputy Judge Advocate, for the Colony, that we should Protest as to the necessity of our coming to Port Jackson, and on the 18th. the Following Protest and general Statement of the voyage, was made by myself Officers & Part of the Crew.

★ ★ ★

[1] From this point begins the page illustrated in the frontispiece.
[2] Atkins figures in all accounts of early New South Wales; see, for example, P. Serle, *Dictionary of Australian Biography* (Sydney, 1949).

Protest Barque Nautilus

By this Public instrument of Protest, be it known unto all Men who shall see these presents, that on 18th day of May, in year of our Lord one thousand seven hundred and ninty Eight, Before me, Richard Atkins Esquire His Majestys Acting Judge Advocate of the Territory of New South Wales and its dependencies, Personally appeared Mr Charles Bishop, Master of the Barque Nautilus now lying in Sidney Cove[1] in Port Jackson in the Territory aforesaid, Roger Simpson, Co-agent, Robert Sutherland, Chief Officer, John Harbottle, Second officer, George McClay, Carpenter, William Sparks and Robert Hinch Seamen, who being duly sworn on the Holy Evangilist of Almighty God, did Solomnly depose to be true, the Sundry matters and things, hereafter mentioned in this Instrument of Protest, vizt.

The journey from Canton to Formosa; the attack; renewal of the voyage; shortage of water and firewood; haven at Kamchatka; departure thence, and the fearful storm; decision on 15 October to return to Kamchatka.

That in consequence of this determination we tried every means in our power against an Almost continual gale of wind to effect it untill Tuesday 24th. but without Success. On that day in a heavy snow storm, as we attempted to Clew up the frozen Sails to heave the vessel too, the Clewlines gave way and we nigh lost our best suit of sails. Fearful of such an event taking place, although we where not more than 60 Leagues from the Port, it was judged prudent to give up the Attempt and bear away for the Sandwich Islands when the following note was entered in the Log Book

'From the great severity of the weather, the state of the Crew, nearly half of whom are sick and the danger of loosing our sails it appears to us and every person on board impracticable to regain our wish'd for Port, and altho' the Sandwich Islands from the wrecked state of the vessel is by

---

[1] Sydney Cove lay on Port Jackson's southern shore.

no means a desirous or safe place for refitting yet it is the only one in our distress which offers without giving up the voyage and returning to Macao. We have now been 11 days Attempting to regain the Harbour of St Peter and Paul without advancing nearer to it than what a ship in the usual course of winds and Sailing might be expected to do in one days beating and the weather still continnuing bad, with little hope of changing for the better at this inclement season, together with the inability of the vessel to beat against these severe storms, that the undersigned are induced to give up the attempt and bear away for the Sandwich Islands.

(Signed) Charles Bishop & Roger Simpson'

That it was not untill 1st December we arrived at the Island owhyhee one of the Sandwich Islands our passage having been much retarded by the inability of the vessel in her wrecked state to bear the quantity of sail we should otherwise have carried—that on Friday 8th we anchored in Karakakooka bay in that Island where began to refitt the vessel, Employing an European Carpenter resident on the Island with four or five native Carpenters, also a Party of Natives under the direction of 2 Europeans also resident on the Island to Hew plank stantions and rails and the Kings smith to repair the old and make new spare Pump Geer with nails and other Iron work.

That on Sunday 24 December having been informed that otter Skins could not be bought on the Coast of America last season under two fathems of Cloth each and in other articles proportionally dear the undersigned Commander and agent thought it good for the concern to make the following resolve and which is entered in the log Book for that day, vizt 'Having heard that otter skins are so advanced in their price on the Coast of America, that with our investment after paying the vessels Expences here, we should not perhaps be able to procure more than 6 or 7 hundred skins, and having several people on board aquainted with the sealing buisness one of whom has been to the Island Masafuera when in about 5 months they killed and dried 35000 seal skins, the undersigned think it good to proceed as before our misfortunes of Kamschatka they intended to that Island and procure 20000 seal skins, as soon as the vessel can possibly *be* got ready, and relinquish going to the Coast of America altogether.

Signed Char*le*s Bishop & R. Simpson'

That in consequence of this determination every exertion was made to get the vessel ready and by 2^d Jan*uary* 1798 new stantions rails and Bulwarks was fixed strongly round the vessel, the sides bends and gunwalls caulked, the rigging & Sails refitted, two Cannoes purchased to aid bringing off the skins from the Island to the vessel and 5 Sandwich Islanders taken on board in addition to the Crew, several of whom vizt Alex*ande*r Dobson, Boatswain, Sam*ue*l Reid, Gunner, John Bartlett and one Cruiz Seamen, having behaved in a mutinous and disorderly manner, refusing their Duty and by their Conduct setting a bad example to the rest of the Crew where discharged and turned on shore and three other seamen shipped in their room. That on the night of the 2^d Jan*uary* we sailed for the Island Mowee to fill up our water and afterwards to Owhahoo and Attooi to compleat our Stock of Provisions and finally left the Sandwich Islands 31 Jan*uary* keeping to the S E*ast* as much as the winds would permitt

That the Goods expended in the Equipment and repair of the vessel at the Sandwich Islands amounted to the Sum of Two hundred dollars or thereabout at invoice price of the Investment—(Exclusive of Provisions) (vide Page 121)[1]

That on Sunday 25 day Febr*uary* being in Latt 7° 40' S and 212 East Long, a serious leak was discovered about 10 feet before the mainmast on the star*board* side in the wake of a Timber. This leak with two others (one on Each bow) had commenced since leaving the Sandwich Islands, and the

---

[1] See above, p. 279.

vessel made 18 Inches water in two hours—and the vessel had been found very weak in the break of the Quarter deck it opening and shutting very alarmingly with the motion and which is believed to have been caused by the force of the heavy Seas falling on her off Kamschatka 14 October 1797 as several of the bolts was found broken short off, and that in Consequence it was judged prudent to touch at the Island Otaheite then lying nearly in our rout, for the purpose of getting two strong Peices of timber as riders along the Gunwales over the break of the deck to be fastened to the beams and stantions, and also to Careen the vessel to try and stopp the leaks. That we arrived at Otaheite Tuesday 6 March and found a Society of Brittish missioneries resident there who had arrived from England about 12 months before for the purpose of converting the natives to Christianity. These people kindly assisted us in supplying our wants and in watering and getting the vessel ready for sea. We recieved from them two pieces of Timber suitable to the above purpose of securing the Break of the deck, some Bolts nails and Carpenters tools, and having stopped the leaks we sailed Saturday 10th, intending as Hogs was scarce at that Island to touch at Huhainu for a Supply of them and Yams. Five of the Sandwich Islanders deserted from us at Otaheite and no inducement we could offer the King was sufficient to get them restored—owing to light baffling winds we did not arrive off the Island Huhainu untill 16th. which day was spent in making bargains with the Chiefs, who where to have brought off the Hogs and vegetables the day following, but a heavy Gale of wind commencing in the night from the North West prohibited any farther Intercourse with the natives and this gale continued with unabated Fury untill Tuesday 20th. in which time the leaks that had been caulked at Otaheite opened afresh and the break of the deck worked so alarmingly, that it appeared Evident to all on board the vessel in her present state is unfitt and unsafe to encounter the voyage to Masafuera dureing the winter months now Commencing, and the storm having driven us in Sight of Otaheite, it was judged prudent to repair thither again and Stop the leaks as we should be able to Careen the vessel in Matavy bay under the protection of the society of Miss*ionar*ies without much danger of the natives attacking us in that Situation. We anchored there Sunday Evening 24 March, on that night two seamen, viz Mich*ae*l[1] McDonald & Tho*m*as Reidson stole the only boat we had and deserted the vessel. The boat was recovered again the next day from the natives by the missioneries who also sent a Deputation to the King to demand the deserters, but the natives Seized the Deputation, stripped them naked and almost murdered them, and which in all probability would have been Effected if the Kings father had not inter-fered and saved their lives. That it appearing too great a risque of the vessel cargo and lives of the Crew to proceed farther on the voyage to Masafuera untill the ship could be repaired it was resolved for the Interest of the Concern by the Commander and Agent, to proceed to Port Jackson in New S*outh* Wales and repair the vessel there during the winter months in the Southern Hemisphere and take such farther steps as the necessity of the case should require. That this step having been previously resolved on, an application by the Society of missioneries, as they concieved their lives Eminently in Danger from a proposed Attack of the natives that we would recieve them and their families on board and as much of their effects as we could convienently and with Safty of the vessel carry, agreeing that they would make good any Extrodinary Expense of Provisions &c which our re-cieving them on board and conveying them to Port Jackson might occasion, which we acceeded to as well on the score of Humanity as a return to the kindness we had previously recieved from them...

Departure from Tahiti; loss of anchor; Port Jackson reached; summary of the Protest; signatures of deponents.

★ ★ ★

Report of a Survey held at Sidney 19th May 1798 on the Barque Nautilus by Messrs. Thomas Moore, master Builder

---

[1] The man's forename is given variously as Michael and James.

of the Kings yard, George McClay Carpenter, Charles Bishop Master and Roger Simpson Co-Agent and 2^d Command, all of the Said vessel who are unanimous in opinion, that before the Nautilus can be put into a fitt state to proceed to sea on her voyage it is necessary to give her the following repairs and Equipment—, vizt:

To shift about 20 feet plank on Each side and fill up two midship ports in the between decks—

To putt 16 new knees to the beams which were formerly knee'd with Iron and were broken or insufficient—

To putt a new Breast hook below the lower deck

To seal the hold with Inch board and the insides between the decks with 2 Inch plank—

To Ripp off all the torn Copper sheathing from the middle upwards between the Keel and Wales. Caulk the bottom and sheath it with Inch Cederboard to Caulk and pay it, and mend the remaining sheathing of Copper

To Caulk the upper works and Decks

To fitt new Channels fore and aft

To fix a Capstern—and make new Pumps

To make new Combings to the Hatches, new hatches & Companions

To putt new shear plank on the Gunwalls, New Stantions & Bulwarks

To build two new boats—

To Repair & Refitt the Rigging & sails

To repair the water Casks—

To Procure two bower anchors and a Cable

Now to the Truth &c &c &c

Signed Thomas Moore, George McClay   Charles Bishop, Roger Simpson

Signed Witnesses William Cummings
              Peter Thompson

★ ★ ★

By the Sales of the N W*est* investment we were enabled to commence the repair and Equipment of the vessel, and altho' stores of every Denomination where excessively dear, and scarce, yet by the assistance generously granted to our request by Government, in supplying us with Pitch and other necessary stores not to be procured otherwise we were once more Enabled to put to sea in a comfortable state 7th October 1798.—Previously, on the 20th Sep*tember* I wrote the following letter to Mr Teast by the Barwell bound to China & London

★   ★   ★

Twentieth letter to Teast, from Port Jackson, 17 September 1798:

That the Nautilus should be here will no doubt awaken your Attention with forlorn Ideas as to the success of the voyage. The inclosed Copy of Protest which Contains the particulars of our proceedings since leaving China until our arrival here, will inform you fully on that Subject, and render any other relation, except what has transpired since unnecessary—

On our Arrival, shattered and leaky as we were, we thought proper to have a survey on the vessel by the Master builder of the Kings yard, whose report I also inclose as to the repairs necessary to render the vessel sea worthy, which you will percieve were Considerable, and to do it we have been under the necessity of disposing of the North west investment in addition to 270£ we recieved from the missioneries for conveying them from Otaheite to Port Jackson an Account of whom you Can peruse in a letter inclosed for the Directors of their Society left open for that purpose, which I beg you will be so good to inclose and send to them

Agreeable to the builders opinion and advice we have given the vessel a thorough repair, and she is in every respect as to her hull much stronger than ever she has been before, but as work of this kind is excessive dear, it has so far

Exceeded our purse, that we have been under the necessity of taking up 200£ from Captain John Cameron of the Barwell now going to China for bills of Exchange drawn on James Drummond Esquire at 5/- per Dollar which we trust he will honour, in the ashurence of our being in China in 7 or 8 months with a large Cargo of Dry Seals skins

From the Commander and sad remains of the Crew of the ship Sidney Cove of Bengal,[1] who where obliged to run their ship on Shore after doubling the South Cape of New Holland to save their lives, we learn that the Islands thereabout abounds with Fur Seals, and it is our intentions to proceed from here about the 25th of this month for those parts with a Strong crew of 25 men and two whale boats to kill and dry skins for China, and boil out seal oil for this markett, proposing first to secure the ship in a good Harbour and then divide the People in Seperate Parties, to the different Islands, under the command of myself and officers, keeping a few of the Crew boiling oil which we expect to procure to the quantity of 3 or 4000 Gallons and which will doubtless sell here well at least 5/- per Gallon perhaps more, and it is further proposed that when we have got about 2000 Gallons and 10,000 Skins to leave 2/3 of the Crew under the officers and proceed here with both articles we have procured, sell the Oil, and lodge the skins as so much property secured, then take in a fresh stock of Provisions and return to the Seal Islands the distance not being more than 3 or 4 days sail, and then to Employ the time untill the end of February when we propose sailing direct to China from hence—and should we be so fortunate, which with ashurence we have every reason to expect, to procure a double Cargo of Seals Skins, as the Nautilus will not carry More than 25,000 to leave them in respectable hands here to send on to China by the first Ships for Teas—

Our Expences will amount I believe to about 1200£ all of which we have been Enabled to pay out of the money arising

---

[1] For the wreck of the *Sydney Cove*, Bishop's friends at Sydney, and the sealing voyage generally, see above, pp. xl ff., and Map I(*a*) and I(*b*).

from the Sale of the N West Investment and the money we recieved from the missioneries except the 200£ we have drawn for on Mr Drummond and great part of this Expence has been incurred for settling the wages of the former Crew, which is more than 2/3^{ds} paid and the present Crew being on shares, no farther Expence will be incurred on that head, the whole hire of the Crew amounts to about 35 per Cent—

I trust yet to be able to render our Melancholly voyage if not successful at least a saving one—& inclose to you the attested Copy of the protest & report of the Survey, and shall by the next opportunity send you the Cost of Equipment—my letter from Kamschatka you probably before this have recieved—

I beg you Sir! to accept my sincere prayers for your health and I hope to be with you in 12 or 14 months and be ashured Sir! I shall always conduct myself with Integrity and Zeal—

★ ★ ★

A Similar letter was written to James Drummond Esquire for the Information of Mr Conseequa—CB

★ ★ ★

Articles of Agreement made and Entered into Between the Master officers Seamen and mariners of the Brig Nautilus whereof Charles Bishop is at present master, now lying in Sidney Cove in Port Jackson in His Majestys territory called New South Wales, and bound from thence to certain Islands and Places in the Pacific Ocean in quest of a Cargo of Seals Skins, and having procured such Cargo to proceed to Macao or Canton in China where, or 24 hours after the Sale and Delivery of the said Cargo, the voyage shall cease and end and the Parties to these presents, having fully performed their duty agreeable to tenor and meaning of these articles shall be intitled to such share of the neat proceeds, as against each respective name shall be affixed on Signing these presents, and which is to be considered, recieved and taken in lieu of Monthly or other pay or Emolument whatsoever—

Statement of conditions as in Agreement framed at Canton (see above, pp. 263-4), down to and including penalties for plundering or embezzling cargo.

And moreover it is agree'd by and between all the Parties subscribing these presents, that if it should at any time appear in the opinion of the majority of the Crew on board the Said brig that any person or persons shall be indolent, slothful or Idle, and not perform his or their proper task share or proportion of work in a suitable and Seamanlike manner, that then the Said Majority so deciding shall have power by and with the aprobation and Concent of the master or Commander, to fine such offending person or persons in such Sum or Sums of money not Exceeding his or their full share or proportions of the proceeds of the said voyage as shall be deemed proper and Expedient, by the Commander and Majority of the Said Crew, and which fine or Mulct, shall be equally divided between the rest of the Crew who shall be found to do their duty Dilligently and faithfuly—And it is further understood and agree'd by all the parties to these presents, that no Officer Seaman or Mariner shall demand or expect his or their share or Proportion, in Skins—but the whole shall be sold and disposed of together by the Said master or such person as he shall appoint to sell and dispose of them, and Each person paid his Share or proportion according to the rates affixed to each name respectively. Oil and every other article obtained in the voyage, except ship stores and Provisions, shall be considered as Cargo, and each person to be intitled to their Share or Proportion of the Proceeds of the Same—

Agreement to obey Simpson in case of Bishop's incapacity, Simpson then undertaking Bishop's guarantees; formal conclusion to Document.

★ ★ ★

Entry	Names	Station or Quality	Shares	Discharge &c
6 October 98	Charles Bishop	Master	4 per Cent Commission }	Discharged 15 September 1799
Do	Roger Simpson	Co Agent	4 per Cent Commission	
Do	Robert Sutherland	1st officer	1/30th	Discharged for Mutinous Conduct
Do	John Harbottle	2d officer	1/30th	China 15 September 99
Do	George McClay	Carpenter	1/70th	Do—13 September 99
17 September 98	James Miln	Able Seaman	1/100th	Do—13 September 99
30 August 98	James Cordell	Do	1/100th	Do—13 September 99
17 September 98	George Appelton	Do	1/100th	Do—13 September 99
30 August 98	Daniel Cooper	Do	1/100th	Cape Barren
Do	William Mackey	Do	1/100th	China 13 September 99
Do	John Ash Smith	Do	1/100th	Do—13 September 99
Do	Joseph Oliphant	Do	1/100th	Cape Barren
6 October 98	William Sparks	Do	1/120th	Cape Barren
30 August 98	Edward Hogan	Do	1/120th	Died 11 December 98 at C Barren
Do	John Steward	Do	1/120th	Run Port Jackson
Do	Thomas Lee	Do	1/120th	Discharged Port Jackson 31 December 98
Do	Hugh Dougherty	Do	1/120th	Do—Do—27 May 99
Do	Samuel Clews	Do	1/120th	China 13 September 99
6 October 98	Robert Hinch	Do	1/120	Discharged C Barren
Do	William Baker	ordinary Seaman	1/140th	China 13 September 99
Do	George Shedrick	Cook	1/140th	Discharged Sick Port Jackson 3 January 99
Do	Thomas Lythgo	ordinary Seaman	1/140th	China 13 September 99
Do	Michael Murphy	Do	1/150th	Discharged Do 27 May 99
1 September 98	Stephen Lawless	Do	1/150th	Do Do 27 May 99
6 October 98	Charles Wood	Able Seaman	1/180th	China 13 September 99
6 October	Samuel R Chase	ordinary Seaman	6 Dollars per Month	Cape Barren
Do	Boxo of Bengal	Taylor	8 Dollars per Month	Port Jackson 25 May 99
Do	Chinese Taylor	boy	4 Dollars per Month	China 31 August 99
Do	Amowee Chinese	Sandwich Islander	4 Dollars per Month	China Do
Do	Namahama	Do	6 Dollars per Month	China 13 September 99
Do	Oneehehow	Able Seaman		Do Do—
31 December 98	William Smith Bradlee	ordinary	1/100th	Do Do—
12 January 99	George King	Volunteers for their Passage to China	1/140th	Port Jackson 27 May 99
Entered } 28 May }	{William Roberts {John Rogers {Joseph Cowdry {William Morice {George Shedrick			Discharged in China with the rest of the Crew

293

With much difficulty we at length put to sea 7th October
in better condition than I had expected, and in a fortnight
arrived at Cape Barren Island where we found Fur Seals
pretty abundant and by the 20th December we had procured
near 5000 Skins with about 350 Gallons oil, when it appearing
we should not have provisions for the whole Crew more than
a month, we resolved to Proceed to Port Jackson with what
Cargo we had already Collected and take in a Fresh Supply,
leaving 14 able hands under the Command of that Excellent
officer Mr John Harbottle to collect skins while the vessel
should be absent—and as a farther encouragement for them
to be diligent and attentive to their Duty, We agree'd to give
them an additional half share for all the Skins and oil they
should collect—we arrived at Port Jackson 25th. and by the
5 January were again ready to putt to sea—the following
letter was left to be sent on should any opportunity offer to
Mr Teast at Bristol—

★   ★   ★

Twenty-first letter to Teast, from Port Jackson, 4 January 1799:

In my letter to you by the ship Barwell 17 September 1798
then bound to China I informed you by the inclosed protest
of the untoward Events of my voyage, and the distresses
which had arisen and brought us to seek shelter and repair at
this Port, and of my intentions to proceed to the Southward
along this coast in quest of a Cargo of seal Skins which I am
happy to say will most probably be accomplished by the
latter end of March—we sailed from hence the 7th October
in Company with a small vessel fitted out by Governor
Hunter to explore the Southern parts of this immense Island,
and arrived safe at the Port of our desire in about a fortnight,
where I had the happiness to find the Fur Seal of the best
quality in such numbers that we could average 200 Skins a
day—unluckily however there is no harbour nearer to their
place of resort than one from 20 to 30 miles distant, where
we moor'd and Sicured the vessel—we continnued sealing
unto 12 December and received on board 5200 Skins ¾ of
which is of the best quality, when provisions beginning to

294

grow short—for owing to the great Expence we had been at refitting and repairing the vessel, I could not lay in but 4 months Provisions and having a Stout Crew I judged it prudent to leave two months provisions with 2ᵈ officer and 14 Chosen men of the Crew, and proceed back to Port Jackson with the skins we have procured, and also 300 Gallons oil—I had hoped to have gott 2000 Gallons—which selling here for 5 or 6 Shillings per Gallon, would have raised a sufficient sum to have defrayd all Expences, but owing to the distance of the vessel from the Sealers we found it work enough to get the cured skins round to the ship at the intervals of fine weather—but I am still in hopes to accomplish even that part of my plan, by setting up the boilers where the seals are killed, and putting the oil into Casks, then when the Cargo is ready, go round with the vessel and Cruize off untill it is all on board. Believe me Sir! I spare no pains or Exertion either of Body or mind to bring the difficulties I have encountered in this disasterous voyage to an happy issue. We arrived here Christmas day, we should indeed been up to the harbours mouth in 50 or 60 hours after we left the Sealers, but a strong North wind took us aback about 50 miles to southward of the port, and kept us out so long, that the last provisions in the ship, was served out to the Hungry crew as we entered the Harbours mouth—I have now laid in 5 months stock and are nearly ready to sail again—for these supplys I am much indepted to William Kent Esquire Commander of His Majesty's ship Supply—This Excellent person is Nephew to Governor Hunter, having perused the sad and distressful Events in our Logbook He stepped forward with his whole influence, in our behalf—stores of every Discription could not be procured for money, the little there was in the Colony, was in the hands of Government. He interested the Governor and the worthy veteran seemed happy in assisting us—on my offering to settle with the Store keepers I was informed the Governor only wished to have a bill upon you to pay for the articles at such price the Navy board should think proper to Charge, probably bills that will not come to hand before I am in England, as he told me he would not send them till we had left the Coast for China and if they should 50£ will be I think the utmost amount—Captain Kent has again stood my friend, thro' him I have Obtained 5 months stock of dry Provisions and a Ton of Salt meat. This with seals asslett[1] Kangaroo and Wild Fowl, will I trust be sufficient. Spirits now is very dear and we go intirely without Grog and have done so this 4 months. Mr Kent indeed now and then gives me a little wine—He has just been with me and desired me to draw upon him for any sum I may want to pay for the Provisions and is Contented to take my note of Hand 'till I come back and If I should not procure a sufficient sum by the sale of oil and Hair skins to pay him, to accept a bill on Mr Conseequa for the Amount. I believe I shall owe him about 260£. He has been so good to suffer us to leave the 5000 skins we brought on board his ship carefully stored and I have begd him should any ship arrive bound to China before we come back to send them on to Mr Drummond, not doubting from the Excellence of the Fur and the smallness of the Cargo that they would in that Instance fetch 2 Dollars per skin if not 3— beside which we should be enabled to carry a greater number in the Nautilus for I have scarcely a doubt of returning full or with 15000 more—Thus I hope shortly to finish my anxious concern, and after disposing of the skins and vessel at China to remit home to you the proceeds, and return to settle my accounts and revisit you and my Dear friends, with a mind Enlightened by Experiences Nautical and Mercantile, Knowledge of the seas and Commerce of the great Pacific, not doubting but that in one voyage of 2 years fitted out from England on the plan I shall have to propose, of redeeming all the failures of a sad 5 years adversity—I pray God that you have your health and that you are happy, and when I have the pleasure of seeing you, I trust and hope Sir you will judge of my conduct, not by the success of my undertakings but by my Zeal integrity and perseverence—as no ship is here immediatly bound towards you I shall leave this letter in Hands of Captain Kent to forward by the first opportunity—whom I have beg'd also to write to you should he send on the skins that

---

[1] Haslet.

you may inshure if you think proper. I think inshurence ought to be low, as the passage is pretty well known and no fear of meeting an Enemy.

★ ★ ★

Disbursments and Expences Repairing the Nautilus at Port Jackson

		Dollars	& Cents
May 15 1798	1 Bushel Corn	1	0
	2 Fowls @ 5/-	2	0
	vegetables	1	0
	Bread	1	0
16th	Paid light house men	5	0
	1 Cwt Potatoes	2	50
17	1 Gallon Rum	16	0
	1 lb Candles	1	60
18	1 lb Butter	1	20
20	2 Bushels Corn for Stock	2	0
	1 Gallon Beer	1	60
	1 lb Candles	1	60
21	1 lb Butter	1	20
	1 Cwt Potatoes	2	50
22^d	1 lb Candles	1	60
	1 loaf Bread		20
	2 Bushels Corn	2	0
23	1 Cwt Potatoes	2	50
	4 lbs Sugar	3	20
	1 lb Tea	16¹	0
	6 Fowls	3	0
25th	½ Cwt Potatoes	1	25
27	1 lb Wax Candles	1	60
Raffities Bill from 19th to 29th	{ 3 Quarts Rum	9	92
	77 lbs Salt Pork	23	10
	1½ Gallons Rum	22¹	0
	1 Fowl 3 lbs Pork	1	0
	1½ Dozen Eggs		90
29th	1 lb Candles	1	60
	1 Quart Rum	3	20
Bakers bill this Month	{ 181½ White loaves @ 8^d	24	20
	113 Brown D^o @ 6^d	11	30
	12 lbs Flour	1	20
	Fire Wood		30
Butchers Bill	{ 315¾ lbs Pork @ 30 Cents	94	71
	34¾ lbs Mutton @ 1/8	13	60
	4 lbs onion	—	80
	Fish this Month	3	50
	Month May 1798 Spanish Dollars	284	8

¹ When scarce, provisions were extraordinarily dear at Sydney. Soon Bishop was to be buying tea there for as low as two Dollars per pound. Rum had a more enduring preciousness, having great importance in the colony's social and economic life. Bishop himself took advantage of this, and paid many costs with liquor, making a profit thereby (see below, p.310).

		Dollars & Cents	
1st June 1798	1 lb Candles	1	60
	1 Boat load Fire Wood	4	0
	20 Gallons Cape Brandy	88	0
	20 Gallons Cape Wine	40	0
	6 lbs Sugar, 1 lb Tea	16	80
3d June	1 lb Candles	1	20
4	1 Hog—60 lbs	15	0
5	1 lb Candles	1	60
9th	6 Ducks	3	60
	1 Goose	1	50
	132 lbs Pork	33	0
12	Hogs Fry 1 lb Candles	2	60
14	1 lb Candles	1	60
16th	1 lb Do	1	60
	House Rent	20	0
	1 Bushel Corn	1	0
18th	6 Chairs 1 Dozen W Glasses	10	80
	2 Dozen Plates 6 Rummers	7	0
	1 Tureen 2 Dishes	3	70
	6 Bottles Vinegar	3	70
	4 Cwt Potatoes	8	0
19th	30 lbs Kangaroo 1½ Dozen Eggs	2	70
	6 Fowls	3	0
	2 Boats fire wood	4	0
27	2½ Dozen Eggs	1	60
28	2 lbs Tea—5 lbs Candles	11	0
	1 Dozen Ducks	6	40
	Fish this Month	6	10
Bakers Bill	⎰ 207 White loaves @ 8d	27	60
	⎨ 156 Brown Do @ 6d	15	60
	⎱ 24 lbs Flour	2	40
	217 lbs Pork @ 1/6	65	10
	1 Hog 205 lbs @ 1/-	51	0
	134 lbs Mutton @ 1/8	44	67
	2 Sheeps Heads	2	0
	2 Cwt Potatoes	4	0
	20 lbs onions	1	50
	Month June 1798 Spanish Dollars	506	97

---

1 July 1798	1 Large Tarpaulin	11	0
	6 Knives & Forks	5	0
	8 Large Rummers	8	0
10th	359 lbs Cordage @ 6d	35	59
	20 Bundles Twine	14	0
	1 Cask bengal beef	13	60
	2 Hides for Rigging	5	40
11th	1 Barrel Tar	7	20
	343 lbs new Europe Cordage	49	70
16th	1 Tea Kettle	2	50
19th	100 Salt Fish	7	20
	1 Hog 83½ lbs	16	70
	14 lbs Candles	8	40

		Dollars	& Cents
20th	4 new Chain plates	4	20
	1 Copper Kettle	4	0
	1 Tierce of Slush	19	60
	House Rent	20	0
25	1 Hog 116 lbs @ 10^d	19	33
	Paid Cooper of Supply	4	0
	Oysters fish & vegetables	7	0
26	3 Muscovy Ducks	3	0
	1½ Cwt Potatoes	4	50
28th	11 Fowls 3 Ducks	11	0
31	2 Cwt Potatoes	8	0
	6 lbs Mutton	2	40
Bakers bill	159 White loaves @ 8^d	21	20
	156 Brown D^o @ 6^d	15	60
	3 lbs Flour		30
Butchers bill	86¼ lbs Mutton	28	75
	Keeping our Hogs	5	0
	22 Gallons Rum @ 9/-	39	60

Total   Month July 98. Spanish Dollars 401 77

1st August	54 Gallons Rum @ 9/-	97	20
	Repairing Tea Kettle	2	0
4th	225 lbs Potatoes	5	50
	Fish	1	50
	157 lbs Pork @ 10^d	26	18
6th	4 Firkins Butter	76	67
7th	184 Gallons Rum @ 9/-	331	20
	238 lbs Nails	83	55
	112 lbs Shott	13	50
	6 Barrels Salt Pork	156	0
	1 Deepsea line	4	20
	1 Iron oil Boiler	15	20
	1 Water Butt	2	80
	repairing Chairs	2	0
	3 Dozen Eggs, 7 lbs Mutton	3	15
	2 Dozen Sealing Knives	11	0
	116 lbs Pork @ 1/-	23	20
	oysters & 10 Fowls	8	0
	63 lbs Potatoes, 1 Dozen Eggs	2	50
11th	Oppossum & Kangaroo	9	0
	171 lbs Pork @ 10^d	29	83
12th	4 Fowls—2 Ducks	4	0
	Paid Cooper Account	48	90
	469 lbs Sugar @ 8^d	62	54
15th	227 lbs D^o @ 8^d	30	27
	8 lbs Tea @ 10/-	16	0
	50 lbs Candles @ 1/6	15	0
	2 Dozen Trucks[1] &c	11	20
	1 Hand lead & line	2	0
	100 Gunny bags	19	60
	2 Water Casks, 2 tin Potts	4	80

[1] Wooden blocks used in rigging.

		Dollars & Cents	
19th	64 Gallons Rum @ 8/-	102	40
	80 lbs Pork @ 1/-	16	0
20th	72 lbs D^o @ 9^d	10	80
	House Rent	20	0
23^d	186 lbs Pork @ 10^d	31	0
	Fish at Sundry times	8	0
27th	179 lbs Pork @ 10^d	29	83
	3 Ducks & vegetables	4	0
	Paid Gunner of Supply	4	0
30th	6 Cwt Potatoes	16	0
	a Cabin table	4	0
	1 Large Iron Boiler	1	60
Bakers bill	⎧ 184 White loaves @ 8^d	24	54
	⎪ 242 Brown D^o @ 6^d	24	20
	⎨ 4 lbs Flour		40
	⎩ 147 lbs Pork @ 11^d	26	95

Total Month August 98 Spanish Dollars 1442 41

1 September 1798.	99 lbs Pork @ 10^d	16	50
	1 Roasting Pig	2	0
	Cleaning the House	4	0
2^d	7 Ducks, 1 Fowl	8	0
	10 Cwt Potatoes	24	0
4th	105 lbs Pork @ 1/-	26	0
5	Fish	2	0
8	12 Seizing lines	12	0
	2 boat load of wood	6	0
	3 Squares of Glass	1	20
9th	2 Ducks—2 Fowls	4	0
	oysters, 1 Dozen Eggs	2	0
11th	60 lbs Pork @ 1/-	12	0
	61 lbs D^o @ 1/-	12	20
	6 Dozen Fish Hooks	2	0
	200 Pounds Salt Meat @ 1/3	50	0
13th	131 lbs Fresh D^o @ 10^d	28	0
	3 Ducks	2	0
14th	oysters & Fish	3	0
	200 lbs Salt Fish	8	0
	Kangaroo	9	20
	Paid for Spiles for Ship bottom	2	0
	1 Small Bower Anchor	28	20
	3 Cwt Jirked Beef	18	0
	2 Gallons oil	1	80
20th	200 lbs Pork at 10^d	33	35
	Sealing geer	22	0
	Fish	1	0
	1 Dozen vinegar	6	0
	Oysters and Fish	3	0
23^d	Six oared Gigg	100	0
	Timber Cart	1	0
	Rope making & Pins	3	0
	1 Dozen Glasses	6	0

		Dollars	& Cents
25	122 lbs Pork @ 1/-, 21 lbs Mutton	32	80
	Fish Hooks, lead & line	4	0
	Currents, fish & blocks	7	0
	10 Honing Knives	10	0
	20 lbs Slush for Rigging	2	0
26	3 Fowls, 1 Dozen Eggs	4	0
	Fish & 10 Pumpkins	5	20
27	vegetables	3	0
	131 lbs Pork	26	20
	2 Tierces beef, 2 D⁰ Pork	175	70
	102½ lbs mutton, 2 Ducks	42	40
	185 White loaves, 372 Brown	61	87
	1036 lbs Flower	75	67
	299 lbs Pork @ 1/-	58	60
	106 lbs D⁰ @ 10ᵈ	31	0
	Total Month September 98 Spanish Dollars	998	97

		Dollars	& Cents
1ˢᵗ October 1798	Paid Carpenter, 77 Days @ 5/-	77	0
	D⁰ D⁰ — 88 Days @ 8/-	140	80
3ᵈ	Building Wale boat	84	0
	Stock of Poltry	12	0
	Salt Fish	9	0
	111 Gallons Rum @ 8/-	177	60
	1 Ton Rice paid in Rum	—	—
5ᵗʰ	15 Cwt Potatoes @ 12/-	36	0
	2 Tarpaulins	11	0
	8 Bolts Canvas @ 50/-	80	0
6	Ship builders bill	943	40
	Blacksmiths D⁰	104	35
	Thomas Foster D⁰	26	20
	Tinmans D⁰	8	40
	200 lbs Corned Pork	40	0
	1 Sow with Pig	15	20
	6 Small Hogs	32	0
	Pilotage in & out	28	0
	2 Cwt buiscuit	20	0
	5 Cwt Coarse D⁰	40	0
	Paid assisting Seamen } & others heaving down }	40	0
	Month October 1798 Spanish Dollars	1924	95
	September—	998	97
	August—	1442	41
	July—	401	77
	June—	506	97
	May—	284	08
Total Cost of Repairs &c		5559	15

Errors Excepted
Charles Bishop

Port Jackson
    7ᵗʰ October   1798

*   *   *

Disbursments & Expences at Port Jackson 1798–9

		Dollars	& Cents
26 December 1798	195 lbs Pork at 10^d	32	50
	6 Pint tin potts	3	0
	1 Cooks lanthorn	3	0
27th	2 Quart tin potts	1	20
	26 lbs onions	2	60
28	1 Quart of Rum	2	80
	4 Gimlets	1	0
29	Fish & 80 Salt D^o	4	20
	3 Knives & Forks	2	40
31st	5 lbs Sugar	2	0
	410 lbs Salt Bakon @ 1/6	123	0
	1 Gallon Rum	10	0
1st January 1799	1 Bottle to light house Men	2	80
	4 lbs Pepper & Fish	2	80
	Glaizing the Skie lights		40
2^d	3 lbs Sugar	1	20
	12 Sealing Knives	5	0
	148 lbs Pork @ 1/-	29	60
	672 lbs Salt Beef @ 8^d	89	60
	640 lbs Salt Pork @ 9^d	96	0
3^d	200 lbs Sugar @ 1/-	40	0
	repairing Boat	34	40
4th	1 Cwt Potatoes	2	40
	2 Barrels Salt Pork	72	20
	1500 assorted nails	3	0
	6 Padlocks	7	50
	12 Sealing Knives & steels	8	20
	1 Bottle Rum	2	80
	34 Gunny Bags	13	60
	100 Bushels Wheat @ 10/-	200	0
	1 Iron Flour Mill	29	40
	35 lbs onions @ 6^d	3	50
5th	1 Quart of Rum	2	80
	1 Hog	8	0
6th	216 lbs Pork @ 1/-	53	30
	Blacksmiths bill	50	70
	48 lbs Onions	4	80
	25 Bushels Wheat @ 10/-	50	0
	52 Bushels Corn @ 5/-	52	0
	39 Gunny bags	15	60
	Medicines	3	0
	5 Cwt Potatoes	15	0
	Tinmans bill	2	40
8th	30 lbs onions	3	0
	Bakers bill, 1 Cwt buiscuit	10	0
	2 Cwt Flour	13	34
	52 White, 112 brown loaves	18	14
	260½ lbs Pork @ 1/-	52	10
10th	Pilotage in & out	8	0

2^d Tripp total Spanish Dollars	1194	28

★ ★ ★

3^d Tripp Expences at Port Jackson

		Dollars	& Cents
8th March 1799	Coopers bill 2^d trip	16	0
	2 Bottles Brandy to lightHouse Men	8	0
	240 lbs Pork @ 1/-	48	0
	Fish & vegetables	2	40
10th	3 Quarts Rum	8	40
12	1½ Cwt Potatoes	5	40
	4 Hogs about 400 lbs	68	0
	171 lbs Pork @ 1/-	34	20
13th	17 lbs D^o @ 9^d	2	55
	1 Bottle Brandy	2	40
15	Cabages		60
16	200 lbs Pork @ 1/-	40	0
	3 Bottles Brandy	6	80
	Fish this trip	4	50
	25 White loaves @ 8^d	3	34
	160 brown D^o @ 6^d	16	0
	Pilotage in & out	8	0
	Total Cost 3^d Tripp Spanish Dollars	274	59

★ ★ ★

Norfolk Island

		Dollars	& Cents
29 March	1 Hog	14	0
	20 lbs Potatoes, 6 Melons	2	0
30th	5 Cwt Potatoes, 6 Melons	11	0
31	11 lbs Mutton @ 1/-	2	20
	2 lbs onions		30
1st April	1 Hog	9	0
	vegetables	1	50
2^d	1 Hog	14	80
	122 lbs Potatoes	2	32
7th	3 Hogs	30	0
	110 Ducks @ 2/6	55	0
	3 Dozen Fowls	14	40
	32 lbs Mutton	6	40
	103 lbs Potatoes	5	15
8th	16 Hogs	130	0
11th	26 Hogs	174	80
	1 sheep	16	0
	14 Fowls	5	60
	4 Furkins	4	0
	5 Cwt onions	10	0
12th	1100 feet 1 Inch board	22	0
	2 Hogs	18	0
	136 fowls	54	40
	40 melons	8	0
	Cost, 610.75 paid in goods =	340	87

★ ★ ★

Expences at Port Jackson fitting for China 1799—and at Macao & Whampoe

		Dollars	& Cents
27 April 1799	1 Cwt Potatoes @ 16/-	3	20
29	1 Bushel Corn @ 5/-	1	0
30th	126 lbs Pork @ 1/-	25	20
	4 lbs Tea @ 10/-	8	0
4 May	2 Bundles twine	9	0
	8 Bolts Canvas @ 11½ Dollars	92	0
	1 Gallon Spirits	3	60
	195 lbs Sugar @ 8ᵈ	26	0
	60 lbs raisons @ 2/-	24	0
	267 lbs Potatoes @ 3ᵈ	13	35
8th	2 Bolts Canvas @ 12½ Dollars	25	0
9th	1½ Gallons Gin	6	0
	47 Gallons Rum @ 2 Dollars	94	0
	858 lbs Sugar @ 8ᵈ	114	20
	1 Case Gin	20	0
	32 lbs Tea @ 2 dollars	64	0
	12½ lbs Candles @ 2/-	5	0
	151 lbs Fresh Pork @ 1/-	30	20
	31 lbs Butter @ 2/6	15	50
10th	320 lbs Cordage @ 5ᵈ	26	67
13th	1 Case Gin	32	0
14th	149 lbs Pork @ 10ᵈ	24	83
16th	2 Barrels Salt Pork	80	0
17th	Paid Cooper	6	20
	151 lbs Fresh Pork @ 10ᵈ	25	18
20th	98 lbs Pork @ 9ᵈ	14	70
	10 lbs mutton @ 2/-	4	0
22ᵈ	12 Bushels wheat @ 10/-	24	0
	121 lbs Fresh Pork @ 1/-	24	20
	7 Gunny Sacks	3	50
23ᵈ	Paid Comisarys Bill	100	65
	Sailmakers Account	19	40
Mr Rhodes Bill	3.2.0. Cwt Ship bread @ 30/-	21	0
	1 Swival Gun	8	0
	2 Water Butts	7	20
	1 Shott Mould	1	0
	2 Cartroush Boxes	1	0
	1 Brass steering Compass	4	20
23ᵈ	10.1.4 Cwt Potatoes @ 15/-	30	87
24	16½ Bushels wheat @ dollars	33	0
	6.1.0 Cwt Potatoes @ 15/-	18	75
	26 yards painted Canvass	5	20
Captain Ravens[1] Bill	2 Cases Gin @ 32	64	0
	1 Dᵒ Rum	42	0
	6 Bottles mustard	4	20
	2 Tierces Pork—£34.1.0	136	20
25th	151 lbs Fresh Pork	30	20
	Letter of Marques Commission	40	0
	6 Bottles vinegar	4	80

[1] William Raven, once a whaler, now employed by the government.

		Dollars	& Cents
26	4½ Bushels wheat	9	o
	Paid Rope Maker	12	o
27ᵗʰ	20 Bushels wheat	40	o
	4 Dozen Sail needles	4	o
	130 lbs Corned Pork @ 1/-	26	o
	5 Hogs	48	98
	Blacksmiths bill	80	o
	2 Tierces Pork	136	35
	Bakers bill	16	80
28	Pilotage	8	o
	Spanish Dollars	1797	31

★ ★ ★

Expences at Macao and Canton 19ᵗʰ August to 15 September 1799—

		Dollars	& Cents
19 August	Fruit &c	2	o
29ᵗʰ	Peter & McEvoys bill	244	75
30ᵗʰ	Do Do	13	75
	Pilotage to Whampoe	40	o
	Postage letters	7	o
	Boathire	4	o
	Hoppomans account	4	o
		315	50

★ ★ ★

General Statement of Nautilus Expences

		Dollars	& Cents
Month May 1798	—	284	8
June	—	506	97
July	—	401	77
August	—	1442	41
September	—	998	97
October	—	1924	95
December	—	187	70
January 1799	—	1023	38
March	—	259	59
Norfolk Island	—	340	87
Port Jackson for China	—	1797	71
Macao & Canton	—	315	50
		9481	70

Errors Excepted

Charles Bishop

★ ★ ★

Account of the wages of the Crew of the Nautilus in her Voyage in the Pacific Ocean 1797. 8. 9.[1]

Names	Quality	Monthly Pay	Entry	Dis-charge	Whole Wage	Advance	Amount paid in Stores & Cargo	in Slops	in Cash	For-fieted	General Particulars Dollars & Cents
Charles Bishop	Master	60	22 ii 97	15 ix. 99	1842.0	—	77. 3	—	1764.50	—	Whole Wages of the Crew 8410.79
Roger Simpson	Factor	60	10 v 97	15 ix 99	1690.0	203.17	202.50	—	1283.25	—	
Robert Sutherland	Chief Officer	50	7 iv 97	6 x 98	900.0	114.25	86.75	3.0	444.0	252.0	Paid in Advance 1044.17
John Harbottle	2ᵈ Officer	40	22 ii 97	6 x 98	780.0	40.0	35.0	51.33	653.75	—	in Stores &c 1158. 3
Alexander Dobson	Boatswain	18	24. ii 97	30 xii 97	188.0	78.75	91.25	10.0	—	—	in Slops 263. 3
George McClay	Carpenter	18	22. ii 97	6 x 98	350.33	116.0	73.50	16.75	144.0	—	in Cash 5197.55
Samuel Reid	Gunner	18	24 ii 97	2 i 98	166.75	76.0	29.50	18.75	—	41.50	Forfieted by Deserters 746.55—8409.63
William Sparks	Able Seaman	12	24 ii 97	6 x 98	232.80	53.0	51.0	27.0	102.0	—	Errors 1.16
William Clare	Dᵒ	12	24 ii 97	21 i 98	130.75	56.0	45.75	15.50	13.75	—	
John Bartlett	Ordinary Seaman	10	22 ii 97	2 i 98	103.0	35.50	28.0	10.50	—	29.0	Canton 29 September
Robert Hinch	Dᵒ	10	22 ii 97	6 x 98	195.0	46.0	55.75	5.0	88 -	—	1799
Thomas Reidson	Dᵒ	10	7 iv 97	24 iii 98 Run	115.60	36.0	69.50	3.75	—	6.40	Errors Excepted
John Block	Dᵒ	10	22 ii 97	22 vi 98 Run	160.0	29.50	12.0	8.50	6.0	103.90	Charles Bishop
Antoney Harvey	Dᵒ	10	22 iv 97	20 v 98 Run	129.0	31.0	2.0	7.50	—	89.0	

Note:

In this account of the wages of the Crew of the Nautilus it may be observed that I have charged on account of myself 60 Dollars per month, whereas I engaged in the voyage with Mr Teast for 6½ per month or 24 Dollars—and should never have Charged more, if it had not been necessary to admit another person in the adventure, and it appearing good for the Concern that Mr Simpson should go with me in the vessel to take Charge in case of Death or Accident to me I was obliged to give him 60 Dollars per Month to induce him so to do, and therefore wrote down against my own name 60 Dollars, the difference of which from 24 Dollars Per Month I always meant to deduct from my Credit in settling with Mr Teast so far as respects his particular Share in the outfit. Thus stated it will be

60 Dollars per Month, 30 Months	
21 days give	1842
24 Dollars per Month Do	737
Do	
Difference Dollars	1105

If amount of the outfit 16788 is charged with the Difference 1105, Mr Teasts Share 9044 dollars is charged with 595 ¾⁴ of dollars too much, and hence credited in my Private account Current.

Name	Rating	Entered	Mo.	Discharged / Run	Amount	Rate				
Juan Delos	Do	15 v 97	10	Run 20 v 98	121.60	24.50	10.25	5.50	—	81.25
Marihildo De Santos	Do	15 v 97	10	Run 20 v 98	121.60	24.50	2.0	0.25	20.0	74.75
Juan Cruiz	Do	30 v 97	10	23 xii 97	67.75	20.0	47.50	0.50	—	—
Simon De Rossa	Cook	30 v 97	10	Run 7 x 97	42.75	20.0	—	7.0	—	15.75
Owhyhee Cocos	Landsman	22 iv 97	6	Run 6 iii 98	63.0	12.0	8.0	7.25	—	35.75
Kahowee	Do	1 v 97	6	20 i 98	52.0	—	52.0	—	—	—
Oneehehow	Captain's Servant	22 ii 97	4	15 ix 99	123.0	—	11.50	17.25	95.0	—
Assancoo	Taylor	30 v 97	8	30 viii 99	216.0	28.0	—	9.0	179.0	—
Amowee	Landsman	16 vi 97	4	30 viii 99	105.0	—	4.25	9.0	91.75	—
James McDonald	Ordinary Seaman	23 xii 97	10	Run 24 iii 98	33.33	—	16.0	—	—	17.25
James Furgusson	Do	2 i 98	6	3 vi 98	30.20	—	14.75	—	15.50	—
James Cordell	Do	12 i 98	10	6 x 98	88.33	—	14.50	15.50	58.0	—
Samuel Chase	Able Seaman	21 i 98	12	6 x 98	102.0	—	52.75	2.50	46.75	—
James Stowe	Gunner	5 i 98	18	27 i 98	13.50	—	13.50	—	—	—
4 Sandwich Islanders	Landsmen	22 i 98	24	Run 6 iii 98	40.70	—	40.70	—	—	—
Bengal Boxco	Landsman	17 xii 98	6	22 v 99	28.80	—	—	—	28.80	—
John Hammond	2d Officer	28 v 99	30	15 ix 99	108.0	—	—	—	108.0	—
Nemahanna	Sandwich Islander	2 i 98	4	15 ix 99	70.0	—	10.50	4.0	55.50	—
					8410.79	—	1158.3	263.33	5197.55	746.55

¹ All cash figures in this and following tables are in Dollars.

Abstract Account of the Crew of the Nautilus on her sealing voyage, with their shares &c &c &c and Wages to Norfolk[1]

Mens Names	Quality	shares	Entry	Discharge or Run	Whole Shares Skins	Oil	Wages for voyage to Norfolk Island	How Paid in Skins	in Oil	in Cash	in Slops	in Stores	Forfieted by Seaman	General Particulars
Charles Bishop	Master	4 per Cent	22 ii 97	15 ix 99	374¼	33½	80.0	—	—	658.0	—	—	—	N.B. Those names marked * staid at Cape Barren while the vessel went to Port Jackson for Provisions and have according to agreement an additional half share upon the skins and oil collected during the absence of the vessel, 3157 Skins
Roger Simpson	Factor	4 per Cent	10 v 97	15 ix 99	374¼	33½	80.0	—	—	658.0	—	—	—	
Robert Sutherland	Chief Officer	1/30th	6 x 98	For Mutiny 18 iii 99	312	28	—	—	—	—	—	—	312 Skins 28 Oil	
*John Harbottle	2 Officer	1/30th	6 x 98	15 ix 99	361	28	80.0	—	—	647.50	—	—	—	
*George McClay	Carpenter	1/75 of 5966 1/57 of 3157	6 x 98	15 ix 99	131	11	40.0	—	—	240.0	14.50	—	—	—
William Sparks	Able Seaman	1/120th	6 x 98	26 ii 99	78	7	—	—	—	4.0	9.50	89.50	—	
Robert Hinch	Ordinary Seaman	1/120th	6 x 98	26 ii 99	78	7	—	—	—	3.0	6.50	87.50	—	Whole Shares of the Crew
*Samuel Chase	Able Seaman	1/80th	6 x 98	26 ii 99	134	12	—	—	—	45.50	13.50	80.25	—	
Joseph Oliphent	Do	1/100th	6 x 98	26 ii 99	94	8½	—	—	—	16.0	9.50	90.0	—	In Skins 3334½
*Daniel Cooper	Do	1/100th	6 x 98	26 ii 99	104	10	—	—	—	18.25	7.50	87.50	—	In Oil 298½
James Cordell	Do	1/100th	6 x 98	15 ix 99	94	8½	24.0	—	—	171.0	—	—	—	Dollars Cents
*James Miln	Do	1/100th	6 x 98	15 ix 99	104	10½	28.0	—	10½	172.0	13.25	—	—	Paid in Cash 3844 —
*George Apellton	Do	1/100th	6 x 98	15 ix 99	104	10½	28.0	—	10½	173.0	6.0	6.0	—	paid value in stores 573. 25
*William Mackey	Do	1/100th	6 x 98	15 ix 99	104	10½	28.0	—	10½	176.50	8.50	—	—	paid in Slops 178. 75
														4596 —

308

John Ash Smith	Dº	1/100th	6 x 98	15 ix 99	94	8½	28.0	—	8½	147.0	21.0	—	—	*paid* in Skins 127
Edward Hogan	Sea*man*	1/120th	6 x 98	Died Cape Barren 18 xii 98	43	2½	—	—	—	—	1.50	—	42 skins 2½ oil	*paid* oil — 102 Forfieted Skins — 432
*John Steward	Dº	1/120th	6 x 98	Run 10 iii 99	78	7	—	—	—	—	—	—	78 skins 7 oil	Dº Oil — 37½
Tho*mas* Lee	Dº	1/120th	6 x 98	31 xii 98	43	2½	—	27	2½	16.0	—	—	—	Paid Cash for the Run to Norfolk Island & back — — Do*llars* 596
Hugh Dougherty	Dº	1/120th	6 x 98	28 v 99	78	7	24.0	1	7	13.0	20.0	53.0	—	
Sam*uel* Clews	Dº	1/120th	6 x 98	15 ix 99	78	7	24.0	—	7	140.0	1.50	—	—	
*William Baker	Or*dinary* Sea*man*	1/140th	6 x 98	15 ix 99	82½	8	24.0	—	8	142.0	—	—	—	
George Shedrick	Cook	1/140th	6 x 98	2 i 99	37	2½	—	18	2½	28.0	—	20.0	—	
*Thomas Lythgo	Or*dinary* Sea*man*	1/140th	6 x 98	15 ix 99	82½	8	20.0	—	8	127.0	8.0	7.0	—	
Mich*ael* Murphy	Dº	1/150th	6 x 98	28 v 99	62	6	20.0	52	6	20.0	16.0	—	—	
Stephen Lawless	Dº	1/150th	6 x 98	28 v 99	62	6	20.0	—	6	17.0	9.0	42.50	—	
*Charles Wood	Dº	1/150th	6 x 98	15 ix 99	68	7	20.0	—	7	123.50	5.0	—	—	
Will*iam* Smith Bradlee	Sea*man*	1/100th	10 i 99	15 ix 99	40½	5	28.0	—	5	81.0	8.0	—	—	
George King	Or*dinary* Sea*man*	1/140th	10 i 99	29 v 99	29	3	—	29	3	—	—	—	—	

Canton 29 Sep*tember* 1799

Except Errors
Char*les* Bishop

In the Com*missions* I am to observe that I was alowed by Mr Teast 6 *per* Cent on the neat sales of the Cargoes, but to induce Mr Simpson to go with me I relinquished 2 *per* C*ent* alowed by Mr Teast to Chief officer, and 1/3d of one *per* Cent to 2d officer of the Ruby together with 2/3ds of one *per* Cent charged in addition to the Concern made our Commissions equal, Namly 4 *per* Cent, as by bond of agree*men*t with Mr Simpson —

C B —

[1] All figures relating to oil are in gallons.

Debtor Brig Nautilus in Account Current: Voyage in Pacific Ocean for Seal Skins.

September 1799	To the anexed bill of Disbursments—	9481 . 52
	To Whole Wages of the Crew 21 February	
	97 to 15 September 99	8410 . 79
	To Amount of Cash paid the Crew for	
	their Shares	3844 . 0
	To Amount paid the Crew for the Run to	
	Norfolk Island taken up on freight 149£	596 . 0
	Amount Paid the Crew in Part of their	
	Shares of Seal Skins by Slops	178 . 75
	belonging to C. Bishop	

Head Debtors[1] 22511 . 6
28971 . 66

Ballance Creditors Spanish Dollars 6460 . 60

per Contra Creditors

May 1798	Freight & Passage of the Missioneries		
	from Otaheite	1080	0
	by Whole Sales of the N West Investment		
	at Port Jackson	2639	75
	By sale 180 large skins there	169	0
January 1799	By Sale of seal oil at Port Jackson	450	0
March	By Freight to Norfolk Island	2000	0
	By Demurrage &c of the vessel	252	0
	By Sale 16 pair Rough Oars @ 5/-	16	0
	By Sale 500 feet Norfolk Island boards	39	0
May	By Sale of 7 Hogs grown poor & unfitt to	92	0
	Kill		
August	By Sale of Seal Skins at Macao	14000	0
September	By Sale of vessel to Robert berry[2] Esquire	4000	0
	By Money Advanced the Crew at Macao		
	on account Wages	1044	76
	By Wages paid in Cargo on the voyage	1157	7
	By Wages & Shares forfieted by	746	55
	Deserters &c		
	By Amount of Shares paid in Stores &c to		
	the Party left at Cape Barren	545	25
	By Profit gained in paying for many Articles		
	in the bill of Disbursements with Rum &c	740	28

Creditor Spanish Dollars 28971 66

★   ★   ★

[1] This appears a more meaningful reading of the abbreviation than 'Dollars'.

[2] Simpson continued as master of the *Nautilus*, in Berry's employ. Berry at one time 'had Swedish protection' (Greenberg, 27–8), yet must now have been a British subject to satisfy the supercargoes as a purchaser of the *Nautilus* (see below, p. 317). Bass and Bishop maintained contact with him (Bowden (1952), 99).

If the Produce of the Amount of the outfitt 16888[1] Dollars be 6460:

Mr Teasts share of 1ᵗ Am*ount*, 8976 D*olla*rs gives only 3433.50
Conseequa D° — 7195 D*olla*rs—D°— 2752.20
Cha*rle*s Bishop D° — 717 D*olla*rs—D°— 274.90

★ ★ ★

Agreement and Bond with Capt*ain* W*illia*m Campbell:
Freight to Norfolk Island—[2]

Conditions of agreement between Capt*ain* William Campbell of the ship Rebecca and Capt*ain* Charles Bishop of the
Brig Nautilus,

Article 1ˢᵗ: To Recieve onboard the Nautilus such goods as
Capt*ain* W*illia*m Campbell shall chuse to put on board her
not Exceeding 50 Tons
2ᵈ—To convey with all possible dispatch the said goods to
Norfolk Island and Land and dispose of them in such manner
as the agent appointed by Capt*ain* Campbell shall think
proper at his risque & Expence
3ᵈ—Capt*ain* Bishop and Roger Simpson are not at liberty to
sell or suffer to be sold any article of their own, while there
shall be any of the Same denomination remaining unsold in
the Investment of Capt*ain* Campbell, except his agent shall
refuse to sell such Article, Now the full meaning of this
Article & Condition is, that in all things Capt*ain* Campbells
agent shall have the first offer of the markett
4ᵗʰ.—All risques, dangers of the sea or Enemy or other unavoidable accident happening to the Said investment shall
be wholly on account of Capt*ain* W*illia*m Campbell—
5ᵗʰ. For Conveying the Said investment to Norfolk Island
Seven Landing days after the arrival of the Nautilus off that
Island, Capt*ain* Bishop and Roger Simpson shall be at liberty
to draw from the agent of the Said Capt*ain* Campbell Five
hundred pounds Sterling to be paid in the Gove*rnme*nt bills

---

[1] This is fifty-eight dollars more than the costs of equipping in China
(see above, pp. 266–71), but omits debts incurred at Kamchatka (pp. 275–
6) and Sydney (pp. 290, 295). All items in the credit account have a tick
beside them in the original.

[2] For Campbell, and the trip generally, see above, p. xliii.

of the Island or such private bills as they shall choose to accept, and Captain Campbell shall instruct his agent to pay such Sum without any DEDUCTION WHATEVER

6th. The Nautilus shall not be Obliged to remain off Norfolk Island more than Seven Landing days, altho' the whole of Captain Campbells investment should not be sold, and the Said Commander & Co Agent shall be at liberty to proceed back to Port Jackson—

7th. It shall be Esteemed a landing day when the colours are hoisted at Either of the landing places for that purpose

8th. Captain Bishop shall be at full Liberty to freight his vessel back to Port Jackson in Such manner he shall think proper reserving room and proper storage for any of Captain Campbells remaining investment, which shall be brought back, dangers of the Sea and Enemy Excepted, freight free

Now for the full performance of the within written Conditions and agreements the Parties signing these Premises mutually bind each other in the penal sum of Two Thousand Pounds sterling money of Great Brittain

Signed Sealed and Ratified at Sidney in His Majestys Territory of New South Wales this 18th day March 1799, in presence of the Subscribing Witnesses—

Signed, Charles Bishop —

(Signed)   Roger Simpson—
Philip Fergusson
Bartholomew Kent   William Campbell

*   *   *

Articles of Agreement made and entered into by the Commander officers Seamen and Mariners of the Brig Nautilus—done at Sidney in New South Wales 16th March 1799.

312

1st: That the persons signing these Articles shall proceed in their several stations as heretofore in the Said vessel, from hence to Norfolk Island, off which the Said vessel is to Cruize, untill a Cargo of Sundry merchandize now about to be taken on board is there disposed of and from thence back to Port Jackson

2dly. That the Said officers Seamen and mariners shall demean in all things agreeable to the Articles of agreement entered into at Sidney aforesaid in October 1798 or in default thereof be liable to all the penalties therein specified—

3dly. The Commander doth hereby agree to pay or Cause to be paid such Sum of Money as shall be affixed against each respective Name hereunto sett on the vessels arrival at Port Jackson which is to be taken in the room of wages shares or other Emolument, Provided always that the 1st and 2^d Articles are fully complyed with and performed by the Said officers seamen and Mariners.

Now in Witness hereof we the Commander Officers and Seamen have hereunto sett our names or Marks the day to Said Names affixed and in the year of our Lord 1799 in Presence of Each Other,

16 March 1799

Charles Bishop	Master	} 4 per Cent Commissions	
Roger Simpson	Co Agent		
John Harbottle	Acting 1st officer	—	20£
George McClay	D^o 2 officer	—	10£
William Smith Bradlee	Seaman	—	7£
John Ash Smith	Seaman	—	7£
George Appelton	Seaman	—	7£
William Mackey	Seaman	—	7£
James Miln	Seaman	—	7£
Michael Murphy	Seaman	—	5£
Hugh Doughterty	Seaman	—	6£
Samuel Clews	Seaman	—	6£
William Baker	Seaman	—	6£
Stephen Lawless	Seaman	—	5£
Thomas Lythgo	Seaman	—	5£
Charles Wood	Seaman	—	5£
James Cordell	Seaman	—	6£
Joseph Jinkins	Cook	—	4£

Signed

We the underwritten Names or Marks do hereby Certify that we have recieved in full of all Demands for our services on board the Nautilus according to the within written agreement Sidney 27 April 1799.

Signed George McClay
&c &c &c as above

★ ★ ★

Request of LETTER OF MARQUES Commission

To His Excellency John Hunter Esq*uire* Governor General and Commander in Chief in and over His Majestys Territory of New South Wales and its Dependancies and Vice Admiral of the Same.[1]

Sir! Being about to proceed on my voyage as licensed by the Hon'ble East India Company, the direction of which lying near part of the Spanish dominions, and Concieving the vessel I command may have an opportunity of annoying the commerce of the Enemy, I have to request of your Excellency to grant me a letter of Marques Commission of reprisal against the subjects of the King of Spain the Enemies of my King & Country ashuring you Sir that the force I direct shall in no wise act dishonourable to the Brittish Flag

Herewith I transmit to your Excellency the Particulars of the vessel I command, trusting you will take into Consideration that altho' our force is Small much may be done by resolute and determined Minds

Messrs. Kent & Williamson has permitted me to use their Names offering to become shurties for my conducting myself agreeable to the Term and meaning of the Commission and Instructions I may recieve from your Excellency

[1] Proof of the grant of this petition is Bishop's listing the fee (see above, p. 304). A letter from Bishop to Atkins, 15 May 1799, gave data from which the commission could be prepared. The only extra item was in supplement to the muskets, '& Bayonets with Pistols and Cutlasses' (Supreme Court of New South Wales Papers, item 1163).

The Particulars of the vessel are,

Brig Nautilus, Built at Bengal
     Burthen 60 Tons per Register
     owner—Sidenham Teast Esquire
     Master, C. Bishop

Carries—3 three pounders brass Cannon
    2 Two Pounders D°
    1 one Pounder D°
    6 ½ lb Swivals
    15 Musketts
    25 Men Exclusive of the Master

I have the Honour to be &c &c
Port Jackson   Signed Charles Bishop
6 May 1799.
     ★ ★ ★

Provisions and stores being excessively dear and scarce at Port Jackson[1]—
     ★ ★ ★

Bishop to Hall and Supercargoes, at Canton, 5 September 1799:[2]

I have the honour to address you with the particulars of the voyage I have performed in the Nautilus, trusting that my conduct therein will appear satisfactory to you that I have not infringed on the Hon'ble Companys licence you were so good to extend the Period of untill I should be enabled to return here

Relation of voyage since leaving Canton, right through to the Nautilus *making Port Jackson and trying the fisheries.*

We continnued on this business untill the beginning of March 99, when having procured about 9000 Seals Skins

---

[1] This half-sentence began a page otherwise virgin. It probably was meant to introduce an outline of the venture which Bishop and Bass undertook in due course.

[2] This correspondence may be followed in the East India Company's 'Factory Records—China' (**126**, 132–8).

with little Probability of getting more that Season we returned to Port Jackson, refitted and laid in a Store of Provisions for our passage here, and finally left the Coast of new Holland 27 May 1799, and without stopping any where but one day at the Ladrone Islands arrived at Macao 18th August—

I have thus Sir and Gentlemen related faithfully the particulars of my voyage, Long anxious, and replete as it as been with adversity and distress, and have now to solicit the favour in behalf of my owner and self that you will permit me to dispose of the vessel, in order that I may save as Early as possible the expence of keeping up the Establishment of the Nautilus, and return myself to Europe to render an Account to my owner and the Honourable Court of Directors of my proceedings and I the more earnestly intreat your Compliance with my request as I have no other means of Saving the remaining property invested with me from total loss...

★ ★ ★

Bishop to Hall, 5 September 1799:[1]

I have the honour to inclose to you a letter to yourself as President and the Gentlemen of the Select Committee relative to the particlers of the voyage I have performed in the Nautilus also conveying my request that you will be pleased to permit me to sell the vessel, relying Sir in your liberality that you will as heretofore favour my Endeavours to render the ill success of my voyage as little felt as possible...

★ ★ ★

Hall, Peach, and F. Turnly[2] *to Bishop, from Macao, 9 September 1799:*

We have recieved your letter of the 5th Instant requesting our permission to sell the Brig Nautilus, and have now to

---

[1] The 'Factory Records—China' copy of this letter has a postscript offering Hall a perusal of Bishop's log-book.
[2] Bishop's transcription is 'Trunby'.

acquaint you in Answer, that we are willing to comply with your request, Provided the purchaser is a Brittish subject, TRADING UNDER THE LICENCE AND PROTECTION OF THE HON'BLE COMPANY, but it is not in our power to grant you permission to sell her to any person not of that discription.[1]

★ ★ ★

Agreement with Ponqua, Houng Merchant

It is agreed this day between Ponqua, Houng Mer*chan*t of Canton, & Messrs Cha*rle*s Bishop and Roger Simpson Co agents of the Brig Nautilus, for themselves & Concern as follows.

The Said CB and RS sells to Ponqua the Cargo of the Nautilus, consisting of nine Thousand Seals Skins or there about, for and in consideration of Ponqua paying and delivering to them on board the Nautilus at Whampu' Three Thousand yards of broad blue wollen cloth,[2] such as is usually Carried to the North west coast of America together with seven thousand Spanish Dollars in Cash to be paid on Demand and Four Thousand Dollars in a Transfer on the Hon'ble English Company as soon as their Treasury is open for granting bills on the Court of Directors in England.

The Quality of said Seals skins having been Ex*amine*d and aproved of by Said Ponqua, who has advanced in part Payment 2000 Dollars cash, and having desired that the above Cargo be Delivered to him at Whampu', Hereby agrees to defray the Port Charges of admeasurment, the Present to the Hoppo, ship and house Compradores and Linguists fees and Pilotage of the vessel also to furnish Messrs. Bishop and Simpson with a Factory at Canton

[1] The 'Factory Records—China' include a letter from Bishop to the supercargoes, thanking them for this and other favours.
[2] The accounts (see above, p. 310) state simply 14,000 Dollars as the price.

In Witness whereof the Contracting parties have hereonto set their Hands & Seals at Macao this 28ᵗʰ August 1799, in Presence of the Subscribing Witnesses

Signed in Chinese by Ponqua

Witnesses, two Chinese Merchants

Charles Bishop

Signed in Chinese

R Simpson

BIBLIOGRAPHY

Note. The Bibliography cites all sources mentioned in text and notes, with a few others of exceptional interest.

I. BOOKS AND ARTICLES CONCERNING
NORTHERN HEMISPHERE

Anderson, B., *Surveyor of the Sea* (Seattle, 1960). Concerns George Vancouver.

Bancroft, H. H., *History of the Pacific States of North America: the northwest coast. Volume I. 1543–1800* (San Francisco, 1884).

Beasley, W. G., *Great Britain and the Opening of Japan 1834–1858* (London, 1951).

Benedict, R., *Patterns of Culture* (London, 1949). First published 1934.

Boas, F., '...On the Indians of British Columbia': a series of Reports in *R.B.A.A.S.* as follows: 1888, 236–42 (preliminary); 1889, 801–93 (general); 1890, 562–715 (The Songish; the Nootka; the Kwakiutl; the Shushwap; crania; linguistics); 1891, 408–49 (the Bilqula; physical characteristics); 1894, 454–63 (tribes of Lower Fraser River); 1895, 523–92 (physical characteristics; Tinneh; Nass River Indians; linguistics); 1896, 569–91 (Kwakiutl); 1898, with L. Farrand, 628–88 (physical characteristics; the Chilcotin; the Haida; linguistics; summary and index).

Bradley, H. W., 'The Hawaiian Islands and the Pacific Fur Trade, 1785–1813', *Pacific Northwest Quarterly*, **30**, 275–99 (1939).

British Columbia Pilot (Canadian edition), vol. I: Southern Portion, 6th edition (Ottawa, 1959); vol. II: Northern Portion, 4th edition (Ottawa, 1961).

Broughton, W. R., *A Voyage of Discovery to the North Pacific Ocean* (London, 1804).

Colnett, J., *The Journal of Captain James Colnett aboard the Argonaut from April 26, 1789 to Nov. 3, 1791* (ed. F. W. Howay) (Toronto, 1940).

Colnett, J., *A Voyage to the South Atlantic and round Cape Horn into the Pacific Ocean...* (London, 1798).

Cook, J. and King, J., *A Voyage to the Pacific Ocean...for Making Discoveries in the Northern Hemisphere...*, 3 vols. (London, 1785). First published 1784.

Dalrymple, A., *Plan for Promoting the Fur-trade...* (London, 1789).
Dawson, G. M., 'Report on the Queen Charlotte Islands', pp. 1–239 in Geological Survey of Canada, *Reports of Explorations and Surveys 1878–9* (Montreal, 1880).
Densmore, F., *Nootka and Quileute Music* (Washington, 1939).
Dixon, G., *A Voyage round the World...* (London, 1789).
Drucker, P., *The Northern and Central Nootkan Tribes* (Washington, 1951).

Earnshaw, J. W., *Thomas Muir* (Sydney, 1959).
Elliott, T. C., 'The Journal of the Ship Ruby', *Oregon Historical Quarterly*, **28**, 258–80 (1927).
Elliott, T. C., 'Journal of Captain Charles Bishop of the "Ruby" in 1795', *Oregon Historical Quarterly*, **29**, 337–47 (1928).

Forde, C. D., *Habitat, Economy and Society* (London, 1963). First published 1934.

Gill, W. C., *Merchants and Mariners of the 18th Century...* (London, 1961).
Goodwin, G., *Vancouver. A Life 1757–1798* (New York, 1931).
Gowen, H. H., *The Napoleon of the Pacific* (New York, 1919). A biography of Kamehameha.
Greenberg, M., *British Trade and the Opening of China 1800–42* (Cambridge, 1951).
Greenhow, R., *The History of Oregon and California, and the Other Territories on the North-west Coast of North America* (Boston, 1844).

Harlow, V. T., *The Founding of the Second British Empire 1763–1793*, 2 vols.: I (1952) and II (1964), London.
Harlow, V. T. and Madden, F. (eds.), *British Colonial Developments 1774–1834. Select Documents* (Oxford, 1953).
Howay, F. W., 'Indian attacks upon maritime traders of the North-West Coast, 1785–1805', *Canadian Historical Review*, **6**, 287–309 (1925).

Howay, F. W., 'Early followers of Captain Grey', *Washington Historical Quarterly*, **18**, 11–20 (1927). Concerned chiefly with Bishop.

Howay, F. W., 'Early relations between the Hawaiian Islands and the Northwest Coast', pp. 11–38 in A. P. Taylor and R. S. Kuykendall (eds.), *The Hawaiian Islands* (Honolulu, 1930).

Howay, F. W., 'A list of trading vessels in the maritime fur trade', *Royal Society of Canada. Proceedings and Transactions. Third Series:* **24**, ii, 111–34 (1930); **25**, ii, 117–49 (1931); **26**, ii, 43–86 (1932); **27**, ii, 119–47 (1933); **28**, ii, 11–49 (1934). Covers the period 1785–1825 and is an invaluable record.

Howay, F. W. (ed.), *Voyages of the 'Columbia' to the Northwest Coast 1787–90 and 1790–93* (Boston, 1941).

Howay, F. W. and Elliott, T. C., 'Voyages of the "Jenny" to Oregon, 1792–94', *Oregon Historical Quarterly*, **30**, 197–206 (1929).

Innis, H. A., *The Fur Trade in Canada* (Toronto, 1962). First published 1930.

Jenness, D., *The Indians of Canada* (Ottawa, 1958). First published 1932.

Jewitt, J. R., *The Adventures of John Jewitt...* (ed. R. Brown) (London, 1896). First published 1807. Jewitt was one of two survivors from the *Boston*, captured by the Nootka people in 1803.

Kuykendall, R. S., 'A Northwest trader at the Hawaiian Islands', *Oregon Historical Quarterly*, **24**, 111–31 (1923).

Kuykendall, R. S., *The Hawaiian Kingdom* (Honolulu, 1947).

Kuykendall, R. S. and Day, A. G., *Hawaii: a History* (New York, 1948).

Latourette, K. S., 'The history of early relations between the United States and China', *Transactions of the Connecticut Academy of Arts and Sciences*, **22**, 1–209 (1917).

Macartney, G., *An Embassy to China* (ed. J. L. Cranmer-Byng) (London, 1962). First published 1797.

McCracken, H., *Hunters of the Stormy Sea* (London, 1957).

Manning, W. R., 'The Nootka Sound Controversy', *Annual Report of the American Historical Association...1904*, 279–478 (Washington, 1905).

Meares, J., *Voyages Made in the Years 1788 and 1789...* (London, 1790).

Mills, L., 'The real significance of the Nootka Sound incident', *Canadian Historical Review*, 6, 110–22 (1925).

Minchinton, W. E. (ed.), *The Trade of Bristol in the Eighteenth Century* (Bristol, 1957).

Minchinton, W. E. (ed.), *Politics and the Port of Bristol in the Eighteenth Century* (Bristol, 1963).

Morse, H. B., *The Chronicles of the East India Company Trading to China 1635–1834*, 5 vols. (Oxford, 1926). Vol. II covers the period 1775–1804.

Norris, J. M., 'The policy of the British Cabinet in the Nootka Crisis', *English Historical Review*, 70, 562–80 (1955).

Ogden, A., *The Californian Sea-Otter Trade 1784–1848* (Berkeley and Los Angeles, 1941).

Parkinson, C. N., *War in the Eastern Seas 1793–1815* (London, 1954).

Parkinson, C. N. (ed.), *Trade in the Eastern Seas 1793–1815* (Cambridge, 1937).

Parkinson, C. N. (ed.), *The Trade Winds* (London, 1948).

Péron, P. F., *Mémoires du Capitaine Péron sur ses Voyages...* (ed. L. Brissot-Thivars), 2 vols. (Paris, 1824).

Phillips, P. C. and Smurr, J. W., *The Fur Trade*, 2 vols. (Norman, 1961).

Portlock, N., *A Voyage round the World* (London, 1789).

Pritchard, E. H., *The Crucial Years of Early Anglo-Chinese Relations 1750–1800* (Washington, 1936).

Ray, V. F., 'Lower Chinook ethnographic notes', *University of Washington Publications in Anthropology*, 7, 29–165 (1938).

Restarick, H. B., 'The first clergyman resident in Hawaii', *Hawaiian Historical Society 32nd Annual Report*, 54–61 (1923). Concerns John Howel.

Rickard, T. A., 'The Sea-otter in History', *British Columbia Historical Quarterly*, II, 15–31 (1947).

South-East Alaska Pilot, 4th edition (London, 1959).

Sproat, G. M., *Scenes and Studies of Savage Life* (London, 1868). Concerns the Nootka people.

Strange, J. C., *James Strange's Journal and Narrative of the Commercial Expeditions from Bombay to the North-west Coast of America*... (ed. A. V. Venkatarama Ayyar) (Madras, 1928).

United States Coast Pilot, 7. *The Pacific Coast*, 8th edition (Washington, 1959).

Vancouver, G., *A Voyage of Discovery to the North Pacific Ocean*... 3 vols. (London, 1798).

Wagner, H. R., *The Cartography of the Northwest Coast of America to the Year 1800*, 2 vols.; pagination continuous (Berkeley, 1937).

Wilbur, M. E., *The East India Company*... (Stamford, 1945).

Williams, G., *The British Search for the Northwest Passage in the Eighteenth Century* (London, 1962).

Woodward, A., 'Sea Otter hunting on the Pacific Coast', *The Quarterly of the Historical Society of Southern California*, **20**, 119–34 (1938).

Yanaga, C., *Japan since Perry* (New York, 1949).

II. BOOKS AND ARTICLES CONCERNING SOUTHERN HEMISPHERE

Anson, G., *A Voyage round the World*... (London, 1748).

Atkins, B., 'Australia's place in the "Swing to the East", 1788–1810: Addendum', *Historical Studies. Australia and New Zealand*, **8**, 315–18 (1958).

Bladen, F. M. (ed.), *Historical Records of New South Wales*, vols. I–VI (Sydney, 1892).

Blainey, G., 'Gold and Governors', *Historical Studies. Australia and New Zealand*, **9**, 337–50 (1961).

Blainey, G. *The Tyranny of Distance* (Melbourne, 1966).

Bostock, J. *The Dawn of Australian Psychiatry* (Brisbane, 1951).

Bowden, K. M., *George Bass 1771–1803* (Melbourne, 1952).

Bowden, K. M., 'George Bass, 1771–1803, surgeon and sailor', *Bulletin of the Post-Graduate Committee in Medicine, University of Sydney*, **17**, 33–56 (1961).

Boxer, C. R., *The Golden Age of Brazil 1695–1750* (Berkeley and Los Angeles, 1962).

Clark, C. M. H., *A History of Australia*, vol. I (Melbourne, 1962).

Collins, D., *An Account of the English Colony in New South Wales*, 2 vols., I (1798) and II (1802), London.

Cook, J., *The Journals of Captain James Cook...* (ed. J. C. Beaglehole), vols. I (+Atlas) (1955), and II (1961), Cambridge.

Cumpston, J. S., *Shipping Arrivals and Departures, Sydney, 1778–1825* (Canberra, 1963). Gives information concerning home ports, officers, places visited and intended.

Dakin, W. J., *Whalemen Adventurers* (Sydney, 1938). Second revised edition.

Dallas, K. M., 'The first settlement in Australia, considered in relation to sea-power in world politics', *Tasmanian Historical Research Association Papers and Proceedings*, 2, 4–12, 15–16 (1953).

Davies, J., *The History of the Tahitian Mission 1799–1830* (ed. C. W. Newbury) (Cambridge, 1961).

Dunbabin, T., *Sailing the World's Edge* (London, 1931). Concerns sea-faring from early Sydney.

Flinders, M., *Observations on the Coasts of Van Diemen's Land, on Bass's Strait and its Islands, and on Parts of the Coasts of New South Wales* (ed. G. Mackaness) (Sydney, 1946). First published 1801.

Flinders, M., *A Voyage to Terra Australis...*, 2 vols. and Atlas (London, 1814).

Greenwood, G., *Early American–Australian Relations* (Melbourne, 1944).

Hawkesworth, J., *An Account of the Voyages Undertaken by the Order of His Present Majesty for Making Discoveries in the Southern Hemisphere...*, 3 vols. (London, 1773).

Hill-Reid, W. S., *John Grant's Journey* (London, 1957).

McNab, R. (ed.), *Historical Records of New Zealand*. Vol. I (Wellington, 1908).

Maude, H. E., 'The Tahitian Pork Trade: 1800–1830', *Journal de la Société des Océanistes*, 15, 57–95 (1959).

Maude, H. E., 'Post-Spanish Discoveries in the Central Pacific', *Journal of the Polynesian Society*, 70, 67–111 (1961).

Metraux, A., *Easter Island* (tr. M. Bullock) (London, 1957).

Naval Intelligence Division (of Great Britain), *Geographical Handbook Series. Pacific Islands*; vol. I: General Survey; vol. II: Eastern Pacific; vol. III: Western Pacific (Tonga to the Solomon Islands); vol. IV: Pacific Islands (New Guinea and Islands Northwards) (London, 1943–45).

O'Brien, E. M., *The Foundation of Australia (1768–1800)* (Sydney, 1950). First published 1937.

Rhodes, F., *Pageant of the Pacific*, 2 vols. (Sydney, 1937).
Roe, M., 'Australia's place in "The swing to the East", 1788–1810', *Historical Studies. Australia and New Zealand*, **8**, 202–13 (1958).

Serle, P., *Dictionary of Australian Biography*, 2 vols. (Sydney, 1949).
Sharp, A., *The Discovery of the Pacific Islands* (Oxford, 1960).

Ward, J. M., *British Policy in the South Pacific (1786–1893)* (Sydney, 1948).
Watson, J. F. (ed.), *Historical Records of Australia*, series I, vols. II–VII (Sydney, 1914–16).

III. MANUSCRIPTS

J. Banks Papers (Mitchell Library, Sydney, call number A 85).
G. Bass Papers. Typescript copies of letters to, from, and concerning Bass, from the originals held by family descendants (K. M. Bowden, Melbourne).
J. Boit, The Journal of a Voyage round the Globe (Massachusetts Historical Society, Boston).
East India Company Papers (Commonwealth Relations Office, London).
J. Grant Papers (National Library of Australia, Canberra).
R. Hassall Papers (Mitchell Library, A 860).
W. House, Transactions on Board of the Armed Colonial Brig *Norfolk* at Otaheita 1801 and 1802 (Mitchell Library, C 229).
J. Ingraham, Journal of the Voyage of the Brigantine *Hope* from Boston to the North-west Coast of America (Library of Congress, Washington).
London Missionary Society Papers (the Society, London).

P. G. King Papers (Mitchell Library, A 1980–2).
W. Paterson Papers (Mitchell Library, D 144).
G. W. Rusden Papers (Trinity College, University of Melbourne).
South Sea Company Papers (British Museum, London).
Supreme Court of New South Wales Papers (Archives Office of
New South Wales, Sydney).

IV. NEWSPAPER

Sydney Gazette, and New South Wales Advertiser, 1803–9 (Mitchell
Library).

INDEX

INDEX

Where items are repeated time and again (e.g. Macao and Canton, Bishop, Teast), entry is selective and consolidated. Places are entered according to their distinctive name, even when that normally follows 'Cape', 'Port', 'River', etc.

Barnett, William, master of *Mercury*, 94 n., 95, 103, 140
Barros, M. V. de, Portuguese merchant at Macao, 246, 247, 255, 267, 271
Bartlett, John, seaman, 222, 265, 269, 285, 306
Bartolome, Cape, 87 n., Map IV
Barwell, storeship at Sydney, 289, 290, 294
Bashee, *see* Batan Islands
Bass, Elizabeth (Waterhouse), wife of George, xlvi
Bass, George, observations in Bass Strait, xl, xli; Bishop's trading partner, xliii–l, 310 n., 315 n.
Bass Rocks, *see* Marotiri
Bass Strait, Map I (*a*)
Bass's Reef-tied Islands, *see* Maloelap
Batan Islands, 220, 222, Map V
Batavia, 1
Baudin, Nicolas, French explorer, xlix
Beale, Daniel, British businessman at Canton, xx, xxxix, 262
Bears, —, sailor held captive by Cumshewa, 84, 96–8
Beauchene Island, 29, 31
Beaver, George, seaman, 189, 193
Beaver Passage, 69 n., Map IV B
Behring's Bay, *see* Yakutat Bay
Bengal Fur Society, xix
Beresford's Isle, 90 n.
Berkeley Sound, 29
Berry, Robert, merchant at Canton, 310
Bishop, Charles, literary style, xi, xvi; his illustrations, xiv–xv, 42; early life, xvi, 83; naval career, xvi, 201, 228; personality traits apparent in Journal, xxix; religious beliefs, xxix, 85; poet and patriot, xxix–xxx; an innocent abroad, xxxii; a man of candour and truth, 68 n., 225; an optimistic planner for future, 261, 296, 315; yet sometimes beset with misgivings, 227, 231, 236; pioneer agriculturist, xli, 58, 124; betrothal, xlv; physical ill-health, xlix, 32, 183, 212, 282; madness, lii; departure from Sydney, lvi
Bishop, William, brother of Charles, xi, xii, xiii, xlvi, lvi, 111, 112, 152

Bishop's Islands, *see* Tabiteuea
Bishop's Junction Islands, Map III
Black, John, seaman, 42, 43, 189, 192, 193
Blanco, Cape, xiv, 51, 52
Blanco Reef, 52 n.
Bligh, William, governor of New South Wales, lv
Block, John, seaman cook, 222, 265, 269, 306
Böa Vista Island, 7
Boca Tigris, anchorage at Canton, 191
Boddam, East Indiaman, 237
Boit, John, master of *Union*, 99 n., 173
Bolton, Thomas Orde-Powlett, first Lord, 'a friend of Bishop's', xlvii
Bones, Stephen, seaman, 257
Bonilla Island, 90 n., Map IV
Bonnar, —, merchant at Canton, 189
Booth, John, surgeon, 5, 144–5, 162, 182, 189, 192, 193
Bosman, —, businessman at Canton or Macao, 166
Botany Bay, 100, 174
Bougainville, L. A. de, French explorer, xxviii
Bounds, Richard, seaman, 182, 189, 191, 193, 194
Boxo of Bengal, seaman, 293, 307
Boyd, *see* Boit
Boyd, Benfield and Company, insurance brokers, 248, 250, 262
Bradlee, W. S., seaman, 293, 309, 313
Brazil pebbles, 14
Breakers Point, *see* Point Estevan
Britannia, East Indiaman, 199
Brodrip, —, Bristol merchant, 14
Broughton, W. R., carries the Journal to Britain, xii, 262; commands *Chatham* and *Providence* on Nootka expeditions, xxiii, xxiv, 95; off Sandwich Islands, xxxi, 135, 136, 137, 160
Brown, William, proceedings as master of *Butterworth* at Sandwich Islands and his death there, 101, 102, 103, 141, 154; presumed outrage at Formosa, 274
Brown Passage, 74 n., Map IV B
Browne, Henry, East India Company supercargo at Canton, with whom Bishop conducted official

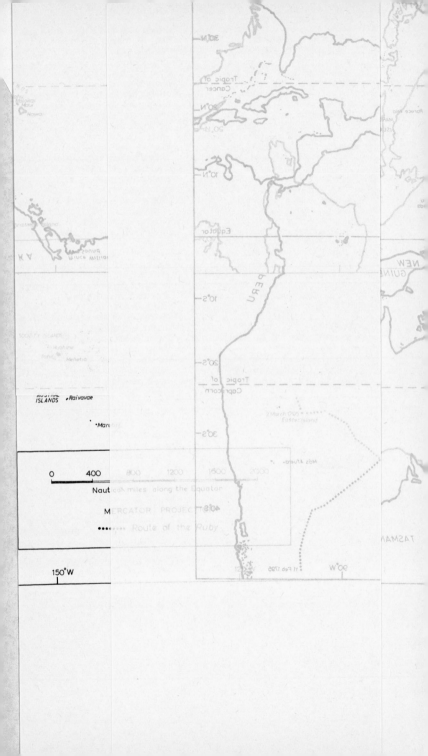

for Port Jackson, passing by Lord Howe Island
port 14 May. The subsequent two trips back
Furneaux Islands may be followed on Maps
From 5 March to 24 April 1799, the *Nautilus*
trip to Norfolk Island. On 27 May she left
passed through the Gilbert and Marshall Islands
and mid-July, touched at the Marianas, and re
18 August. Bishop then returned to Britain.

The *Venus* reached Cape Town on 3 June 180
made Port Jackson 29 August. She sailed for Tah
ber) and *en route* touched the south coast of
Raivavae in the Austral Islands, and the Ma
before turning north to pass by Mehetia be
Tahiti on 24 January 1802. On the return trip
14 November), the *Venus* probably stopped a
Tonga, and Fiji Islands. On 15 October 1809,
left Port Jackson for Britain, carrying Bishop a

DATE DUE

GAYLORD			PRINTED IN U.S.A.